Now, in the summer of 1949, my wife was pregnant. My plans would have to change. I had intended to finish up at USC and then start studying law. Suddenly I had to face up to supporting a family.

We were living in a crummy little apartment off Sunset Boulevard. I had gone through a succession of part-time jobs, driving trucks and, for a year, working in a service station pumping gas. Even so, I was seriously in hock.

One day I ran into Dick Eckenwieler, a friend I hadn't seen much of since high school. To my utter astonishment he told me he had joined the LAPD.

"Listen, if you need a job, why don't you become a Los Angeles police officer?" Dick said.

"What?"

"I'm serious, Daryl. It's a cinch. The Police Academy is only three weeks. And you make two-ninety a month."

"Two-ninety a *month*?"

That seemed like an incredible amount of money in those days. Two-ninety? Why, I could sign on for a while, pay off my debts, and finish USC through night school.

I actually considered this for a moment. Then I came to my senses.

"No way in the world," I said, "will I *ever* become a dumb cop."

—From *Chief*

MY LIFE
IN THE
LAPD

CHIEF

DARYL F. GATES

WITH
DIANE K. SHAH

BANTAM BOOKS
NEW YORK • TORONTO • LONDON • SYDNEY • AUCKLAND

CHIEF

A Bantam Book

PUBLISHING HISTORY

Bantam hardcover edition published July 1992
Bantam paperback edition / February 1993

ISBN 0-553-56205-3

Published simultaneously in the United States and Canada

Bantam Books are published by Bantam Books, a division of Bantam Doubleday
Dell Publishing Group, Inc. Its trademark, consisting of the words "Bantam
Books" and the portrayal of a rooster, is Registered in U.S. Patent and Trademark
Office and in other countries. Marca Registrada. Bantam Books, 666 Fifth
Avenue, New York, New York 10103.

PRINTED IN THE UNITED STATES OF AMERICA

RAD   0 9 8 7 6 5 4 3 2 1

To the members of the LAPD family,
past and present,
who have made this department
the finest in the world . . .
and
to my own long-suffering family—
all of them.

Contents

CHIEF

Prologue

It had been a miserable flight from Washington, delayed three hours by weather and bumpy the whole way across. By the time we began the descent into Los Angeles it was nearing midnight. Monday, March 4, 1991.

On Thursday I'd gone to Harvard for a seminar on community-based policing. A group of thirty-five police chiefs, mayors, city managers, and Harvard professors had been meeting regularly for two years to discuss this concept, which is designed to build a partnership between the police and the community.

Frankly, I was bored with it. The LAPD had pioneered community-oriented policing in the early seventies and by now I felt the group had explored all there was to explore and it was time to move on—to something, maybe, like crime. But I could never get a discussion going on crime, or what we ought to be doing about it.

Sunday, I flew to Washington for Attorney General Richard Thornburgh's conference on violence. I had been asked to speak on the prevention of narcotic usage, specifically about the Drug Abuse Resistance Education program—or

D.A.R.E.—which the LAPD and the Los Angeles Unified School District had designed and which was now taught in elementary and junior high schools throughout the United States. President Bush was scheduled to address the conference on Tuesday and I was tempted to stick around for that. But I always grow edgy when I'm away from L.A., so late Monday afternoon I headed for Dulles Airport.

Before boarding the plane I phoned my office. "Everything's fine, Chief," I was told. "You don't have to worry at all."

■

The chief's official car is a dark-blue Oldsmobile, and it was waiting on the tarmac at LAX.

I carried my bag off the plane, slipped through the door that maintenance people use, and descended the metal stairs to the field. But the relief I felt at being on the ground vanished immediately as my security aide, an eleven-year veteran of the LAPD, switched on the ignition.

"I've got some real bad news for you, Chief," Gerry Sola said. "There's a video of officers taking a suspect into custody. They administered a beating to him and the whole thing was caught on tape and shown on TV." Gerry hesitated. "I'm afraid it's really bad, boss."

Even before I heard more, I knew what videotape meant. Whatever had taken place would be carried into the living rooms of every home in Los Angeles, and any visual depiction of force can appear worse than it is. People are quite naturally repulsed by violence—unless it's part of a Hollywood-produced show. Then it's considered entertainment.

The video had been shot from a second-floor apartment balcony by an amateur photographer, who sold it to a local TV station. KTLA had aired it that night on the ten o'clock news. As he drove, Gerry described the contents of the tape. "I have to tell you," he concluded, "what those officers did sickened me."

When I got home, my wife, Sima—whom I call Sam— told me that Assistant Chief Bob Vernon had phoned to say that he had asked Internal Affairs to start an investigation. Since it was after 1:00 A.M., I decided not to disturb him. Instead I called my secretary, Mary Miller, whose candor I respect. Mary was much more descriptive about the video than Gerry had been, and far more pessimistic.

"It was horrible, just horrible," Mary said. "They hit him a few times and he went down on his knees and they still kept beating him for the longest time. He was bleeding and not resisting at all. And then one of the officers went over and kicked him in the head. I almost threw up."

"White, black, Hispanic?" I inquired.

"Black."

This meant the incident would automatically evoke a greater response than if the man had been white or Hispanic. Long ago I had come to realize that when an incident involved a black person, race is often interjected and can become a significant factor when really it shouldn't be.

"Chief," said Mary softly, "I didn't see anything that could possibly justify what those officers did to him."

Troubled, I hung up. I pushed my disturbing thoughts aside and spoke to Sam of other things. I had learned long ago not to anguish over matters I could not immediately control. At two o'clock in the morning there was little I could do. Jetlagged, and exhausted by the turbulent flight, I fell immediately into a deep sleep.

■

By seven the next morning, I was in my sixth-floor office at Parker Center downtown, being briefed by Bob Vernon on the events leading up to the beating. A copy of the videotape, delivered by KTLA, perched in my VCR.

A man in a white Hyundai had sent two California Highway Patrol officers on a high-speed chase over an empty stretch of freeway in the San Fernando Valley at 12:30 A.M. Sunday, Vernon recounted. The driver was Rodney G. King, a twenty-five-year-old parolee who had been released from prison three months before, after serving time for second-degree armed robbery. He had two male passengers with him. Several LAPD squad cars from the Foothill station joined the pursuit. King left the freeway, ran four red lights, and finally pulled over across the road from an apartment complex in Lake View Terrace. By then, more LAPD units and a police helicopter had arrived at the scene.

I switched on the VCR. The tape slowly came into focus,

showing King already out of his car. Four men, whom we later identified as a sergeant and three uniformed patrol officers, surrounded him; others—it was impossible from the camera angle to tell how many—stood in a blur at a distance. A thin wire was sticking out of the suspect's back. The sergeant, Stacey Koon, had apparently attempted to use a taser gun on King. The taser shoots a pair of high-voltage darts, which are supposed to immobilize a suspect temporarily, allowing officers to handcuff him. But Koon's taser appeared to have no visible effect on the heavyset King.

He charged one officer. A baton blow was struck to ward off the charge and then another. As the three officers closed in on King, he dropped to his knees. The officers began whacking him with their batons, administering blow after blow after blow. The man rolled on the ground as they repeatedly struck him across the legs, the back, and about the head. One officer kicked him five times. Another stomped on his head.

I stared at the screen in disbelief. I played the one-minute fifty-second tape again. Then again and again, until I had viewed it twenty-five times. And still I could not believe what I was looking at. To see my officers engaged in what appeared to be excessive use of force, possibly criminally excessive, to see them beat a man with their batons *fifty-six times*, to see a sergeant on the scene who did nothing to seize control, was something I never dreamed I would witness. It was a very, *very* extreme use of force—extreme for any police department in America. But for the LAPD, considered by many to be perhaps the finest, most professional police department in the world, it was more than extreme. It was impossible.

I sat there watching, terribly shocked.

Feeling sick to my stomach, sick at heart.

■

As the nightmarish morning wore on, reporters and TV crews staked out the elevator area on the sixth floor and spilled along the corridor toward my office door.

I had faced countless crises during thirteen years as chief of police in Los Angeles, and numerous calls for my resignation. But nothing on the morning of March 5, 1991, suggested to me that this incident—revolting and unconscionable as it was—would be the one that would force me to fight for my dignity and ultimately my job or, worse, send the entire LAPD hurtling into a bottomless pit of distrust and public disfavor.

As the tape was run, and rerun, in my office, and was starting to flicker across the nation on CNN, the President of the United States was—at that very moment—addressing the conference on violence at the White House, where I was supposed to be.

"If you want to look at an all-American hero," George Bush said, "then look at Police Chief Daryl F. Gates."

I read about it in the papers the next day.

1

Streetfighter

That I came to be known as a police chief "who shot from the lip" is ironic. For one thing, I was such a quiet little kid, really shy. For another, my early encounters with the police hardly portended a future with them.

I was born August 30, 1926, at a time when many Americans were experiencing some prosperity and had every expectation for more. My family was among them.

We lived in Glendale and were not rich by any means. But we could afford to live in a spacious house up Adams Street hill on a block with well-tended lawns and plenty of shady trees. We were, by the standards of the day, a typical American family. My father, Paul, was in the plumbing business with his father, and doing fairly well. My mother, Arvilla, stayed home. I had my own room, and so did my brother, Lowell, who was four years older.

In 1930 my world changed. Without explanation we moved west to the other side of Glendale, almost to the Burbank city line, past cornfields and grape orchards and into a tired and ramshackle frame house that was quite small. Suddenly, Lowell and I found ourselves sharing not only a room but a single bed. Even more disconcerting, my mother wasn't home anymore. That was the most shocking thing in my memory: my mother going to work.

As a four-year-old, I didn't understand why. But once again we had become the typical American family—ravaged by hard economic times. The stock market crash of 1929 had brought American industry almost to a standstill. Nationwide, the unemployment rate hit 25 percent. In Los Angeles, conditions were no better. Beggars appeared on street corners and long bread lines were common as sales skidded, banks closed, and businesses disappeared overnight.

One of them was my father's. As the devastating Depression took its toll on his livelihood, the bottle began taking a toll on him. He would vanish mysteriously for days on end; when he reappeared he would sit around the house in a boozy haze. With my mother gone and my brother at school, I was, in effect, home alone.

As the Depression deepened, food became a daily concern. In our backyard on Raymond Street we raised turkeys, chickens, and rabbits, and we ate them. My father had a big hatchet and I remember how he would bring it down on a chicken or a turkey for our dinner. I couldn't stand to watch him kill a rabbit, though; rabbits were so cute and cuddly. But I didn't hesitate to eat them. My mother had a way of frying them so they were very crisp on the outside, with moist, tender white meat inside. I've tried to cook rabbit myself once or twice, but I've never been able to match hers.

To supplement our meals we depended on government handouts. Once a week I would go with my father along San Fernando Road to an empty lot just outside Burbank. We would join a long line of other recipients. Inching forward, I would hold my gunny sack while people tossed in potatoes, cabbage, and lettuce. I always felt a little embarrassed, thinking it wasn't right, people giving us things. I felt the same way at Christmas when the school would come by to deliver a Christmas basket to the Gates family. Again, I had those ambivalent feelings; I was delighted, but a little uncomfortable at being singled out.

The sting of poverty followed me to school. I can remem-

ber the godawful sandwiches my mother made for me. The
other kids brought theirs in nifty little lunchboxes. I was so
envious. To have a lunchbox with a thermos inside was
something I wanted more than anything. Instead, I'd take
my wrinkled paper bag out to a corner of the schoolyard
and eat by myself, worried the kids would make fun of my
food. Often it would be a bean or mashed-potato sandwich.
Sometimes, when things were really bad, my mom would
mix sugar, cocoa, and canned milk into a thick paste and
spread it on a piece of bread. Ugh. Greedily I eyed the other
kids' sandwiches from a distance. *Peanut butter and jelly.* It
was a delicacy I yearned for but was never able to have.

Milk was another scarce commodity in our house. I loved
milk. And I couldn't help but notice how most of our
neighbors had it delivered in bottles on the doorstep. I
always wondered why we were only able to get it occasionally at the store.

One day Lowell and I bought a quart of milk and we
were ferrying it home on top of our jerry-built skate coaster.
The rickety wheels hit a stone. The bottle toppled over, hit
the sidewalk, and broke. I cried—talk about crying over
spilt milk—I literally stood there and cried because it was
not a question of getting another five cents and returning to
the store. For us, there wasn't going to be any more.

Shoes were a problem too. When my one pair would
wear out, my mother would take me to Kress's, the five-
and-dime store, and she would buy these ready-made
patches. At home she would cut the patches to fit the holes
and glue them on. That's how my shoes were resoled.

By then my mother had become the backbone and sole
support of the family. A strong woman, she didn't take
anything from anybody, but she was always kind to everyone, and incredibly tolerant of my father. My brother and I
became very, *very* protective of her. Even kids can see the
pain, and we knew how hard she worked. We knew what
time she left in the morning and what time she came back at
night.

She would be gone when I woke up, already clanking
toward the garment district on the Red Car—the old electric
streetcar—an hour long ride from Glendale to downtown
L.A. She worked on Los Angeles Street—actually, about

eight blocks from where Parker Center is now—and every night she would trudge a mile to the Grand Central Market at 3rd and Broadway to buy groceries before taking the Red Car home. Lowell and I waited for her, often in the dark, at the Glenoaks and Western Red Car stop, many long blocks from our house.

As a nonunion laborer in a dress factory, she put in, I suspect, nine or ten hours a day. It was tough work. Her job was to lay a pattern on a thick stack of material and, using giant scissors, cut through all the fabric. Later, after they switched to electric cutters, she often came home with her hands bleeding and fingers gashed.

I don't recall that she ever complained. Sometimes, when I think back about what kept me on the straight and narrow, I think it was a fear of disappointing her. She had such faith in Lowell and me and, later, my little brother Steve, eleven years younger than I—in our abilities, in our sense of right and wrong, and in our goodness—that it almost radiated from her. The last thing we ever wanted to do was cause her to question her belief in us.

My father kept us in line out of sheer fear.

When he was sober we were scared to death he would whip us. He did that only a couple of times, but we were always terrified that he might do it again. Basically, Paul Gates was an easygoing man who liked to laugh. With his self-deprecating humor and an ability to tell a funny story, he made everyone else laugh too. But he also had a real temper—whew! And that kept us in line.

Unfortunately, much of the time he was inebriated. Before we moved I don't recall that he drank, though I do remember him making beer in the bathtub. This was during Prohibition, and every six months a group of his Irish Catholic buddies would come to the house and make beer. I used to watch them bottle it. They had some kind of device that put caps on the bottles. After we moved to the new house the men still came to make beer, but more and more my father wouldn't be there.

Where he was, what he was doing, I never knew. The Glendale police, however, apparently did.

One of my worst memories was the first time they came for him. There was a knock on the door, a loud knock, and out front stood these large, uniformed people. It was just devastating to a kid. Drunk or not, my dad was still the authority figure in the family, and there he was, scurrying out the back door into the blackness of night, while these massive uniformed people were beating on the door, rushing in. In those days they didn't stand on ceremony. They just pushed in, past my mother . . . *Where is he?*

The scene came to be repeated many times. I learned never to ask questions. I don't know if they were marshals serving papers because we had terrible debts, or if it was the Glendale police coming to take him to jail for drunken behavior. But I formed a very poor opinion of the police—*very* poor. And that opinion didn't change in later years, when the police would stop him for a traffic violation. I found them smart-alecky and unnecessarily abusive. I thought they were just a plague on society. In fact, I didn't see the need for any policemen *at all*.

Over time, my father's unsteadiness grew more trouble-some. One morning when I was about seven, I woke up with a strangely puffy face. Lowell studied it and declared, "You better not go to school. There's something wrong with you."

I went to show my father. Already drunk, he just shrugged me away. Unsure of what to do, I stayed home. But that afternoon, when my brother returned, I followed him into the backyard to play baseball with the kids. By now my face was about twice its normal size. The kids made fun of me because I looked so funny with my eyes nearly swollen shut. Even I began to laugh. A while later my father came out to join us, but he never said a word. Then my mother got home. "Oh, my God," she exclaimed. The doctor arrived right away.

What I had was an acute kidney condition. There had been, several days before, an athletic competition at Thomas Jefferson Elementary, and I had won the gold medal. A fast and daring second-grader, I had managed to accumulate more points for the various chinning, running, and jumping contests than anybody in any grade. In fact, I broke the school records in all events. But in doing so, I had somehow pulled a kidney loose. Now the kidney was bleeding and my face—it was so long ago I can't remember why—blew up as a result.

"He'll have to go to the hospital," I heard the doctor say, followed by my mother's pleading that she couldn't afford that. Instead, I was sent to bed and sternly warned not to get up except to go to the bathroom. For the first two weeks I couldn't even do that. Someone had to carry me.

It took me a long, long time to forgive my father for his neglect. Letting his kid run around, face all bloated, while he shined it on, viewing me through the blurry eyes of an alcoholic and not those of a father at all. For three months I lay in bed. No one came in to look after me. With my mother at work and my father again mysteriously gone, I had to amuse myself. There were books, but not many. So I waited impatiently for Lowell, who ran home from school and did little things to brighten my day as best he could.

About a year after my kidney problem, we inexplicably moved again. This time to Highland Park, an area of northeast Los Angeles just below the Glendale line. It was a working-class neighborhood with a fairly mixed ethnic makeup: a lot of Italian and German families, a mixture of Catholics and Jews, many Hispanics, some Japanese and Chinese. I don't recall any blacks.

It was now 1935, and my father had finally hit bottom. Picked up for public drunkenness, he had been thrown in jail—again—by the Glendale police. But this time, as he told me many years later, when he woke up in the drunk tank he had such a terrible case of the DTs that he thought he was going to die. Wished he *could* die. "It was at that point," he said, "I decided I had to do something or I'd be dead."

He stopped drinking, cold turkey. And though he wolfed down chocolate bars like a fiend, craving the sugar, I never saw him take a drink again.

Our lives improved immediately. He took a job with a plumbing company and once again showed what a skilled plumber he was. For the first time we had our own transportation: Dad's company truck. It was an old clunker, the racks for pipes and tools rattling in the back. But now we could go off as a family anywhere we wanted to.

Over the next few years I came to know my "new" dad, a bright, witty, extremely well-read man who liked nothing better than to hold court at the dinner table, delivering his Depression-era harangues on the economic and governmental injustices against the common man. He was staunchly pro-F.D.R., staunchly Democrat, and fiercely pro-union, forever railing against the arrogance of management over underdog labor. I remember the comic sight of him as he piled up platters and bowls on his plate, so engrossed in his own words that he would forget to serve himself. Soon, we would pass him our empty plates, and my father, still intent on his pontifications, looked blankly around for a place to put them as we tried to stifle our laughter.

More important to this teenager, he taught me to box. He made a pair of dumbbells for me by filling two cans with cement and running a piece of plumbing pipe through the cans. Then he showed me what he thought were good exercises for somebody who wanted to fight.

By the time I was fifteen, I announced—to the horror of my mother—I intended to be a professional fighter. I joined a school boxing club that met on Wednesday nights, and when matches were held on the playground, I boxed then too.

Unfortunately, I got into a number of unscheduled fights. I don't think I was a bully. I wasn't a bad kid; just—a little bit the way I am now—mischievous.

For example, one Halloween, Lowell and I went to the costume party at the Highland Park playground. I don't remember my costume, but I do remember I had a bean shooter up my sleeve. And *pfttt!* I'd shoot beans at people.

Not appreciating my act, one of the big kids came over and told me so. He told me with a shove. Up flew my fists and the crowd formed. I was probably losing badly when Lowell came elbowing through. Lowell was the great arbitrator. One stern look from him usually did the trick. He told us to knock it off. Obediently, I backed off, but the other kid was having none of it. Suddenly, the kid's father came busting through, yelling at Lowell to stop pushing his kid around.

"Hey, I'm just trying to break up a fight here," Lowell protested.

The father shoved Lowell. Whereupon Little Helpful here came flying over and hit this father—boom!—right in the gut.

When we dragged home, my brother's costume was half ripped off, and I was in terrible shape with a bloody nose. Absolutely furious with me, Lowell grabbed my bean shooter and snapped it in half. But the lesson he intended to teach me fell upon deaf ears. I could not keep my fists to myself.

A clash of teenage contradictions, I was outwardly shy and soft-spoken, inwardly brimming with competitiveness and ego. The latter qualities I used productively on the football field, where I played fullback and outside linebacker for Franklin High. At five feet nine and 165 pounds, I enjoyed hitting and tackling and scrambling hard for yardage. But off the field, I carried with me the indelible feeling of being an outsider that poverty instills in a child. My father's son, I was quick to sense an injustice, and even quicker to resent a bully.

And in my mind there was no bigger bully than a cop.

When I was finally able to scrape up enough money for a used 1936 Ford, they were always pulling me over for something—speeding, signals, boulevard stops, and to each citation was added "loud muffler." I resented every citation, dead certain the police were secretly saying to themselves: *Ha ha, another one!*

Why, I furiously wondered, couldn't they just *warn* me?

On a Sunday night in 1942, with my girlfriend beside me and my buddy in back, I stopped my car in front of the Highland Theater. Every Sunday night they showed a Hopalong Cassidy, and my buddy Pete Ciulla went in to see what time the next show started. We were sitting there, my car parked just a little bit out from the curb, when suddenly a squad car slammed to a stop behind me. Because of the war, the LAPD had been forced to hire emergency wartime officers—among them, it turned out, these two. One strolled over and whipped out his pad.

I jumped out of my car. "What are you doing?"

"Writing you a citation."

"Come on, what for?"

"You're double-parked."

"But my friend'll be right back!"

And it deteriorated from there.

Pete came out and said a couple of things. This got the

other officer out of the car. He was trying to move Pete aside when Lowell walked out from the just-ended show. As usual, my brother tried to talk my way out of this one, but the officers roughly pushed him away.

Which is when I lost it. I punched one cop, and my buddy punched the other one. And we all ended up in the Highland Park jail.

Pete and I, sixteen-year-olds, were herded upstairs to Juvenile division, where they forced us to sit on the floor, handcuffed. My brother stayed downstairs, where they dealt with adult troublemakers. Luckily, two Juvenile officers happened to walk in who knew Lowell through his work with kids in sports activities. Since Lowell hadn't really been involved, they were able to plead for his release.

My case was different. "We don't know what we're gonna do with *you*," said the Juvenile officers, shaking their heads. "*You* hit a police officer."

Because they liked Lowell, Officers Gilbert Burgoyne and Lee Chapman went off to confer with the two policemen Pete and I had hit. They came back with a deal. All charges would be dropped if we would apologize to the cops we'd belted. Pete agreed, but I would not.

"No way!" I protested. "The guy was wrong, not me. He pushed my brother. No way in the world am *I* gonna apologize."

We went round and round, getting nowhere. Finally Lowell was brought in to beat some sense into this kid's brain. All he said was, "You're gonna apologize."

And I said, "Oh, okay."

But by then the officer had gone home and I was told to return the next day. God, how I dreaded doing that. Just dreaded having to apologize to that officer, because I didn't think I was wrong.

Still wrestling with myself, I gloomily returned the next morning. Resisting every step, I dragged myself up to the desk and asked for the officer. He was in roll call, I was told. Someone went to get him. Looking as if he still wanted to smack me, the cop sauntered over.

It wasn't much of an apology. But then it wasn't much of an acceptance either. Practically nose-to-nose, I mumbled, "Uh, sorry. Won't happen again."

He said, "Okay, kid," wheeled, and left.

Little did I know how fateful that little drama would prove.

■

The following fall, having graduated from high school and worrying that World War II would end without me, I joined the navy. An impatient seventeen-year-old, I signed up for the shortest school the navy offered, two weeks. By the first of the year I was settling in aboard the U.S.S. *Ault* D.D.698. Soon we were steaming through the South China Sea as one of the destroyers in Admiral William Halsey's legendary Task Force 38 and 58. In our role during bombing missions against Japan, the *Ault*—along with several other destroyers—would form what we called The Screen, which protected the aircraft carriers in the center of the task force from submarines and the dreaded kamikaze air attacks.

Thinking back, I must have been crazy to be so eager to go overseas. As one of two hundred men on board, I was assigned to a 40mm ack-ack (or antiaircraft) gun. My job was either to load it or keep the weapon pointed in the right direction. On one memorable mission in March 1945 we took three destroyers and a couple of cruisers into the mouth of Tokyo Bay. The idea was to show the Japanese that we could penetrate the bay if we felt like it.

The newspapers really played this mission up: United States fleet bombards Japan. Well, hell. What we did was go in under cover of darkness in a pretty low fog, run into the bay a mile or two, and bombard . . . I don't know what. I'm not sure any of us knew. Then we turned the ships around and ran like hell.

By the summer of 1945, even though the handwriting was clearly on the wall for Japan, it was still possible that the United States might have to stage a full-fledged invasion. I remember reading some of the plans that had been drawn up for an attack; the official estimates of casualties were enormous. More than one million Americans were expected to die. So even though the bombing of Hiroshima and Nagasaki was dreadful, I can't help feeling grateful that we did not have to invade.

When the Japanese surrendered on August 15 we all

gathered on deck to listen to Admiral Halsey on the radio as he gave thanks for our victory. While he was speaking the Japanese kamikaze were still attacking our task force. Obviously they hadn't received the official word to surrender, or were ignoring it. So Admiral Halsey—in what had to be one of the strangest victory speeches ever—told us "not to shoot them down vindictively, but in a friendly sort of way."

On September 2 the *Ault* slipped into Tokyo Bay one last time, pulling to within shouting distance of the *Missouri,* and from this ringside seat we watched history being made as General Yoshijiro Umezu and Mamoru Shigemitsu, the frail Japanese foreign minister, came aboard the *Missouri* and, standing alongside General Douglas MacArthur, signed the peace treaty with the Allies. Afterward, I was chosen by my shipmates to go ashore and buy souvenirs. A wad of Japanese bills was jammed into my hands and off I went. I found some trinkets, paid for them, and received change in yen. Somehow, by the time I got back to the ship, I had more money than I left with. No one quite understood, including me, how they ended up with souvenirs *and* a bonus. This is probably the last time we had a favorable balance of trade with Japan.

I served my two years and came home a Seaman First Class, the same way I'd left. I can't say I was at all sorry to get out. Never again, I swore, would I stand in line, or say *"Yes sir, no sir"* to anyone, ever. Still, the navy taught me something valuable about myself. I learned about my ability to take on a challenge and to meet it. And I learned how to handle fear. I watched others who were terribly afraid and saw how badly they reacted.

I could be terrified and still handle it.

■

Thanks to the GI Bill, I was able to go to a fancy private school like the University of Southern California.

Exactly what I was going to do with this education, I had no idea. I ran the gamut. I was going to be a psychologist for a while. Then I was going to teach. But when I did my practice teaching at Franklin High in Highland Park, I realized this wasn't going to work. The boys drove me buggy; I wanted to punch each one of them out. And the girls . . .

well. *All* the girls looked good to me and I kept thinking, *Gosh, this is terrible. I'll be in trouble in no time at all.* So I scratched teaching. At last I figured it out. I would become a lawyer.

As I prepared to start my senior year I applied to law school. The problem was, I plain old needed a job right away. In the fall of 1946 I had enrolled at Pasadena City College and met Wanda Hawkins. She was the very attractive blond friend of a friend, and our first date, as I recall, was when I drove her home. I was the football player and she was the song leader and the following spring we were married.

Now, in the summer of 1949, my wife was pregnant. I was not happy about this in the least. I had planned to finish up at USC, where I had since transferred, and then start studying law. The kids, I always figured, would come at some opportune moment in the future. Suddenly I had to face up to supporting a family.

We were living in a crummy little apartment off Sunset Boulevard, trying to make ends meet on the small amount the GI Bill paid veterans and the meager funds from Wanda's job, which she would soon have to give up. I had gone through a succession of part-time jobs, driving trucks and, for a year, working in a service station pumping gas. Even so, I was seriously in hock. And now I would need to find a nicer place to live; no kids were allowed in that crummy building.

One day I ran into a friend I hadn't seen much of since high school. Dick Eckenwieler had been the textbook bad boy in many respects, but like me, he was now going to school and needing a way to pay for it. To my utter astonishment he told me he had joined the LAPD.

"Listen, if you need a job, why don't you become a Los Angeles police officer?" Dick said.

"What?"

"I'm serious, Daryl. It's a cinch. The Police Academy is only three weeks. They encourage you to go back to college. Even help you to pay for it. And you make two-ninety a month."

"Two-ninety a *month*?"

That seemed like an incredible amount of money in those

days. Two-ninety? Why, I could sign on for a while, pay off my debts, and finish USC through night school. After two or three years, when I had saved up enough money for law school, I could leave the stupid police department and commence my ascent to millionaire attorney.

I actually considered this for a moment. Then I came to my senses.

"No way in the world," I said, "will I *ever* be a dumb cop."

2

Rookie

On September 16, 1949, I became a Los Angeles cop.

In the end, enticed by the $290 a month, I hustled to change my plans. I had already started my senior year at USC and now I had to drop out. I was so embarrassed to tell people why that I kind of mumbled I had taken a job. Eventually I confided to a few friends: "Well, I'm going to be a police officer *for a little while.*"

I did not start off auspiciously. On the way to Hollywood High to take the civil service exam, my car broke down and I nearly said, *Forget it. I'll never make it, and I don't want to be a police officer anyway.* But as the fates would have it, a streetcar rattled by just then and I found myself hopping aboard.

Inside the high school I was astonished to find five thousand other applicants crammed into the auditorium. That astonishment turned to skepticism weeks later when the test results were posted. I could not believe that I ranked *ninth* on the list. Was it possible? Eight prospective dumb cops scored higher than me? Somebody, I thought sourly, must have some major pull around here.

Wary and suspicious, I went for the background interview conducted by personnel. A rough, tough, no-nonsense lieutenant named Ken McCauley took down my answers to his questions.

"You ever been arrested, booked, anything like that?"

"No, sir," I replied truthfully.

" 'Cause we don't take guys with records."

I gulped. If my brother and those two Juvenile officers hadn't gotten me a deal, I realized, I would have been out the door in a second. "I don't have a record," I said uncomfortably.

"Okay. Report to the Academy on September sixteenth, seven A.M.," McCauley gruffly told me. "You'll be there till nine at night and your training will last for thirteen weeks."

What? This was news to me. "Well, I can't," I said.

"What do you mean, you *can't*?"

"Someone said the training lasted three weeks."

"We changed that."

"Uh—at night too? I mean, I got things to do."

McCauley gave me one of those slitty-eyed stares that cops are so good at. "Look, kid, you don't want to be a police officer, tell me right now. 'Cause a lot of guys out there want this job."

Not liking his tone, not to mention how they were already changing the rules on me, I was tempted to tell him what he could do with his stupid badge and his gun. Or what I would. Hell, I'd find another way to pick up some dough.

Instead, I heard myself saying, "I'll be there on the sixteenth, sir. No problem at all."

And so I found myself on the morning of the sixteenth, staring dubiously at the words inscribed on the Police Academy wall: THE MORE YOU SWEAT HERE, THE LESS YOU WILL BLEED ON THE STREET.

I shrugged at the motto—yeah, sure. We had already taken our physicals. When the statistics showed five eleven and 205, the Police Training doctor said, "For your height, two-oh-five is too heavy. But don't worry—as you go through training you'll quickly drop the extra weight." Another bit of stupidity. I was 205 pounds of *muscle*. No way would I lose *that*.

Actually, it was one of the few times I turned out to be

right. Thirteen weeks later I weighed 200; the muscle just got harder. Other cadets called me The Bear, a nickname I admit I relished. But more than on my physique, I prided myself on my intellect.

In no time at all my ego plummeted to earth. To my continuing amazement I was not the smartest guy in the class, nor the best educated. There were some cadets with towering IQs and superb educations. One guy, John McAllister, had a degree from Berkeley, two years of graduate work, and was an army air force pilot. The guy on my right had a master's in chemistry; the guy on my left had finished two years of law school. And *they* actually viewed police work as a legitimate career. It was still a mystery to me how anyone with a brain could. But their dedication opened my eyes. I realized I could never give the impression that I wasn't here for the duration; if I did, I would be out the door in a minute.

Equally surprising to me, the Police Training staff included brilliant instructors. Lieutenant Tom Reddin, who eventually became chief, provided outstanding lectures in law, as did Officer "Buck" Compton, the attorney who, twenty years later, would prosecute Sirhan Sirhan for the assassination of Robert Kennedy, and would ultimately wind up on the Appellate Court bench.

As the weeks flew by I also began, for the first time, to get some sense of what the police were all about. Maybe, I thought, they weren't all Neanderthals, cowboys, or fascist Republicans. Maybe they actually played an important role in society; maybe they even performed some essential functions. Maybe.

■

The Los Angeles of 1950 boasted no Dodgers, no building taller than twelve stories except for City Hall, which was twenty-seven stories, no streamlined San Diego or Santa Monica freeways, and no street-corner mini-malls. It was still a sprawling, often dusty, horizontal city, broken up by large empty spaces. Horseback-riding trails could be found all over the city, including along the middle of Sunset Boulevard in Beverly Hills, and South Central L.A. was still a pleasant middle-class neighborhood inhabited by many people I knew. But signs of a Los Angeles on the move were everywhere. The end of the war had brought new optimism, prosperity, and a rapidly growing population. Thousands of servicemen and defense plant workers who had spent the war years here decided to stick around. Tract houses were blossoming overnight, decorated with brightly colored banners and signs advertising prices as low as $7,000.

But with the manufacturing plants and the huge influx of automobiles came the smog, choking brown air that obliterated the clean outlines of the distant mountains I had so often gazed at as a child. The crystal blue skies were rarely that any longer; more typically they were soup. Los Angeles had another big problem in 1950 as well. We had, even then, traffic.

Which was my first assignment as a Police Academy graduate.

Feeling awkward in my stiff new uniform and trying to maneuver under the weight of all my equipment, I took up my post at the busy intersection of 3rd and Broadway downtown. Los Angeles has always been depicted as a city without a downtown, but in the boomtown days after the war, and before the blossoming of Westwood, Century City, and the San Fernando Valley, "downtown" was where people came to work. Most of them, it seemed, came through 3rd and Broadway.

Although it was my first day on the job, I was, to my annoyance, more in debt than before. Not until we were sworn in at the Academy did anybody bother to mention that each officer had to purchase his own uniform and equipment.

They said, "Look, you have to have a uniform and you have to have a gun and you have to have all these other things to be a police officer—and we'll get you a good deal!"

So the first thing most of us did was run over to the credit union to take out a loan. Then we went down to Foreman and Clark to buy, well, everything. One uniform wasn't enough. You needed at least two; one at the cleaner's and one that you wore. You also needed two pairs of uniform shoes and black socks. And rain gear—a rain hat and coat and jacket. You needed to have what they call a Sam Browne, the belt that holds your equipment—baton, handcuffs, gun—all of which you also paid for. And of course, you have to buy a hat, and bullets for your gun. Today, all these things are issued and paid for by the city, but then it was up to you. The only thing the department provided was a key to open up callboxes in emergencies.

This little shopping spree cost me $175. Twelve bucks a month on credit, for eighteen months.

The gun I purchased was a Colt .38 revolver with a big, thick barrel that resembles the gun Dirty Harry used. Like most new officers, I went through a phase of wearing this gun everywhere I went, off duty or on. And since I couldn't afford a nice holster, I rigged belts in the oddest contortions to keep my gun strapped on. After a while, I realized how uncomfortable it was to have this thing clamped on to my body day and night and how unlikely it was that I was going to need it for all the emergencies I had conjured up.

My off-duty compulsion didn't last long. But habits are habits. I still keep a 9mm semiautomatic in my briefcase, but I don't make a fetish of carrying it.

On my first day it didn't seem likely I was ever going to need a gun, since I was almost fired before I had my uniform on. Because I had once driven a truck, two lieutenants and a captain decided I should go undercover as a driver for the Teamsters' Union. To make the scam work, I was to be "fired" from the department.

"So don't report to work or anything," they told me. "We'll contact *you*."

That morning, Lieutenant Marion Phillips from traffic called my home, wondering where the hell was I? I tried to explain.

"You don't show up in, say, fifteen seconds, Gates, you are fired," the lieutenant stormed.

I went crazy. I started calling the other lieutenants to find out what was going on. Sorry, they said. Operation's off. Forgot to let you know.

Now, standing in the middle of traffic, in the rain, I felt like a pack horse. The Sam Brownes back then, as opposed to those we use today, had a shoulder strap that came across your chest and attached to your belt, which held up all your equipment. I must have been wearing ten pounds of stuff, and soon my shoulder began to ache. I felt conspicuous as hell, as if everyone in Los Angeles was ogling every move I made.

I was given a split shift—morning rush hour and evening rush hour. Directing traffic is more complicated than it looks. I like to think that because of my skill at keeping things running smoothly they stuck me at one of the busiest intersections in Los Angeles. I had streetcars coming in from two directions down the middle of Broadway. On either side of the streetcars ran two lanes of traffic, two flowing north and two running south. And I handled the whole thing. Just stood there, like I was conducting a traffic symphony.

After two months I was transferred to Accident Investigation, known as AI. In those days the police investigated every accident. If it was a fender-bender, we investigated that. Traffic deaths, traffic injuries, hit-and-runs—whatever it was, full traffic report. By comparison, the only accidents investigated today are those involving death, serious injury, and hit-and-run. All the others, we just make sure everybody exchanges information, if we respond at all.

Seeing firsthand what terrible damage motorists did to themselves, and to others, I began to understand why, as a motorist, I had been given no breaks. In Los Angeles in 1950 there were more traffic deaths than homicides. Our whole economy, our whole social structure depended on the car. It still does. When a little fender-bender can tie up traffic for hours, the driving public must be disciplined or the entire city can be brought to a standstill in minutes. Studies by the police department showed that issuing a warning had no deterrence whatsoever; the only effective way to make people drive in a way that did not cause mayhem was to issue a citation.

I also learned, to my surprise, that officers hated giving tickets, just hated it. They had to be hit over the head, told all the reasons why it was necessary, or they wouldn't bother.

One evening I received a particularly chilling lesson in why the police must enforce all traffic laws, especially the law against jaywalking, which the public hates. Receiving a radio call that an automobile had struck a man in a crosswalk, my partner and I pulled up at the scene just ahead of the ambulance.

The victim was shrieking inside his own bloodbath. He had crossed against the light. The speeding auto had closed in. The pedestrian, hearing the sound, turned, and instinctively threw out his arms in futile self-protection. Now both of his arms, ripped off at the shoulders, were jammed grotesquely into the auto's front grill.

Jesus, that thing has stuck with me all these years. The shock in the poor man's eyes. The mangled, gushing stumps. I don't know what became of him, whether he lived or not. But it's one of those moments a police officer never forgets. Nor could I forget the anguish of the driver, wailing, "It's not my fault—oh, God."

From Accident Investigation, I transferred to patrol. LAPD has carved Los Angeles into fourteen divisions, each anchored by a station house. Three watches work out of each division—day watch, night watch, and the early-hours morning watch. Three patrol officers are assigned to each car per watch; only two work at one time, rotating with the third for days off. Every car keeps a "hot sheet," which lists the license numbers of stolen vehicles that we had to be on the lookout for. At roll call before a shift began, the sergeant in charge would update that sheet, announce new suspects on the loose, and alert us to anything important happening in our area. Then you and your partner got in the car and began your rounds.

Even then, LAPD seemed too small for the city it protected. We had a force of only 4,300 officers responsible for the safety of nearly 2 million residents spread out over 462 square miles. But at any one time, one third of the force would be on days off. Others had desk jobs or special assignments, such as tracking mobsters or working Internal Affairs. This left roughly 400 to 500 officers available for patrol or to respond to a call at any one time of the day. As a result, unlike other cities where officers simply drive around waiting for something to go down, we always were saddled with specific tasks. Warrants for arrests, for instance, or stolen vehicles to locate. And we did. On average, 10,000 cars were reported stolen each year in the early fifties and we managed to recover 92 percent. By 1991, when 70,000 auto thefts occurred annually, we were recovering only 55 to 60 percent.

The shift would take on a tempo of its own. You would cruise the streets, actively looking for problems. We might drive by a bar known for rowdies and fights, make sure all was calm. The crackling of the police radio would alert us to a "211" (robbery) or a "459" (burglary) in progress, and off we'd go. There were always plenty of knifings too. But unlike TV police, who need a whole hour to get a job done, sustained action for a patrol officer rarely lasted more than fifteen minutes or produced any real drama.

Feeling self-important in my sharp LAPD uniform, I manfully set out to make my first arrest. But as my eyes roved the streets for ne'er-do-wells, I noticed this guy sitting on a shoeshine stand slumped over. He was nicely dressed and wore a big ring on his finger. *Gee,* I thought, *what's wrong with this guy?* I shook him. Nothing happened. *Oh, God, the guy's sick.*

Concerned, I called for a radio car. A few minutes later an old-time beat officer rolled up, got out of the car, and said, "What is it, kid?"

"We got a man over here—he's ill. I think we'll probably need an ambulance right away."

The officer went over to take a look. To my astonishment he pulled out his sap and whacked the guy on the bottom of his shoes. The guy sat up. In a drunken voice he said, "Oh. What is it, Officer?"

I signed the arrest myself. My first arrest—nothing but a plain old drunk.

Domestic disputes were far more worrisome, potentially dangerous because you never knew what an emotionally overwrought couple might do. One day my partner and I got a call over the radio: "Domestic dispute—shots fired."

The address took us to Bunker Hill, an area of downtown distinguished by turn-of-the-century tenements and boxlike wooden houses, largely inhabited by Filipinos. Before our arrival the woman had fired shots at her husband on the street. He raced into the building, into their first-floor apartment, and grabbed a meat cleaver. When we arrived she was standing behind a locked bedroom door and he was pounding on it. Both were screaming at the top of their lungs. Despite our uniformed presence, the man totally ignored us.

The problem was sticky. If we clobbered him, we didn't

know what she would do—maybe shoot *us*. Which has been known to happen. Unlike today, when officers routinely call for backup from their car, we just looked at each other and shrugged. Then I tackled the man. While I was fighting him for the cleaver, my partner kicked the door in. I got hold of the cleaver and the man, and the woman, seeing us, obediently put the gun down. After chastising them both, we picked our way carefully through the topsy-turvy living room—where, apparently, the battle had begun—and left.

Like other police officers, I learned to harden myself against what I saw day in and day out. Walking in on a husband beating his wife, seeing the frightened eyes of a child cowering in a bedroom doorway. Rushing to the side of a terrified woman in labor—a total stranger—and helping to deliver her baby. Or barging into a Skid Row saloon, reeking of vile odors and littered with broken men, to drag a troublemaker off to the drunk tank.

Patrolling the low-rent areas of downtown, I was continually thrust into the lives of people without means or a glimmer of hope. People, oftentimes, who had never learned to settle a dispute verbally—only physically. The people I encountered on my daily rounds were no poorer than I had been during the precarious days of the Depression. Yet the differences made a deep impression on me. Even in our most desperate moments—when the electricity would be turned off again because we couldn't pay the bill, or when my mother would plead with the landlord to give us a few more days to come up with the rent—our home was never without hope.

In a college sociology class I had learned that people develop a pattern of conduct and mores at an early age. And even if you move them into a new environment, they are unlikely to change. I walked into homes that were pigsties and felt revulsion: *Hey, what's the matter with you?* But this feeling was always supplanted by one of pity. These people never had what I did: someone in the home to brighten it up. Someone like my mother, to offer tremendous support. To lay down the rules and instill certain values. Our home was always spotless. One week I would wash dishes, and Lowell would make the beds. The next week we would switch. We were taught responsibility and respect for others. You didn't steal from your neighbor. You found ways to deal with troubling situations in a fairly civilized way. This type of socializing process, inculcated in me at the earliest age, had made it possible for me to pull myself out of my circumstances. Many of the people I encountered on the job were forever mired in theirs.

I got used to seeing the results. I got used to the ripped flesh of a knife wound, though I never got used to the smell of blood. I have no idea how doctors manage. I've never smelled blood in an operating room, so maybe it's not the same. But the blood on the street had a stale odor that always stuck with me for long hours afterward.

■

As I came to the end of my rookie year I waited anxiously for a transfer to motorcycles. That was the glamour beat in my eyes, and if I was going to stick around the department a while longer, I intended to do it on my own terms. My friend John McAllister and I had signed up for motors and I had already taken the oral exam. This consisted mainly of telling three tough old motor sergeants on the other side of the desk a lot of lies about why I wanted the duty. They had nodded and grinned back at me, saying, *Yeah, yeah, uh huh*. But when the test results were posted, I ranked only second on the list—John was first. Now I would have to wait for an opening.

One night, when I had my uniform on and one foot out the door to go to work, my old high school buddy Pete Ciulla showed up with a used motorcycle he had just bought. It had a real hopped-up engine and I only half-listened as he told me about the suicide clutch and the quarter acceleration. The clutch allowed you to change gears faster than normal and the quarter acceleration meant you only had to hit it a little bit, and voom!

Itching to try it, I took off down the street, really burning rubber. Straight ahead was a dead end with a hard right. I hit the clutch to move down into second gear for the turn, and then I hit the throttle. At once I understood the meaning of *quarter throttle*. Hitting it too hard, I was practically wide open and I knew there was no way to make that corner. So I charged straight ahead through a wall of hedges into this lady's backyard. She was sitting in her living room looking out the bay window and here came this fully uniformed police officer flying through her hedges and crashing onto her lawn.

People poured out of their houses. "Who's he chasing?"

There I was, on all fours, hurting like hell all over, uniform torn up, legs torn up. I still have the scar.

My wife, who saw the whole thing, raced up, breathing hard, thinking I was dead. Pete thought I was dead; everyone thought I was dead. Seeing I was not, Wanda berated me all the way home. "You are not, absolutely *not,* going on motors."

Ordinarily, I would not have heeded her admonition, but I hurt so badly that I paid attention. I will never forget the look on that sergeant's face when I told him the next day: "You know, I've just decided that I don't think riding motors is the thing I want to do in my career right now."

∎

Every day brought home some new lesson or experience. I tried to act in a more measured way, less impulsively. I learned I could often control a situation with my words instead of my fists. And as the weeks sped by I found—to my continuing amazement—that police work was revealing, rewarding, thrilling, and ever-changing. One moment you're barreling down the street, gaining ground on a suspect; the next, you're chaperoning a lost kid home. Within three hours you can deliver a baby and witness someone getting killed. I had a very high arrest rate. Back then, that's how the department judged you, so I made a lot of them. I learned to act with authority—the command presence they taught at the Police Academy. But once I had a suspect subdued, I never tried to intimidate him. I could see how frightened most were and I always tried to make them as comfortable as possible going to jail. Besides, it made good sense. A happy, smiling arrestee wasn't going to fight you all the way to the jail door.

The car radio became like a magic box that dealt you your next chance. The call that always got the adrenaline flowing was *Officer needs help.* This didn't mean "assistance," such as backup; it meant the officer's life was in danger. And it evoked a tremendous response. Every officer who heard that call raced full-bore to the scene. And they continued to pour to the scene—from all over the city—until a Code 4 went out, which meant everything was under control. There was no greater feeling than seeing the way officers responded. It filled me with pride. No matter who you were or where you were, if you were an LAPD officer and you needed help, you were going to get it.

Still, the job had not yet become a narcotic. Soon I would quit and go to law school. And I have no doubt I would today be an attorney . . . had I not come to know William H. Parker.

A stern, cantankerous man with a reputation as a bully, Parker had just been jumped over a lot of high-ranking officers to become the newly appointed chief of police. A sort of gloom descended over the department. None of the people I worked with had encountered him. But word had it that Parker was a tyrant.

A week after Parker was sworn in, Sergeant Floyd Phillips from Internal Affairs, who had taught one of my physical training classes at the Academy and apparently was impressed with me, asked if I would like to serve as Parker's driver/bodyguard.

I said, "God, no."

The last thing I wanted was to be somebody's toady, bowing and scraping along in the chief's ceremonial wake. I had seen that routine firsthand a few months before, when I had worked security detail the night of the Oscars. The previous chief, William Worton, was a retired marine general who used to strut around as if he'd never left the corps. What I remembered most about the Academy Awards that night was Janet Leigh coming out of the auditorium looking absolutely ravishing. I stared openly as she glided over to Chief Worton and they stood talking. After a while a deputy chief asked one of us on security to tell Worton's driver to take the chief to the Beverly Hills Hotel. As if the deputy chief couldn't personally tell the driver, or Worton couldn't tell his own driver. I mean, the chain of command was ridiculous.

"No, thanks," I told the sergeant again.

Ten days later I was standing on the sidewalk in front of

the Central Division police station when up drove Sergeant Phillips. Not even stopping, he rolled down his window and yelled, "You're on the transfer!"

"What?"

"You got the job!" he shouted, and roared off.

Oh, God.

Well, back to the military, I thought.

3

Parker

In 1950, police headquarters were still located in City Hall, at the corner of Temple and Spring. The mayor entered his office on Spring Street. The police chief entered his on Temple. My first day on the job, in full uniform, I went through the proper door and reported in. A supervisor showed me to a small desk outside the door boldly stenciled OFFICE OF THE CHIEF OF POLICE. Dutifully, I stopped the first guy who tried walking into the inner sanctum. He looked vaguely familiar, but I couldn't take any chances.

"Excuse me, sir, may I ask your name?"

He thrust out his steely hand. "It's Parker," he said.

▪

William H. Parker had been sworn in on August 9, 1950, in the wake of a major police department scandal. The year before, several high-ranking police officials had been indicted by a county grand jury for giving protection to Brenda Allen, a well-known madam with Mafia connections. In addition, allegations surfaced that members of the Gangster

Squad, LAPD's task force assigned to combat the Mafia, were instead dining at expensive nightspots as guests of L.A.'s most notorious gangster, Mickey Cohen, who graciously picked up the check.

Chief of Police C. B. "Jack" Horrall and Assistant Chief Joe Reed were among those indicted, obviously with too much haste, for the indictments were quashed almost immediately. Both immediately resigned. The mayor chose marine Major General William Worton to come in and sweep up the mess.

The mess hardly glorified the reputation of the city, coming on the heels of what had been the worst political scandal in L.A. history, due to the very corrupt administration of the Shaw regime.

Frank L. Shaw, a one-time wholesale grocery salesman and later city councilman and county supervisor, was elected mayor in 1933. No sooner did he toss his fedora onto the hatrack than he demanded the resignations of the five-member Police Commission, which counts among its duties the appointing of the police chief. Shaw wanted to reorganize the internal structure of the LAPD, he said. He then usurped the responsibility of the disbanded Police Commission by reappointing James E. Davis as chief, after which he restocked and reactivated the Police Commission.

The same summer, Joe Shaw, the mayor's brother, decided to invent a new job—boss of both the police and the fire departments—and appointed himself to the post. Joe, who also served as Frank's secretary and worked out of Frank's office, then began selling promotional examinations to police officers. Included were sergeant's exams, which went for as much as $500, but which guaranteed instant promotion. This proved to be only one of the many schemes the Shaw brothers hatched to extort money.

It fell to the L.A. County grand jury to clean up the corruption. Undaunted, the Shaw regime was able to control even the grand jury by making certain appointments to it. For the next few years the Shaw machine and the underworld held almost complete control over the city of Los Angeles by its manipulation of that grand jury.

A reform-minded restauranteur named Clifford Clinton somehow got himself on the grand jury and found several sympathetic jurors. When the "bought" jurors issued a report proclaiming no evidence of corruption in Los Angeles, Clinton's group did something unheard of: It issued a minority report alleging underworld contributions to financial campaigns of all principal municipal offices and accused the district attorney, the sheriff of Los Angeles County, and the chief of police of Los Angeles of working in total harmony with the underworld. Clinton's home was mysteriously firebombed.

Even this might have been ignored, but an ex-LAPD cop, who was employed by Clinton's group to investigate corruption, tried to start his car one morning only to have it blow up. Miraculously, he survived. It was then discovered that LAPD had this ex-cop under surveillance. After a police captain was tried and convicted of attempted murder, the city responded by initiating a recall action against Frank Shaw. In 1938 he became the first mayor in America ever to be thrown out of office.

Now, eleven years later, came this new scandal. The hard-bitten General Worton did get rid of many bad eggs in the department, but because he had been brought in from the outside and was not a sworn police officer, Worton was forbidden by the City Charter from serving more than one year.

Normally, a new chief is selected from the highest ranks of the department. But as Worton began to search for his successor, he kept hearing about a rebellious, stubborn, scrupulously honest inspector named Bill Parker.

General Worton promoted Parker to the rank of deputy chief and made him head of the feared Bureau of Internal Affairs. From that position Parker took the Civil Service exam for chief and placed first.

For four months the Police Commission bickered bitterly over which of the three top-scoring candidates on the exam should become chief. Parker brought with him twenty-three years of LAPD experience, a degree from Southwestern Law School, and the prestige of having devised the police and prisons plan for the European invasion under General Dwight D. Eisenhower. A decorated veteran, Parker helped Munich and Frankfurt set up democratic police systems after the war.

The squabbling over the three contenders raged on. In the end Parker won out, when one of his detractors on the Police Commission died, tilting the vote in his favor.

Parker was a trim man with thinning brown hair and a reputation as a cold, aloof loner. At forty-seven, he was old enough to be my father.

Not recognizing him was only my first faux pas of the day. That night when I went to drive Parker home, I scrambled to open the back door for him, as I had seen my predecessor do for General Worton. Smoothly, Parker stepped in front of me. "Oh, I'll ride in the front," he said, pulling open the door before I could.

More nervous than ever, I dashed around to my side and jumped into the chief's official car, a brand-new Buick Dynaflow. I fumbled for the ignition and finally found that. But my feet could not find a clutch on the floor.

I floundered around for what seemed an eternity.

"You've never driven an automatic shift," Parker said finally.

"No, sir. I don't have the slightest idea how to drive this car."

"Well, get out."

We traded places. In his civilian clothes Parker drove himself to his hillside home in Silver Lake. After climbing the steep set of stairs to his house and speaking briefly to his wife, a frowning Parker came loping back down. And taught his new driver how to work an automatic transmission.

■

He never once called me Daryl—it was Gates, always Gates—but I felt Bill Parker's fondness. Few people were able to see the Parker that I did. To most of the force he was a real iron-ass, a tough disciplinarian with no heart at all, who picked on officers, was arbitrary in his decisions, ran roughshod over people, and had not an inkling of understanding of the cop on the beat.

The truth was, he understood all too well.

I saw that as we drove around the city together. To me, he was friendly, down to earth, and a man who, above all else, was dedicated to elevating law enforcement into a respected profession. I couldn't know then, in the fall of 1950, that over the next sixteen years he would mold the LAPD into the world-recognized, aggressive police force that it is today. Even now, nearly every guideline in our police manual reflects Bill Parker's ideas on law enforcement. What I received, during my fifteen months with him, turned out to be more than a primer on policing.

It became a tutorial on how to be chief.

■

My unofficial lessons began each morning as he slid into the front seat. With Parker, you didn't just sit there like a lump and drive. He talked continuously, and he expected a response. Not the response of a callow twenty-four-year-old factotum, but of an equal. I was finishing up my degree in public administration at USC night school and he grilled me on what my instructors taught, engaged me in discussions on law enforcement and philosophical concepts as if I were one of his deputy chiefs, asked my opinion on current events, and passed along ideas he had culled from his eclectic reading.

"You know," he said one day, "everyone believes the chief of police has Civil Service protection and cannot be fired. Pick up the City Charter, Gates—you'll see the chief can be fired very easily."

Unlike Chicago or New York, in Los Angeles the police chief does not report directly to the mayor. Standing between the mayor and the chief is a five-member Board of Police Commissioners, appointed by the mayor and confirmed by the City Council. This body is, by law, "head of the department," allowed to make LAPD policy, hear complaints against officers—and their chief—and hold the department accountable for its actions. Made up of civilian volunteers, the board meets one afternoon a week. This system, fairly common in younger western cities, is designed to insulate chiefs from the machine-style patronage and political intimidation so prevalent in the East.

To fire a police chief, the Charter states, a public charge is required and must be proved at a hearing of the Board of Civil Service Commissioners. Even if the board can demonstrate "good and sufficient cause" for removal, the chief may appeal to the California courts.

Unlikely as removal seemed, Parker was not about to take a chance. "You have to build a power base," he told me. "If you don't, the chief can be swept out of here in no time at all."

From the beginning Parker set out to build one.

Since most homes in 1950 did not have television, he took to old-fashioned campaign-style stumping. Twice a day, every day, Bill Parker gave speeches, and some nights he gave two more. On weekends he would deliver three. He accepted any and every request: large group, small group— it didn't make any difference. Parker went.

He wrote out by hand every speech he gave. I still have a compendium of them at home. He was a dynamic speaker who adopted a faintly Harvard, faintly Bostonian accent and he could captivate an audience just by the majestic way he swept into a room. His delivery was riveting as he spoke of what the police were like, what their role in society was, how often they were misperceived or misunderstood. I never once saw anyone yawn.

Those speeches had a major impact on me. When Parker explained how the police were a minority, with all the injustices heaped upon a minority, I began to have a sense, finally, of what police officers were all about. The public, Parker would lecture, with its typically American underdog sympathies, automatically placed the police in a no-win situation. The amount of force necessary to restrain someone might, for instance, be judged by an onlooker as being greater than was appropriate to the situation. This happened, he said, because the public's perception of the situation, and what was needed to deal with that situation, were entirely out of sync with the reality.

The reality—how the suspect behaved, what he said, whether he was under the influence of narcotics or alcohol, what he might already have done that led to use of force— could not be accurately judged by an onlooker at a distance. "When violence has occurred, there is the inevitable attempt to blame the police," Parker said.

Misunderstood, the police banded together and, like a true minority, developed instinctively a minority's mentality: Us Against Them.

Wouldn't it be better, Parker suggested, if the public could view the police not as its nemesis but as its employees? Paid by the people to do what the people wanted done. But didn't care to do themselves.

■

I became totally smitten with Bill Parker. He was, I suppose, a kind of father figure—though, sadly, he was a paternal image in more ways than I would have liked.

After trying to absorb Parker's brilliance by day, I would, too often by night, drive him home drunk.

And I mean loaded. He drank until his words slurred and stairs became a hazard. He would repeat the same thought over and over until he became a terrible bore. Some nights he would attend a function and not touch a drop. Other nights he drank heavily and smelled embarrassing to me as he stumbled getting into the car, and stumbled getting out. From the street to his house required negotiating a steep hill and I often had to help him up.

Those who knew of his weakness for bourbon deluxe called him Whiskey Bill. And most of the department knew. So did the press. Luckily, in those days personal peccadilloes weren't written about, and anyway, most of the reporters drank heavily too. Parker never drank during the day, so I can't say it impaired his thinking. But I always worried that one night something might go drastically wrong and it would taint him, and the department as well. Apart from the bad long-ago memories Parker's drinking triggered in me, it was just an incredible thing to watch this man, who carried himself with such dignity and presence, lurching around really loaded.

Once, his drinking did affect his behavior the next day. And mine too.

New Year's Day, 1951, Parker and I were to pick up Mayor Fletcher Bowron at 7:00 A.M. and drive to the Elk's Club for breakfast. From there we would all go to the Rose Parade and afterward to the Rose Bowl game.

Parker, of course, had been out late New Year's Eve and had gotten himself snockered. By the time I got the chief home, and then me home, I had only two hours sleep before I had to be back at Parker's door.

When I arrived at the bottom of the hill, pooped, I switched off the engine and waited. From my vantage point below, the house looked dark. But I figured, *Oh, he'll come out any minute. I probably just can't see the lights.*

But Parker didn't appear. Getting up all my nerve, I hiked up the hill and pounded on his front door. Eventually it creaked open and Parker, barefoot, unshaven, and wearing rumpled pajamas, stared at me through bleary eyes.

"Chief, the mayor. We've got to pick up the mayor."

"Oh, my God," said Parker, and slammed the door.

Fifteen minutes later, shaved, but I'm not sure showered, and dressed in a dark-blue suit, Parker reappeared. Realizing he was going to be late, he had phoned Bowron. Mrs. Bowron answered and explained that the mayor, who lived up another steep hill by the Hollywood Bowl, had already left the house and was down on the corner waiting.

The mayor was not someone to be kept waiting. Fletcher Bowron was a pompous man who, after Frank Shaw had been removed, had swept into office on a campaign promise to clean up the city's scandals. He had. But being this very mayorly person, he was often the object of ridicule. Short and on the chunky side, he was called "Old Chubby Cheeks" by reporters at City Hall. He was an honest man at bottom, but if he possessed a sense of humor, nobody had yet encountered it.

It was a freezing cold morning. And as we barreled up, a half hour late, there stood the mayor in his little black suit and black overcoat, with his white hair sticking out of a bowler hat, and his nose an ominous red. Big clouds of hot breath issued from his mouth, coming out in even greater bursts because of his anger. I mean, you could practically see steam coming out of his ears.

Parker giggled. Then I let out a little giggle. Which only got Parker going all the more. The harder we tried to stop, the more uncontrollable the giggling became. Dutifully, Parker jumped out of the car to help the mayor into the back seat, chuckling the whole time. I was behind the wheel trying to repress my giggles—and not succeeding.

"Don't you realize," seethed Bowron, "I'm the mayor of this city?"

Every time the mayor remonstrated, Parker apologized

profusely. Then he would give off a little giggle. And I would giggle. And the mayor got madder and madder. By the time we finished breakfast, stopped by the parade, and reached the Rose Bowl, the mayor was so angry that he stormed off and sat with another party. Which only made Parker and me giggle even more. Like lunatics escaped from an asylum, we laughed through the entire game. Afterward, lips pressed together, I ceremoniously opened the back door of the chief's car for Bowron.

"Officer, I'm not riding home with you," the mayor declared furiously. "Matter of fact, I hope I never have to ride with you again!" Turning on his heel, he stalked off to his own car, which had somehow materialized in the parking lot.

■

In his more characteristic moments, Parker was tearing up the department. He streamlined what had been an unwieldy organization, reassigning manpower according to the times of day and the neighborhoods in which the most crimes were being committed. He ordered the writing of our first departmental manual, upgraded training procedures, lengthened the time spent at the Police Academy, and put in "schools" for new sergeants, lieutenants, and captains. He reduced the department's use of separate forms from 757 to 300, by designing new, multi-purpose forms. He created a new division, Administrative Vice, to audit the vice units at every division and to keep an eye on what Intelligence was doing. By having Ad Vice, Intelligence, and Internal Affairs all report to him, he could coordinate their activities and make sure each division was doing its job. For instance, if Intelligence, in monitoring organized crime, by chance discovered a major prostitution ring, Parker would wait and see if Ad Vice, whose responsibility prostitution was, did something about it. If it didn't, he'd know there was a screw-up somewhere and he could act.

He also insisted on adhering to LAPD policy of promoting officers according to how they scored on Civil Service exams; when in 1950 Officer Vivian Strange ranked near the top on a sergeant's exam, he promptly elevated her to become the first black female sergeant in the country, over the strenuous objections of many among the departmental brass.

Most importantly, he instituted the concept of pro-active policing. Many police departments operate on the theory that you simply react. A crime is committed; you find the perpetrator. A bomb goes off; go after the bomb setter. A neighborhood known for trouble is routinely patrolled—until it erupts; then you march in. But due to the small size of LAPD, Parker thought it would be far more effective to try to stop crime before it happened. In a troubled neighborhood, we knew who the troublemakers were. If a man was suspected of a burglary, we put him under surveillance. If someone looked out of place in a neighborhood, we had a little chat with him. If a description of a thief could be obtained, we stopped everyone fitting that description, even if it meant angering dozens of innocent citizens. We actually sat down and tried to figure out what the criminals were doing, where they were likely to strike, and when. Using these pro-active tactics, LAPD would become the most aggressive police department in the country.

A real taskmaster, Parker determinedly stayed detached from the men and women of LAPD. He came down hard on anyone who breached departmental policy. He was feared by most, liked by few, but respected by all.

Still, as the *Los Angeles Times* never tired of pointing out, the average life of an LAPD chief was only two years. Undaunted, Parker plowed ahead, determined to keep his promise "to make this department the most respected in the United States." His quest for professionalism started at the lowest ranks.

We were no longer cops. We were police officers.

■

Innovative, daring, and inherently fair, Parker nevertheless jumped from one frying pan to another.

An officer-involved shooting made front-page headlines weeks after he was sworn in as chief. During a routine traffic stop, a reserve police officer shot and killed an unarmed eighteen-year-old college honor student. Parker took incredible flak for that.

The following year came the "Bloody Christmas" scandal. Two beat officers, responding to a "trouble call" at a bar on Riverside Drive in the Valley, tried to eject a group of rowdies. A fight broke out and the outnumbered officers were badly beaten. Backup units arrested seven merrymakers and hauled them off to the main jail in Lincoln Heights. There, about one hundred officers were enjoying their own Christmas party. Hearing that one of the injured officers might lose an eye, a group of enraged policemen marched to the holding cell and beat the seven men with wet towels and gloved fists until the floor and walls were covered with blood.

Parker went after those officers tooth and nail. A county grand jury indicted eight of them and issued an interim report that—as I read an old press cutting four decades later—sounds like a precursor to the one the Christopher Commission would issue in 1991.

"Definite and remedial action by Police Chief Parker to insure the citizens of Los Angeles will be secure in their person, and their rights properly protected," was recommended, the article said, as part of the grand jury's continuing investigation into police brutality.

The jury further found "a general lack of proper supervision and control of some subordinate leaders, a definite failure on the part of sergeants and lieutenants to report violations observed and disclosed.

"Thus the rights and privileges of citizens have been ignored by some police who consider their badge as a license not only to flout the constitutional safeguards but to violate common rules of courtesy and proper procedure." Eventually, two of the officers were convicted of assault, a third was convicted on a misdemeanor charge, and charges against the other five were dismissed.

Parker survived the incident and the report, bolstered by a pledge of support from Mayor Bowron. But several years later, when a Santa Fe train derailed and police officers physically removed reporters who got in the way of the rescue effort, Parker was again excoriated in the *Times*.

In the thirties, forties and fifties, the *Los Angeles Times* was the most powerful entity in the city. It elected mayors. It brazenly decided City Council issues—literally. A political reporter named Carlton Williams, the paper's ex-officio power broker, would attend City Council meetings, Parker and others told me, and gesture to some councilmen how to vote. The *Times* could get anything done it wanted to—and several times it wanted to remove Bill Parker. (In a move that hardly improved his popularity, Parker had the slot machines in the Los Angeles Press Club taken out. They were the only slot machines in California, where gambling was illegal.)

Still, Parker was smart. He appointed the first police department press-relations officer in the country. I don't mean public relations, someone who hands out press releases. Inspector Eddie Walker was a high-ranking officer who was close to the chief and whose job was to assist the press in getting a story, especially a breaking story. Until that time, reporters had been given no special access. But Parker understood the need to accommodate them. The press corps loved Walker—as Parker, in slyly picking the charismatic inspector, knew it would. Parker also developed a training course, which exists today, for police officers on press relations.

His ability to understand what the media needed saved his job more than once. His neck was another thing.

Early in 1951, word came down through our organized crime people that the Mafia was planning to murder Parker that night. The Senate's Kefauver Committee had arrived in Los Angeles for two days of hearings on organized crime and Parker was expected to testify the next afternoon.

The hit, according to the information, would take place at 8:00 P.M., on the road to the Breakfast Club in Griffith Park, where Parker was scheduled to speak. Using extra security and taking a different route, we delivered Parker safely to the dinner. I was behind the wheel.

Accompanying him inside, I, along with other officers, wandered through the dining room, scanning the crowd. In those days L.A. was very much a small town and we were able to recognize most of the guests by sight.

Jittery nevertheless, we went back outside and waited. Eventually, Mrs. Parker came out and I escorted her to the Buick. No Fainting Fanny, Helen Parker was willing and able to use the shotgun Parker kept loaded on the back seat. Time passed. But the chief did not emerge. Dreading the worst, I hurried inside.

He wasn't in the banquet hall.

I ran out and yelled to the other security officers. Cautiously, we searched the building.

When we finally found him, it was not with a bullet in his head but with a bourbon in his hand. Someone had cornered the chief and had led him into a hidden, private bar.

Once again I feared for him. This drinking was bound to do him in. Already Parker had created a lot of enemies. Many people lay in wait, hoping for the one serious misstep that would lead to his downfall as chief. That night it seemed to me, more than ever, that Parker's drinking would one day cause him to stumble.

Years later I would become part of a plot to get him to stop drinking. Eddie Walker (Parker's press relations officer, best friend, and loyal subject), I, and one or two others, knowing the direct approach would never work, urged a doctor to help us. This doctor warned Parker that his health was not the best, that he might want to drink less because of his heart, and then he described some terrible encroaching ailment. Talk about sheer willpower. Parker walked out of that doctor's office and never had another drink. He stopped smoking the same day.

For the next several months he couldn't have been more miserable to be around.

■

By October 1951, I knew it was time to move on. Driving for Parker those fifteen months had been exciting, interesting, exhausting, and I had learned an enormous amount. I knew I was going to stay on the force a while longer. Not only because of Parker—Parker was the icing on the cake—but because I was challenged by the work and chastened by a whole group of dedicated men and women, many, to my continuing disbelief, far more intelligent than I.

That November, I was reassigned to the field.

I was ready. Really ready.

4

Gamblers, Drunks, Prostitutes, and Scumbags

I was told to report to Central Station, a crumbling, rat-infested building at 1st and Hill Street that had been condemned by the city twenty years before. The stairs leading up to the second floor were so rickety they threatened to disintegrate beneath you. Then there were the rats. If you didn't see them, you could hear them. I checked inside my locker for them several times a day.

The building fit the neighborhood. Central Area encompassed a much larger territory then, stretching east to Chinatown and the Los Angeles River, and west to Vermont Avenue. It was a melting pot in 1951, as it is today, a mixture of blacks, Hispanics, Asians, and whites, many of them newly arrived immigrants. The station itself stood decaying on the edge of downtown. It policed Skid Row, Main Street—with its B-girl bars and burlesque theaters—to East 5th and 6th Streets and Bunker Hill. The skyscrapers and beautiful condominiums that clog the area today were not even a line on a developer's drafting board. Then it was a bunch of beaten-down, dilapidated old tenements, rife with crime, narcotics, gambling, drunks, prostitutes, and wholesale scumbags.

My first taste of the streets, post-Parker, was Juvenile patrol.

The struggling families who lived in these inner-city neighborhoods had to worry about their kids mingling with all these elements. Day in and day out I saw nothing but troubled kids. José was one I saw often. I don't know how many times we picked up José. A nice little kid, thirteen or fourteen, he was already a master at his craft, burglary.

One day my partner and I heard over the radio that a window had been smashed on the other side of the division, five or six miles away. Probably any of two hundred kids could have done it. But we glanced at each other simultaneously.

"José."

José lived in a house at the end of an alley. We parked the car, walked down the alley, and hid behind some trash cans.

Ten minutes later, along came the kid with his arms loaded. We stepped out. "Hey, José. You been shopping?"

José dropped the stuff and turned to run. Then he thought better of it. "Okay, you got me," he sighed, and off to jail we went. Each time this happened his mother watched teary-eyed and his father just shook his head.

Even then there were kids like José, lost to society before they grew up. Today, there are just more of them. They are more unanchored; many operate with guns in their hands and drugs in their systems. Four decades later, society still has not found a way to turn the hopeless ones around. Still, times were so different then. The people were different and the laws were different. Often, you'd haul a kid in, chew him out, and call his folks. Father would come down, bawl the kid out. You'd never encounter that kid again.

One kid we picked up for stealing a motorbike. We took him in, booked him for theft, and planned to release him to his parents. The kid's father showed up and I'll never forget how he hit that kid right in the mouth—I mean, just clobbered that kid, knocked him to the floor. We had to grab the father and almost booked *him*. That was one kid, believe me, I never saw again.

We spent a great deal of time talking to kids, with amazing success. The police had more power then. We had our own in-house probation system that allowed us to skip the courts and put kids on probation ourselves. Officers assigned to this duty would develop individual programs for kids while working with the parents. Also, LAPD had a vast youth-services program with camps, and something called the Deputy Auxiliary Police. These were kids, nine to twelve years old, who were given special badges and could participate in organized activities. Between our youth services program and DAP, we had the ability to reach out and assist the kids—and their parents—to stem the tide of Josés.

I wasn't involved in that end of the business. As a young patrol officer, my job was merely to answer the calls. I was never able to have a lasting relationship with any of them, but it was a sign of the influence of parental authority that I rarely had to haul in any kid twice.

After a few months I was transferred to Hollywood. Although it was at the height of its glamour years, with its boulevards boasting elegant theaters and nightspots, even then this part of town had its seamy side. The promise of fame and fortune attracted runaways from the East Coast and the Midwest, thirteen- and fourteen-year-old kids, just ripe for being hustled for every damn thing. When we found runaways, we'd pick them up. We could detain them for forty-eight hours and that gave us time to contact their parents. We'd do our best to get them back home, and in almost every instance we did. The parents would send money and we'd put the kid on the train or the bus. If money wasn't sent, we'd scrounge around and raise it ourselves to send the kid home.

Today, the police can't do that. In the mid-1960s, children's rights advocates lobbied for laws giving minors adult rights. Now we pick up a runaway, even a twelve-year-old, and there's nothing we can do except take the child to a halfway house, where he or she can be detained for twenty-four hours. If we can get a lead on the kid's family and contact them in twenty-four hours, fine. But even for those twenty-four hours we can't make the kid stay in the house. At the same time, budget cutbacks eliminated the Youth Services Program and DAP. Children are being frightfully neglected, and as a result many continue conduct that leads to criminality. Today, crime prevention means "hardening the target"—installing better locks, putting in alarm systems, having more police on the street. Rather than stopping the development of a criminal, we try to stop the crime. In those days, I really believe we were much more helpful in preventing crime by turning kids around.

In one case, though, I may have been a little too helpful.

We had encountered a sixteen-year-old girl living on her own. A typical arrival, she was hoping for the big break. But on the streets of Hollywood anything could happen to her, so when we'd spot her we would stop and talk, or sometimes we'd go by her room to check up on her. I tried to give her all kinds of fatherly advice, and I guess she kind of fell for me.

One day I was thumbing through a batch of crime reports, when I noticed one for rape. I picked it up and—oh, no—it was the girl. Next I saw the suspect's name. *Me.*

Oh, my God, I thought. Instinctively, I checked the date of the rape, and the time, trying to remember . . . what the hell was I doing then?

Suddenly I looked up. A bunch of detectives were standing there laughing, thinking they'd played a pretty good joke on me.

Their joke had scared me to death.

I continued to keep an eye on the girl, long after I'd moved on. The last I knew, she was putting herself through college. Whether my protective watchfulness was a factor, I can't say. But hers was one of the happy-ending stories I still recall today.

■

From Juvenile, I transferred to Vice. I was reassigned to Central to work the same downtown area as before, from Skid Row east to the gambling dens of Chinatown. But it could have been a different planet. With the kids, I was trying to change their lives and to present myself as a model. Given the scumbags involved in vice—the prostitutes, addicts, drunks, gamblers, and habitués of after-hours joints—it was a whole different clientele that we served.

Dick Eckenwieler, the high school buddy who "recruited" me, was my new partner. Giving me the rundown my first day, he told me first off that the complaints a Vice officer most dreaded were those involving homosexuals. Under the law (since changed) oral copulation was a felony, even in the privacy of one's home. Usually the sex acts we heard about would occur in a public restroom in a park where kids played, and their parents would call us, irate.

We had no choice but to go check out the complaint. Under Parker, the LAPD had instituted a strict, nearly foolproof system of investigating vice complaints. For each complaint that is called in, a written report must be taken, numbered, and filed. Many police departments do not have this kind of control. They do not make a written report and can claim a complaint was never received. If someone asks, they say, "Well, we didn't know about this." But in LAPD, vice is so carefully monitored that superiors routinely phone in—or "stiff in"—bogus complaints just to make sure we are checking everything out.

So when Dick and I got a "318"—a vice complaint—for Echo Park, we knew we had to go.

Oh, how we hated those things—I mean, absolutely hated them. To work a homosexual complaint, you either had to operate the homosexual or catch him in the act.

To "operate" a homosexual, you had to stand at the urinal and wait for an overt act, meaning letting the guy grope you. It wasn't enough to observe him getting an erection and stand there manipulating it. You'd get to court and the judge would say, "Well, that's just kind of a natural thing for an individual to do." Frankly, being touched by a homosexual . . . We weren't about to do that. So the only other choice we had was to catch them in the act.

To do this, Dick would climb up into a small crawl space overlooking the commodes, which was hardly the most sanitary or the nicest-smelling place to be—plus, there were always spiders.

Between the commodes were walls through which holes had been drilled. Two homosexuals would go into adjoining stalls, sit on the commodes, and establish eye contact through the holes. If they liked what they saw, one would stand up and put his penis through the hole and the other would orally copulate him.

My job was to stand somewhere outside and watch who went in. I could see Dick up under the roof, and if he observed an act he would signal me and I would come trotting in and make the arrest.

This particular day in Echo Park, Dick observed two guys go through this routine. He signaled me and I made the arrests. In time, we received our subpoenas to testify in court. "I know this sounds crazy," Dick said to me, "but I have this awful feeling that the guy's gonna wind up without a penis."

"What are you talking about?"

"I just have this terrible feeling that somehow this guy is not gonna have a penis. And I'm going to have to testify that he was orally copulated and somehow he won't have a penis."

"Let's check the records," I said, humoring him.

One of the two men did have a criminal record and we studied it for abnormalities, such as possible amputations. None was reported. Still, Dick would not be mollified. He was still unnerved by the recent case of a Vice officer testifying that he had observed an act of prostitution through a hole in a hotel door. For some reason, the judge ordered the door removed and hauled into court. No hole. The officer, who had probably confused the case with one of his numerous other ones, was charged with perjury. This made a huge impression on everyone. Given all the arrest reports we wrote, and the number of court appearances we made, the fear of this kind of mistake haunted us all.

I said, "You saw the act."

"I saw the guy start to orally copulate the other one," Dick agreed, "but I didn't want to watch the damn thing. I gave you the signal, yeah, but I didn't watch. So I know he's gonna wind up not having a penis."

For a week and a half my partner put himself through living hell, imagining this guy standing up in court, saying, "He couldn't have seen what he said, Your Honor, because I don't have a penis."

The guy never did get up and testify; he pleaded guilty as charged.

I guess he had one.

■

Oral copulation and sodomy are now legally permissible in the privacy of one's home, and have been reduced to misdemeanors if committed in public. But Vice officers rarely get such complaints anymore. Although Los Angeles actually has more parks than it did in the early fifties, fewer people use them. Once the scene of happy family picnics, children at play, and young people taking an evening stroll, parks are now more often the province of rowdy gang members and gun-toting drug dealers. Concrete barriers have been erected at the entrance to some parks to prevent these elements from driving in. But even so, with graffiti on the restroom walls and picnic tables smashed, the carefree feeling parks once engendered is gone. To the police, this in itself signals a crime: the crime of debasing the quality of life.

LAPD Vice policy has always been geared to maintaining quality of life and is guided by the "Three C's": Commercialization, Complaints, and Conspicuousness. An office football pool or a poker game at home are not commercial or conspicuous activities, so the police don't care. A street corner where drugs can be bought—they do care. Not only because drugs are illegal, but because people who live on that block are afraid to walk down it and that devalues their quality of life. Same thing with prostitutes. Their carrying out their business conspicuously makes passers-by uncomfortable. "Don't want to walk down that street, see those women selling themselves, maybe get hustled myself."

When people complain that the cops should be going after murderers, not bookies or prostitutes, they miss the whole point. Few people in Los Angeles will ever be touched by murder. The quality of life touches everyone, every day.

■

Having a plan is the first lesson they drum into you at the Police Academy. Any time you step out of your patrol car or walk through a door, you and your partner better know what you are going to do. Otherwise, they warn, you can't believe how quickly a situation can turn on you. Tactics—always think tactics. Those who don't, get killed. That's what they hammered into us, over and over again. But one night . . . Well, it sounded like another routine call.

Two policewomen, as they were then called, radioed for assistance. At the time, female cops were firmly instructed never to do anything dangerous. These two had spotted several suspicious-looking characters in a parked car and they wanted to check them out.

My partner and I arrived, saw that the people were not doing anything, and sent them on their way. We then lingered for a moment, chatting. It was a chilly night and my partner sat in the car with the two women while I stood on the sidewalk with my hands shoved into the warm pockets of my topcoat.

A call came over the radio: man with a gun in a bar. I looked up, and there was the bar, *right behind me*.

"I'll go," I said, and wandered through the swinging doors, hands still in my pockets. Slowly, as my eyes adjusted to the darkness of the place, I realized that all the customers were staring at me. I glanced at the bartender. He was staring at me too. Behind him, the mirror on the wall was shattered. Then I realized that the people weren't looking *at* me—they were looking *behind* me.

I turned.

Suddenly, a guy was shoving the barrel of a gun into my belly.

Apparently this nut case had walked in minutes before I had and started arguing with the bartender. Figuring he'd settle it once and for all, the guy stepped back and fired a shot at the bartender. He missed, hitting the mirror instead. Then the bartender picked up a beer mug and threw it at the guy, also missing. A patron sneaked out and called the police. And into this standoff I waltzed, hands jammed into my pockets.

The room fell silent. I could hear, through the doors, one of the policewomen jabbering with my partner. The jabbering grew louder and I thought, *Oh, no! My partner's coming through the door with the policewoman and this guy's for sure gonna shoot one of 'em.*

Sliding my right hand out of one pocket, I began pushing against the door, trying to keep my partner out, while I fumbled with my left hand to unbutton my coat. My partner, feeling the pressure, started pushing harder.

"He's got a gun! He's got a gun!" I yelled, still fumbling to unbutton my coat and whip out my revolver. I couldn't do it. So I did the only other thing I could think of: I hit the arm of the guy with the gun—whump!

And then, *after* his gun bounced onto the floor, *then* I managed to get my gun out.

I also managed, by the grace of God, not to get my partner killed or the policewoman killed. Or me killed.

Pretty clever game plan, I always thought.

■

Detectives and undercover officers handle the cases that inspire the fiction writers, but for a cop on the beat the life becomes one long series of blurred incidents arranged around stops for doughnuts, coffee, and dinner, coffee again, maybe another doughnut.

I worked the morning watch, 11:30 P.M. till 7:30 A.M., the same hours as my quarry. One night, as my partner and I were preparing to leave the station to begin our duty three teenage boys came in to file a complaint. Aged sixteen, eighteen, and nineteen, they had found rooms to rent in a house owned by an older man. According to their story, no sooner had they moved in than the man pulled a gun and warned them that if they left the house he would find them and kill them.

Although the boys were terrified enough to remain prisoners of this man for three weeks, they managed to fend off his attempted sexual attacks. An hour before, deciding to risk it, the boys escaped after the man went out.

Being somewhat goofy teenagers, they couldn't remember the number of the house, but they told us the street and gave us a description of the premises.

"If you ring the bell, he won't answer," the boys said. "He never answered the door the whole time we were there."

We got the man's phone number from the operator and left it with the desk sergeant. We calculated how long it would take us to drive to the house and told the sergeant to call the number ten minutes after that. If the man wouldn't answer the door, maybe he'd answer the phone and we'd know he was inside.

My partner Jack Horrall, son of the former police chief, and I found the house without any trouble. It looked eerie from the street, completely dark inside, and no outside lights were on either.

We knocked on the door. "Police officers. Open up."

No response. We rapped harder. Suddenly the door inched open, making such creaking noises that I expected Boris Karloff to leap out at any moment.

Switching on our flashlights, we stepped quickly inside, flattening ourselves against the walls. Still, no one appeared. Jack pointed in one direction, indicating he'd go that way. I started off in the opposite direction. It was pitch black and, despite my flashlight beam, spooky as hell. Cautiously, I moved from one room to another. Every floorboard groaned. Then, just as I was rounding a corner, there came the piercing jangle of the telephone.

I jumped.

Jack grabbed the phone. It was the desk sergeant, whom I'd forgotten all about. Still breathing hard from the scare, I switched on the lamps. The guy was not there.

He was picked up two days later while driving his truck. His gun was right on the seat beside him. He was booked for kidnapping and assault with a deadly weapon.

It became just one more entry in a patrol officer's log.

■

Soon the rough, honky-tonk streets became my home away from home. The speeches Parker had delivered on how the police resembled a minority at last began to hit home. We were the guys everyone wanted around but nobody wanted to see. People who spotted a police officer standing over a motorist, with his dark glasses and his unfeeling manner, writing a traffic citation, instinctively identified with the motorist. No one ever thought about the guy being a menace on the road—until he cut them off in traffic. Then, "Where's the cop? A cop's never here when you need him!"

At times it made you want to scream, "Yeah, well you should see where that cop is right now, buster. Down in the gutter somewhere, rolling around in the dirt with some scumbag. Seeing things you never have to see." And after a while, an officer's biggest problem is not giving in to the cynicism, recognizing that everyone out there is not a bum. But no matter how hard you try, you know you are seeing a world different from anybody else's. Soon you begin to take that home. I would try to relax with our friends, only to find everything had changed. Whenever we went out socially, someone would start beating on me about the department or complain about a ticket he got or some other damn thing. And you would get so tired of hearing this. With other cops, you never had to listen to that crap. And you could always trust a cop. In play, at work, whatever you did, you could always trust another cop. But you couldn't trust anyone else . . . completely.

In time, you cut yourself off. The more you hung out with other cops, the more inbred you became, believing that anyone not a cop was a son of a bitch and a no-goodnik. In later years, understanding how that Us Against Them mentality built, I worked hard to break this attitude down. We encouraged officers to grasp the importance of having a wide circle of friends; we emphasized that there were people out there who needed to know them—and that they needed to know those people back.

But as a fourth-year man on the department, I had just about given up all other friends except police officers. One of them, Charlie Guzman, became my partner in Vice.

■

"Listen, kid, you're not going to wear a gun, all right? You keep your weapon in the glove compartment."

But that's against departmental rules, I protested.

"Girls always reach around and hug you to see if you're a cop," Charlie said knowingly.

Being relatively new on the beat, I was expected to arrest a lot of prostitutes. Mine was a new face they didn't know. Eager to be as convincing as possible, I bought the thickest glasses I could find that didn't totally drive me crazy, yet made my eyes look strange. I wore funny-looking clothes; I acted half-drunk. I walked every street of Skid Row and operated every B-girl joint on the Main Street strip. And always it was the same.

Prostitutes barely flicked me a glance, then sighed, "Cop."

I never had a single taker—not one.

Charlie was a master at it. He could operate anybody anywhere. He only had to walk a block and prostitutes would be grabbing on to him. Once, after we arrested two prostitutes and two johns, Charlie went to get the car. He returned with three more prostitutes. "What's this?" I said.

"They just kind of followed me," said Charlie with an impish grin.

■

Everything in Vice became a challenge. It was exciting, interesting; I'd have to say fun. Almost a kind of game—how can I outsmart this guy? The one thing you tried never to do was to make moral judgments about the people on the streets. Most of them were pathetic; some were real bastards, not worth wasting your effort or your time on. But once in a while, you'd encounter someone you really grew to like.

Lolly the Handbook was one.

A skinny little guy, Lolly was a bookmaker who worked a few square blocks around East 5th Street. The nicest guy in the world. Always wore a clean white shirt, light-blue denim trousers, and tennis shoes. Always had a friendly word for us. And no matter what Charlie and I did, we could not catch Lolly.

There he would be, standing on the sidewalk, available to take bets on sporting events from his regular clientele.

"Hey, fellas!" he'd yell as we drove by.

Over and over we'd see him doing business. But it never helped us catch him. Lolly knew every building, every passageway, every stairway, and he could disappear just like that. I mean, we'd see him with a guy and it was clear the guy was placing a bet. We'd watch Lolly writing the bet on a scrap of paper. Then we'd look again and he was gone. Vanished.

It became a matter of pride that we were gonna put Lolly in jail.

Several times we actually thought we had him, going up, grabbing Lolly, ready to haul him away. But the markers weren't on him. We had no idea what he could have done with those scraps of paper so quickly, but without the bets, there was no evidence to book him. So we waited and tried again. But all we seemed to accomplish was to build up a relationship with him. Once, as we stood chatting, he idly asked what we liked to drink. Neither Charlie nor I drank much, but we played along and told him our preferences. In those days, we never bothered to lock our squad car, and one day we came out and there on the back seat was a case of liquor for Charlie and one for me.

"God," we said. "Lolly."

We jumped in and took off. When we found Lolly, he denied knowing anything about the liquor. Charlie and I dumped the cases on the sidewalk and warned the book-maker never to do that again.

■

At the time, we were on the day watch, 7:30 A.M. till 4:30 P.M., and because we were working Vice, we called in regularly to the desk sergeant to let him know what was going on. Late one afternoon Charlie made that call. He came back to the car looking somber. "They want us to come in," he said, sliding behind the wheel. "They want to talk to us about something."

I could tell he was upset. Thinking maybe we had done something wrong, I rode in silence. When we got to the station, our sergeant sat me down. "I have some real bad news for you, Daryl. Lowell's dead."

Like anyone hearing shocking news, I am unable to remember what went through my mind. My brother, married and with two young children, was still my best friend. He worked for a plumbing company, supervising the work on one of those big tract developments that were springing up all over. That morning, he and my younger brother, Steve, had gone surfing at San Onofre, not far from San Clemente. Still the daredevil, Lowell had waded out into an area known for its hellacious waves, while Steve joined a group of surfers in less treacherous waters nearby.

Occasionally the surfers would pause to watch Lowell. Then, suddenly, his surfboard shot up without him. When he did not surface, they took off, paddling hard. They found him floating, not breathing at all. Efforts to revive him at a nearby hospital failed. What had caused the accident, the autopsy did not reveal. But my brother had drowned.

Wanda had alerted the sergeant, so she knew. I drove to my mother's house to break the news to her. She wasn't home. As soon as I heard the car pull up, I pushed open the screen door.

She took one look at my face and said, "It's Lowell, isn't it?"

I was devastated. But in the haze of those wrenching, painful days afterward, I remember a huge wreath arriving at the house. A beautifully written card to my family accompanied it. The wreath was from Lolly. That a two-bit gambler would make this gesture to a cop who was working desperately to put him away deeply touched me.

But it didn't stop Charlie and me for a minute.

By now we'd been chasing Lolly for more than a year and we had run out of ideas on how to catch him.

"I got it," Charlie said one day. "We'll get a big box and put it on the back of that old truck I have. We'll drive the truck up and park it right where Lolly does business, and you are gonna be in that box, overhearing him taking a bet."

The next day, we drove the truck to the appointed spot and warned the regular beat officer: "For God's sake, don't impound our truck!"

For nearly three hours I sat inside that box on the hottest day I can remember. Lolly, completely unaware, casually leaned against the truck and took several bets. Through a peephole I watched him walk over to the stairway of an apartment building and quickly slip the pieces of paper inside the banister. Sonofagun. I notified Charlie on my walkie-talkie. "We got him."

Poor Lolly was so flustered when we confronted him, and when we went straight to the banister and pulled out the markers, his face just fell. After all we'd been through, it made me sad to be finally putting him away.

As it turned out, it wasn't all that sad. When the case went to the IRS, it was discovered that Lolly had made a small fortune. He owned a beautiful home in Laguna and another big house in Covina. He ended up paying huge fines to the government for not reporting income, but he didn't spend much time in jail.

■

At times, you had to be half-monkey to work Vice. Many nights, with nothing special on tap, we'd climb to the top of a four- or five-story building, look through a pair of binoculars, and see what we could see. When you've been in this business for a while, you learn to spot all kinds of activity that the average person might not notice. Two people talking on a street corner might look innocent enough. But we could tell at a glance if one of the two was getting down a bet. Ever on the lookout for lawbreakers, we found that roofs offered a front-row seat.

I was on top of a building on East 5th Street one night, with a partner other than Charlie, when we spotted two men standing outside a hotel. They went in. Soon two others went inside, then two more. After eight or nine men had entered the hotel, we said, "They've got a game going, obviously."

We scrambled down the fire escape, crossed the street, climbed up the fire escape of the hotel and then down through the building to the room where we thought the game was in progress. The door was closed. Using a gimlet, a crude T-shaped device similar to a corkscrew, we bored a hole in the door. It was just big enough to look through— and lo and behold.

On the floor in the middle of the room was one small pile of heroin and a second, much bigger pile of marijuana.

Men were sitting on the bed, folding small amounts of heroin into little pieces of paper and stacking them. Others sat on the floor filling small plastic bags with marijuana. They were jabbering away. Each of them, when they thought nobody else was looking, would slip a packet up his sleeve or into his own pocket.

When they finished, we kicked the door open.

Successful door-kicking, I ought to mention, requires a well-practiced technique. In the movies, they bust the door down using their shoulder. Uh-uh. You kick a door in by kicking, aiming the whole bottom of your foot at the door handle. A good door kicker is a valuable person, especially if you can kick hard enough to break down a door with a dead-bolt lock. That night, weighing 210, I kicked the door right off its hinges.

Moving quickly, we collected the packets and the bags piled on the bed. Then we went up to each man. "Are you holding anything?"

"Absolutely not!"

And I reached into the precise place I had seen each guy stash a packet and pulled it out. "You son of a bitch!" someone would scream at him. Now, they were not only angry at us, they were angry at each other. And growing angrier by the minute.

We sat them on the floor facing away from us. Then my partner pulled me over to the corner.

"I don't have a gun, Gates. So you watch 'em and I'll run down to a telephone and call for backup."

"Uh, I don't have a gun either."

"You're kidding!"

I told him I wished I were. "But you go ahead," I said. "Just get somebody up here quick."

I turned back to the men. "Okay, my partner's getting help, and I'm telling you right now, I'm by myself and if one of you moves, I'm gonna shoot you, that's all there is to it. Just blink, I shoot. I'm not gonna take any chances. There's nine of you and there's one of me and I'm gonna shoot you."

Off went my partner. He was halfway down the stairs when I heard a loud thump, as if he had tripped. Then came the unmistakable sound of him tumbling all the way to the bottom. And I thought, *Oh, my God,* because the men had heard it too. They started to get up.

"I told you, I'm gonna shoot," I barked, edging out the door and calling down to my partner: "Are you okay?"

Up the stairwell came all this moaning and groaning. Followed by an unsteady, "I think so."

"Then get to a phone!"

Somehow, he crawled out to the sidewalk. Naturally, there was no phone anywhere. But a black-and-white happened to be cruising by. He hailed it and we hauled all nine of them in. I made a sardonic mental note to thank Charlie Guzman for training me not to carry a gun.

■

Still, what I remember most vividly were not the moments of danger but the sad cases we encountered.

There was one prostitute, for example, whom I still recall. Whenever I hear people argue that prostitution is a victimless crime, I get angry. It is not. The women are always victims.

A complaint came in about this particular prostitute, whom Charlie and I both knew. She was a hype—a heroin addict—a nice, really lovely woman who turned tricks to take care of her habit. Charlie and I could not bring ourselves to operate her, and since she conducted business in an inside bedroom, we weren't able to climb in a window and catch her in the act.

"We'll just have to go in when she's out," Charlie said, "and hide."

The only place to hide was her closet. It was fairly large, and Charlie stood way in the back while I sat on the floor by the door, peeking out. We waited. Forty-five minutes later she returned. By then I was feeling terrible. The closet seemed to grow rank and for some reason my eyes were watering. But here she was with a trick.

They haggled over the price and what he was going to get for it. Finally they made a deal. She began to disrobe. All of a sudden, she stopped. She stared at the closet, looking—I was sure—straight at me. Then she opened her mouth and cried, "Fire!"

The trick, half out of his pants, jumped up and flew out the door, while the woman quickly began to dress. We came bursting out of the closet in a cloud of smoke and I'm thinking, *What the hell is on fire?*

It was Charlie's cigar.

All this time, unbeknownst to me, my partner, an inveterate cigar smoker, had been standing in the back of this dark closet puffing away, making the closet stink and my eyes burn, until the smoke came billowing out.

We lost her. The trick was long gone and we had no evidence to book her. In truth, I felt relieved. The poor woman had offered me her body, offered me anything I wanted on a regular basis—would I like her to be my snitch?—if only I would leave her alone. But I couldn't help her. I wouldn't have anything sexually to do with a prostitute and I couldn't make her a snitch. Even if she were able to come up with information, I could not offer her protection. Only pity. I just felt sorry for her.

One prostitute I had no use for was Verdelle Reese. We picked her up on a routine street arrest. It stopped being routine when Verdelle suddenly took off.

I chased her down East 5th Street, past darkened doorways where figures lurked and knives were known to suddenly appear, and finally grabbed hold of her, a big, tough, rawboned woman growling obscenities at me. A crowd formed. She began flailing her arms at me, and as I was wrestling with her, her pimp jumped on my back.

One of the two of them—I think Verdelle—started whacking me on the head with a knife. Any time you get a cut on the head, the blood really spurts. I was bleeding profusely when, quick as a fox, Verdelle clamped down and bit me. Bit my arm to the bone. Aw, Jesus, the pain was incredible.

Through the blood streaming into my eyes, I saw a car plow into the crowd, heading toward me. It was Charlie. We managed to subdue the pimp and book him, but somehow we lost Verdelle. I had no intention of letting her escape, so we came up with an old cop's ploy to get her. Every time we arrested someone, whether it was for prostitution, gambling, or narcotics, we would tell the suspect: "Verdelle Reese gave us the information."

It didn't take long for Verdelle to come screaming into Central, begging us to *puleeze* take her to jail; *anything* to get her off the street.

■

Verdelle's attack on me was the only time I was seriously injured. Bumps, bruises, scratches, an occasional cut were pretty routine. It was as if street violence had not been invented yet. Despite all the pimps, burglars, drunks—even murderers—we encountered every day, most of us did not feel the need to walk the streets of Los Angeles carrying a gun. I had a deputy chief named Mert Howe, who used to say, "In my day, if you had a good partner, you wouldn't care whether your partner was armed or you were armed or not. You'd go out and handle anything out there without a gun. Long as you had a good partner."

In the 1950s it was still true. Drawing my gun was the last thing I thought about, even when I had one strapped on. I may have fired mine a couple of times; never hit anybody. Never had to. In later years, when I went out in the field as chief, I was always a little shocked at how quickly guns were drawn. I would probably get myself killed very quickly on the streets today, because I don't have the instincts about safety that officers routinely learn.

Instead, I was taught that you draw your weapon only for known felons or armed suspects. You were expected to rely on physical force, particularly if you were in uniform. A uniform meant something then, as did your presence. I remember getting a call one night that a giant-size sumo wrestler was menacing people over by City Hall.

The first two officers arrived and jumped out of their car. The guy lunged at them and they dived back in and rolled up the windows. The wrestler climbed on top of the car and began beating the roof with his enormous fists.

Next, a beat officer came along and headed straight for the wrestler as he lumbered down off the car. I drove up at that moment and thinking, *Oh, my God*, I started running toward them. The beat officer marched right up to the wrestler, looked him in the face, and whacked him on the back of the head with his sap. Whump. The sumo wrestler went down.

We handcuffed him and that was that.

■

If my recollections of life on the streets seem oddly lighthearted, it is, perhaps, because they reflect a more halcyon time. Although we had as many as one hundred homicides a year, most were committed by people who knew their victims, and random violence was almost unheard of. In an odd way, the police and the villains then played a slightly more sophisticated kid's game of cops and robbers. Friendships developed out of mutual respect. When the cops arrived, more often than not, the bad guys graciously gave up.

I remember particularly the gambling dens of Chinatown. Some of the most respectable people in Chinatown ran the games of *Pai Gow*. When we'd come busting in, they'd shrug and say, "All right, how many?"

"Twenty," we'd say. And the man in charge would pick twenty players for us to haul off to jail.

At the same time, we needed evidence. Many of the ornate, ivory *Pai Gow* tiles were quite valuable, often family heirlooms, so we cheerfully accepted old, beat-up ones kept on the premises for just that purpose.

Criminals were a better class of people then. They operated according to a code of honor, even robbers. Occasionally, a stickup man would kill someone, but generally if the victim handed over his money, the robber wouldn't shoot. LAPD ran its own jail at Lincoln Heights, and prisoners were let out as trusties. They would work as janitors at the police stations or as shoeshine men. The stations were immaculate and the trusties often complained when their time was up and they had to leave. Today, we no longer have trusties; criminals aren't trustworthy enough. Most are under the influence of drugs.

The truth is, since the fifties, the quality of the bad guys has fallen off . . . criminally.

5

Climbing (and Learning) the Ropes

I began studying for the sergeant's exam a year and a half before I had to.

According to departmental regulations, an officer needed four years on the force before he or she could attempt to move up a rung to sergeant. Because I had joined LAPD mid-year, and because they only gave the exam every two years, I couldn't take the test until my sixth anniversary. The wait seemed interminable. By then I had decided I would climb the LAPD ladder as fast as I could. Not that I had committed to a life as a police officer; I was always open to opportunities from the outside. But as long as I was carrying a badge, I wanted it to be the highest-ranking badge I could manage.

This, I knew, would present problems. By nature of my relationship with Parker, I was branded the fair-haired boy, someone who had a direct pipeline to the chief. I didn't. I would never pick up the phone and call him; I mean, I wouldn't do that. And he wouldn't have respected me if I had. But this was the rap. As a result, I always had trouble with officers holding me at arm's length. Each time I had a new assignment, I would have to break down this impression of me, and let the others know I was a regular guy, that I didn't have anything special going for me, that I worked hard and was a damn good police officer.

Knowing that I would be held suspect at every promotional step, I set out to move up the chain of command in a way that would leave no doubts. To be promoted to each new rank—sergeant, lieutenant, captain, inspector (now known as commander), and deputy chief—you must take a written exam, which accounts for 60 percent of your score, and an oral exam for the other 40 percent. To avoid the favoritism label, I knew that I could not be promoted on the basis of an outstanding oral score alone. I needed to do well on both.

So I worked my butt off. I sat in my bedroom for hours every night and studied for the better part of a year and a half. When I took vacation time, I studied ten hours a day. On the bus to work, I read. Having had courses in teaching, I understood the learning process, how you use every one of your faculties. At dinner I would talk a blue streak, lecturing my wife and two daughters, aged four and five, on forgery and its famous cases while they all just sat there and looked at me. I talked to the people at work. "Say, did you know . . . ?"

This helped me put what I read into my own words, and it became a pattern for my promotions: read and talk. As the time neared for the sergeant's exam, I became more determined than ever. It was important to finish as high on the list as possible, because promotions were awarded only when a vacancy occurred, and then according to position on the list. If they hadn't dipped down to your number within two years, you had to take the test again. No way I was going to do that.

The written portion of the sergeant's exam was a grueling all-day test, 180 questions in the morning, 120 more in the afternoon. But it was the oral that I dreaded. And there was no clear-cut way to prepare for that.

Several weeks after I had taken the written exam, I was summoned to an interview room on the second floor at City Hall. Who would be awaiting me, I didn't know. Because two hundred officers were taking the sergeant's test, they had assigned three panels to handle the load, each panel consisting of one inspector and two captains. We knew who these officers were, but not to which panel we would be assigned. One of the inspectors had the reputation of being an impossibly tough grader. If you were Jesus Christ, the rumor went, he'd give you a 90.

Just my luck, I thought, I'd get the panel with *that* guy. Sure enough, I did. There he was, seated behind a long table, flanked by the two captains. I gulped and sat down.

The purpose of the oral is to judge a candidate's ability to express himself or herself. It's also designed to make the candidate as uncomfortable as possible to see how he or she handles it. I was expected to start out with an opening statement. For several minutes I told them how I'd prepared myself to be a sergeant—what books I'd read and issues I'd studied, what experience I had that would make me a good sergeant, and why I believed I would make a fine supervisor.

On the table in front of me I noticed a quarter. It had been put there, I knew through the grapevine, to see what I would do with my hands. I ignored the coin and kept my hands in my lap.

For the next half hour they fired questions at me, trying to put me on the defensive. If this situation came up, one captain would say, what would you do?

Answer.

But suppose . . .

Answer.

Really? But what if . . .

This went on until they had backed you into a corner—or tried to.

When they finally finished, they asked me to make a closing statement. You were supposed to tell them, I knew, what a mature, stable person you were, always in control, a shining model for those you would supervise, capable of giving sound advice, and so on.

"Oh, I am all those things," I cockily assured them—reciting my husbandhood, fatherhood, high arrest record, exquisite manners and courtesy to scumbags of all kinds—"and more." I left the room, grateful that the tough inspector hadn't shredded me alive, and waited anxiously for the results to be posted.

My hard work paid off. I finished with the highest written score of anyone and the highest score overall. My name appeared number one on the list.

After that, I came out first on every exam I took all the way up to chief, not through favoritism or because I was smarter, but because nobody worked harder at preparing for exams than I did.

There would be no way, I vowed, anyone could ever say I moved up because I was Bill Parker's boy.

■

Overnight, I transmogrified from an order-taker to an order-giver. This took some getting used to. Police officers who had been friends since the Academy looked at me a little differently. Some spoke to me not at all. Even though I was twenty-nine, I still lacked the kind of judgment that arrives only with age and experience. Therein lies one of the most significant problems in any police department. Generally, officers younger than twenty-seven or twenty-eight have the desire, energy, and enthusiasm to do the job, but not the maturity. As a boss, I still wanted to jump on my horse and go every time a call came in.

A sergeant is like a coach. You spark enthusiasm among your officers and make sure they know and abide by the rules. If they're deficient in some skill, you must train them. In addition to the reports you seem always to be writing up, you spend a good deal of your time in the field, in uniform, driving alone, supervising the officers assigned to you. I was one of three sergeants operating out of Central Division nightwatch and among the things I supervised were the drunk wagons and foot beats. I also oversaw two or three F cars, or felony cars.

Detectives would alert us to felons operating in our territory. Because detectives carry such a huge workload, and because many of their days are spent testifying in court, they would ask us to locate the felon and bring him in for questioning. I would tell the officers in the F cars which felons to track down. If they needed advice or guidance, they would contact me over the car radio. I was also there to provide backup. If a call went out about a robbery in progress, a sergeant was expected to arrive on the heels of the patrol officers to make sure the situation was handled properly. I, in turn, reported to the watch commander, who was a lieutenant. Sometimes I would fill in for him.

Once a month this particular lieutenant delivered a talk on ethics. It was an important ritual for him, and frankly, his lectures always impressed me. He was a tough taskmaster and a real stickler for regulations.

One evening, when I was still trying to make a good impression, I went to change into my uniform. I opened my locker and found, to my dismay, that my hat was missing. Baffled, I looked around. And there was my hat in the wastepaper basket.

When I saw this lieutenant later, I said, "The funniest thing happened—did you see anybody go into the sergeant's locker room?"

"No."

"Well somebody went into my locker and dumped my hat in the wastepaper basket."

"That was me."

"You're kidding," I said.

"One thing you better learn, Gates. My sergeants don't have frayed hats. Get a new one."

Chastened, I bought a new hat. Soon after, we were both on morning watch, and around 2:00 or 3:00 A.M. this lieutenant invited me to join him for "lunch."

I drove. He directed me to a warehouse area on the east side of town. At this hour it was deserted. "I thought we were going to eat," I said.

"We are. Turn left."

We pulled up in front of a warehouse and he jumped out of the car and banged on a sliding metal door. A man peeked out, opened the door, and motioned us inside. It turned out to be the warehouse for Thrifty Drug Stores.

Somewhat confused, I followed them to a cavernous refrigerator. In those days, Thrifty had soda fountains and lunch counters in its drugstores, and inside this refrigerator hung great big hunks of cheese and slabs of lunch meats. I stood there wondering as I watched my lieutenant pull out bread and cheese as if he owned the place.

"Hey, come on, Gates. Make yourself a sandwich."

And I'm thinking, *But this is crazy. Here is a guy who*

lectures on ethics once a month, and he comes to a warehouse to get a damn sandwich?

I fixed something to eat and didn't say anything. But after that, whenever he said, "Let's get lunch," I'd say, "No. I've got something to do." I just couldn't get over this stickler for ethics who was blinded by those big baloney sandwiches he'd gorge himself on.

What to accept and what not to is a universal problem all police officers must face. Free meals always present a dilemma. People like to make jokes about cops and free meals. They especially make jokes about cops and free doughnuts. They say, "You need a cop? Call the local doughnut shop."

And there's a certain amount of truth in that. Often the owner of an establishment is quite willing to provide the police with a doughnut, a cup of coffee, or a meal, just to have officers present. This may make good business sense for the owner, but it creates a disturbing problem for a police administrator. How do you make it clear that your officers are not on the take?

To categorically outlaw all gratuities under all circumstances isn't feasible or fair. At Christmas a little old lady goes up to an officer who has walked a beat for years and hands him a pair of socks she has knitted. You can't have that officer say, "Sorry, ma'am. I can't accept a gratuity." We're not that cold. Often, it becomes a judgment call.

What LAPD has always tried to do is to make the officer think hard about ethical considerations: What are you giving away for that free cup of coffee? The policy is blindingly clear: You do not accept gratuities if there is an expectation of some kind of service in return, period. Given that, it is almost impossible to implement.

Years later, after I had become captain of a precinct, I asked my adjutant to suggest a place for lunch.

"There's a great Mexican place," he said, and told me how to find it.

I arrived, wearing my uniform, and had lunch by myself. When I took my check to the register and plunked down my money, the cashier pushed the bills back. "It's taken care of."

"No," I said. "I want to pay."

"I'm sorry, you can't pay."

"I insist. Here's my money."

"I'm not going to argue. I'm going to call the manager."

I thought, *Fine. This will be a good time to talk to the manager about this because it's obviously a problem with my officers.*

The manager came storming out. "Listen, you do your job as a police officer and I'll do my job as manager of this restaurant," the irate man told me. "I work hard to entice people in here and I want the business of your police officers. It saves me the price of hiring private guards. And there's nothing you can do about it because it's not illegal."

I told him he was right. I couldn't do anything to stop him offering free meals. But I could talk to my officers about it in terms of *their* integrity.

"What integrity?" the man shot back. "They enjoy my food. I don't ask for anything. I've never asked for anything. I just want them to be seen here enjoying my food."

The manager had it all figured out. Which still left the problem of what his other customers thought when they saw police officers getting special treatment. If nothing else, it is the old problem of not necessarily what you do, but what people's perceptions are of what you do.

Since there are no absolute rules you can apply, and no amount of bluenose talk is going to change anything, LAPD tries to stress the pride an officer must have in himself; how it is assumed each officer has enough pride to want to be his own person and not be obligated to anyone.

Which doesn't necessarily work either. As chief, I was out on patrol with some officers and they asked if I'd like to stop at a fast-food place called Tommy's Hamburgers. I said, "Great. I haven't been to Tommy's in years."

So I went up to the counter, got hamburgers for all, paid for them, and sat down. All the officers were grinning at me.

"Why are you smiling?" I asked.

"Because," an officer replied, "you only paid half price for the hamburgers."

"I did?"

"They charge us half price, and we knew if we told you, you wouldn't do it."

Even as chief of police, I took a gratuity—cut-rate burgers at Tommy's.

■

Far more tarnishing to a police officer's image than the odd doughnut is the widely held perception that we are sworn members of a Brotherhood of Silence. A sort of "I won't report your dirty deeds if you don't report mine" credo.

It may have existed in Serpico's day in the New York Police Department, when officers covered up one another's illegal deeds, but it does not exist, and never has existed, as written or unwritten policy in LAPD. We do not preach, teach, or condone a Code of Silence. Officers are reluctant to come forward and finger a partner for minor infractions, just as colleagues in other lines of work are. Occasionally, serious misconduct is covered up.

But not dishonesty. Known for its incorruptibility, LAPD instills in each of its officers from day one the pride of being a member of the department and of upholding its principles and values. Breaking *that* code results in tough discipline. But there is no Code of Silence, as much as the media loves the sound of it. Actually, the Code of Silence that exists in America's media regarding its mistakes, its imperfections, its misdeeds makes the police in Los Angeles look like saints.

What does exist in LAPD is a complicated concept that is often misunderstood. When two people work together day in and day out, depending as they do on each other for their lives, they will build a loyalty, unquestionably. Sometimes it's as strong as the loyalty one feels for a spouse or child. It is similar in other professions—medicine, law, journalism—where peers work closely together. But just as these people are expected to report a colleague's wrongdoing, so are we.

Right away I learned that if you caught your partner doing something wrong, the first thing you did was to call him on it. "Hey, knock it off. You participate in that, I'm gonna let somebody know."

Where every officer gets hung up is on the use-of-force issue. This is such a troublesome area because it is difficult, even for experienced police officers, to discern if the force used is greater than it should be. Everyone believes in such easy answers. But officers must make split-second decisions. They are well trained to do this. But much later, long after an officer has whacked a suspect with his baton, the rest of us sit back in our cozy arenas and go through this deliberative effort to determine if the split-second decision was a good one or a bad one.

A police officer, watching his partner use force, may well wonder if "enough" was too much. He's thinking, *Damn, I wish he hadn't hit him a second time with a baton, but I do understand. The suspect gave him a hard time. So I'm not going to run in and say, "Sergeant, you know he hit him an extra time with a baton."*

Every year we have officers coming forward when it goes beyond that, when a partner has inflicted unnecessary injury. And every year Internal Affairs investigates and disciplines hundreds of officers for violating departmental rules. But what becomes tricky are the borderline cases, or those slightly over the border. Perhaps it's one or two extra whacks, a kick, or one punch—it shouldn't have happened, but it isn't that bad. It produced a bruise or two, but no real injury. A temper was lost, it became a heated situation, and the partner realizes that. He won't report it, not because of a Code of Silence but because he has made a judgment: There's no big deal here, and certainly no pattern of excessive behavior.

One case I was supervising concerned a rash of burglaries in Central's territory. The burglars hadn't provided us with enough of an M.O. to really get a fix on them. So this particular night, I was out driving with no specific plan in effect.

A call came over the radio: "Kidnapping, rape, robbery." The victim, who had phoned in the report, and her boyfriend had just been dumped out of a car. They said the driver had kidnapped them, raped her, and taken all their money. A description of the suspect's car had just come over the radio when—lo and behold—I saw the car in the distance, zooming along a cross street. It was going like hell. I flicked on my siren and took off after it.

The pursuit didn't last long. The guy went barreling around a corner, the back end of his car hit the curb, and he bounced into a light pole. He bailed out of his car, I bailed out of mine and we met in a weed-filled vacant lot.

It was pitch dark. From the moment he jumped out of his car I had my eyes glued to his hands, looking for a gun. Kidnapping, robbery, rape—he must have had a weapon. But I didn't see one.

Faster afoot than he, I caught him in the middle of the lot. We wrestled around a bit before I finally got him handcuffed and put him in the back seat of my car. Then I went to his car to look for a weapon.

A pair of uniformed officers and a team of detectives came screeching up. I told them I couldn't find a gun, that probably he had dumped it, either in the empty lot or somewhere along the way.

"I'll find out," one of the detectives offered. And he walked over to my car, opened the door, stuck his head in, and asked the guy where the gun was.

The guy said, "What gun?"

The detective punched him in the gut.

I didn't see it, but I heard the thump and when I looked back, the suspect was gasping.

"Where's the gun?" the detective repeated.

The suspect could hardly talk. And wham! The detective hit him again.

This was the first time I had seen anything like it. I didn't know if officers behaved differently around me due to my association with Parker, but I doubted this kind of behavior happened very often. It pissed me off. I grabbed the detective and pulled him off the guy, fuming, saying, "My prisoner. Get out of here."

I'm not against punching somebody if he needs to be punched—if you're fighting with him—but this guy was handcuffed.

In the end, we found the gun in the field and we were able to prosecute the guy successfully. I probably should have taken additional action against the detective, but all I did was confront him again.

"I can't believe you would do that to a prisoner and expect me, as a sergeant, to stand there and let it happen," I said.

"Well, he's a no good S.O.B., just committed a rape and a robbery, and we needed that gun for the prosecution. And that was a way to get it."

"You didn't get anything," I snapped. "We got the gun. You didn't need to do that."

From then on I was extremely tough on discipline anytime force was used against someone in handcuffs or under restraint. I just have no patience for that whatever.

■

I was promoted to lieutenant in 1959, taking the test as soon as I was eligible to and coming out number one on the list. This promotion put me right back into Parker's office, as his adjutant—which didn't thrill me. I much preferred the action in the field.

Serving as his right-hand man, I kept him abreast of internal issues, wrote memos, and made sure staff work was complete and accurate. I was later upped to his executive officer, another administrative job in which I became his link to people outside the department and those in the top echelons within.

Immediately I found that my relationship with him had changed ever so subtly. By now, I had mastered most of the books on police administration, so I had a better understanding of his lectures to me nine years before. This gave me the confidence to test some of his philosophies and argue those I didn't think were correct. Not that Bill Parker ever once conceded my points. But occasionally I would notice little changes in his speeches or, to my private delight, actually hear him strongly defend one of my positions.

That was probably the good news. The bad news was that I had to serve as his messenger. "Go tell Deputy Chief So-And-So . . ." he would command, and off I'd trot. The problem was, I had to speak Parker's words at a lieutenant's level or I'd lose my head.

One time Parker sent me off to see two deputy chiefs concerning their expense accounts. "I think they're cheating," Parker said flatly. "I don't believe they really spent what they said. If they did, they spent too much."

Oh, my God, I thought as I returned to my desk to think this one through. I had to phrase Parker's accusations in some way that would be acceptable coming from a lieutenant. Swallowing hard, off I went. To the first deputy chief I said, "Um, you know I find myself in a very awkward situation. I hope you understand I'm only communicating a message. But the chief believes perhaps a little better accounting is needed of how you spent the city's, er, money.''

My lessons in diplomacy continued to be forced on me. Most of the time, Parker was his usual self, energetic, ornery, and miserable to deal with. He frightened everybody. Why he never frightened me I don't know. I was always very respectful around him and I watched him like a hawk. One thing I learned: He was eminently fair-minded—unless you crossed him.

A sergeant named Tom Bradley did.

Although our paths rarely crossed, I had watched Bradley move quickly up the ranks. (It would be some time until he moved all the way up to the rank of mayor.) Parker had terrific confidence in Tom, a smart guy who, Parker believed, would be capable of providing strong leadership. He began sending Bradley out in the mid-fifties to speak to dissident groups, hoping this polished, articulate sergeant could defuse some of the hostility these groups felt toward police officers.

One day an intelligence report came back. Parker told me the report said that Bradley, instead of talking the department up, was providing negative information to dissident groups, saying unfavorable things about Parker and the LAPD. That changed Parker's view of him just like that. Bradley, he fumed, was an absolute traitor to the department.

Although hurt and disappointed, Parker never added this information to Bradley's personnel packet. Instead, Parker retaliated by transferring him out of a trusted position into one as an also-ran lieutenant. Bradley wound up as a watch commander of Wilshire division, where, I've since been told, he wasn't trusted very much either since he was viewed as taking care of his friends rather than supporting his men.

■

I came to know all of Parker's habits. I knew that he came to work each morning aware of everything that was going on in Los Angeles because he read the papers carefully. If you wanted his respect, you had to know what was going on too.

This led to more embarrassing moments for me. Parker would call in two or three, or maybe all, of his seven deputy chiefs and he would hold court on a certain issue. He would ask questions: "What do you think? What should we do?" Then he would buzz for me.

"Gates," he would say, "we've just been talking about . . ." whatever it was. And then, right in front of these deputy chiefs, he would ask me, a lieutenant—an inferior by three ranks—what I thought.

That these seven deputy chiefs would one day sit on my oral board for captain did not escape me. I had no desire to offend them or show them up, but Parker was forever doing this to me. So I would tactfully give him the answer I knew he wanted, because I was well attuned to his thinking and I, too, had read all the papers.

Parker would say, "*See!* Gates knows all about it. Gates reads the newspapers."

I, cringing inwardly, would leave the room, thinking, *Oh, my God!*

■

Despite this, four years later I did make captain. I was now eligible for command of one of the then fourteen uniformed patrol divisions. Unfortunately, the only vacancy available in February 1963 was the last place I wanted to be: Highland Park.

Never dreaming I would voluntarily return to the station where I'd been brought in for punching a cop, I showed up for work, eager to continue trying out my talents as a boss. As a sergeant, I had overseen 20 officers at most; as a lieutenant, 65 to 70 on a watch. As commander of the Highland Park division, I would be overseeing 170 officers, and reporting to Inspector Jack Collins, in charge of Area #3, and to Deputy Chief Roger Murdock, the head of patrol. Two days after I arrived, I called in my three lieutenants to set forth my objectives.

One of the lieutenants was an old-timer named Harry Fremont. Harry had been a great detective, a hard-nosed detective, who had run into problems with Parker years before. Namely, he had been one of the eight officers involved in the 1951 Bloody Christmas beatings at the Lincoln Heights jail. As punishment, Parker had yanked him out of robbery and banished him to uniformed patrol, banished him to Highland Park.

Harry walked into the meeting with a cup and saucer—unusual, since most officers use mugs—and Harry could not keep that cup and saucer still. They chittered and clattered; I mean, it was as if we were having a small earthquake at all times. I tried not to pay any attention, but it was so obvious, all this rattling of china. And you could see the coffee inside; I was sure it was going to fall out, so badly was old Harry shaking.

I thought, *Holy Cow,* as I brought my eyes up from the trembling cup to Harry's florid face. He was a nice-looking man with an Irishman's round face, but his skin was kind of blotchy and his nose quite red. Nice smile, bright eyes. But he couldn't keep that coffee cup still.

Boy, I thought, *Harry must really be drinking, coming to work at this hour, already a little bit smashed.*

I edged closer. I didn't smell any alcohol and he talked reasonably well. Okay, so the guy was obviously *very* nervous. After the meeting, I thought more about Harry, and I finally put the shaking down to his having had too much to drink in his life, so that he'd reached a point where he had delirium tremens.

Still, every time I encountered him, he almost came unglued.

It occurred to me then that Harry believed Parker had sent me to Highland Park just to get Harry Fremont. Clearly his days were numbered, he thought. He was absolutely frightened to death. And nothing I could say seemed to reassure him.

At the time, we had a burglar working Highland Park, a daylight burglar who was just ripping us apart. Every day there were two, three, four burglaries. I called Harry in.

"This burglar is driving us crazy, Harry. And you have forgotten more about police work than those kids you've got working for you will ever know. I want you to catch that burglar, Harry. You put together a plan, we'll have this burglar in jail. I want you to do it, Harry."

He gave me an odd look, as if to say, *Oh, God, this is it. It's all over. I'm gonna fail and somehow he's gonna turn it around and get me.* What he actually said was "Yes, sir."

Two days later Harry walked into my office with the biggest, broadest smile you ever saw, eyes twinkling. "Captain, we got the burglar!"

"I knew you would, Harry. There was no doubt in my mind that you could do it," I raved. "This is fantastic work."

I praised Harry to the skies. I talked about him at roll call. I wrote up the case in my progress report and I threw Harry bouquets he hadn't received in years. He changed overnight. He stopped drinking. The DTs disappeared. His appearance improved. No more blotchy skin or red nose. He became the most attentive lieutenant I had. His wife told me: "I don't know what you did to him, but Harry's a new man."

That experience taught me a valuable lesson: that you can't give up on people, that there is plenty of good in people even though they might make a mistake from time to time. Harry Fremont was a perfect example. He died a few years ago, but I will always carry fond memories of Harry as a good man I think I saved—rather than destroyed.

■

It didn't take long for the sheer weight of my new responsibilities to hit me. As Captain of Highland Park, I was in charge of a station, *my* station. I was forever coming in, checking, looking for signs of breakdowns, looking for dishonesty, unethical conduct, or even just officers sleeping instead of patrolling on the morning watch. The station, and the area, represented my little piece of the city. I took great pride in my building, inspected every nook and cranny for cleanliness. *This station belongs to me*, I would tell myself. *And so does everyone in it.*

I was also aware, as I drove daily through the community, that I was the guy 170,000 people turned to for police protection. Every crime, every traffic accident in my forty-two square miles reflected upon me. I studied the pin map in my office carefully, charting where each crime and accident occurred. This was also the first job that I had to take home with me. I learned to respond instantly to the ringing of the phone in the middle of the night. As captain, I was always on call.

I would be for the rest of my days with LAPD.

6

Intelligence

I had been at Highland Park only four months when I got a call from Parker. "Get ready to be transferred," he said. "You're going to run Intelligence."

I was astonished. Jim Hamilton, the captain of Intelligence, had been Parker's man in that position from day one and I had assumed Jim would never leave. But the National Football League was having terrible problems with gambling. "Pete Rozelle thinks the mob's shaving points on football games and he wants to hire a director of security who knows organized crime," Parker said. "Robert Kennedy suggested Jim."

I knew why Parker had selected me. Head of Intelligence was one of the most sensitive jobs in LAPD. Other than the deputy chiefs, only the captains of Internal Affairs, Administrative Vice, and Intelligence reported directly to Parker. More than any position, the captain of Intelligence had to give total allegiance to the chief of police, the kind of unwavering loyalty that would never be questioned. For inevitably, this captain will come across information so politically sensitive that it could lead to disruption within the department. Often this information would involve top-level people in LAPD. The chief had to be absolutely certain that his Intelligence captain had loyalties only to him, and to no one else.

On June 6, I transferred back downtown into police headquarters. In 1955 we had moved out of City Hall and into a new glass-and-steel structure called the Police Administration Building. Nicknamed The Glass House, and made famous on *Dragnet,* the eight-story LAPD headquarters on Los Angeles Street would one day be renamed Parker Center. My office was on the seventh floor, up one from the chief's. As head of Intelligence, I had to educate myself fast.

The seventy-man division was making quite a name for itself across the United States. Its main job was to monitor organized crime in Southern California—or maybe I should say, discourage it. The success it was having in keeping the mob out was causing other police departments to take notice.

During Parker's reign, the Mafia had become a weak and ineffectual outfit in Los Angeles. In the late 1930s and throughout the forties, Bugsy Siegel and, later, his lieutenant Mickey Cohen, and their powerful rival Jack Dragna had gained a strong foothold in the local gambling, prostitution, and narcotics businesses. Given the wealth in Southern California, the attractive real estate and the movie studios, L.A. was ripe for mob action. And indeed, a steady stream of East Coast Mafiosi came through to scout the territory. After the Brenda Allen scandal and the indictment and resignation of Chief Horrall as a result, various stories surfaced as to how deeply involved LAPD was with these hoodlums. I never learned the truth.

All I knew was what happened once Parker became chief: He took off after organized crime, particularly the Mafia, like a general attacking an enemy army. It was full-scale war every single day. From the big boys to the street-corner bookies, LAPD was on top of them. Down the hall from my office was a room that resembled an army command post. Charts up on the walls depicted Mafia family trees, traced back to Sicily, and named every key Mafia figure in every major U.S. city.

We knew who they were and we knew who they knew. We had thick loose-leaf notebooks crammed with the most detailed information about these men. Who was seen talking to whom, where, on what date, cross-referenced with previous meetings between the same pair. In short, Intelligence knew the precise whereabouts of every Mafia figure in Southern California and what he was doing at almost any given moment.

That summer, I studied the Mafia and other aspects of organized crime like a college student cramming for a final exam. Having worked in Parker's office, I already had some insight into organized crime, but not much. As a result, I took home every book I could find on the subject and every article, and I devoured them. I went through thousands and thousands of police files. I ate, drank, and slept organized crime.

There were two other units I oversaw, as well.

One, deep within Intelligence, was unknown to most. This unit dealt with Communism, Communists, and other subversives. It kept a small office at Wilshire division that was filled with files but rarely occupied. The top guy was Lieutenant Carl Abbott, who had been undercover in the Communist party for years. Carl had actually spent time in the Soviet Union working as an undercover officer for us. Few people in LAPD even knew Carl Abbott existed. He reported directly to me, or to Parker.

The third function of Intelligence was to provide security for visiting dignitaries and heads of state. Another area I had to master quickly. For not long after I arrived, President Kennedy flew in to deliver a speech.

There had been problems when JFK had come in for the Democratic convention three years before. His helicopter had landed on the first tee of the Los Angeles Country Club, just across the street from the Beverly Hilton Hotel, where he would stay. A staunchly Republican membership watched in furious silence as the helicopter made a huge indentation in the grass, and out popped the Democratic hopeful, who strode jauntily across their manicured course—which was pretty funny. But the next day, standing on a crowded elevator, Kennedy wanted to make room for a couple of aides. So he physically pushed two police officers assigned to his security out—which was not funny. Hearing this, Parker angrily grabbed the phone and called Bobby Kennedy.

"You tell your brother if he ever puts his hands on a Los Angeles police officer again, I will pull all—do you hear me?—*all* the security off the Democratic convention. All of it! Uniforms—everybody—will walk off the job. Now, you *tell* him that!"

Two years later, the President returned. After again infuriating the L.A. Country Club set with his arrival, Kennedy was escorted to his room. I immediately phoned Parker and told him the President was safe and recited his schedule.

"I'm going to be down there at four o'clock," Parker responded. "Would you tell the President I'd like to talk to him?" He hung up.

Oh, shit, I thought. *I'm going to march in to the President of the United States and tell him* when *my boss wants to see him, rather than ask him? How am I supposed to do that?*

Trying not to panic, I found the agent in charge of the White House detail. "What the hell am I supposed to do?" I asked.

Jerry Baines looked at me skeptically. "Does he know the President?"

"Oh, yeah. He knows Bobby, too, and Pierre Salinger."

Baines said he'd see what he could do. Ten minutes later he returned. "He'll see him at four." And I thought, *Whew!*

At 3:40, Parker came bouncing in and together we went to Pierre Salinger's room. Pierre came to the door in his boxer shorts, T-shirt, and black socks, with a big cigar in his mouth and a snifter of brandy in his hand. We went in and chatted until four, when I signaled Parker.

I rode up with him to the President's room and stood there while they talked. Nobody introduced me. It wasn't until we were riding down in the elevator together that Parker did. Kennedy said, "You're awfully young to be captain."

I laughed. "You're pretty young to be President." Kennedy grinned.

Three days later, as we were escorting the President onto Air Force One, all of the security detail and motor officers

lined up to shake his hand. When he got to me, he said,
"Captain Gates, I appreciate very much all the assistance."
And I thought, *My God, this guy remembered my name.*

This time when Kennedy arrived, in the summer of 1963,
I was shocked. From what I could perceive, good protection
for the President was sorely lacking.

The field was not entirely new to me. In 1960, I had
worked security at the Democratic national convention. I
had also helped out on the detail when Soviet President
Nikita Khrushchev visited Los Angeles in 1959. I could
remember vividly the tremendous amount of attention that
went into planning Khrushchev's protection. When he demanded to go to Disneyland, a KGB general marched into
Parker's office to discuss it. I was there and I listened as
Parker emphatically laid down Parker's Law. He said, "Absolutely not. I can't protect him and that's that." So the
leader of the Soviet Union didn't go. Now, only four years
later, here came the President of the United States, but the
same meticulous planning was absent.

The President's protection then consisted of a pickup
team organized by an understaffed Secret Service and composed of various federal agencies, most of which had no
idea what adequate protection entailed. Agents came from
Internal Revenue, from the FBI, some from Customs, a few
from drug enforcement, and all were ill-prepared.

The Secret Service didn't appear much better suited. I
won't say they were inept. These were dedicated, hardworking men and I felt sure that if a grenade were to be
thrown at the President, they would have instantly jumped
in front of him and fallen on it.

The problem was, I didn't see anything that would prevent a grenade from being thrown.

At the Palladium in Hollywood, where the President was
to deliver his speech, no one had done anything about high-
ground security, which is the first thing one does today.
Even then I was conscious of a need to get people up on
roofs, and when I looked around, not a single soul was on
top of a building.

The agent in charge of the Secret Service in Los Angeles,
Guy Spaman, was nowhere to be seen either.

"Don't expect Guy to be on the scene," said Pat Boggs,

the second in command, when I inquired. "Guy gets so nervous at these things, he can't bring himself to show up. You need him, you'll find him pacing back and forth two or three blocks away, worrying about what's going on here."

Worse, if possible, was the inability of anybody to control the President. No cover had been provided for him when he came out of the Palladium. Instead of having his car waiting at the entrance, it was parked in the lot. So Kennedy walked through the lot to the car, and as he was getting in, he spotted Senate Majority Leader Mike Mansfield.

The President got out of the car, in the open, and walked over to Mansfield, saying, "Hey, Mike, I want to talk to you," and they stood there—again, out in the open in downtown Hollywood—with no Secret Service surrounding them, no cover whatsoever. I was simply amazed.

Several months later, President Kennedy was assassinated.

I remember noting there was no high-ground security in Dallas either.

■

By coincidence, Lieutenant Jack Revel of the Dallas police department phoned me two days after the assassination on a different matter. "Are you sure you've got the right guy?" I couldn't help asking, referring to Lee Harvey Oswald.

"Oh, don't worry, Daryl," he said. "We're putting the nails in his coffin right now."

Hours later Oswald was shot to death by Jack Ruby. I phoned Revel back. "Is *that* what you meant, Jack?"

"Oh, God, no," the mortified lieutenant said.

■

The following year, security had improved significantly when President Lyndon Johnson came through, campaigning for reelection. Even so, you couldn't do much with Johnson. I will never forget his arrival at LAX. Air Force One had landed and he was escorted to an armored limousine across the tarmac. It took a while for everyone in his traveling party to get to the proper cars. We were still waiting for part of the motorcade to move into place when Johnson stuck his head out the roof window—actually, he stuck half his body out of the car—and shouted, "Let's get this fucking thing going!"

I thought, That's *the President of the United States?*

We took him downtown along Broadway, past a mass of humanity—which we argued against, but Johnson insisted. He wanted to make speeches along the way and end up outside City Hall. Frankly, I was surprised that he made it up to the podium, because he was drunk, absolutely loaded. Later, he went on to Salt Lake City and some local people there told us afterward that it was hard to get him off the airplane, so snockered was the President.

Interestingly, one of the people we spent the most man-hours protecting was not a head of state, but the Reverend Martin Luther King, Jr. In 1965 he made five trips to L.A. amid all kinds of rumors that he was going to be assassinated. We gave him the kind of security we would give a President, even though it was unheard of at the time to provide such heavy security for a black leader. But given the rumors, I wanted to do the intelligent thing.

I, personally, went on the security detail during his first visit. And yes, it was true, there were some escapades at his hotel involving women. We paid no attention to that; his relationships with women were well known. Still, I remember hearing many unflattering stories about him. Yet when I met Dr. King, I was terribly impressed with his extraordinary intelligence. I heard him speak on five different occasions, always without notes. And each time, he gave a different speech, geared to that particular audience.

One speech took place at a synagogue, and his education really came through. He was able to talk to a Jewish audience because he knew enough about the Old Testament and Jewish doctrine to speak with great force and great insight. I think everyone who heard him came away deeply impressed.

■

Using every free moment, I continued to study the Mafia. I was fascinated by how they operated. How they muscled into bookmaking operations, wrested small businesses away from their legitimate owners, and infiltrated big-city police departments. In time, I became a national expert. Of course, I had a national expert as my tutor. Lieutenant Marion Phillips was a veritable walking encyclopedia of facts on organized crime, and if there was something he didn't know, he knew where to find it. But even in those first few months I could boast that I knew more about the Mafia than the FBI.

This was because J. Edgar Hoover refused to recognize that there was a Mafia. He absolutely would not admit there was an Italian crime machine with ties to Sicily operating within the United States. Some people speculated that he chose to ignore the Mafia because he feared the FBI could not effectively stop it. This may have been partially true. The other part, I always suspected, was his jealousy of Bill Parker. By then, after thirteen years as chief of police, Parker had become the most famous lawman in America next to Hoover, and Hoover deeply resented that.

The bad blood between the LAPD and the FBI began when Parker, as the new chief, demonstrated that he was his own man and that he would not be beholden to J. Edgar. I'm not aware of a particular incident; in fact, I don't believe the two men ever met. But Parker made his thoughts on law enforcement clear through his numerous speeches, articles, and the direction in which he was taking the department. All of this was duly reported back to Hoover through the local head of the FBI, whom Parker tended to ignore. In the forties, I am told, Hoover enjoyed visiting L.A., hanging out with movie stars and studio chiefs. His visits abruptly ceased after Parker became chief.

In time our officers were excluded from the three-month training academy run by the FBI. It was always our impression that the real purpose of the academy was not so much to educate police officers—the stated purpose—as it was to build an allegiance to the FBI. A police officer who "graduated" from the academy was expected to have a loyalty first and foremost to Hoover.

In effect, without changing the laws, J. Edgar Hoover was trying to nationalize the police in America. But he couldn't fool Parker. Parker simply ignored him.

With Hoover steadfastly refusing to recognize the Mafia,

a vacuum existed in this country between local intelligence units. Encouraged to trust only Hoover, police departments were suspicious of one another. Seeing a need for some kind of Mafia intelligence network, Parker and my predecessor in Intelligence, Jim Hamilton, helped create the Law Enforcement Intelligence Unit in California in 1955. Through this network, Mafia and organized crime information was exchanged among the San Francisco police department, LAPD, and the L.A. County sheriff's department, which policed all unincorporated areas, plus any city that lacked its own department and contracted for the sheriff's services. Soon, this network began to expand nationwide. For the first time there was a way of bringing together police specialists who, for years, had been fighting organized crime on their own.

Hoover dismissed the network, just as he managed to dismiss the Mafia until the Kennedys came to power. For the first time since becoming FBI director in 1924, Hoover was under an Attorney General who had more access to the President than he did. As a result of Bobby Kennedy's badgering, Hoover eventually acknowledged an organization that he stubbornly referred to as La Cosa Nostra.

Our experts just laughed. "La Cosa Nostra? What in the *hell* is that?"

Parker merely shrugged. "I don't care whether they call it the Italian Birdwatchers' Society," he declared. "It wouldn't make any difference." To get more information we sent Sergeants Pete Bagoye and Stu Duncan to Washington, where the Attorney General allowed them to interview Valachi, who in testimony revealed for the first time the existence of La Cosa Nostra. After Bagoye and Duncan returned, they told me how unimpressed they were with the depth of Valachi's information concerning organized crime.

Today the FBI works closely with local law enforcement on organized crime, and the M-word is no longer forbidden. But this happened only after Hoover's death in 1972, for I am sure I never once heard him say "Mafia." I'd love to go back and see whether you could ever put Hoover and the word *Mafia* together. I doubt that you could.

By the mid-sixties, mob influence in Southern California was minimal. We had one local boss, Nick Licata, who in his younger years ran gambling enterprises for Jack Dragna. But now, at age seventy, Licata was living off income from several apartment houses he owned and legitimate businesses he had infiltrated, and he spent his days at the racetrack issuing orders to lesser hoodlums. We had a few Gallos. Sam Giancana out of Chicago still wielded a great deal of clout. Mickey Cohen had gone to prison for income tax evasion in 1962, for the second and final time.

We helped put him away. By then, the feds had decided the only way to get Cohen was to prove "conspicuous consumption." If they could show he spent far more money than the income he accounted for, they'd have him. Our Intelligence people had jumped on the case. Painstakingly, using our contacts around the city, they documented where he dined and how much he spent. How many suits he purchased. What pieces of jewelry he bought for his wife. What he paid for his cars, and so on. This evidence sealed the case.

For Cohen, it must have seemed ironic that Bill Parker's department provided the information that convicted him. In Cohen's book, *In My Own Words,* he reports that in 1950, when the selection process for chief of police was going on, he was advised by an associate to get out of town for six weeks. He went to Chicago. When he learned that the dreaded Parker had been selected, he phoned his associate in Los Angeles. "What happened?"

"Our man on the Police Commission died," came the response.

With Cohen locked up, this left, according to our numbers, only thirty major Mafia figures operating out of Los Angeles. Primarily they owned, controlled, or influenced through extortion, bars, produce wholesalers, vending machines, macaroni and garment manufacturers, loan companies, bakeries, unions, pizza parlors, and large apartment houses. They were heavily into gambling. Also, they acted as enforcers or executioners for eastern "families." These thirty were associated with maybe another hundred lower-echelon persons known as soldiers.

By the end of 1964 the number of key figures had

dropped—due to deaths, convictions, and deportations—to twenty-three. But the Mafia could not reasonably be expected to disappear as if by magic. Like a small vigilant army, we took up our posts in the fort, always on the lookout for the next attack.

Often it came from the East. New York and Chicago hoodlums, ever eager to make the big score, would come out hoping to set up operations. Through our contacts, we usually knew when to expect them. We had men permanently stationed at the airport to alert us to arriving mobsters. Before they could claim their luggage, we had LAPD officers out there to greet them. We said, "You're not wanted here—get out. Go get your ticket and leave." We literally put them on the next plane home.

There's no way, of course, we could get away with that today. We would be hauled into federal court for violating somebody's civil rights. But at the time, it was one of our most effective tactics.

We had a whole arsenal. Heavy surveillance was a favorite. If we didn't send a visiting hoodlum home, we dogged him everywhere he went. This undoubtedly hampered the guy's efforts to contact local sources, and after several days the hoodlum would leave. One leader of the Gallo mob out of New York grumbled, "I will never return to Los Angeles because of the heat placed on my visit." Time and again, eastern gangsters would pack up and leave, cursing our suffocating surveillance.

We used surveillance on the local mob, too, and they knew it. To most, our surveillance was blatant. For instance, Nick Licata knew we went by his place every day. Each morning, we'd drive to the home of Angelo Polizzi, whom we suspected of a couple of murders, and follow him to work. At night we'd trail him home. We did this with a lot of them, letting them know that *we* knew what they were doing at all hours. It drove some of them absolutely crazy. They would complain to an officer: "Hey, I'm not involved in anything. Why are you bothering me?"

Some were afraid to use their telephones. Although by law we were not allowed to wiretap, we did regularly check with the phone company to find out whom they called. Hoping to outsmart us, a guy would leave his house, which we were watching, get in his car, and drive to a pay phone. He would then call another guy we were also watching. The second guy would drive to a phone booth and wait for the first guy to call him back. So we still knew who was calling whom—and when.

At times we preferred not to have a person know he was under surveillance. Trying to watch someone who knows he's being watched, without letting him see you, is hard work. To follow a guy down the freeway, for instance, took three or four cars. One car drops off, another picks him up.

Even so, suspecting a tail, they would elude us. They would go down the fast lane of the freeway at seventy miles an hour, then whip over to the off-ramp. And there was our man, stuck in the far left lane. He couldn't stop a line of cars behind him, so he had to pass his off-ramp, get off at the next one, turn around, go back and try to find his man.

Rarely did we bother to book these guys, for they would be out on bail in no time. They had the money and the lawyers to get out, so arresting them was not a useful harassing tactic. Back then, it was simply muscle on muscle.

Talking, at times, like the bad guys on TV, we convinced these gangsters that late some night they would wind up in a dark alley, where the LAPD would gladly take care of them.

We had one fellow in our department, Roger Otis, who was a master at intimidation. A tall, bare-knuckled guy, Roger could put the fear of God into these people. They really believed he would corner them in a dark alley and beat the shit out of them, leaving them to die.

Roger would saunter into a bar and, man, there was dead silence. He would walk up to some hoodlum. "Wanna talk to you." And the toughest of the tough meekly got up and followed Roger into the alley. When the guy would come back to the bar he would be very subdued. And Roger never laid a hand on him.

So the whole Mafia and organized crime structure remained weak; weak in terms of the amount of money they brought in, weak in terms of violence—hardly any violence at all. But we still felt a need to monitor their activities closely. Southern California was so attractive, a land of fast opportunity if you knew how to play your cards. There was all that real estate, ripe for a scam. And Las Vegas money was only a four-hour drive away. Thus, whenever we saw muscle that we recognized as Mafia—or organized crime— muscle moving in on a business, we jumped in to try to stop it.

One guy I decided to stop myself.

Sam Farkas had a carpet business on Wilshire. We knew he used to run with Mickey Cohen, and now we were hearing Sam was trying to strong-arm several men into joining a bookmaking operation in the Wilshire area. Because of his name, and because of his past association with Cohen, his threats drove fear into a lot of people.

So I had Sam Farkas picked up and brought downtown to me.

I sat in my office waiting, expecting a big, rough, tough guy to come swaggering in. But the man who showed up looked more like a teddy bear. I told him to "siddown." Then, using some fairly strong language, I explained to Sam that he was going to stop doing what he was doing.

" 'Cause if you don't stop, we're gonna come out and make sure you stop," I told him. We would use the kind of pressure that he knew we could use, and not only would he be out of the bookmaking business, *all* of his businesses would end.

I sounded like Jimmy Cagney in a bad movie. I was using the same kind of coercion on Sam Farkas that organized crime used to coerce others. It amused me for a moment.

Sam swore up and down that all he had going was his carpet business. But he also swore up and down that if he *were* doing anything else, he would cease and desist immediately.

I gave him more Cagney; then I began to feel silly using such tough language on a nicely dressed man who was staring at me like a genial grandfather. Most mobsters, I learned, never looked like hoodlums engaged in murder, mayhem, extortion, or the rackets. They were not the stereotypes you see on TV. They were more polite to us, typically, than the guy we pulled over for a traffic violation. Moreover, many of them were quite well read, sophisticated in every respect. And some of them were awfully good businessmen.

Sam Farkas smiled kindly. In his soft-spoken, friendly way, he assured me there was no problem. And if there *were* a problem, honest to God, the problem would end.

As a matter of fact, it did.

■

Occasionally we resorted to using undercover agents, but only on a short-term basis.

Undercover work is difficult and tricky. LAPD policy has always been that working undercover does not give an officer license to break the law. A traffic violation, you might get away with. But you cannot assist, aid, or abet in any kind of major crime. Yet if you infiltrate and form a close relationship with a lawbreaker, how in the world can you operate effectively unless you participate when they pull off something major?

I was amused by the TV show *Wiseguy,* where the hero, a federal agent named Vinnie Terranova, goes undercover from one assignment to another. I always wondered how he could get involved in so many illegal dealings and still have any credibility. In our department, if an undercover officer gets involved in something, he's lost his credibility with us and we can't keep him on the force. So if we do send someone undercover, the job has to be quick and clean.

We did rely on informants, though. Heavily. Sometimes these would be sleazy characters lurking in alleys. But the best information always came from legitimate people: restaurant owners, barkeeps, waitresses, parking lot attendants, airline ticket agents, the manager of a produce market, theater owners, prop men—people who were in a position to see who was doing what and talking to whom.

We kept an up-to-date file of Mafia hangouts. Tracton's, a steak house on the west side, was where you could find a major hoodlum any night. Wednesday through Sunday nights, lots of activity along the Sunset Strip. Sneeky Pete's was a sure thing, mainly because Eddie De Stefano, the host, was seen as a friend to every burglar, pimp, bookmaker, gambler, and headbuster in town. Sherry's on the Strip, the Losers, the Laurel Inn, and The Scene were also spots where officers could observe gangsters of repute. So was The Four Trees. The Red Velvet Supper Club, meanwhile, was the "in" place for assignations between pimps and apprentice prostitutes. Toluca Lake in the Valley had its hangouts as well.

Our informants worked all these places. Occasionally, we were asked to stay away. Sometimes a bartender feared that a mobster would see him talking to us. More often, an owner worried that our presence would scare big-spending hoodlums away. So we alerted our people to that. Also, periodically, we circulated within the department a list of spots we did not want officers to frequent. Walking into a known mob hangout, an unsophisticated officer could easily be glad-handed by the proprietor—dinner checks picked up, for instance—or by the hoodlums themselves. "Here's my card—call me." The card would identify the hoodlum as the owner of a meat market. "Come in some time, buddy. I'll give you a deal."

Despite the ready supply of honest informants, police officers instinctively searched for dishonest ones. Their theory was that an informant involved in crime had to be better than one who was not. Actually, this is almost never the case. I had two officers in Intelligence who got quite close to a bookmaker. They weren't taking payoffs; they just fell in love with this guy. He made their job easier. They simply sat down and wrote reports based on what he was telling them.

What they refused to see was that the informant expected something in return. In this case, protection. And he got it. Instead of zeroing in on him as a major bookmaker, these officers were letting him operate because he fed them tidbits, some of them good, most of them worthless. In return, he used the officers as muscle.

This is how it would work: Say you are a bookmaker and you want to pressure a guy to work for you. You say, "Listen, I've got protection. I've got a couple of cops I take care of—they take care of me. I'm telling you, you don't work for me, I'm gonna bring these coppers in and they're gonna take care of you."

Guy says, "You're lying."

You say, "I'll prove it. I'm coming over with these cops tonight."

So you call the cops. "I've got some good information for you. How about meeting me at such-and-such location?"

Then you call the guy back. "I'm coming out with my muscle and either you sign up with me or I'm gonna sic 'em on you."

And the guy says, "Fuck off."

You and the cops meet, and the guy is watching from across the street. He sees you shake hands, jabber a bit. You're probably giving the cops some bit of worthless information. The cops leave and you stroll over to the guy. "See? I told you. Those guys are working for *me*. So any time I give the word, they're gonna get *you*."

This happens all the time. And the cops are so in love with the informant that they fail to see how they're being used. In this case, the officers were knowledgeable, street-wise men. But they forgot the informant was not handing them information just because he liked them.

To put an end to this one situation, I called in another team of detectives and said, "Put their informant in jail. He's making book."

Then I held a division meeting. "Anybody who gets too close to an informant is in deep trouble," I warned. "You've got to recognize what informants are."

I laid out a new policy, which the officers hated, requiring them to reveal to us the names of the informants they used. Only the commanding officer sees this information, but at least the person's name is on file. It gives us a means of judging how good the information is. Still, the problem never goes away.

Nor did the problem of wiretaps.

The one tool we did not have and could not get was permission to wiretap.

Unlike New York and Illinois, California made it a felony to tap a phone. This made it nearly impossible for law enforcement to prosecute any of the Mafia. So much of their "business" is conducted by phone that without wiretapping, we had no effective means of gathering the evidence to indict them.

Every session, Parker would trek up to Sacramento to ask the State Legislature for court-approved wiretapping. As chief, I tried, too, and finally in 1989 the Legislature granted us court-approved wiretapping, primarily for narcotics cases. This ignores a whole spectrum of criminal activity, but then, the majority of California legislators still have their heads up their asses.

Forced to resort to other tactics, we often relied on bugging. We had our own electronics expert, Vince Kelly, who planted bugs in the homes of major bookmakers for LAPD while moonlighting for Howard Hughes (making sure no one was bugging *him*). But after one big trial in 1955, the California Supreme Court ruled we couldn't introduce evidence obtained through a bug, arguing that we had to enter the premises to place the bug, and this constituted illegal search and seizure.

We continued to bug anyway, for our own edification. Vince Kelly left the department and went to work full-time for Howard Hughes.

■

Our whole approach to the Mafia was a shining example of Bill Parker's pro-active stance. Stop 'em before they do something, if possible. But for all of our hoodlum-obsessed activities, Parker was most fearful that they would somehow infiltrate LAPD.

In every other city where they operated, buying cops, prosecutors, and even judges was their ticket to success. You simply can't go out each week and collect "protection" money from a bar owner or a dress manufacturer if that owner knows he can go to the police. In Chicago and New York, nobody ever knew who was on the take—what cop, what district attorney, what judge. Rumor had it that one New York bookie paid off five hundred cops each week.

LAPD was clean. People who feared Mafia muscle knew they could come to us and they wouldn't be double-crossed by a dirty cop. Such was our reputation that, in a kind of weird turn of events, we even had bookmakers asking for our help. In the days before narcotics became big business, gambling and bookmaking were the lifeblood of organized crime. By "recruiting" hundreds of handbooks across the country, the Mafia raked off a fortune. The "recruiters"—known as legbreakers or headbusters—would approach a bookie and flatly announce, "You work for me now. You are part of my organization."

Parker put a stop to this. He wanted to keep bookmakers

independent entrepreneurs—and put them in jail as independent entrepreneurs.

Knowing this, and knowing they could trust us not to disclose where we got our information, the handbooks would tell us if they were being pressured by "organizers." Then, without any evidence at all, our intelligence people would pick up the hoodlum who was doing the organizing and scare the living daylights out of him. "Don't want to see you on the street. We know what you're doing and you can't do it in this city. Get out."

Running this kind of operation required a police department above reproach. To keep the department honest, Parker had installed his intricate system of checks and balances.

At the lowest level are the Vice units that operate out of every division, such as Central Vice downtown. Next up the ladder is Administrative Vice, which is run out of police headquarters. Ad Vice monitors the big-time operations—major bookmakers, major pornographers, major madams—and has the resources to conduct long-term investigations.

Ad Vice also audits and monitors the division Vice units. It is Ad Vice that "stiffs in" phony 318 complaints to insure that local units are not allowing anything to slip by. In addition, Ad Vice runs its own intelligence network. It might hear that Chinese gambling is expanding, that the tongs are coming down from San Francisco and moving in. Ad Vice would check to see what Central Vice is doing about it. If Central Vice appears to be on top of the situation and arrests are being made, Ad Vice will give its stamp of approval to the chief of police.

In this way, if a Vice officer in Central is accepting bribes to let a gambling ring operate, Ad Vice would find out, theoretically.

Finally, you had Intelligence, my division, which was responsible for gathering information on organized crime and which checked on Ad Vice, while Ad Vice, to some extent, checked on Intelligence. Over and above that, there was Internal Affairs, which kept watch on everybody. So while the system was not foolproof, its point and counterpoint made it the most sophisticated system of any police department in the country. In short, it was pretty hard to be a corrupt L.A. cop.

Then we got a major scare.

We noticed that a bookmaking operation in Central's territory was suddenly expanding. No one had come to us complaining of being muscled. Instead, it appeared that this small-time bookie in the 3rd Street area had set out to organize other bookies. Business had gotten so big that he was now laying off bets and operating out of a back office.

The only way this bookie could expand to such an extent was if he was under the protection of someone in Central Vice. And the person in Central Vice, to offer that protection, would need the help of someone in Ad Vice. This was because an officer trying to protect a gambling operation could not "run" a telephone number from a back office through the phone company on his own authority. He would need someone in Ad Vice or Intelligence to go to the phone company and get the name of the party the number belonged to, plus records of calls made from that phone. And this dirty cop would want to know if Ad Vice had already run the number and was wondering why no one in Central Vice had brought it to Ad Vice's attention.

We were tipped to the possibility that we had been infiltrated by Joe Gunn, a young detective in Ad Vice. New to the LAPD, and not quite sure what to do, Gunn nervously confided to his lieutenant that his partner, Henry De Maddalena, had asked him to participate in a scheme to protect this group of bookies. For $200 a month, all Joe had to do was make a series of phone calls whenever the protected bookies were about to be raided.

Gunn seemed to be honest, but he was Italian and he was from the East Coast and there was concern that maybe he was trying to set something up within the department. Henry De Maddalena, on the other hand, was a top-notch bookmaking specialist whom I'd worked with in Central Vice years before. I always thought Hank was totally straight, so our suspicions shifted to Gunn.

Meanwhile, we began to fear that the bookmakers also had a contact in Intelligence. If they had someone in my division, someone in Ad Vice (like Gunn), and someone in Central Vice, they would have all bases covered and our system of checks and balances would be useless.

Clandestine meetings were held daily in Parker's office.

They were attended by the captain of Ad Vice, the captain of Internal Affairs, and me. We were so fearful we had been infiltrated that we each took a different route to Parker's office and did not tell our secretaries where we were going or for how long. We called it the "Black Investigation."

Suspicious of Gunn, but having no alternative, we began to feed him information to pass to his partner, De Maddalena. To our surprise, Hank led us to a sergeant in Central Vice named Pete Stafford. We then told Gunn to tip off De Maddalena that Ad Vice was running the back-office telephone number. If they knew we had that information, they would know the phone company would also give us the office location.

Actually, we already had it, and we set up a stakeout. Two detectives and I waited near the back office in an undercover car. Because we could tap our own phones, we listened to De Maddalena in Ad Vice place a call to Stafford at Central and pass along Gunn's information. Then Stafford went to a pay phone and dialed the back office, which we had bugged, and warned them we were about to raid it.

As the three bookmakers fled the building, we arrested them. Pete Stafford was convicted and sent to prison. A tough guy, hard as nails, he timidly and graciously came up to me years later after I spotted him working security for the Music Center during the Academy Awards. Henry De Maddalena was also convicted. He was an alcoholic, a really sad case. Just a total wreck who came unglued.

For Joe Gunn, this was his initiation into LAPD. He had come out here believing that ours was an ethical department of great integrity and suddenly he was confronted with this situation and wondered if he was about to be killed. Instead, Joe went on to get shot as a sergeant, lived, and ultimately became one of our most outstanding commanders. When he left LAPD, he wrote and produced episodes of *CHIPs*. Fortunately, because he came to us right away, we were able to hit this thing hard. We were never able to prove the bookmakers had a contact in Intelligence; I suspected one officer and I moved him out of the division.

This was the only time I know of that someone was almost able to corrupt LAPD.

We believed it could never happen, and it almost did.

7

Watts

In the spring of 1965, I was promoted to inspector, again coming out number one on the list. In June, Chief Parker appointed me to the command of Patrol Area 3.

The city of Los Angeles was sectioned into four patrol areas, with the fourteen divisions divided among them. Patrol Area 3 covered the middle and northern parts of the city and included Highland Park, Hollywood, Hollenbeck, and Central divisions. As area commander, I was in charge of all uniformed officers in those divisions. I was to make sure that departmental policies were carried out consistent with the other patrol areas and that all patrol operations ran smoothly. Once again, I had become a bureaucrat, but at least I was a field bureaucrat.

It had been an insufferably hot summer. Wednesday, August 11, 1965, was no different: another day of oppressive heat gripping Los Angeles. Unlike summers in the East and the Midwest, our nights are cooled by ocean breezes and the humidity stays relatively low. But this heat wave had settled in on us with a drenching humidity that made everyone miserable, including me.

Shirt sticking to my back, I was driving along Imperial
Boulevard in the early evening, heading for the Harbor
Freeway. The inspector in charge of Patrol Area 2—south
central and southwest L.A.—was on vacation and I had
been temporarily ceded his territory to command along with
my own. I was on my way to Harvey Aluminum, located in
an industrial area southwest of downtown and just east of
Torrance, where a strike was in progress. The strike had
turned violent, the police had been called in, and I wanted
to see how things were going.

I was in plain clothes, grateful that I didn't have to wear
a hat, but I was still soaking wet. Without air conditioning,
I began to look forward to the freeway and the hot air that
would blow through the car. But just before 8:00 P.M., as I
slowed to turn onto the freeway, a "major 415" crackled
over the radio. A 415 call means a disturbance of the peace.
A "major 415" means a lot of people are involved.

The report was coming from 116th Street and Avalon
Boulevard, less than a mile from me and only blocks from
an area called Watts. I changed course quickly. I would see
what the disturbance was, stay for five minutes, then continue on to Harvey.

I ended up staying for five days.

■

Watts is a tiny area, no more than one square mile. If
you had driven through it, on another day, you would have
had the feeling of passing through a small town. There is a
little City Hall and a little police substation with a park
behind it. Kids playing in the park would go into the police
station to buy candy bars out of the vending machine. A
"business district" of shops and storefront offices ran along
a two-block stretch of 103rd Street. Some of the streets in
Watts were well tended, with single-family houses, grassy
lawns, and cars in the driveways. Other streets looked
shabby, with decaying two-story apartment buildings and
homes in disrepair. Yet not even these blocks displayed the
squalor often found in big-city slums. Reporters who came
out from the East, perhaps expecting to see block after
block of broken-down tenements with cramped quarters,
shattered windows, and garbage strewn on the streets, had

difficulty understanding how so much violence could erupt in a neighborhood with leafy trees and tricycles parked in driveways.

Yet it just exploded.

It exploded far beyond the actual boundaries of Watts, covering, in the end, 46.5 square miles. Before the seven days of riots were over, 10,000 black people had joined in the mayhem. I have always tried to point out that of the 400,000 blacks who lived in that area, only a tiny percentage participated. Most of the people stayed inside, locked their doors, and were just scared to death.

I followed the radio call to a gas station off Imperial, where a police command post had been hastily set up. Less than an hour before, Lee Minikus, a California Highway Patrolman, had tried to arrest a twenty-one-year-old black man named Marquette Frye for drunken driving on the outskirts of Watts. Frye's brother Ronald, twenty-two, was also in the car. Marquette was given the standard sobriety test and failed. Minikus, who was on motorcycle, radioed for a patrol car to take Marquette to jail and a tow truck to take the car to a pound.

Ronald, only two blocks from home, went to get their mother so she could claim the car. By the time he returned with her, the patrol car and the tow truck had arrived, and so had a crowd of several hundred bystanders.

Miserable from the suffocating heat, people had taken to the streets that night, searching for relief. Little, if any, air conditioning existed in the Watts area; in fact, not much air conditioning existed anywhere in Los Angeles. No one felt like sweltering in front of their TVs, so they had come outside to try to cool off, maybe have a beer. And because so many people were out, sitting on their front steps or mingling on the sidewalks, it was easier for them to get caught up in the action.

The sound of sirens attracted their attention. Marquette began resisting arrest and playing to a crowd becoming increasingly hostile to the police. His brother got into it and his mother jumped on the back of one of the officers. Soon, all the Fryes were under arrest, and as they were driven away a woman in the crowd spat on one of the officers. Another arrest was made and eventually the police pulled out.

Rumors spread like wildfire. The cops had beat up somebody's mother—or something. Ignited, small groups roamed the streets, throwing rocks, bottles, and, as we began arriving, angry epithets at us. Tempers, already frayed by the heat, snapped.

As the substitute inspector of Patrol Area 2, I was put in charge as field commander. Using the seventeen or twenty patrol cars we now had at the scene, we tried to make a perimeter around the eight-block area where the rioting was heaviest. But it was hopeless from the start. A kind of crazed carnival atmosphere had broken out. Laughing, shouting, hurling anything they could find, people were running helter-skelter through the streets. Cars—ours and those of unsuspecting motorists—were pelted with rocks and bottles. No single mob had formed. It was a few people screaming and yelling on this street, none on the next, more on a third. A pair of officers would break up one group and move on to the next, only to have another group form in the same spot moments later.

We had no idea how to deal with this. There were seventy of us, eight hundred of them, maybe a thousand as the night wore on. We were constantly ducking bottles, rocks, knives, and Molotov cocktails. One officer was stabbed in the back. Guns were poked out of second-story windows, random shots fired. The rioters uprooted wooden bus-stop benches, pulling them out of their concrete bases and setting them on fire. Firemen could not get through—or wouldn't, terrified of being shot at. Two or three television mobile units were damaged, along with fifty to sixty vehicles. It was random chaos, in small disparate patches.

Working out of the gas station, I was continually on the radio, trying to get instructions from Deputy Chief Roger Murdock at police headquarters a few miles away, but it was impossible to describe to him what was going on. Over at 77th, the division that handled this area, the phones were ringing off the hook, with citizens needing assistance or wondering what the hell was going on.

"Bring in more cars," I kept repeating to Murdock.

What few they could round up they sent in. But since the cars came from other areas of the city, their radios were not set to the right frequency to communicate with the frantic calls going out of 77th station.

Undermanned and overwhelmed, we responded cautiously. Guns were not to be used unless an officer clearly felt his life was threatened. Arrests were not encouraged.

At three o'clock in the morning, or maybe it was four, Murdock ordered us to retreat. The rioting had lessened somewhat; because the police were thought to be the objects of rioters' ire, the prevailing wisdom at the time was that if the police backed off, things would quiet down.

It turned out to be faulty wisdom, but, ordered to withdraw, we did. I felt pretty shitty about this, thinking it was an unwise decision.

Then again, it was obvious we were not equipped to deal with the situation at all. We had gone through long sessions of riot training, but the marauding we encountered on the outskirts of Watts was hugely different from what we had been taught to encounter. In a riot, you imagine a large group of people marching down the street, bent on some kind of destruction. You meet them. You mass up your officers into a formation and your tactics are well developed on how to split off the rioters in two directions and disperse them down two different streets. We knew how to do that.

We did not know how to handle guerrilla warfare. Rather than a single mob, we had people attacking from all directions. They were completely disorganized. We were just as disorganized. Although we arrested thirty-two persons, we had nineteen injured officers. Amazingly, nobody died.

By dawn the streets were nearly deserted, and the last of us pulled out, thinking that maybe our poorly executed tactics had actually worked. Among the command staff at headquarters a general euphoria broke out; we had prevailed.

Well, we hadn't prevailed at all. The rioters hadn't given up; all they had done was gotten tired, gone home to get some sleep, and prepare for the next round.

As I drove away, hot, clammy, and exhausted, it suddenly hit me that I didn't have a uniform to wear.

Six months before, I had separated from my wife, and since my duties did not require me to wear a uniform, I hadn't bothered to take mine with me. Now, because I would undoubtedly return to 116th Street—even if only to check on things—and because any officer going into the area would want to be a visible presence, I had to go back to my old home to get them.

The house was in Monterey Park, a comfortable middle-class neighborhood east of downtown, and as I headed into the morning rush hour, I looked forward to seeing my three kids. I had been having a difficult time trying to maintain a relationship with them. The girls—Debby, sixteen, and Kathy, fifteen—seemed increasingly engrossed in their own lives. I did manage to spend quite a bit of time with Scott, my nine-year-old, by coaching his Pop Warner football team.

He had come as an unplanned but welcome surprise. I had completed my degree at USC, but I was taking graduate courses, hoping to earn a master's degree in business. We had just moved, from the little garage apartment I had built on to the back of my mother's house, into a house we had purchased in Monterey Park, and I felt that two children were all I could support on a police officer's salary.

Still, when Scott arrived, two days after Christmas 1955, I admit I was overjoyed to have a son. I visualized him as a terror on the football field, as well as a scholar, and all those things fathers expect from a son. Because he filled me with pride, I took great care to lavish attention on my daughters. I didn't love them less; I was just excited about having a boy.

Scott was one of those kids nobody seemed able to resist. He was a little towhead with tawny skin and luminous blue-green eyes, the All-American boy. He was friendly and kind. He got good grades. As an athlete, he was strong and fast. Naturally, I taught him to box. When he was eight he signed up for Pop Warner football and I found myself attending his practices as well as his games. He was a running guard and he could go out, blast open a hole, and allow the running back to make yardage all day long.

I remember taking him for a pizza after one game, and in the car he said, "Dad, what's a touchdown?" The season was almost over and I laughed. "You don't know what a touchdown is?" So I explained a touchdown and other football fundamentals, and after that he put all the elements of the game together and he only got better and better.

Even after the separation, I saw him often as his "coach." When I went on vacation I took the children with me. But trying to be the dad who was always there for the three of them could sometimes be tough. Seeing no need for divorce, I was paying all of their bills. I was broke, and living with my mother in Highland Park as a result. On top of this, I had a lot of turmoil in my professional life; as a new inspector, I didn't know what the hell I was doing.

Still, I knew I had done the right thing by splitting up with my wife; to stay in a bad marriage seemed worse. Thinking back, I can trace the problems in our marriage to the beginning. We were young and I was very ambitious. We had an understanding, I thought, that I would finish college and work my way through law school. But Wanda wanted to get pregnant and buy a house, like her friends. I didn't want those things then. I just wanted to study and get ahead.

Wanda was a good wife and mother, but she could be as single-minded as I was. I would tell her of my plans to prepare for an exam and we would reach an agreement over my study hours and the curtailing of our social activities. She would say, "Okay, I'll keep the kids from bothering you while you study." And she would—for a while. Then the interruptions would come and the arguing would start all over again. I am not good at arguing; I simply withdraw. So we would sit down and talk again. And I would explain again. "I'm going to pass this exam high up on the list," I would tell her. "That way I'll get promoted right away. I don't want to take the test again."

Over time, we just kept moving apart. She would see other police officer's families, officers who didn't work as hard as I did, and wonder why her life couldn't be like theirs.

And then we committed the fatal error. We decided to remodel the house. They say you should never, *ever* remodel; remodeling destroys marriages. And that's what happened. We hired an incompetent contractor and I ended up doing much of the work myself. It was a drain and a strain and I finally came to the conclusion that this was not the way I wanted to spend my life. Still, the breakup hadn't been easy on any of us and I missed my kids terribly.

It was 8:00 A.M. when I pulled up to the house. After knocking on the door and getting no answer, I used my key and went in. Nobody was home. With another hot day forecast, they were probably heading for the beach. I searched everywhere for my uniforms, getting hotter and stickier by the minute. Finally I realized Wanda had packed my things away and I rummaged through box after box before I finally found them.

Actually, I found only parts of my uniform. I drove home and took a shower. Then, before reporting to work, I stopped at the uniform store. I needed a belt and tie, and my uniform pressed.

■

The summer before, major riots had erupted in Detroit, New York, Chicago, Philadelphia, and Jersey City. But the problems black people faced in those cities did not seem the same as those in Los Angeles. Our housing conditions weren't nearly as bad as those in the East. One third of the houses in black neighborhoods, for example, were owned by the occupants. Most had jobs. The majority of those subsequently arrested in the riots were employed. In fact, a study by the Urban League ranked Los Angeles first among the sixty-eight cities it examined, in quality of life for African-Americans.

So while it was not out of the question that we could have unrest here, too, we still naïvely believed that what occurred Wednesday night was no more than a fraying of nerves brought on by the hot weather and fueled by this feeling of "Hell with it. Let's go out and have fun."

Deputy Chief Murdock, Inspectors John Powers, Pete Hagan, and I, with our aides, spent the day on the sixth floor at police headquarters working on a plan to keep south central Los Angeles quiet. It seemed reasonable to assume that if trouble erupted again, it would erupt in the same eight-block section it had the night before. Therefore, we decided to flood the area with two-officer units. We would bring in additional units from around the city and deploy them, if needed, from the 77th Street station. We would also borrow some sheriff's deputies and we would deploy people heavily on foot. The mere presence of so many officers, we believed, would be enough to maintain order.

While we were working out the details, Watts, as we had predicted, remained quiet. Surely, we thought, everyone had slept it off and had awakened with a new perspective. By late afternoon a few complaints filtered in about damaged automobiles, but no major incidents were reported. We were so confident the worst was over that we went to a popular restaurant called the Rodger Young Auditorium and ate a leisurely dinner. Afterwards, I headed for 116th Street.

Our plan was simple: John Powers would lead a contingent on foot to the area south of Imperial Boulevard, where the trouble had occurred the night before; I would take my contingent in cars to the area north of Imperial. We would form a perimeter. Either we would keep people in or we'd keep them out. But for sure, we'd keep the streets peaceful.

I wasn't on the scene an hour when it became clear that everything was going to hell.

Already all of the officers were engaged—again in this guerrilla warfare. They were trying to break up groups, ducking bottles and rocks. Shots were being fired, windows were being smashed, fires were erupting, and the radio in my car was just going crazy. Officer needed help here; officer needed help there. So fast were the calls coming in that the people at 77th could not even plot them.

It was impossible to describe the utter chaos, or how confused we felt, having been schooled in riot control and realizing our schooling was useless. I kept searching for a great big crowd that I could confront with all the tactics I had learned, and instead, once again we had people all over, running out of alleys, running down streets, through backyards, climbing onto roofs. And it was clear to me that our wonderful field deployment that evening was a total failure—I mean a complete abject failure. It was awful.

My driver that night was a sergeant named George Morrison. Moving through the turbulent streets, we tried to respond to radio calls but we couldn't begin to keep up with them. Finally, we turned off Imperial onto a little street called Lanzit, and I'll never forget the sight as we made the turn: police officers and sheriff's deputies hugging the wall of a building, pinned there by rioters on the roof raining bricks and chunks of concrete down on them.

"Keep driving," I said to George.

When we were halfway down the street, rocks started hitting our car. We bumped across a railroad track and found ourselves in the middle of a large field. Still we were getting hit from all sides—bottles, rocks, and I mean big rocks, things that would break your head open.

George braked hard. "Now what?"

I surveyed the darkened field. "This is as good a place as any. We'll set up our command post here."

"Are you joking?"

"I don't know what else to do," I said. "We're not going anyplace, that's for sure, and I need a place to work from. So let's set up a command post here."

Setting up the command post meant hauling out a shotgun and radioing for assistance.

"Got no units available," came the staticky reply from headquarters.

"Repeat. I need to set up a command post," I radioed again.

In time, they rounded up twenty Highway Patrol officers in ten cars and rushed them out to me.

"Your job is to let me run this command post," I told them.

Poor fellows. Their job, ordinarily, is to give traffic citations and this was a little beyond what they normally had to confront. I imagine they were sent because they were the only officers equipped with shotguns. They ringed their black-and-whites around my car—talk about circling the wagons—and their very presence, standing there, shotguns poised, became effective in turning people back.

As I communicated with headquarters on the radio, I could hear, in the distance, the steady sound of gunshots. The sirens of fire engines grew more insistent, and from time to time a mob would rush by, shouting and yelling and throwing things. I became very adroit at sidestepping and dancing and ducking, but I was pelted with rocks all the same. And, increasingly, I had this sinking feeling. I didn't know what the hell I was doing; worse, neither did anyone else.

"I gotta take a pee," I finally told Morrison.

With George trailing me, I wandered out into the field and was just starting when suddenly I was aware of a sound that sends shivers through any police officer: the distinctive click of a round being jacked into the chamber of a shotgun.

Nothing does damage like a shotgun—nothing. You don't even have to aim it; you just shoot. I'd rather be hit by bullets from an assault rifle than be torn to pieces by spray from a shotgun. And to hear this gun being loaded gives you a feeling of terror like none other.

It stopped my peeing just like that.

"What was *that*?" I yelled to George.

"Er, just loading my gun, sir. Is something wrong?"

■

Back at my command post, I continued radioing for units. The cars we already had were racing from call to call on a fairly random basis. If they drove out of their sectors, we lost communication with them. We were effective neither in stopping the marauding nor containing it.

I finally got hold of a lieutenant with twenty motorcycle cops. I gave him instructions on how to reach us, using what I thought were the safest streets. But by then, there were no safe streets. And these cops came roaring up, absolutely furious. Motor officers take such pride in their bikes, forever washing them and polishing them up. And here they came, windshields smashed, dents in the bikes, headlights broken, shards of glass all over. They slammed on their brakes, just glowering at me.

"Park your bikes," I said, making them even angrier. "We're going to do this on foot."

By now, bedlam had broken loose, and among the things I had to contend with was Chief Parker barking out orders on the radio.

"Get everybody out of their cars!" he kept bellowing. Because by then, our cars were getting heavily damaged, turned over and set on fire.

For all of his good intentions, it was impossible for Parker to visualize how widespread and out of control the rioting had grown. He was still envisioning one big riot, two or three thousand people storming up and down 103rd Street. That was only one of the locations. Even I had problems with the logistics, just in my own little corner of the riot. Down the street from me was one of the worst housing projects in the city, not to mention a whole series of problems breaking out in the surrounding area. I wanted to deal with these first. Then we would move on.

Meanwhile . . . "Everybody out of their cars!" Parker kept yelling. "I'm ordering you, get everybody out of their cars!"

From my vantage point, I could see the two-man patrol cars driving around. They would spot something and one guy would hop out to deal with it. But one officer remonstrating with six or eight people, trying to get them to move or stop throwing rocks, wasn't working. And he and his partner knew if they both got out of the car to deal with the crowd, another group would arrive, turn the car over, and ignite it.

Parker was still bent on trying to save the cars. But there was no way to communicate with many of them, and there was no preplanned place for officers to leave their cars in safety.

"Turn that radio off," I snapped at Morrison, thinking: *Forgive me, Chief, but I have to turn you off.*

■

Around midnight, word came down. The comedian Dick Gregory wanted to talk to the rioters. It was just what I didn't need.

"Don't let him come," I said over the radio. "It's not safe. I think we're finally having some success. Don't send him down."

Pretty soon Gregory arrived. I called the command post at police headquarters. "You're ordered to allow him to go in and see if he can reason with the rioters," I was told.

"He can't help," I again protested. "These people are out of control. We're only going to get control through sheer numbers and sheer force. I want more cars, not a comic."

My pleading was ignored. What I really resented, shorthanded as I was, was that I would now have to dispatch some of my officers to escort Dick Gregory in.

Off Gregory went, with his bullhorn, two aides, and a contingent of my officers. He wasn't gone long. No sooner did he begin pleading with the rioters to stop than . . . boom! He was shot in the leg.

The wound wasn't serious, we escorted him out of there, and that was that.

Although the rioting seemed to be going on everywhere, it was not going on in the area where it had started the night before. The 120 officers John Powers had taken below Imperial Boulevard had walked around for hours with nothing to do. Finally, we pulled them out and brought them to my command post. By now, I thought I understood the tactics we would need to gain control. Chasing them willy-nilly, shouting at them to get off the streets—go home!—would never work.

Gathering every available officer—around 250 at this point—I formed scrimmage lines of helmeted officers and marched them shoulder-to-shoulder down Avalon Boulevard. This cleared Avalon. But the rioters merely scattered onto side streets. So, a scrimmage line here, another one there. And it just kept getting rougher. One of the motor officers came back, shot. Fortunately, the bullet had smashed into the cartridge case on his belt and not into his gut.

We continued to move with extreme caution, reluctant to draw our weapons or to slap someone with an arrest. The same thinking prevailed—that perhaps a lot of good citizens had become caught up in the rioting and we ought to see if we couldn't get them off the streets by using reason. All night long, ministers, social workers, community leaders trooped in to plead with them, and departed in frustration.

At one point I approached a weathered old sergeant for a situation report. I was wearing a construction worker's hard hat, since riot helmets hadn't been issued to the brass. The sergeant looked at me skeptically. "Why do you want to know, kid?" At thirty-eight, I didn't look old enough to be an inspector. In the middle of Watts, I had to explain why I wanted to know. I had to explain it many times.

By 4:00 A.M. the streets had at last quieted down. Some one hundred people had been injured, a number of stores on Avalon looted and burned, and estimates of the number of rioters now rose to seven thousand. On a final reconnoiter of the area, I sensed the worst was over. We had gained control of the housing project and several other ravaged blocks. Surely, I thought, this is the end. They would not continue with the same intensity. Their common sense would grab hold, and with a good night's sleep, the riotous mentality would dissipate. I told this to the media. "The situation is under control," I stated emphatically.

Once again, the people had scattered to go home to bed. I went home, too, but only to shower and to put on another uniform.

Then I went back to the office to prepare for the next night.

■

The next night arrived early the next morning. On Friday, August 13, everybody woke up and went straight to town, looting.

We were holed up at headquarters, trying again to formulate a plan that would make some sense of our deployment. We still had not found a way to gain control. While we struggled, looting went on. Most of the looting took place in the commercial section of Watts; two blocks of 103rd Street and north on Central Avenue. For much of the morning the looters cruised the streets, grabbing everything they could get their hands on and loading up the trunk. Newspaper photographs would show people walking out of stores carrying stolen goods while police officers stood by, watching. Badly undermanned, there was little they could do to stop the looting.

By early afternoon, the looters began burning the buildings they had just cleaned out. Fire trucks hung back, unable or unwilling to plow through sniper fire. As the afternoon wore on, the disturbance began to spread as far as fifty blocks to the north. The looting moved with it, to a business district on Broadway.

Given our ineptness the night before, and given our lack of presence that morning, a psychology was building, I think, that all restraints had been totally removed . . . and anything goes. So people continued to drive their cars, their station wagons, their trucks, right up onto the sidewalk and load them up with everything that wasn't nailed down. Even when it was, they unnailed the item and took that. Then they burned the place down.

The armchair quarterbacks who rushed in afterward

maintained that the burning of the stores reflected the anger of the people at exploitive merchants. I have always been skeptical of "experts" who arrive to analyze a riot after the fact. I always believed the burning was intended to cover up the looting. Now no one would ever know how much was stolen and how much destroyed by fire. Many of the markets that were leveled were not individually owned businesses, but chains, owned and run by people from a distance. Some of the stores had credit accounts. So I had the feeling also that some of the burning was designed to wipe out debts. But mainly I think the looting and the burning was the result of a mass psychology: the carnival atmosphere, the feeling that anything goes—burning and looting just for the sheer hell of it.

By late afternoon, with fires raging and bullets flying, we finally convinced ourselves that if we didn't take stronger action, the riots could pose a serious threat to larger areas of the city. Belatedly, we understood the police would have to be deployed in force. Not two officers to a car, but four. Four officers, four shotguns. They would be deployed in squads of two cars, bolstered by a third car containing a sergeant and a police officer driver. The presence of eight shotguns sticking out of two cars in tandem would make an impressive sight, we hoped. Only we didn't have enough shotguns. We put out calls to other police departments and they began to fly in shotguns from around the country. There still weren't enough. By now, other cities were worried about what might happen in their communities and they were reluctant to part with their guns. We finally collected two hundred. Many officers brought rifles from home. Some we purchased. You actually saw, later that night, police officers holding guns with price tags still affixed.

We also decided to move the command post to an elementary school on the other side of the Harbor Freeway from Watts. The north-south freeway formed a natural barrier that would contain the riot in the east. So we all moved in there, only to discover that police officers were of course too large for the children's desks. We moved the desks out and began hauling in our own equipment, including what was needed to set up a makeshift jail for mass bookings.

This was my idea. I had told Parker it was essential that

we start making mass arrests, that if we didn't we would never seize control of this thing. It was still an unpopular tactic. Some of the brass continued to argue that making arrests would only inflame the demonstrators more. Fortunately, Powers and Murdock, who had been in the field, were present and could describe what had taken place. "Mass arrests," they insisted, "are essential to control."

Parker listened to both points of view. Then, "Okay. Start making arrests."

Late that afternoon, as officers arrived for their shifts I briefed them in the school auditorium.

"We're taking the gloves off," I said. "There will be mass arrests. If people fail to disperse after you tell them to, arrest them. The penal code allows us to arrest people for unlawful assembly and rioting. Arrest them for throwing a bottle at someone, or breaking a window. You see looting, arrest them. Arrest them for whatever charge you can."

Then I explained how we were going to deploy them, four men to a car, two cars to a squad, a third with a sergeant and a driver. There would also be buses filled with twenty-five to thirty officers. "You won't have to worry about the cars. Now you will be able to leave enough people behind to protect them while you go out in force. Each group should be able to handle twenty, thirty people at a time. Plus, we will have mobile jails sent out to pick up your arrestees so you won't have to leave your sector of patrol."

With some 1,500 officers assigned—roughly half LAPD, half sheriff's deputies, some Highway Patrol—and the National Guard starting to arrive, we went out to face the worst hours of the riots. The first deaths had been reported, a sheriff's deputy, followed by that of a looter.

Sometime that night, I don't remember the time, Inspector Pete Hagan took a large force into Watts and I led one into the area around Manchester and Broadway, several miles northwest. We went in on foot, forming a wedge, moving shoulder to shoulder, making a sweep of the streets.

Talk about utter stupidity. I had two forces: one, a group of LAPD officers; the other, miscellaneous police officers who had come in to help, including some Highway Patrolmen. I lined up the Highway Patrol at one end of the troubled area and LAPD at the other and sent them forward in a kind of a pincers movement. Every time I think about it, I cringe; deploying people so that they were coming in facing each other. If any shooting had gone down, we would have been firing at one another. Somehow, this never entered our minds.

Miraculously, no shots were fired and we did clean those areas out. We were incredibly lucky on that venture, because everywhere else that violent Friday night, everyone was shooting at everyone else. Hundreds of sniper calls came into the 77th Street station. Someone would stick his head out of a darkened second-story window and fire once at a police officer. We had no organized response to snipers, so the police would shoot back indiscriminately. By the time I would arrive, everybody was blasting away. It was not easy to get them to stop. I remember the words I used most often: *"Cease fire!"* Or, *"Stop firing!"* I had a megaphone and I just kept yelling those words all night.

By midnight, or maybe later, the first of the National Guard arrived. Governor Pat Brown had been vacationing in Greece and the Lieutenant Governor had been slow to respond to Parker's request for help. What the Guard enabled us to do was to park an armed presence in an area we had cleaned up. Before, short-handed and running from scene to scene, we had no men to leave behind, so the rioters came back and started again. We were also able to use the Guard to ride shotgun on the fire trucks. Firefighters have always amazed me. They have such a dangerous job and they show such incredible courage. I remember being struck by the fact that while they weren't in the least bit frightened when battling a fire, they were scared to death of being attacked by the crowds or shot by a sniper. And I didn't blame them.

By Saturday morning, although violence continued, the tide had finally turned, this time for good. There were no more stores to loot. With 13,000 National Guardsmen, we now were able to use the Highway Patrol to rim the area and keep people out. An 8:00 P.M. curfew was imposed, and by Sunday we were beginning to pull police out of the area.

Meanwhile, other riots were erupting—San Diego, Pasadena, Pacoima. On Sunday night I took a contingent of police officers down to Long Beach, which is twelve miles south of L.A., and helped clean up the trouble down there. Then, for the first time since the riots broke out, I went home to sleep. I slept for twelve hours.

■

When the final tallies were in, Watts—as it would be forever known—proved to be the worst of the sixties riots; and none since has matched it for size and intensity. Thirty-four persons were killed, including one fireman, one sheriff's deputy, and one Long Beach police officer. There were 1,032 reported injured, including 90 L.A. police officers, 136 firemen, and 773 citizens. More than 600 buildings were damaged by burning and looting; millions of dollars lost. Arrests—3,438 persons, nearly half of whom had never been arrested before.

Peace was restored by the following Tuesday, but the effects of the riots had a long reach into the future. They had an especially long reach into the LAPD. And they gave my own career a new direction.

For the next month I stayed in south central Los Angeles, commanding a special force and working twelve-hour shifts. Pete Hagan and his contingent worked the other twelve-hour shift. We were there to provide security until, little by little, we were able to pull out completely.

As summer turned to fall the scars left by the riots did not heal. Watts would become a sad chapter in the history of Los Angeles that I don't think will ever be righted. Nor will it ever be totally explained.

The McCone Commission Report, ordered by Governor Pat Brown and chaired by former CIA director John A. McCone, absolved the police of many accusations that were heaped on us in the aftermath of the riots. Higher up on the list of what went wrong, the commission pinpointed a number of factors, including the hopeless downward spiral that people in the poorest black neighborhoods endured throughout their lives.

But what I read in the ensuing months did not fit what I saw, nor what I experienced. Say all you want about social causes, I don't believe they accounted for what occurred. Face it, people gorged themselves with a heady diet of unrestrained conduct, stealing, burning, rock- and bottle-throwing—destroying and flouting the authority of government. The saddest part was the general belief that everyone living in south central L.A. had participated, when only a small fraction had. Nationally, all manner of long-winded reviews were spewed out, along with dozens of recommendations, most of which were never enacted.

Marquette Frye's story proved equally disheartening. In the decade after the night of his arrest in Watts, he was arrested numerous times, mostly on minor charges which were later dismissed. He's had trouble keeping a steady job. He once told a reporter he didn't even know about the riot until he got out of jail the next day. He said, "I heard on the radio about how many people had died, and I just started to cry."

8

SWAT

The Los Angeles of 1965 was still an endless sprawl of two-story wooden and stucco buildings, but the city's face was changing nevertheless. The Hollywood, Harbor, and Santa Monica freeways sluiced through the core of the city, replacing the clanking of the trolleys and the groaning of the Red Cars. To the west of downtown, the towers of Century City would, in a few years' time, rise on what had once been the back lot of Twentieth Century-Fox. The Century Plaza Hotel was already up and signaled a westward move in population, particularly to Brentwood, West Hollywood, and Santa Monica. The city had grown to 2.7 million people and with it, the LAPD to 5,181 sworn officers.

The people were changing, too. Due to the postwar baby boom, we saw a huge increase in the number of teens and people in their early twenties—the most predominant age group for criminals. Crime soared. The drug culture was established and national civility just broke down.

Watts marked the beginning of what would become a terrible and troubled decade for LAPD. In a country racked by turmoil and civil unrest, the police became the ultimate hated minority. We were "the pigs." We were universally despised. Whatever we did.

What we tried to do first, in the fall of 1965, was to improve relations with the younger members of the black community. Although we had been building good, strong ties for years with the black population in south central L.A., these were not the people who had participated in the riots. Now we knew we were going to have to build a bridge to the younger people, starting with programs introduced in the schools. But as time went on, even communication became a struggle. All over the country, black activists were doing their best to break down relations with whites, so you had a tug-of-war in progress for the hearts and minds of the black community.

As chief of police, Parker was continually under attack. Many blacks old enough to remember him will insist to this day that he was the cause of all police brutality and that he hated blacks, when in fact it was Parker who desegregated the department and refused to assign black officers only to black neighborhoods. During the riots at one point, some politician demanded that more black officers be sent immediately to Watts, and we told him black officers were dispersed throughout the city and we had no centralized way of knowing who they were.

Relations only grew more strained.

In December, I got word that black officers in one of my patrol divisions planned to boycott the Christmas party en masse. When you hear rumors like that, you know something is wrong, so I promptly called a meeting.

The black officers complained they were unhappy because they couldn't work together. "White officers can work with white officers, but we can't work with black officers. Have to be white."

I told them I knew that.

"We'd like to be able to pick our partners too."

Parker had made it policy that black officers work with white officers in an attempt to break down patterns of discrimination within the department. But apparently we were working at cross-purposes with the officers we were trying to help. They misperceived Parker's intentions, and mine, viewing this policy as another form of discrimination.

I told them I understood. I tried to explain that we were in a transition period and I knew it wasn't easy for them. But that we were trying to break down informal barriers that had existed in the department for years. I said I thought everyone would benefit, and that soon they would be allowed to pick a partner from time to time. "I know it's a sacrifice on your part," I offered, "but let's just try to get through this period."

Begrudgingly, they accepted that it was their responsibility to themselves, not to mention the department, to try to work with us to erase discrimination as best as we could. They came to the Christmas party.

From Parker's first days as chief, he had worked conscientiously to break down patterns of racism inside LAPD, yet he was still viewed as a hard-nosed guy with no sympathy for minorities. And relations with the community only grew worse.

The strain began to show in Parker. He hadn't been well in recent months. He'd been in and out of hospitals, first having an aneurysm repaired, then with bleeding hemorrhoids. When a white officer shot and killed a black man in south central L.A., and our report indicated that the gun had gone off accidentally, Parker blew up. "This was deliberate . . . It's murder!" he cried.

I had never seen him so upset. I realized then he was reacting to the cries of racism that he knew would be hurled at him. And because he had been ill he just wasn't up to it.

■

Almost every week now I was hopping a plane to go somewhere. Because of my role in Watts, I became—improbable as it sounds—LAPD's resident expert on riots and a national expert on riot control. Despite the fact that this "expertise" had been gathered in about two muddled days, I was now in demand as an adviser on riot control. Law enforcement agencies all over the country invited me to teach them what I knew. U.S. Attorney General Ramsey Clark organized a series of seminars for police chiefs and invited me to lecture. In addition, I was writing a riot control manual for the President's Commission on Civil Disorders, and another manual for LAPD on procedures to handle major disruptions of any kind—riots, earthquakes, fires, bombs, or any conceivable disaster that could potentially frazzle Los Angeles.

Both manuals are still operative. Yet despite this expertise I supposedly had, I knew there were serious tactical problems LAPD had not licked.

This became sadly evident not a month after Watts, during an incident known as the Surry Street shootings. Surry Street is in Los Feliz, an area of northeast Los Angeles not far from Griffith Park. Hollywood division handled that territory, and as commander of Patrol Area 3, it fell into my bailiwick.

Late in the afternoon, Officer Ron Mueller responded to a disturbance call at 3031 Surry. The house sat up on a little rise, as so many older homes in the hilly areas do. There was a low cement retaining wall that formed a perimeter around the grassy area. Mueller climbed the three steps to the lawn, then moved along a short walk and up a couple of steps to the front door. He knocked.

A man opened the door and—boom!—shot Mueller, just like that.

Badly wounded, Mueller crawled onto the lawn just as another officer, K. A. Shipp, drove up. As Shipp was getting out of his car the man stepped out with a .30 caliber Winchester and fired. The bullet drilled through the car doorpost, grazing Shipp's head and blowing off part of his ear. So now we had two officers down. Then a citizen named Billy Richards, attempting to help ambulance drivers move Mueller, was also shot and lay seriously wounded in the grass nearby. Hearing the gunfire, neighbors phoned the police and an all-units call immediately went out.

With the suspect barricaded and blasting away from inside, there was some heroic action by the police and two ambulance drivers who dragged the wounded officers and Billy Richards out of the line of fire. Meanwhile, the house was surrounded by fifty more officers. Which is when I pulled up.

Captain Charlie Crumly was hunched down behind the low retaining wall, walkie-talkie in hand, trying to direct the operation. I crawled up on my belly beside him, and while we were talking strategy, I felt a movement right next to me.

Cautiously, I turned. "So, Inspector," boomed a radio reporter, shoving his microphone at me, "what do we have here?"

"Get that damn thing out of my face. I don't know. Let me find out."

By now, the guy in the house, Jack Ray Hoxsie, was dashing from one window to another, running from the front of the house to the side to the back, shooting off an arsenal of weapons. The police were shooting back. The captain was pleading with everyone: "Cease fire, cease fire, cease fire!"

I agreed with him. "My God," I said, "you've got to get everybody to stop firing or we're gonna get another officer killed."

No sooner did I say that than a third officer was shot in the left hand. I have always suspected he was hit by one of our own, but there was no way to prove it.

The insane shooting continued. Many of the officers still had weapons in their trunks from Watts, so out came a lot of rifles and shotguns. Instead of the 00 buck we normally use in a shotgun, these officers had shotgun slugs. The slug is a piece of lead that's encased in a shotgun shell. Instead of having a spray of buckshot going out in a spread pattern, you have a single explosive piece of lead. These slugs were boring right through the walls of this wooden house and up through the roof. It was horrendous.

I called for tear gas. But we had trouble lobbing it in from a distance. An officer named R. D. Johnson and Sergeant Chuck Higbie, a tough ex-marine, volunteered to move closer to the house.

They put on the body armor of the day, which was like Knights of the Round Table stuff. They strapped on this thick piece of metal that ran from the chest down to the thighs and calves, making it nearly impossible to walk. Then Higbie clanked up to a broken window and lobbed in some cannisters of tear gas. A lot of good that did. By then there were so many holes in the house that the tear gas began spewing out faster than it was going in.

Johnson waited only a minute. Then he kicked in the front door. He and Higbie, without gas masks or proper body armor, bravely entered the house. Hoxsie was lying in a rear hallway, wounded but not incapacitated. He had a 30-30 rifle by his side and a .41 caliber magnum revolver inches from his hand. He reached for the revolver. Johnson shot Hoxsie in the chest and he was taken into custody. As is often the case with individuals who suddenly pull out a gun and go crazy, it was never determined what set Hoxsie off. He was convicted of attempted murder and sent to prison.

The incident alarmed me. Surry Street was hardly a textbook operation: three officers, a citizen, and the suspect all wounded. Later, as I analyzed how we had responded, I realized again, as I had during Watts, that we were going to have to devise another method for dealing with snipers or barricaded criminals other than our usual indiscriminate shooting.

Without official authorization, several of us—Commander John Powers, Lieutenant Frank Brittell, Sergeant George Morrison and I—began reading everything we could get our hands on concerning guerrilla warfare. We watched with interest what was happening in Vietnam. We looked at military training, and in particular we studied what a group of marines, based at the Naval Armory in Chavez Ravine, were doing. They shared with us their knowledge of counterinsurgency and guerrilla warfare. In time, our little group came to include some brilliant tacticians. Sergeant John Nelson became our specialist in guerrilla warfare. Mike Hillmann, now a lieutenant, was our liaison with the marines; after Delta Force had been formed to get the hostages out of Iran, Mike worked and shared his expertise with them. Bob Smitson also contributed great know-how. So did Pat McKinley, now captain of Metro, and Ron McCarthy, longtime sergeant of training and tactics. Then there was Jeff Rogers, who would become the premier SWAT leader anywhere in the world. Many others assisted.

Nobody in the department seemed interested in our pursuits. Marines at Camp Pendleton and at the Armory did. Once we attended several marine sessions on guerrilla warfare and there were a few chuckles over what we were trying to put together.

What we were trying to put together were highly-trained anti-sniper teams. We searched the department for the best marksmen. During their off hours we took them to a range and allowed them to practice with their own rifles. We brought in military people to teach them how to respond to sniper fire. But we were not able to organize these men into a special unit. They remained scattered throughout the department.

■

On July 16, 1966, Chief Parker attended a banquet at the Statler Hilton Hotel. He had just accepted an honor from the Second Marine Division Association, and as flags waved and the Marine Corps band played he walked back to his seat amid a standing ovation. Then he sat down and keeled over. The aneurysm repair job had broken. William Parker was dead.

I had just gotten home and was in bed when the call came, a little after eleven. It was a terrible shock. I mean, he'd been ill and we knew he'd been through a particularly trying period. But it was still terribly wrenching to me that Bill Parker was gone.

His funeral was something this city had never seen before, and hasn't seen since. The procession was five miles long. Thousands jammed into Saint Vibiana's Cathedral for the requiem mass, including governors, mayors, politicians of every stripe, and police chiefs from sixty cities across the United States.

Bill Parker left a rich legacy to law enforcement—and an invaluable legacy to me.

■

Meanwhile, the streets of America's cities had become a foreign territory. Urban riots signaled one kind of disorder, but we also had civil rights actions, sit-downs, and student uprisings and protests of every kind. In 1967 a whole variety of forces pulled and tugged at our society. The police were caught in the middle.

With the "Establishment" tugging on one side and a litany of causes pulling on the other, we had the responsibility for maintaining order. In most instances we were supposed to maintain it in a sensitive and careful way, while being confronted by people who weren't the least bit careful or sensitive to the police. We were supposed to intervene respectfully—"Hi, I'm Officer Bill!"—while they swore, spit, hissed, kicked, fought, and threw things at us, which occurred every single day. Many of these were miserable people: pot-smokers, college dropouts, wayward and lost human beings, people who had absolutely no interest in anyone's rights but their own. They were bent on pursuing their personal indulgences in pot, LSD, uppers, and downers, and many were bent on causing a revolution. They were out there seeking their own self-interests at any cost, any way they could find.

Into this angry and chaotic setting, in the summer of 1967, came Lyndon B. Johnson to drum up support for his Vietnam policies.

From Intelligence we learned that a massive antiwar demonstration would greet the President in Century City. Many in this crowd, our intelligence told us, intended to force their way into the Century Plaza Hotel, where the President would be staying, and disrupt whatever was going on inside. The Secret Service was petrified.

Since I was the resident riot-control expert, it fell to me to prepare a plan to deal with this demonstration.

As 14,000 people surged into Century City, filling up the streets and threatening to break into the hotel, the Secret Service men began to panic. They had drawn up their own emergency plan to get the President out, but now, seeing the crowd, they were fearful they were going to have serious problems with his safety.

Most of the top brass were on hand, including Chief Tom Reddin, who had been selected to succeed William Parker and whom I remembered as one of my most erudite instructors at the Academy. I was in the streets with several top command officers, and at this point my plan dictated that we declare the assembly unlawful. We made the announcement and ordered the demonstrators to disperse immediately. They did not. We made another announcement. In a minute, we believed, the crowd was going to riot.

With 450 officers ringing the area, and more on the way, we moved in. Because of our meticulous planning, we were able to disperse that crowd completely in about fifteen minutes. We moved literally thousands of people out of the area. Unfortunately, some of those we moved were older people and parents with kids who got caught in the middle.

The media had a field day. They snapped pictures of police officers pushing, and using the thrust of a billy club to move people along. This caused a great outcry about police brutality. Many demonstrators might have received a bruise or two, but none was seriously injured. And when you understood the potential danger, when you realized how hard it was for us to deal with a crowd that size, it was a masterpiece of police tactics. And it got the ACLU and every civil rights group in America screaming about the LAPD.

The newspapers vociferously joined the attacks. Traditionally, the *Los Angeles Times,* owned by the Chandler family, and the *Los Angeles Herald Examiner,* owned by the Hearst family, had taken a conservative stance. But conservatism seemed to die at both newspapers as, increasingly, the papers hired young reporters fresh off college campuses. Disdainful of authority, and suspicious of anyone over thirty, these reporters wrote stories that clearly reflected their sympathies.

We were stuck in the middle again.

If we had done nothing, if the demonstrators had broken into the hotel and posed a serious threat to the President, not four years after John F. Kennedy's assassination, the LAPD would have been ridiculed throughout the world. *Dallas West!* Instead, we dispersed this huge crowd with no serious injuries, the Secret Service was ecstatic, and we were angrily attacked in the press as vicious Gestapo.

Or pigs. Cartoons always seemed to show a Neanderthal-sized police officer with a pig's head, combat boots, and a big stick ready to hit some defenseless person holding a WE SHALL OVERCOME sign. If you go back through the newspapers, every single photo of a police officer showed him with his club raised, giving the appearance he was about to break open some poor citizen's head. There was no way to avoid it: We were brutal beasts. We were subhuman. The graffiti of the day jumped out at us everywhere: OFF THE PIGS! KILL THE PIGS!

It was as if the police had been banished from the rest of society.

Moving to play catch-up with the times, Tom Reddin, in one of his first acts as chief, created a unit called Tactical Operations Planning. Its purpose was to prepare for disasters and major events of all kinds. It would be part of my command, operating out of Parker Center. I was also in charge of the business office division, which was the name we used for our twenty-four-hour command post. In addition, I had charge of Metropolitan division, which was housed in a small building called Georgia Street. At the time, Metro numbered only fifty-five officers, who had been used mainly to handle labor disputes and to "shake, rattle, and roll,"—that is, roust—anything strange that moved on the streets.

My first order from Reddin was to "do something" about a series of bus robberies. They were being committed with such frequency, all over the city, that bus drivers were threatening to strike. Not having enough manpower in Metro, I called all the divisions, asking to borrow officers who could come in and follow the buses. Most of the divisions sent me the ten least desirable people they had. We caught the bus robbers and now I had this massive unit of castoffs, whom nobody seemed to want back.

"Why don't you keep the unit together and form a crime task force?" said Reddin.

I sent back the most undesirable, but others I kept. I found that if you gave them some leeway and the opportunity to use their own initiative, they became very resourceful. We were like the LAPD's "Dirty Dozen"—a bunch of castoffs and retreads who, in time, became the elite of the department.

■

Elite was an odd word to be using in the late 1960s. If LAPD had once considered itself an elite organization, it was having trouble maintaining that image.

The few people on the planet who still wanted to join LAPD hardly fit the image of the officer we were trying to groom. A lot of them had questionable backgrounds. Some had come home discombobulated from Vietnam. Many had used drugs.

Having to scrape the bottom of the barrel for officers

wasn't our only personnel problem. Our standards for appearance were eroding. Hair began to grow long, sideburns were forever inching downward, and officers kept testing us every single day. Can't have hair below the collar line? We'll put our hair in ponytails and stick them up under our hats.

How you perform may have nothing to do with how you look, but appearance does mean something when you are in uniform. The neatness of the uniform, the way an officer wears his or her hair, having clean fingernails and shiny shoes and badge—these immediately convey the impression of a person who is in control of himself or herself. When you are trying to convey competence, trying to take control of a situation, you must present yourself in a way that gives people confidence in you. In our training manual we stress that the public's contact is fleeting; impressions are formed immediately.

The one corner of LAPD where we categorically refused to let officers look like flower children was in Metro. Breaking from LAPD tradition, we formed sixteen military-type squads with a sergeant in charge of each ten-man squad, and then we meshed them into two platoons, each headed by a lieutenant.

They were given missions for which they were responsible. They developed the approach and the tactics without direction from above. Their only admonishment was to maintain departmental policy and rules.

At the same time, our work with the anti-sniper group continued. All the research showed that the most effective way to stop a sniper or apprehend a barricaded individual was with a small team of highly disciplined officers using specialized weapons and tactics. By now, we had recruited sixty expert marksmen who also ranked in the upper 25 percent of the department in physical skills. But they were still scattered throughout the department. Late in 1967 we were finally able to bring them into Metro as the third platoon. We now numbered 220 strong.

The sixty marksmen forming the third platoon, called D-Platoon, were organized into five-man teams consisting of a leader, a marksman, an observer, a scout, and a rear guard. Two teams formed a squad, with a sergeant in command of each.

We couldn't know it then, but what we had forged out of D-Platoon would soon revolutionize law-enforcement agencies all over the world.

One day, with a big smile on my face, I popped in to tell my deputy chief, Ed Davis, that I thought up an acronym for my special new unit. Davis was not at all enamored of this unit. He was still, as we all were, glued to the classic concepts of policing, which discourage formation of military-type units. But he realized some changes would have to be made.

"It's SWAT," I said.

"Oh, that's pretty good. What's it stand for?"

"Special Weapons Attack Teams."

Davis blinked at me. "No."

There was no way, he said dismissively, he would ever use the word "attack." I went out, crestfallen, but a moment later I was back. "Special Weapons And Tactics," I said. "Okay?"

"No problem. That's fine," Ed Davis said. And that was how SWAT was born.

■

So I became known as the "Father of SWAT." Not that I developed its tactics—I didn't. I supported the concept and I gave my people the opportunity to develop the unit. I went to bat for them, tried to get them the equipment they needed, and lent them moral support.

They needed it. For a long time they were *persona non grata,* even within the department. That SWAT operates like a quasi-militaristic operation offended some of the brass. I tried to explain the difference. Whereas the military will go in with bazookas and blow the place apart, SWAT's main objective *always* is to get everybody safely out. If anybody gets killed or injured, the operation's a failure, I steadfastly pointed out. To no avail.

Banished from everyday police circles, we kept our training operations secret for years. Deep in the San Fernando Valley, on farmland owned by the city, the five-man SWAT teams rotated in and out, working on their maneuvers. Regularly, we sent squads to train at Camp Pendleton, trading expertise with the marines. We also took advantage of the generosity of Universal Studios in Burbank. The movie studio's back lot was practically a ready-made training center with its many permanent sets. Storefronts, buildings, city streets, and villages—SWAT scaled them all.

The toughest training drills were reserved for the farm. We sent teams out on these miserable exercises that were, in most cases, dangerous and dirty. For example, we would have a "sniper" holed up with a "hostage"—their favorite hostage being me. The SWAT team would come in and plan how to get this hostage out. They would develop tactics, sketch them out on a blackboard or on the ground, like a football game plan. They would climb trees or up onto roofs, crawl into gutters or down into basements, dangle from ladders and ropes. Later, using helicopters, they would rappel down a rope from a hovering craft onto a roof. With rifles, they could hit a bull's-eye from a thousand feet.

What a gutty little ragtag outfit it was. With no money allotted to us, officers were forced to use their own equipment or buy what they needed from the lowest of the low-end surplus stores. By inventing as they went along, SWAT people became masterfully innovative. Before we got a little money to buy AR-15 semiautomatic rifles, they cannibalized weapons they picked up off the streets, using the parts to fashion new weapons. They made ladders to their own specifications. They invented mirrors to see around corners. Many of the devices they jerry-built then are used as standard equipment by SWAT teams all over the world today. The streamlined vans filled with sophisticated electronics, for instance, started out as battered trucks they practically had to push up a hill.

Years later, when the American hostages were seized by Iran, I told Bill Booth, our public relations officer: "I'll take a hundred SWAT guys and I'll go over and get the hostages out."

A reporter picked up my comment, printed it, and the remark made headlines. The U.S. State Department was outraged and I heard indirectly that the White House was too. Months later, when President Jimmy Carter's attempt to get the hostages out failed because the army helicopters broke down, one SWAT member told me: "You were right, Chief. We could have got the hostages out. We're used to shitty equipment!"

In time, our ragtag little outfit melded into a tightly disciplined, highly trained unit, ready for any emergency. A bank robbery is in progress, for example; regular police officers are on the scene. The suspect is inside, armed and holding people hostage. To rush the bank—as we learned from Watts and Surry Street—and fire willy-nilly could be disastrous for everyone. At that point, we call SWAT.

Within thirty minutes a couple of SWAT teams can be put in place. Given the vast geography of Los Angeles, SWAT members can be called to a scene based on where they live. Their equipment stays in the trunks of their LAPD cars, which they are allowed to drive home at night.

Once SWAT arrives, they develop a plan and present it to the field commander. If the field commander approves, SWAT is then in charge. The goal is always the same: Get everyone out safely. Time and again, they have. Their record of saving lives is nothing short of spectacular. Ordinary, old-time police tactics have been mothballed around the world, replaced by SWAT maneuvers.

Still, it wasn't until the 1984 Olympics that the city of Los Angeles agreed to equip SWAT properly. Despite its record and reputation, officials balked at the police using fully automatic weapons. The standard cry was, "Hey, the LAPD is supposed to be a civil police force. They are peace officers. Their job is to *relate* to the community, not put on combat boots and helmets and *assault* the community."

For years we tried to reassure everyone that, yes, we are a civil police force. The people are the police, and the police are the people. And we hold to that.

Though at times, *assault* is not a dirty word.

9

Shootouts in the Streets of L.A.

On Monday, December 8, 1969, SWAT got its official unveiling.

The precipitating event had occurred on Friday evening, November 28. Captain Ted Morton, newly installed commander of Newton division, was strolling along Central Avenue when a young woman stopped him. Could he please do something, she asked nervously, about the noise blasting out of a loudspeaker at 4115 South Central?

Morton had received other complaints about this address. A large, two-story building in a downtown business district, it was occupied, he knew, by the Black Panthers. For months they had been annoying neighborhood business people, frightening them with their tough talk and rough ganglike behavior.

The Panthers had begun drifting into L.A. three years before, declaring themselves the vanguard of the "People's Revolution." By feeding underprivileged children, denouncing police brutality, and catering to the idea of black pride, they hoped to win over the black community.

In truth, the Panthers were modern-day mountebanks, a

rabble-rousing street gang with a bit of Che Guevera political savvy. They never garnered the support of the substantial, mature part of the black community, but they did attract some of the younger people. They also attracted west-side liberals, who thought it was chic to invite Black Panthers to their parties, show them off, and write checks supporting their causes.

But what the Black Panthers really sought was power for themselves, not the people. They were hoodlums, who, I suspect, took checks from their wealthy patrons and chuckled about it, saying, "This is easier than robbing somebody." They were mean. They were violent. And that got them into difficulty with us.

Two months earlier, on a mission to "off the pigs," a pair of Panthers walked up to a squad car, stuck a carbine and a shotgun through the windows, and pulled the triggers. One officer was injured. Both returned fire. One Panther was killed and the other wounded.

The address on South Central was one of three known Panther locations. It was the biggest, and according to Intelligence, it had been fortified like a military bunker. Each interior wall was packed floor-to-ceiling with sandbags. Gunports had been built into the windows and escape tunnels dug out from the basement. When I stared, stunned, at the detailed diagrams we had made, I thought, *What in the world is in their heads?*

People who worked in the neighborhood openly feared the Panthers and had called us repeatedly, saying, "Why don't you *do* something about them?"

Ted Morton was aware of the building tensions. He was deeply involved in developing good relationships with people in the community. After Watts, LAPD had inserted into every division a lieutenant to serve as Community Relations Officer (CRO) in an attempt to improve relations with the public. The CROs were warmly received. One, Sam Wilson, started what was known as the "Wilson Wave." Silly as it sounds, he made it a point to have his uniformed officers cheerfully wave to people as they drove by. Grinning, the people would wave back. Ted Morton, too, was winning the trust of the people in his community, and he kept hearing about these Panthers. So that night, November 28, after speaking with the woman, he decided to drop in, introduce himself, maybe have a little chat—you know, real community-oriented policing.

As soon as Morton was permitted to step inside, a Panther named George Smith pointed a .45 caliber automatic pistol at him. Ted quickly identified himself as a police officer.

"I don't care who you are," said Smith, "I'm counting to three, and you'd better be out of here by then."

Morton turned, and now he was looking down the barrel of a pump-shotgun held by Panther Paul Redd. Redd began to count. Morton left.

He went back to Newton and wrote out a crime report charging assault with a deadly weapon. Arrest warrants were issued for Smith and Redd. But knowing from Intelligence how fortified the building was, not to mention how heavily armed, getting in there to serve the warrants was not going to be easy.

Sometime during the week of December 1, the decision was made: SWAT would undertake its first mission.

It was a tough call. Although we viewed the Panthers as a criminal gang, the police were working hard to establish a better relationship with the black community. Unfortunately, we were guided by some pretty unenlightened ideas, one being that we needed some special way to reach a minority. Ultimately we found out, of course, that most people in the black community wanted the same things everyone else did and if you approached them on that basis, everything was fine. But at the time, we were trying hard not to offend anybody, and since so many younger people seemed to be "signifying" with the Black Panthers, we were reluctant to tear down what they considered to be symbols.

Furthermore, we knew that Black Panthers were being acquitted by juries in other cities. Too often, I think, the police were precipitous in their actions, overzealous in building cases without adequate evidence. In other instances, juries were ruled not by law but by self-imposed guilty consciences over injustices suffered by blacks, and they let the guilty go free.

Nevertheless, we decided to make our move.

By then, I had been promoted twice more, in 1968 to

deputy chief, and in 1969 to one of three assistant chiefs who served one rung below the chief. Tom Reddin had retired after two years, and the new chief, Ed Davis, was in Mexico, trying to improve relations with the Mexican police. That left me in charge.

Long before dawn on Monday, December 8, our entire operation gathered at the Naval Armory in Chavez Ravine. We had a search warrant for 4115 South Central and arrest warrants for Smith and Redd. We had uniformed patrol officers who would be deployed to stop traffic and establish perimeter control of the area. At 5:00 A.M. we began calling the political leadership in that district to alert them to our plans. Against a racially tense backdrop, and because of the position the Panthers held in the black community, we did not want our actions to be misconstrued.

Our plan was simple. A SWAT entry team would go in first, to serve the warrants and make the arrests. We were relying on the element of surprise: Hit them fast and hard, before sunrise, and hope to get out of there without anyone's being injured.

So off went this forty-man assault team, sixteen of them members of SWAT, everybody thinking it would all be over in five, ten minutes. I went on to Parker Center, anxious to hear the results.

At 5:30 A.M. the entry team banged on the door at 4115 South Central, announcing, "There's a warrant for your arrest. Open the door." Hearing movement but getting no response, they tried to force the door. The Panthers were ready for them.

Alerted by their own patrol, the occupants—four males and two females—greeted SWAT with bombs, hand grenades, and twenty-four guns, including a Thompson submachine gun, which they immediately used. Three officers were shot; one was shot six times. While they were being dragged out of there by backup, a fusillade erupted from inside the building.

Scrambling, the LAPD assault team took up positions on rooftops across the street. But the Panthers' building was like a fort, able to resist our onslaught. All it lacked was a moat.

The SWAT entry team had been defeated by the quickness and violence of the Panthers' response. Today, using substantially improved tactics, we would have resorted to a faster, more sophisticated entry. But having failed to get inside, SWAT and its accompanying assault team found themselves digging in for an all-out battle.

Hearing the news that three officers had been hit, and apprised of the standoff, I activated our Emergency Operations Center. This was a room on the first floor of police headquarters, set up to handle crises of any sort. Since then, a more progressive version has been thoughtlessly built into the fourth sub-basement of City Hall East, the reasoning being *God, what if they drop The Bomb on Los Angeles?* That an earthquake presented a more likely emergency did not, apparently, cause anyone to think: *Well, might be a problem with access to the fourth sub-basement.* The result is a room so dark and depressing—even with fake scenery painted on the walls—that few of our four hundred civilian communications staff, who are permanently housed there, ever stay permanently.

As the sun came up and the shootout continued, we now had to consider all the people going to work in the midst of these high-powered weapons being used on both sides. Obviously, we had to evacuate the area. Stopping all traffic in the morning—any morning—in Los Angeles becomes a horrendous problem. On top of that, out came the media in force.

SWAT, meanwhile, worked on devising new tactics. They considered asking the fire department for shape charges—explosives used to blow open a hole from a skylight or roof so firemen can get their hoses inside a burning building. But Intelligence didn't have a diagram of the Panthers' top floor. Also, we had no assurance that the shape charges would even work, given the heavy fortifications inside. So SWAT discarded that one.

Hours passed. High-powered rifles continued to fire steadily across South Central at one another. Whenever you have hundreds and hundreds of rounds being shot off in the middle of your city, your stomach churns. I became desperate to get the damn thing stopped as quickly as possible.

SWAT said, "Well, we need a grenade launcher."

LAPD did not have a grenade launcher. Only the military

had them. They were tantamount then to a rocket device today, capable of firing a mortar shell that would blast a hole in a building. SWAT hoped the first blast would scare the Panthers out. If it didn't, two or three more blasts would surely kill everyone inside.

Putting this operation into motion was a huge decision. As acting chief, I had to make it.

I called the marines at Camp Pendleton to ask if we could borrow their grenade launcher. The commanding officer said, "You're going to have to get permission from the Department of Defense and probably the President of the United States."

This would take time. And Camp Pendleton, just north of San Diego, was a two-hour drive from Los Angeles. The officer must have read my thoughts. "We'll get the equipment together and put it on the road," he said, "so you'll have it if you get permission."

I called Mayor Sam Yorty next and asked if he would make the call to Washington. My words seemed unreal. Anytime you even *talk* about using military equipment in a civil action, it's very serious business. You're bridging an enormous gap. We are not like a military force, going in and blasting a building to smithereens, not caring who gets killed in the process. That's not what the police do. SWAT's objective—our objective—is always to save lives. But having reached this point, we could not see any alternative.

With the same heavy reluctance I felt, Mayor Yorty agreed to phone the Defense Department. I cannot say enough on his behalf. He was a sharp man, very intelligent, flamboyant, but sensitive too. I don't want to call him the Fiorello La Guardia of L.A., but I believe he was the best mayor this city ever had. He had a vision for Los Angeles and he worked hard to put that vision into effect.

"Okay, Daryl. If that's what you think we need, I'll see if we can get permission," the mayor said.

I broke out in a cold sweat, thinking, *Here I am, acting chief. I blow up some place downtown, kill all these people, the Black Panthers are still a force within the community, how am I going to be judged?* The question would be asked: "Was the grenade launcher really necessary?" And all the Monday morning quarterbacks would cry, "No! There must have been another way."

I racked my brain, trying to think of one. When SWAT is involved, it is their duty to come up with a plan, but they can't execute it without approval. SWAT doesn't do anything on its own. So the field commander either says, "Okay, I buy your plan. Go ahead." Or he says, "No, I don't want to do that." Then he must come up with something else. Or I must. By ten o'clock, I hadn't.

The Pentagon got back to us within the hour. We had permission to use the grenade launcher.

From the Emergency Operations Center, I phoned Assistant Chief Bob Houghton, the field commander on Central Avenue. "Tell me again—when's the last time you asked them to surrender?"

"It's probably been half an hour, maybe an hour."

"Okay," I said, "let's *really* get the amplification up so we know they're hearing what we're saying. And tell them again this is their last chance to come out, they're not going to be injured, come out right now. Otherwise we're going to take drastic measures."

I paused. "One last time," I said into the phone. "Warn them one last time."

I stayed on the line. I heard Bob make the broadcast. Then we waited. As I held the phone to my ear, I remember thinking about the lives I was about to put on the line and how I was only *acting* chief. Poor Ed Davis was down in Mexico, and here I was making a decision that could ultimately cost him his job. I wondered what he would have done. Ed always preached restraint. He would say, "Hey, when you get a situation like this, it's time to step back, light up your pipe, and think about it before you do something." I wondered, *Is this something Ed Davis would be highly critical of?*

No, I decided. It had been thought out, we *were* in a situation that was no-win at that point, and we absolutely had to bring it to a close. I had consulted the experts and I had involved the mayor, which was appropriate. In the end, I was going to make a decision for which the mayor would have to take part of the heat, and certainly the chief of police would, and they might look upon me with great disfavor, even demote me, but I had to make a decision and I did.

As I waited, everything in my body seemed to slow down, including my pulse rate. Whenever I think back about an emergency situation, I am always amazed by the almost calming effect that a crisis has on me. I don't know whether this is a chemical reaction or something I developed over the years, but everything just skids into slow motion. I can feel it, feel myself becoming calm—or maybe the word is serene. People look at me and say, "You're so *calm*."

And I will answer, "But what's there to get excited about? So the city's falling apart."

This time, it threatened to.

Over the phone I could hear Bob Houghton broadcasting the warning for the final time. More minutes passed. I was staring at the clock when Bob said quietly into the phone, "I see a white flag."

"You're kidding."

"No, I see a white flag. They're waving a white flag."

"What does that mean?" I asked hopefully.

"I *think* they want to come out."

I took a deep breath. "For God's sake, let them out of there."

One by one they emerged, waving that little white flag, a rag they had tied to a stick, waving it as they came, one by one.

■

We arrested the six of them. Three were wounded, including one female, but none seriously. We confiscated their arsenal: one submachine gun, thirteen rifles, five sawed-off shotguns, and five revolvers.

We were roundly criticized for our brutal activity, even though our injuries were worse then theirs. But nobody, not even the media, ever learned the whole truth. That in a nondescript military vehicle parked on a side street nearby sat one very frightening military grenade launcher. Primed and ready to blast the house to kingdom come.

■

Several months later I did something I swore I never ever would: I got married again.

For three years after I separated from Wanda, I hardly

dated at all. For one thing, I wanted to maintain my image within the department. Most people were not aware that I was no longer living with my wife. I wasn't seeking a divorce; I didn't see the need for one. So I kept the whole thing kind of quiet. Those who knew the situation assumed I was a ladies' man. I was fairly successful; I was, I think, reasonably decent-looking. I had more hair, anyway, than I do now. And women were attracted to me. But in actuality, I spent a lot of time by myself, not going out with women at all. My mother began to worry about me. She knew I wasn't getting out, so she bought me a subscription to *Playboy*. I guess she thought, well, at least he can look at the pictures.

It was in this sort of sorry state that I boarded a plane one afternoon at Dulles Airport.

I was still teaching Ramsey Clark's riot-control seminars in Washington. I would take the red-eye out on Sunday night, lecture Monday and Tuesday, and catch American's 5:30 P.M. flight home.

But on this particular Tuesday, I had to be back in L.A. early, so I ended up on a United flight. I used to be a nervous flier, terribly claustrophobic. Once they close those doors, I think, *This thing can't fly; it's too big,* and, *Why do I put my life in the hands of those two guys sitting up there in that cockpit that I don't understand anything about?* Sweaty-palmed, I watch everything like a hawk. I mean, I know every little nuance. I know exactly when the wheels are supposed to go up and when the plane will bank. Only on this day, the plane used a different flight pattern, so I was more of a wreck than usual. Worse, I was trapped in the window seat next to a guy with whom I was not very enchanted. He was, I think, of a different sexual persuasion from me, and it was very obviously on display as he chatted incessantly at me. Then the movie came on. *Mary Poppins*. I'd already seen *Mary Poppins*, and the guy was showing far more interest in me than in Mary. I escaped to the first-class lounge.

The flight attendant, having picked up on my seatmate's proclivities, said, "Couldn't take it anymore?"

I whined something and we started to talk. As it turned out, she and her two colleagues had been flying together since stewardess school and one of them had a father who was an LAPD sergeant. I had worked with him. So maybe that convinced this one very pretty, dark-haired attendant that I wasn't a rapist, for she agreed to give me her name and phone number.

It's funny how things happen. I looked at the card she gave me and I said, "Baloney." She had written down this name, Sima Lalich, which was ridiculous. I handed the card back. "You've got to be kidding."

She glanced at it and said, "Oh, you're right. I made an error. I gave you the wrong telephone number. I forgot, I just changed it." And she wrote down another number.

If I hadn't thought her name was a joke, I might never have found her again.

I nicknamed her Sam and we went together for two years before we finally got married.

■

My household, after the wedding, consisted of four occupants: Sam; my oldest daughter, Debby; her very large part-Afghan part-standard poodle, Putney; and me.

Once I had finally moved out of my mother's house and into an apartment in Highland Park, Debby came to live with me. She had started college at Cal State Los Angeles and she wanted to be with me, she said. Naturally, I was delighted. Years passed. Debby graduated, I married, and still Debby stayed. Three more years went by, and there was Debby, still occupying the second bedroom.

One day, I said, "Debby, you're out of school. You've got a good job, your own new car, money in the bank. Maybe it's time to find a place to live? Give me back my gasoline credit cards?"

Well she cried and cried. But a week or so later, she announced, "Dad, guess what? I found an apartment."

"Gee, that's great," I enthused. "Where is it?"

"One floor up," my daughter said.

■

Throughout the years, I had continued to see as much of my children as I could. Before I remarried, I tried always to take them with me on vacation. I was coaching Scott's football team. I was a proud father when my daughter Kathy was named homecoming queen. Kathy and Scott frequently came for the weekend, all of us somehow managing in that cramped apartment. So I was a little surprised when, in the spring of 1970, I got a call from my ex-wife Wanda. "Have you noticed any changes in Scott?" she said.

Scott was a great-looking kid with a winning personality and a lot of friends, and the differences were hardly noticeable. True, there had been a drop-off in his schoolwork, he was less attentive to his chores, and for the first time he was growing long hair, which really irritated me. Still, Scott wasn't that different from other fourteen-year-olds we knew. They were *all* acting weird.

Most of us were baffled by our children's behavior. Wanda lived in a good, solid, middle-class neighborhood, where parents went to PTA meetings and participated in school activities with their kids. One of us was always taking a group of them somewhere; it wasn't as if they were being neglected.

So it took a long, long time for the terrible truth to hit. Scott was on drugs.

My first reaction was that of a father in denial. "Of course my son isn't using drugs. *Not my son.*"

"I caught him using pot," Wanda reminded me.

Shocked and angry, I took Scott to one of the best psychiatrists I knew, Dr. Tom Ungerleider at the UCLA Medical Center. He told me that yes, Scott was smoking a little dope, but it was not a serious problem. He'd outgrow it. All Scott needed was a little more guidance, Dr. Ungerleider said. Why didn't Scott come and live with me?

And, God, I would do anything for that kid. With Wanda's approval, I went out and looked at houses I could barely afford. But each time I got ready to make a down payment, Wanda would change her mind. I didn't have the heart to go to court to try to get custody of Scott. So he stayed with his mother.

The guilt ate at me. Was it my fault? Even if I had been living there, I told myself, I wouldn't be spending any more time with him than I already was. *But*—another voice interrupted—*you created a situation that obviously is traumatic to him, that caused him to go out and find some satisfaction in drugs.*

Anxious for a second opinion, I brought Scott in to see our police department psychologist, Martin Reiser. He came back with the same report: the kid will outgrow it.

Little did I realize that Scott had already begun to develop a skill common to many drug users: He had become a consummate con artist.

All I knew was that Scott assured me he wouldn't use drugs ever again.

He would assure me of that many times.

■

By now I had been on the department twenty years and I began to wonder if I would turn into one of those old-timers, forever telling stories from God knows when. *Naw*, I thought, *not* me. *No way*. In truth, I still hadn't committed to a life with LAPD. I was always open to job offers, and I had turned down quite a few, including one with the FBI and one as a professor of criminal science at Michigan State University. Howard Hughes's Summa Corporation was pursuing me at the time. Convinced his people were stealing from Hughes, a group of high-level executives wanted me to replace Robert Maheu, who was about to be fired, and restore order to various parts of the organization. After spending my vacation at the Desert Inn in Las Vegas, appraising what needed to be done, I decided I didn't like any of the people I would be working with. I turned down their $90,000 annual salary—plus the free house, free car, and unlimited travel—and stayed where I was for about a quarter of the money. Besides, I had designs on becoming chief.

I had been having them, actually, since Parker's time. They had been planted in my head by Parker himself. Often he would tell someone, to my embarrassment, "Meet Gates. This officer is going to be chief someday." For years, I figured he was only flattering me and I didn't give it any thought. But in 1965 or 1966, when he was ill, he confided that he might not be well enough to stay on as chief. "You know," he said, "I've always thought you would be the next chief, but if I have to leave now, you're too young. You don't even have your twenty years in."

I was thirty-nine. "What difference does that make?"

"You can't afford to take this job unless you have twenty years, and you have your retirement benefits. Because if something happens, if you're forced to resign, you wouldn't want to stay here at a lower rank. So you'd leave and you wouldn't have anything."

What he was refering to didn't sink in until sometime later. A police officer who retires after twenty years receives 40 percent of his salary. With this to fall back on, a chief could be more independent in his decision-making.

I didn't care. After Parker died I took the exam anyway. This was early in 1967 and I was still an inspector. There were deputy chiefs above me and inspectors with far more tenure, so I knew my chances of succeeding Parker were remote. I didn't study much. I looked at a few books, but didn't do my usual job of immersing myself in materials. When the list came out, I was sorry. I got almost the same score on my oral as Tom Reddin, who became chief.

The following year I took the deputy chief's exam, placed first, and was promoted. In private industry, to achieve a senior vice-presidency in nineteen years would not have been a great achievement. But in police service, with a system that requires you to compete for every position and demands that you spend a specified amount of time in that job before being promoted to the next, I had moved up very quickly.

Tom Reddin served only twenty-six months. So I took the chief's test again and this time I worked hard to prepare. I thought I had done very well. But my oral turned out poorly. I've always believed this was due to my being recently divorced at the time. The application form, which has since been rewritten, required that you indicate marital status. The oral-board members saw me, I'm convinced, as a young single man, and decided they didn't want to risk having me as chief. I may be wrong, but during the oral they dwelt on this issue and I came out with my worst oral and placed number four on the list.

The test was given early in 1969, so even then I didn't quite have twenty years. Meanwhile, I had been offered a job in Washington as an administrator for the newly created Law Enforcement Assistance Administration, which was designed to offer sizable grants to law-enforcement agencies across the country. As deputy chief I was making about $24,000 a year, and the LEAA job paid $36,000. I thought about it hard.

While I was reluctant to move to Washington, far from my mother and children, I was, at the same time, having qualms about staying on the department. The newly selected chief, Ed Davis, was someone I had not always gotten along with, although I had enjoyed working under him when he was deputy chief. Still, I worried what our relationship would be.

As the new chief, Ed was allowed to appoint three assistant chiefs from the ranks of deputy chief. To my surprise, I was one of his choices.

"I didn't select you because I like you," he bluntly told me. "I selected you because I thought you were the best person for the job. I'm looking for competent people. You were the one I thought was most competent."

Hearing this, I immediately brightened. I turned down the job in Washington. Assistant Chief was a big job.

I was ready for it. Each step up the ladder had given me more responsibility. As captain at Highland Park, I had overseen 170 men and women. As inspector, I had control of four divisions—more than 1,000 people. For my brief term as deputy chief, I oversaw, as deputy chiefs did, a function. I was in charge of all training and personnel. Not only did I make hiring decisions, I arranged training programs for new detectives, new sergeants, new lieutenants, and so on. Each new rank requires more hours spent studying and training at the Academy. I had shown leadership, administrative abilities, management skills, and—thanks to Parker—a bit of a knack for diplomacy. I also had completed nearly all of my courses for an MBA (though I would never finish the program). In short, I was building a reputation for getting a job done, having ideas, and making the department function better.

The LAPD is divided into three bureaucratic fiefdoms, each headed by an assistant chief. The first, Office of Operations, includes detectives, patrol, and traffic. The second, Office of Administrative Services, oversees jails, property, budget, computers, communications, and all of the things you need as support functions, including planning and research. The third division, Office of Special Services, entailed Administrative Vice, Administrative Narcotics, Internal Affairs, Organized Crime Intelligence, and Public Disorder Intelligence.

For the first eighteen months, I was in charge of Administrative Services. It's a large but not very exciting operation. One of my duties was budget. I had to go to the City Council and ask for money.

This obviously worried Davis. He took me aside and said, "You know, one of the things you have to do at the Council meetings is be more forceful."

I suppose I was considered a quiet person then, someone who was very thoughtful, very courteous, never abrasive or abusive. At times I could be withdrawn. It was always a relief to me to go to an event with Sam, because I could sit back and not have to say a word. Just grunt occasionally while she did all the talking. And what Ed Davis needed was a live wire to march into City Hall and pound the Council into great financial submission, for at the time, twenty-five police departments in California paid better wages than LAPD. Assuring him I would do my best, off I went.

Conning the City Council out of any amount of money takes work. It took me nearly a year. The plan I presented had been drawn up, after meticulous research, by the Jacobs Company, which the city had hired to analyze the pay scales of LAPD, the fire department, and civilian employees. Historically, police salaries had been set according to rank and tenure, but within only a 5 percent range. The new plan implemented pay grades that reflected specific duties within each rank, for some had tougher jobs than others. A detective, for instance, who didn't want to study to become a sergeant, but who did a crack job, could end up making almost as much as a lieutenant.

My first task was to sell this plan to the Personnel Committee of the City Council. The chairman, Billy Mills, said he would back it as long as I made sure I had the support of LAPD. "I don't want your union coming in here demanding a different plan," Mills cautioned. So back and forth I went, from City Hall to Parker Center, where I tried to keep various factions of the department from engaging in internecine warfare.

The union, known as the Police Protective League, is a potent force, often flying in the face of the chief and—if enough dissension arises—capable of rendering him powerless. This had happened in other cities. When money was tight, unions would bargain for management prerogatives in place of pay raises. For instance, some unions were allowed to determine the makeup of watches. They might choose to do this according to seniority—veteran officers got first pick of their watches—and as a result there would be no experienced officers on 11:00 P.M. to 7:00 A.M. morning watch. Such practices drained power away from the police command and put it into the hands of the union.

In Los Angeles the union hadn't gotten that far. But it had the funds to lobby the City Council directly, contributing money to various Council members' campaigns, buying tables at political fund-raisers, and so on.

My problem was that while the Jacobs plan would raise all police officers' salaries, it would raise some more than others. Hoping to keep the complainers from destroying the plan, I kept steadfastly phoning the union board members, reminding them, "This is a *good* thing."

Once the proposal passed Billy Mills's committee, I began heavily lobbying each Council member. What a chore that was. Six of the fifteen members supported the plan, but I needed ten. So, while making sure the six stuck, I set out to convince four more, phoning them, cornering them in City Hall corridors, or dropping into their offices. Soon I had developed the glibness of a suede-shoe salesman. One councilman I didn't even bother to approach was Tom Bradley, who vehemently opposed the Jacobs plan. While he cited the costs involved and was fiscally conservative at the time, it seemed to me that twentieth-century personnel management was something he was unable to grasp. Using his own brand of glibness, he pressured the Council to veto it.

With nine votes finally in my pocket and five decidedly against, it came down to the vote of its newest member, Pat Russell. I talked to her until I was blue in the face. Apparently, so did Bradley, who had helped get her elected, for at one point this strong woman said, "Daryl, I really want this to pass," and she had tears in her eyes. No one knew what she would do. When Pat voted yes, I was ecstatic.

On my maiden assignment I conned the City Council out of the biggest pay raise in department history. In one day, I put $12 million into the pockets of Los Angeles police officers. Not only did our new plan revolutionize pay grades for the LAPD, it has been the envy of police departments nationwide ever since.

From that point on, I was able to stroll into City Hall anytime and talk the Council into almost anything. Overnight, I suddenly had the reputation of being the department's Mr. Smoothie.

More importantly, I had mastered my political skills; I could dance with the best of them.

■

In February 1974, Patricia Hearst was kidnapped from her apartment in Berkeley. For months the FBI conducted a nationwide manhunt for the twenty-year-old granddaughter of the newspaper magnate William Randolph Hearst, and her abductors, members of the guerrilla-like Symbionese Liberation Army.

These people were lunatics, clearly bent on violence against, as they put it, the "ruling class in the name of the oppressed people." They first came to national attention in November 1973, by gunning down the school superintendent of Oakland, using a bullet tipped with cyanide. Two months after snatching Patty, they held up the Hibernia Bank in San Francisco, wounded two people, and took off with $10,000. Tape from the bank's video cameras clearly showed Patty, who was now calling herself Tania, wielding an automatic weapon. She was being sought as a fugitive as well as a victim.

On Thursday, May 16, 1974, the SLA surfaced in Los Angeles.

That afternoon, a man and a woman, identified as SLA members William and Emily Harris, entered Mel's Sporting Goods Store in Inglewood, and paid $31.50 for sweatshirts and socks. As they were leaving, a clerk saw Harris stuff a pair of socks up his sleeve. The clerk confronted Harris outside. As they began to struggle, Harris's gun fell out of his waistband and another clerk rushed out and grabbed it. The scuffling renewed. Across the street a dark-haired woman in a Volkswagen van pointed a machine gun out the window and squeezed off fifty rounds. Nobody was hit. The Harrises scrambled into the van and took off.

In the hours that followed, the Harrises stole two cars and kidnapped one driver.

That night, the FBI found the abandoned Volkswagen and a parking ticket on the front seat. The ticket cited an address on West 84th Street. Thinking the address might be where the Harrises were staying, the FBI called us. Shortly before 6:00 A.M. on Friday, May 17, FBI and LAPD SWAT teams assaulted the suspected house—too late. The SLA was already gone.

From the beginning the case belonged to the FBI, and its agents had a great deal of time, as well as rightful ego, wrapped up in it. But now SLA members were in our community and we intended to participate in whatever else was planned. That is, I intended to.

I had since been switched from Administrative Services to assistant chief of Operations, so command of detectives, traffic, patrol, and SWAT fell to me. All day Friday, I stayed at my desk fielding reports of SLA sightings, which seemed to drift in from all parts of the city.

At two o'clock, FBI and LAPD brass, along with their SWAT teams, met at Newton division, several miles south of downtown. By now four locations had been targeted as SLA hideouts, all within a few blocks of one another in southeast Los Angeles. The FBI was itching to go in.

William Sullivan, their top man in Los Angeles, was one of the nicest, neatest agents I've ever known. Still, he was a bulldog, a J. Edgar Hoover man down to his socks. Cooped up at Parker Center, I hadn't talked directly to Bill. But Deputy Chief John McAllister had.

He called me from Newton. "The FBI wants their own SWAT people to take them."

"Tell Bill I understand how he feels," I replied, "but the answer is no. If there's going to be any shooting in Los Angeles, it's going to be done by LAPD."

Minutes later McAllister called back. "Bill was livid at first, absolutely shaking with anger," he reported. "But I told him you were adamant, that there was no way we were going to allow them to go in. So finally he settled down. Just said, 'Okay.' "

The FBI had no choice, basically. What were they going to do? They needed the police department to block off the surrounding area, evacuate people, provide resources, and make sure the fire department and ambulances were there. A federal agency can't provide these backup operations on its own. Usually the FBI sails into a small or medium-size city and the chief of police is more than willing to let it run its own operation. But they weren't going to do that here. If people were going to be killed in *my* city, I wanted to be assured it was necessary. I could only have that assurance if my highly trained personnel, who are taught to avoid killing, found there was no other choice.

Once before, I'd had a control problem with the FBI. A flight had been hijacked out of Washington State and was believed to be en route to LAX. I got on the phone to the local agent in charge.

"Are you guys going to handle it?" I asked the agent who answered.

"We'll get back to you," he said.

Time passed while he made the obligatory call to Washington. I phoned again. "Hey, call it. We got SWAT on the way and if you're not going to handle it, we'll take care of it."

Someone rang back saying they were now all in a meeting and when it broke, they'd let me know.

"Fine," I said. "Just tell them we'll handle it. Tell them when the plane comes in, we're going to blow out all the tires. Then we're going to board the aircraft and we're going to take the hijackers off." I hung up.

Thirty seconds later the phone rang. *"We will handle it,"* the FBI said.

That was fine with me; all I wanted to do was get them off the dime, make a decision. Had the job fallen to us, we would have been prepared. For some time SWAT had been practicing on old jets at LAX. They would blow the tires out first, effectively taking any decision-making responsibility off the shoulders of the pilot. SWAT had also been practicing ways of boarding hijacked planes, but those plans necessarily cannot be revealed.

The flight never landed at LAX, but I learned one thing. I learned how to get an answer from the FBI.

At Newton they were making plans to search three of the four suspected SLA locations. Then at 5:20 P.M. surveillance phoned in promising information regarding armed suspects at 1466 East 54th Street. It was a five-room stucco-and-frame house, maybe seven hundred square feet, painted yellow and with a stone front porch. No one had seen, or knew, if Patty Hearst was inside, but SWAT got ready to go in and arrest whoever was.

In the aftermath of the tragedy that followed, many people could not understand how the LAPD could march into this residential neighborhood like an army from hell and assault this one poor little house. It's a difficult concept for an ordinary citizen, difficult even for me. But we were dealing with an outlaw band schooled in sophisticated guerrilla tactics and armed to the teeth; masterminded by sociopaths who didn't mind pulling the triggers. The safest way to arrest them was in a confined place, where we could exert some control over the surrounding area and use our own carefully plotted tactics against barricaded snipers.

And maybe, *just maybe*, they would surrender.

To this end, we brought along an experienced negotiator and, because this house had no phone, a guy from Pacific Bell who could install one.

At 5:30 P.M. we began deploying people from Newton.

Within minutes, 218 police officers moved in and formed a perimeter around the immediate area, sealing it off from traffic and pedestrians. SWAT officers quietly evacuated residents from the surrounding houses. A command post had already been set up at 57th Street and Alba, several blocks away. Fire trucks and ambulances were parked there, waiting.

By 5:35, twenty-five members of SWAT were slipping into their assigned locations. Although SWAT is technically set up into five-man teams, configurations vary depending upon the situation. For this one, Sergeant Ron McCarthy, the squad leader of Team One, deployed eight men in front and to the east of 1466 East 54th Street. They were armed with two tear-gas guns, two 12-gauge shotguns, four AR-180 semiautomatic weapons, one AR-15 semiautomatic rifle, one .243 caliber long rifle, and a slew of .45 caliber sidearms.

The squad leader of Team Two Sergeant Jerry Brackley sent his eight men to the rear and southeast of the house. They were similarly armed. Lieutenant Joe Sonlitner, the SWAT officer in charge, took up a position about forty feet south and to the rear of the house in order to direct both teams' operations.

I figured it was time to go to the scene.

No sooner was I in my car than the thing blew up. With my police radio able to pick up all frequencies, I listened to the drama unfold. The squad leader of Team One, using a bullhorn, bellowed: "Occupants of 1466 East 54th Street, this is the Los Angeles Police Department speaking. Come out with your hands up. Comply immediately and you will not be harmed."

He repeated his announcement. Then a minute later, he broadcast: "People in the yellow frame house with the stone porch, address 1466 East 54th Street, this is the Los Angeles Police Department speaking. Come out with your hands up. Comply immediately and you will not be harmed."

The door opened. Hesitantly, an eight-year-old boy walked out. A SWAT officer led the child away. After that, SWAT made fifteen more surrender announcements in the next eight minutes.

Nothing happened. Now a decision had to be made. Soon it would begin to grow dark, making it easier for the occupants to escape. In addition, it was known that the SLA had stockpiled a large quantity of food. They could hole up indefinitely, dig tunnels—if they hadn't already—or find other ways to escape into the night. The safest and most effective way to arrest them, SWAT concluded, was to try to pressure them to surrender now.

They went for the tear gas first.

Two projectiles were shot through one of the windows. For a long moment my radio carried only silence. Then the SLA answered back . . . with heavy bursts of gunfire from a big, scary automatic weapon called a B.A.R.

I could hear the fusillade of bullets crackling over the radio. Dialing like crazy, I picked up what the field commander was doing. Then I switched to SWAT. SWAT was calling for fragmentation grenades.

Jesus, I thought.

We didn't even have fragmentation grenades. Used only by the military, they explode into body-piercing shards. LAPD relies on "flash bangs." Roll it in, it makes a huge flash and a loud bang, like a firecracker. They are meant only to distract. If they explode too close to someone, the person can possibly be burned. As one of SWAT's favorite practice hostages, I have been, on several occasions, held in a room into which "flash bangs" were tossed. Once, a projectile exploded next to me and burned tiny holes in my shirt. SWAT thought that was pretty funny.

Fragmentation grenades are not funny. They are *meant* to seriously injure people.

The SWAT request was made to John McAllister, the field commander. I picked up the microphone in my car and butted in. "You do not have permission to use fragmentation grenades," I said—in effect telling John what *his* decision would be.

Had I been able to see firsthand what was going on, maybe I would have called the military, made the request. But instinctively, I didn't like a civil police force using a weapon designed for an army.

■

As soon as I got to the field command post at 57th and Alba, I had Commander Pete Hagan brief me. Then I decided to go to the scene. Wearing a suit and tie, and carrying only a .38 caliber revolver, I had no intention of participating. I only wanted to look. But on my first approach to the house I was gagged by tear gas, so I circled around and finally came in from the opposite direction—upwind.

As I turned the corner of Compton onto 54th, I quickly took cover behind a low wall down two houses from 1466. Al Preciado, a SWAT guy, was pinned down right in front of the house. Each time he'd raise his head—*ratatatat*—he'd duck back down.

It was an incredible scene. Here in the heart of Los Angeles was a war zone, something out of a World War II movie, where you're taking the city from the enemy, house by house. I was having trouble adjusting to the frightening reality of what was happening within yards of me. I was briefly amused to notice that the hordes of reporters who had by now materialized were actually keeping their distance—for the only time I can remember.

Cautiously, I moved across the street to join John McAllister, who had come over from Alba Street. He was standing with the Metro captain Frank Brittell, and SWAT leader Joe Sonlitner. Sonlitner was issuing orders to the twenty-four LAPD and five FBI SWAT people, and to the extent they needed additional effort, Brittell would get involved. McAllister was making decisions for the overall operation and I was just there to lend support or advice.

About fifteen minutes into the shooting, out stumbled a black woman onto the front porch. We had no idea who she was. She kind of wandered around acting as if she were drunk. Ducking bullets, a SWAT man grabbed her and walked her to the corner, away from the gunfire. Her name was Christine Johnson and she said she owned the house. She didn't, but she was a hostage of sorts. She had some injuries, so she was taken to the hospital.

It seemed to me that others in the house, seeing that we didn't shoot the woman, might surrender. Instead, they kept blasting away, firing M-1 fully automatic carbines, rifles, pistols, shotguns, and revolvers.

At 6:41, about fifty minutes into the shootout, flames suddenly poured out the front windows. Within a minute, the tiny wood-frame house was consumed by fire.

That's it, I thought. *They'll come out now*. Sergeant Ron McCarthy on the bullhorn was yelling, "Come out! The house is on fire. Nothing you can do. Come out."

Their reply didn't vary: more bursts of gunfire.

The next few minutes were horrible. A fire truck pulled up in front of the house, but the firemen refused to drag the hoses up to it. They stayed planted behind the truck, scared to death of getting shot.

"How about a water drop?" I asked the fire department battalion chief.

"It's too late. By the time we get a water drop over here, this thing's gonna be over."

The water supply was in Culver City and it would take ten minutes to get a helicopter loaded and hovering over the house. Besides, he explained, the weight of the water would crush the people inside to death.

"Can't you go between the houses, somehow?" I tried.

"I'm not gonna get my firemen shot. And the only way they can attack that fire with any degree of effectiveness is to meet it head on, right from the front."

"How about something, *anything?* God, we can't just let this thing rage on."

But we did. How it started, we never knew. Maybe a tear-gas projectile knocked over the can of gasoline later found in the debris. For ten interminable, nightmarish minutes, all we could do was stand there and watch the damn house burn down. It was a terribly helpless feeling. Yet only when the house was a pile of rubble, and all that was left was the concrete foundation, did the SLA guns fall silent. Everybody was dead.

At that moment my main concern was whether Patty Hearst had been inside. I didn't give a shit about the others. Cinque, their leader, whose body was later identified, was a total psychopath; the others were no better—people completely devoid of any empathy or human feeling. I often wondered how they could attract any followers at all. But they had. Even after the shootout, there were people who praised Cinque as a martyr, someone who would go down in history as the champion of a cause—this no-good murderer.

I stayed long into the night, watching the crew sift through the debris. My instincts told me Patty had been inside, but there was no way to know. All the bodies had been charred beyond recognition and it would be a while before the coroner, Dr. Thomas Noguchi, could do his analysis.

Early the next morning I returned to East 54th Street. Many houses were scarred by the firing or explosion of 3,772 rounds of SLA ammunition or the 5,371 rounds expended by us. (The city paid for the damage.) Two pipe bombs, found in the rubble, were being dismantled. But still no word about Patty Hearst.

I drove over to see George Hearst, her uncle, whom I'd known for years as the publisher of the *Herald Examiner*. He said, "I hope to God she's not there." And I remember thinking she had been there, that they were going to identify her any minute. Because if she wasn't there, where the hell was she?

Later, I stopped by Noguchi's office. We had been talking through the night. By now, the FBI had flown in dental charts and Noguchi had made positive identifications of the six victims. He came out and recited their names: Camilla Hall, Donald DeFreeze (Cinque), Nancy Ling Perry, William Wolfe, Patricia Soltysik and Angela Atwood. "They are the six," Noguchi said. "Patty Hearst was not there."

I was tremendously relieved. I believed then, and still do, that she was a victim, that she was coerced or brainwashed into cooperating with the SLA. And I had been wrestling with a nagging thought: *Maybe I should've let the FBI handle it, because if Patty was inside, and did die, it'll be my ass on the line.*

Otherwise, I felt no remorse. We needed to stop the SLA before they could do even more damage, or take more lives. Our aim was not to shoot up the neighborhood, but to make arrests with as little loss of life or injury as possible. Except when you find out you are dealing with really bad people. Then you reach a point where you finally say to your officers, "Hey, if those sons-a-bitches fire, kill 'em."

Still, the memory of the fire devouring six people will always haunt me. I can't help but think there was something I could have done to extinguish it. Maybe I should have put more pressure on the fire department. Most of the gunfire was coming out the back of the house by then, but you couldn't convince a fireman where the gunfire was coming from. And you certainly couldn't insist they go in. Their job is not to put out a fire when somebody's shooting at them. Maybe we, the LAPD, should have picked up the hoses. Me, I could have taken a hose. I think sometimes, *I could have taken a hose, grabbed a couple of police officers, and maybe stood behind a pole or at the corner of the house next door, and tried to train the water on 1466.*

But I wasn't thinking like that at the time. I was only thinking how the fire would surely force the people out. I mean, who would choose to die in a fire?

I often wondered, too, what could have been done differently in terms of our deployment. This group did not want to be taken alive. They wanted to shoot it out, so our options were fairly limited. But none of us came away thrilled. We didn't stand around patting ourselves on the back: "Say, that was a good one!"

Nevertheless, we were roundly criticized. The media, and many citizens, demanded, "Why did they have to do *that?* The police didn't give those people a chance. They just burned 'em down."

Sensitive to the reaction, we announced we would welcome suggestions for other tactics we might have used. One guy went to the governor and said, "The cops should have used water. They could have *floated* the SLA out."

Wanting to be responsive, we asked the fire department to hook up the kind of nozzle the guy had suggested, and try his idea out. It didn't work. "You'd have killed them with the water pressure," the fire department concluded.

Although the media's criticism of us was mild, compared to what it would become in later years, we responded instinctively, as people do when accused. We began boiling up defenses, justifying our actions. You erect this wall of defense and you stand behind it, saying, "God, we did everything in our power, and we did it *right,* and that's the way we'll do it in the future."

One thing was certain. That night, SWAT became a household word throughout the world. They were intrepid; they were brilliant in their deployment; their execution was flawless. Soon, other law-enforcement agencies began mounting their own SWAT teams. The whole nation had watched the shootout—live, on network TV.

Clearly, SWAT had arrived.

10

The Ghosts of
Kennedy and Monroe

Marilyn Monroe's death in her bedroom in Brentwood in 1962, and the assassination of Robert Kennedy at the Ambassador Hotel six years later were two of the most exhaustively investigated cases LAPD has ever undertaken. But our findings, detailed and conclusive as they were, only made us suspect.

I wasn't involved in either investigation. But as I kept moving up in rank, and as the skeptics refused to give up, I would finally become part of the reinvestigations of both.

I was working out of Parker's office when Monroe died, and like the rest of the world, we were shocked. I remember thinking, as I looked at the death-scene photos of her, how I wished that what could remain in my mind were all the beautiful shots of her in the movies, how gorgeous she was. But those images were erased forever, supplanted by the photographs of the actress draped across her deathbed.

In those photos she looked like hell. God, she looked awful. And it wasn't just death that had robbed her of her beauty. I thought of all the women in the world who have said how lucky she was to look like she did, have hair like that, have features like that. And what I was struck by, really, was the lack of good features. Thin hair, for one thing, and brittle. And so many other flaws that women worry about, like surgical scars and veins. But it was the face that upset me the most. Death had not altered it yet. Without makeup and theatrical lighting, Marilyn Monroe had blotchy skin, puffiness, and tiny veins on the bulb of her nose. She looked more like fifty than thirty-six, I sadly noted. The ravages of drugs and alcohol had unmercifully taken their toll.

The LAPD investigation into her death was painstaking, but also routine. Monroe was not the first movie star to die in Los Angeles; we investigate celebrity deaths all the time. And from our standpoint there was nothing puzzling about how she died. She killed herself. Whether it was accidental or on purpose was impossible to tell. But it was clear from our information that a suicidal pattern existed and that she had a lot of problems.

This is what Dr. Theodore J. Curphey, chief medical examiner-coroner for Los Angeles County, concluded, based on a report by the Psychiatric Investigative Team that was brought in after Monroe's death:

> Miss Monroe had suffered from psychiatric disturbance for a long time. She experienced severe fears and frequent depressions. Mood changes were abrupt and unpredictable. Among symptoms of disorganization, sleep disturbance was prominent, for which she had been taking sedative drugs for many years. She was thus familiar with and experienced in the use of sedative drugs and well aware of their dangers.
>
> Recently, one of the main objectives of her psychiatric treatment had been the reduction of her intake of drugs. This has been partially successful during the last two months. She was reported to be following doctor's orders in her use of the drugs; and the amount of drugs found in her home at the time of her death was not unusual.
>
> In our investigation, we have learned that Miss Monroe had often expressed wishes to give up, to withdraw, and even to die. On more than one occa-

sion in the past, when disappointed and depressed, she had made a suicide attempt using sedative drugs. On these occasions, she had called for help and had been rescued.

From the information collected about the events of the evening of August 4th, it is our opinion that the same pattern was repeated except for the rescue. It has been our practice with similar information collected in other cases in the past to recommend a certification for such deaths as probable suicide.

It is my own opinion that her death was accidental. So many times people lose track of how many pills they take, especially if they are drinking—or, enjoying the good feelings the pills bring on, they just keep taking more.

In any event, because of Monroe's association with the Kennedys, we had to keep going back again and again to put to rest all the conspiracy theories. One claimed that Robert Kennedy had asked J. Edgar Hoover to send FBI agents to Monroe's house to remove any evidence linking her to either Jack or Bobby Kennedy, and that Bill Parker closed his eyes while they did. Which was preposterous. Bill Parker would not have closed his eyes for anyone. And J. Edgar Hoover working for the Kennedys? Gimme a break. All the insinuations that shady creatures slipped in and out of her house late on the night of August 4, or in the early hours of August 5, either to kill her or to remove evidence before the police arrived, or to move her body from one room to another, cannot be supported by witnesses, the state of Monroe's body, or anything else.

Time did not diminish the conspiratorialists' fervor. As captain of Intelligence, I had to deal with their questions, and again as assistant chief, and once more as chief, as late as 1985.

The biggest reinvestigation was conducted in October 1975, after *Oui* magazine published an article: "Who Killed Marilyn Monroe?" The author, Anthony Scaduto, suggested she was murdered, alleging a coverup by the L.A. County Coroner's office and LAPD.

Although Scaduto was an investigative reporter, the "evidence" to support his murder theory came mainly from the

book *The Life and Curious Death of Marilyn Monroe,*
written by Robert F. Slatzer, who was once, supposedly,
Monroe's husband.

Slatzer contended Monroe was injected with a lethal dose
of barbiturates on the afternoon of her death. The coroner
and the LAPD, he said, distorted the evidence to protect
Robert Kennedy, who was supposedly present at Monroe's
residence when she was administered the drugs.

Although we doubted the *Oui* article contained anything
but rumors, innuendo, speculation, and obvious discrepan-
cies, Chief Ed Davis agreed to review the case and he turned
the job over to me. I turned it over to the Organized Crime
Intelligence division and Robbery-Homicide.

The problem was that by 1975 little evidence was left to
review. The initial investigative reports had been retained in
our files for ten years, as law prescribes; then, in 1973, they
were destroyed. But we found copies of most, maybe all,
the relevant reports in the private archives of the late Thad
Brown, who had been deputy chief of the Detective Bureau.

As part of the reinvestigation, Kennedy brother-in-law
Peter Lawford was interviewed at his home on October 16,
1975. I quote from that report:

> Mr. Lawford stated that most of what has been
> written by various authors, such as Slatzer, Scaduto,
> Mailer, and others regarding the last days in the life
> of Marilyn Monroe is "pure fantasy." He states that
> Miss Monroe was a regular weekend guest at his
> beachfront home in Santa Monica those last weeks
> before she died.
>
> On August 4, 1962, Mr. Lawford telephoned Mar-
> ilyn Monroe at approximately 5:00 P.M., to ask her if
> she was coming to his house that weekend. She
> sounded despondent over her loss of contract with
> 20th Century-Fox Studios and some other personal
> matters (presumably the romance with Robert Ken-
> nedy). Lawford tried to convince her to forget about
> her problems and join him and his wife, Pat, for
> dinner that evening. She replied that she would con-
> sider joining them.
>
> At approximately 7:30 or 8:00 P.M., Lawford tele-

phoned her a second time to ascertain why she hadn't as yet arrived at his home. . . . Lawford stated Miss Monroe was still very despondent and her manner of speech was slurred. She stated she was tired and would not be coming. Her voice became less and less audible and Lawford began to yell at her in an attempt to revive her. (He described it as a verbal slap in the face.) Then she stated, "Say goodbye to Pat, say goodbye to Jack (JFK) and say goodbye to yourself, because you're a nice guy." When the phone went dead, Lawford, assuming she had hung up, tried several times to redial her number and received a busy signal each time.

Lawford then told [Milton] Ebbins [his agent and dinner guest] he was going to Marilyn's house. Ebbins recommended against it, "You know how agents are," and suggested that he (Ebbins) would call her doctor or lawyer. Eventually, Ebbins was able to reach her attorney.

Lawford stated he often talked to Marilyn on the phone while she was under the effect of downers, and her voice on this evening sounded about the same. For some reason, however, he had a "gut" feeling that something was wrong. He states he still blames himself for not going to her home himself.

Approximately three weeks prior to this event, on a weekend, Lawford states Marilyn was a guest of the Lawfords at the Cal-Neva Lodge in Lake Tahoe where Frank Sinatra was headlining. When Lawford awoke one morning, his wife told him Marilyn had overdosed the evening prior. She was discovered when she fell out of bed and was able to be revived without professional medical assistance.

Regarding Robert F. Kennedy, Lawford is adamant that the attorney general was not in the Los Angeles area on August 4th or 5th. He states that whenever RFK came to town he would come to the Lawfords' home and swim in the pool. Lawford states he has no knowledge of RFK's stay in San Francisco, as alluded to in the *Oui* article.

The truth is, we knew Robert Kennedy was in town on August 4. We always knew when he was here. He was the Attorney General, so we were interested in him, the same way we were interested when other important figures came to Los Angeles.

At the time, in our efforts to thwart the Mafia, we had people at the airport—airline personnel, for instance—who could recognize a well-known person and alert us. We also relied on helpful employees at hotels and restaurants. In keeping tabs on people, we stumbled onto all sorts of information: this man's wife having an affair; this *man* having an affair. But we never went out of our way to see who was carrying on with whom. The fact is—and most people don't want to hear this—we just didn't care.

So while we knew Robert Kennedy was in town that day, we paid no attention to where he went or what he did; whether he saw Monroe or not. Frankly, I never bought into the theory that she killed herself because he dumped her— if he did. My feelings were that she was emotional over many things; a relationship gone sour would be just one of many problems she had.

■

The Organized Crime Intelligence Division, after spending weeks checking out key accusations in the *Oui* article, issued its findings in a ten-page report. Here is some of it:

> *Oui* article: She didn't behave as if she were planning to kill herself; all those that spoke with her on that last day . . . agree that she was happy.

> FACTS: Dr. Ralph Greenson, her psychiatrist, saw Miss Monroe professionally, almost daily for approximately one year prior to her death in an attempt to divorce her from the use of barbiturates. He had met with Monroe twice on August 4, the eve of her death. According to handwritten notes recorded by LAPD investigators on the death scene, Dr. Greenson had asked Eunice Murray (the housekeeper-psychiatric nurse) to stay with Monroe that evening because she was very upset.

Oui: In deaths from barbiturates, in the last minutes before consciousness is lost, there is pain and contortion. It's common to see the body twisted. You never see a body with the legs straight.

FACTS: The source of the above was a quote from Sergeant Clemmons, not an experienced investigator. Dr. Noguchi, Los Angeles County coroner, was interviewed by investigators on October 6, 1975, and stated that an overdose of barbiturates produces a restful sleep which graduates to a comatose state and then on to death. There is no sign of pain or contortion.

Oui: Marilyn could never swallow even a single pill without drinking water . . . yet no drinking glass was found in her bedroom.

FACTS: Investigators obtained photographs taken at the death scene, dated August 5, 1962. The photo clearly shows a drinking glass half filled with liquid on the floor by the bed. Also shown is a ceramic vessel which may have contained a liquid for drinking purposes, as it is covered with an inverted cup.

Oui: . . . when someone swallows an enormous quantity of capsules, a residue is usually found in the stomach; partially digested pills, liquid solution . . . refractile crystals . . . there is always a highly visible trace in the stomach, of the barbiturates that killed.

FACTS: According to Dr. Noguchi and toxicologist Edward Griesmer, M.D., of the Los Angeles County Coroner's office, in only 50 percent of cases where drugs were used to produce death is there any residue of the drug found in the stomach or duodenum. The absence of refractile crystals indicates total absorption. The doctors stated that absorption time decreases when the subject is a frequent user of drugs (as Marilyn Monroe was known to be). The process of digestion continues from time of ingestion to the time of death; even through the comatose stage.

Oui: . . . sources within the LAPD say the original report made at the time of the autopsy was suppressed, and a report reconstructed from memory and omitting many details was substituted.

FACTS: If such sources exist, investigators, after a diligent search, were unable to locate them. Dr. Noguchi labels this statement as "ridiculous."

Oui: Marilyn may have been *injected* with a fatal dose of drugs. . . . The fact is that Marilyn had been given at least two injections in the days before her death. Evidence of those injections would still be on her body after her death.

FACTS: While it is true that the subject had been administered injections on August 1 and August 3, 1962, the puncture wounds, according to Dr. Noguchi, would have disappeared after twenty-four hours. Noguchi adds that any large quantity of barbiturates injected would produce death almost immediately. A large swelling would appear in the area of the injection, and the puncture wound and swelling would remain visible, as the healing process would cease at the time of death. Noguchi stated that because of the absence of residue, he made a diligent examination for needle marks, and found none.

Oui: Had Marilyn swallowed 47 Nembutals, yellow dye from the jacket of the capsules should have been found on the linings of the throat, esophagus and stomach. No trace was found.

FACTS: Dr. Griesmer stated that of more than two hundred overdose cases he has examined, he has never found yellow dye in the stomach from Nembutal ingestion. The only time a dye

is visible is when the subject has ingested
Seconal, which will leave traces of red dye.

Oui: Had Marilyn swallowed that many capsules, she
must have vomited, for suicides by barbiturate poi-
soning always vomit.

FACTS: According to Dr. Noguchi, frequent
users of drugs rarely vomit from overdose.
Marilyn Monroe was a frequent user. If she
had taken an alcoholic beverage or had recently eaten, vomiting would be possible, but
not probable. However, the autopsy disclosed
that her stomach contained neither alcohol nor
food.

Oui: The finger points to Los Angeles Police Chief
William H. Parker. . . . He told journalists that the
records showed Marilyn had called Bobby repeatedly
during the last week she was alive, making eight calls
to his Justice Department office.

FACTS: During the initial investigation, in 1962,
this department obtained long-distance and
toll-call records from General Telephone Company. The records reveal all such calls made
from the phones in Miss Monroe's residence
for the period June 1, 1962, through August 18,
1962. Eight calls were reportedly made from
her residence to a Washington, D.C. number
during this period. Assuming this was RFK's
number, as these were the only calls to Washington, D.C., only one was made within seven
days of Marilyn Monroe's death:

> July 30—8 minutes
> July 23—1 minute
> July 17—duration unknown
> July 17—duration unknown
> July 16—duration unknown
> July 2—duration unknown
> July 2—duration unknown
> June 25—duration unknown

Oui: It has been reported . . . that there exists in the vaults of the Los Angeles Police Department a 723-page report labeled, Marilyn Monroe-Murder.

> FACTS: The author's reference comes from an excerpt from Slatzer's book, wherein Slatzer claims to have held a clandestine-style meeting with a man who identified himself as Jack Quinn. This script is the sole basis for his belief that such a report exists. Slatzer himself admits that the information may not be accurate and that the true identity of his informant is unknown.

The report concludes:

> Many other statements were made by the author with little or no attempt at credibility. Any attempt to prove or disprove some of the author's "speculations" would be an exercise in futility.
>
> Probably the most accurate statement in this literary endeavor: "Some of the evidence is as thin as Depression food line soup."

∎

The assassination of Robert Kennedy produced even more misguided accusations. June 5, 1968, the night he was shot, I had been dining at Inspector John McAllister's house. I had recently been promoted to deputy chief and was, that night, "duty chief." If anything happened, someone in the business office was supposed to alert me. Nobody did.

When I got home, I flicked on the TV and . . . *my God.* Not forty-five minutes earlier, Kennedy had been shot and the coverage was still being broadcast live. It was a shock. I had talked to him on the phone many times. He and Pierre Salinger had spent many hours with LAPD Intelligence in the days when his brother was Senator Jack Kennedy and he was bombarding the Teamsters Union over the corrupt

use of their pension funds. Bobby's politics had changed
since then; he had shifted to the left, taking a far more
liberal stance than his brother had. I knew I couldn't have
voted for him for President, but . . . What was America
coming to?

After a moment my thoughts returned automatically to
the unfolding drama. Immediately I picked up the phone
and checked to determine who had been notified. As it
turned out, the right people had been and were all at the
scene: the captain of Homicide, the chief of detectives, plus
a substantial contingent of detectives and uniform personnel. With the investigation under way, there was nothing for
me to do. After a while I shut off the TV and climbed into
bed. Wondering: what is this going to mean to the city of
Los Angeles?

■

As soon as Kennedy was pronounced dead on June 6,
we knew we were going to have to deal with a conspiracy
theory. I remember discussing it that day with others in the
department. Even though Sirhan Sirhan had been seen firing
the shots by many eyewitnesses and was apprehended on
the spot, we could already anticipate the questions that
would be raised.

Like—*Where were the damn cops?*

We weren't at the Ambassador, that's for sure. Had we
been, I have no doubt we would have preplanned Kennedy's
route from the Embassy Ballroom, where he thanked supporters, to the Colonial Room, where he intended to meet
reporters, and we would have had enough officers on hand
to protect him. Sirhan Sirhan would never have made it to
the pantry; if he had, he would have been spotted raising his
gun. But Kennedy's people were adamant, if not abusive, in
their demands that the police not even come close to the
senator while he was in Los Angeles.

This troubled me greatly, because when he was Attorney
General he had been helpful in so many respects. Whenever
I wrote to him about organized crime, he responded imme-
diately. I think Bobby always had an affection for LAPD
because of the help we gave him. But this was different.
This was politics, Kennedy-style people politics. And in his

bid for the presidency Kennedy had taken the side of the "peaceniks" and the flower children—which, from a political standpoint, was, I guess, very wise.

But in currying favor with liberal elements, Kennedy did not want anyone to think he was in any way connected with the police. This was 1968, not the time to be identified with these miserable *blue people* who were putting down peace movements all over the nation. He wanted no uniforms around at all. None that could be captured in a photograph or on a piece of film. Kennedy desired to be seen as a man of the people, charging into crowds *alone*.

He wasn't the only one. Adlai Stevenson didn't want us. George McGovern, who was Kennedy's main rival for the Democratic nomination, wanted nothing to do with us either. It was a very bitter pill to swallow; to realize suddenly that a *presidential candidate* didn't want the police around. There was no federal protection then, either. Only after Robert Kennedy was assassinated did they assign the Secret Service to candidates.

Having been ordered to stay away, we did. For a bodyguard, he had only Roosevelt "Rosey" Grier, the imposing Rams lineman, as he moved through the pantry at the Ambassador Hotel and into range of the assassin's gun, just after midnight on June 5.

Over the next twenty years we had to explain more than why the hell we weren't there. Despite Assistant Chief Bob Houghton's massive investigation, called Special Unit Senator, in which every lead, rumor, piece or non-piece of evidence was examined, categorized, and dealt with; despite a prosecution conducted by my old law instructor, Assistant District Attorney Buck Compton, which was the most thorough anyone had ever witnessed; despite a jury conviction that Sirhan Sirhan did, on his own, shoot the bullet that killed Robert Kennedy, we still aren't free of suspicions, cast by a parade of conspiracy buffs that never seems to end.

I don't know how many times I have had to go back through the files, bring in investigators, return to the Ambassador Hotel to walk through the whole thing again. And this was after the kitchen was crumbling and we had to walk through, searching for holes in a wall that no longer existed.

One major reinvestigation came in the fall of 1974, at the request of former New York congressman Allard Lowenstein. He insisted a lone assassin could not have fired four bullets into Kennedy, wounded five others, and left three bullet holes in the ceiling with a gun that held only eight bullets.

Right. We'd been through this before. First during the murder investigation itself, then rehashed for film maker Theodore Charach for his 1973 movie, *The Second Gun*, then for County Supervisor Baxter Ward when he campaigned for governor, not to mention for other self-appointed seekers of the truth.

So I put together a new team of five investigators and we rehashed it all again.

Their findings, reported in December 1974, were clear and undoubtedly disappointing (if not suspicious) to Lowenstein.

The eight bullets fired from Sirhan's gun did do the damage cited. Their travels, though cockeyed, were as follows:

Bullet #1: Struck the senator in the right mastoid area.

Bullet #2: Passed through the right shoulder area of the senator's coat and struck Paul Schrade (a union Kennedy supporter) in the forehead.

Bullet #3: Entered the senator's right rear back, exited his chest area, entered the ceiling.

Bullet #4: Entered the senator's right rear shoulder and lodged in the area of the sixth cervical vertebra.

Bullet #5: Struck (citizen) Ira Goldstein in the left buttock.

Bullet #6: Passed through Goldstein's pant leg, ricocheted off the floor, and struck (citizen) Irwin Stroll in the left leg.

Bullet #7: Struck (citizen) William Wiesel in the left abdomen.

Bullet #8: Ricocheted off the ceiling and struck (citizen) Elizabeth Evans in the forehead.

According to District Attorney Joseph P. Busch, who announced the findings, "The questions of bullet trajectory and ballistics which have been raised in recent years are questions based on misreadings of fact . . . which have been fully explored and explained."

No matter. Six months later, Lowenstein demanded another investigation into Kennedy's assassination, accusing the LAPD of "stonewalling" efforts to reopen one, and telling reporters that officials have "ignored, concealed, or distorted" evidence from eyewitnesses and ballistics experts.

At the same time, Vincent Bugliosi, the former deputy district attorney and author, brought suit on behalf of his client Paul Schrade to reexamine the ballistics evidence presented at Sirhan's trial, also certain there had been a second gunman. As a result, a special prosecutor was named to rereview Sirhan's gun to determine once again whether the bullets we said were fired from it were.

To do this they brought in seven ballistics experts, who tried to match the bullets to the weapon, which had been in the county property department and, frankly, not well cared-for. While they couldn't match three of the bullets to Sirhan's gun, they ruled out any possibility they could have come from anyone else's.

This little inquiry cost tens of thousands of dollars and required an enormous amount of the police department's time to dredge up all the materials and the evidence, seven years after the fact.

■

And the accusations *still* surfaced. Among them:

If Kennedy really did order us to stay out of his sight, how come we didn't force security on him? Couldn't we have at least had plainclothes officers somewhere on the premises?

The truth is, we thought we probably should have—in retrospect. We did assign four patrol cars to circle the hotel. But had we, against his wishes, assigned plainclothes officers to work inside the hotel, and especially if Kennedy had lost the primary, his handlers would have accused us either of spying on the Kennedys or trying to ruin his campaign with our presence. This was the mentality that existed, both on the public's part and on our own. And it was very disconcerting to those of us who were trying to do a good job.

We were part of a conspiracy to kill Kennedy; that was the real reason we stayed away.

According to *this* theory, the LAPD was a bunch of right-wingers (possibly with links to the Ku Klux Klan). Other right-wingers, whom the police wanted to protect, killed Kennedy. *That* was why we weren't at the Ambassador. We *knew* something was going to happen. Talk about being caught in a no-win situation. We're specifically asked to stay away, something happens, and we're accused of being part of it because we're not there.

How about those bullet holes in the doorframe, captured in a photo, with those two cops pointing to them?

Indeed, the AP ran a photo the morning after the shooting, showing two uniformed officers crouching near a doorframe. One was pointing to a tiny hole. The caption identified this officer as a technician. The question raised was how come we didn't account for these two or three holes, which certainly proved more than eight bullets had been shot?

The officers, we tried to explain, were not ballistics experts, but patrolmen who had come on the scene for crowd control. A photographer asked them to pose, and wanting only to be cooperative, they did. But the holes were not bullet holes. We dismantled the doorframe and determined that it contained no bullets. Eventually, we threw away the doorframe—an obvious act of covering up, according to some.

On one piece of evidence, we did make a mistake. During the initial investigation, DeWayne Wolfer, our chief forensic chemist, did an elaborate job of matching the bullets recovered from the bodies of Senator Kennedy and the two other people who had been shot that night with seven bullets which were test-fired from Sirhan's gun. Four of those test bullets were then placed into evidence before the Grand Jury along with the Sirhan weapon and the bullets taken from the victims. Since Sirhan's gun was no longer available to him, Wolfer had used a similar .22 caliber revolver found in the LAPD property department to conduct sound level and pattern tests. He didn't recover or retain any bullets from those tests but later, when he put the other three test bullets fired from Sirhan's weapon in an evidence envelope, he mistakenly wrote the identification number for the similar weapon on it. No one noticed the error during the trial, but the mistake came out later and set the conspiracy wheels in motion again. The belief is that the second envelope contained bullets from a *second* gun, used the night Kennedy was shot. No matter how many times we went through this, people remained skeptical.

■

As requests for more investigations poured in through the late seventies and into the eighties, it became more and more difficult to duplicate the events of that night. Most of the people who worked on the original investigation were gone. Only two detectives remained, and I had to call on them each and every time and go through the whole thing.

The media kept raising the conspiracy issue too. For instance, on November 7, 1976, Art Kevin delivered an editorial on KMPC radio, beginning: "This reporter is in receipt of new documents heretofore classified and suppressed, which raise serious new questions about the possibility of a conspiracy in the RFK murder." He then mentioned that two persons, who had been at the Ambassador Hotel at the time of the shooting, had been questioned by us, and how come nobody knew about them?

"As politics '76 thunders on and into the homestretch," he concluded, "details on such information remain locked away in LAPD's Intelligence files, fueling continued speculation of a conspiracy on that California primary morning eight years ago."

Sighing inwardly, I turned the questions over to Major Crime Investigations; the report that came back explained that the two people, who were among hundreds we interviewed, had added nothing helpful toward our investigation.

By now, everyone was demanding to see our files. Personally, I had no objection to opening them up. The problem was, the files contained information given to us on a confidential basis. We had all kinds of personal information from people who were around the senator, what they were doing, who they were with, *private* information. I didn't think we had any right to disregard a confidential relationship. This only added more fuel to the conspiracy theories. "If the police weren't hiding something, they'd let us get into that file. So they're hiding something, they *know* there's a conspiracy, and that's why they won't give us that file."

Finally, I got so sick of this, I recommended the files be placed in the hands of our archivist, pointed out what we thought was confidential, and let him worry what to do about it.

■

In my mind, only one question remains unanswered twenty-four years later. That is: how could you possibly get the police, the FBI, the Secret Service, prosecutors, courts, and special commissions *all* to engage in this cover-up conspiracy?

Maybe a good mystery writer could tell me.

11

Evil

On January 31, 1975, I was called to an address on the east side of Hollywood.

On the drive over I tried not to think about what awaited me. Even so, I could feel queasiness stirring in the pit of my stomach.

A police officer learns to build up a resistance to the blood and gore that intrudes into his or her life. You stand around at the scene of a crime puffing on cigars, making jokes, laughing a little too loudly. Sometimes you make jokes about the corpse. It is a way of ensuring that you don't become emotionally tied to that individual. Human pain and suffering can take over the mind easier than almost anything else. So we all know the tricks. Have to. Otherwise we'd go and blow our brains out.

One thing a police officer cannot do, though, is ever forget. Like grainy photographs in an old album, dozens of images of the dead remain on file in my memory. We all lug them around with us; I sensed I was about to collect another.

For the last two months I had been in charge of a special

investigative task force set up to find a killer known as the Skid Row Slasher. The graphic name told the story. The guy mostly operated along Skid Row and his victims got their throats slashed. So far there had been eight. All male. The first was a forty-six-year-old black man, a transient, who was found in the arcade portion of the Central Library on 5th Street.

Whoever was committing these crimes was an equal-opportunity killer. The next victim was an Eskimo, followed by a Caucasian, a Mexican, two more Caucasians, and two Latinos. But his M.O. didn't vary much. Preying on transients, he would offer his victims money—or force them—to orally copulate him, and while they were on their knees he would reach down and slit their throats.

People in the community who like to scream that the police ignore low-rent murders should have seen the hours the three lead investigators were putting into this one.

The address I was looking for late that afternoon was an apartment house on North Van Ness. I parked on the street, walked past the yellow crime-scene tape and into the ground-floor unit.

Unlike the others, this victim, a thirty-two-year-old Caucasian named Clyde Hay, was not a transient. He was gay and he used to frequent Skid Row bars looking for friends. Thinking he had found one, he had brought his killer home.

His nude body, lying across the rumpled bed, was arranged in the ritualistic manner the others had been. A towel covered his groin. (In the three others I'd seen, the pants were pulled partway down.) His shoes were neatly aligned, the toes pointing toward his bare feet. A considerable amount of salt had been sprinkled over the corpse (a new wrinkle).

I stared at the body an extra long time; then, reluctantly, my eyes traveled to his neck and . . . *Aw, Jesus.*

Clyde Hay's head had been nearly severed from his body, the gaping slash extending from one ear to the other.

And that wasn't all. On either side of the washbasin, two long-stemmed cut-glass goblets were filled with blood. The blood the murderer hadn't drunk.

I left the apartment to the crime-scene experts. The foul, stale smell of blood stayed in my nostrils all the way back to Parker Center.

■

Central division was handling the case, since most of the murders had occurred in its territory. From information collected from various sources, we believed the suspect was black, and a police artist drew a composite based on what we had learned. But then a vagrant had come forward, claiming he had seen a man come out of the bushes where a body had been found. He described the man as white, with long stringy blond hair. Our artist dutifully drew a second composite. But Ed Davis and I were never really happy with that lead; we didn't have much confidence in the witness.

Central did. And somehow the *L.A. Times* got hold of the composite of the white man and printed it as our primary suspect.

Davis blew his stack. He decided that the reporter must have gotten too close to the detectives, and the detectives leaked the composite to bolster their case. Central swore up and down it had not influenced the reporter to print this one composite over the other. But Davis refused to listen. He demanded the detectives take lie detector tests, which I thought was a little harsh. The tests came up clean. But not even this ever convinced Ed.

After the ninth murder, Hay's, there were no more. Suspecting the killer may have left town, we began checking. Sure enough, Chicago police had arrested a guy for a similar murder, although the jury was able to convict him only of a long-ago assault. His name was Vaughn Greenwood; he was black and thirty-two. He turned out to be our man as well. He was ultimately convicted of eleven counts of murder (he'd committed two others in 1964), one count of assault, and five counts of burglary. He was sentenced to life. But not to death.

■

Clyde Hay became another picture stamped indelibly on my mind. And the seventies would produce many more. It seemed as if it was serial-murder time in Los Angeles.

Starting actually in 1969, the Charles Manson murders were the first to horrify us. He was the ringleader responsi-ble for the stabbing, numerous times in the chest and abdomen, of the pregnant actress Sharon Tate Polanski, killing her and her unborn child, as well as four others who were in the house on Cielo Drive. The next day, Manson's four sidekicks murdered two more.

Bracketing the decade were the Bittaker murders, probably the most brutal I have ever seen. Larry Bittaker and Roy Norris would hunt young girls on the beach or walking down the street. At first they simply took pictures. Then they decided to lure one into their van. Between June and October 1979, they lured five, ages thirteen to sixteen. With Bittaker calling the shots, he and Norris cheerfully tortured their victims as they went about raping and murdering them. They used pliers on the nipples and the vagina and, in at least one case, drove an icepick through one girl's ear into her brain. As a final sick twist, they photographed the torture and tape-recorded the whole thing.

I listened to maybe half the recording of one victim, listened to her desperate pleadings, her chilling screams:

BITTAKER: What are you doing? (MORE INTENSE) *What are you doing?*
VICTIM: I'm trying to do what you wanted me to do.
B: What did I want you to do?
V: Suck on it.
B: Suck on what?
V: This.
B: What is this?
V: Your dick.
B: Yeh. Say it.
V: Your dick.
(Later)
B: Tell me what are you doing.
V: I'm sucking on your dick.
B: Do you want to do it?
V: You want me to.
(Slap)
B: You want to, girl. . . . Do you want to suck my dick, baby? Huh? Huh? Hey. Start answering me.
V: Yes.
(Later)
B: You don't sound like you really mean it.

v: I do.

B: Suck on it then. C'mon, suck on it.

(Tape pauses)

B: No matter what you can . . . squeeze hard, you understand. And if all else . . . if it hurts any time, you want to scream, go ahead and scream.

v: Oh, no! (SCREAM)

B: Scream, baby . . . scream some, baby.

v: I can't.

(Later)

B: You want me to come, yeh, want me to come, tell me, baby.

v: Yeh.

B: Huh?

v: Oh, yeh.

(Sound of digging in tool box)

B: Hey, girl, you want me to put a pair of pliers up your cunt?

v: What?

B: You want to make me come, huh, you want to make me come.

v: *(Scream)*

(Later)

B: Where do you want me to come . . . where?

v: Come.

B: Where.

v: All over . . . all over.

(Pause in tape)

v: I think you broke it.

B: I barely hit it.

v: Don't hit it again.

B: Oh, yeh.

v: *No no no no no!*

(Loud sound of hit)

v: *(Scream)* Oh, no no no no!

(Loud sound of hit)

B: How's that?

v: *No no no no no no!*

B: Scream.

(Radio goes up in background)

B: Scream.

v: No No No, Oh, Oh (SCREAM). (SOUNDS OF PAIN)
b: Get noisier, girl. Go ahead and scream or I'll make you scream.
v: *(Moaning)*
b: Oh, yea. Oh.
v: *(Scream)*
b: Keep it up, girl.
v: *(SCREAM)* Oh, oh (Scream). Oh, no. (LONG DURATION WITH APPROXIMATELY TWENTY TO TWENTY-FIVE SCREAMS)

Until, unable to bear it anymore, I told the detective: "Shut the damn thing off!"

The tape was played in its entirety in court. Nothing in the movies could even come close to what that horrified courtroom had to hear.

■

And yet. Something always gets lost along the way. The distance between crime and punishment can be from one end of the earth to the other. You have the police down in the dirt and the grime, right down in the garbage pit. But once the action shifts to the courtroom, it's as if someone has waved a magic wand. Presto! Everything is all cleaned up.

The judge sits there in his magisterial robes, symbolically high up on his bench, as if he doesn't want to touch any of the dirt connected with the case. The suspect's there, all cleaned up, shaven, nice haircut, cloaked in clinical white. Jurors are neatly dressed, respectful and polite. It's an atmosphere as antiseptic as an operating room. And the jury wonders: How in the world could he have done what they said?

Soon the jury starts to feel sympathy for the son of a bitch. Why, look at him! He's the neighbor next door, the nice guy who goes to college, the friendly fellow who works down the street. *My God,* they think, *I'm going to send this guy to the gas chamber?*

The judge sits there in his germ-free surroundings, making all these rulings based upon his vision of the world, or his perception of the world, not having rolled around in the gutter, and he doesn't want to get the court's hands dirty on this tainted evidence that might be offered. "Oh, no, we can't have that! It would dirty this court to have that evidence."

With a serial murderer, it becomes even harder to believe what the guy's done. It goes beyond the pristine setting of a courtroom to a place the normal human mind seems unable to venture. The place is called evil. And it would return to haunt this city two and a half years later.

■

As the seventies progressed, it wasn't only murder and mayhem that preoccupied me. Drugs were constantly on my mind as I helplessly watched my son fall into the life of a chronic user.

Like a lot of parents then, I believed the sheer force of my personality would overcome Scott's involvement in drugs. I believed I had a greater influence on my kid than the drugs did. Big mistake. Scott has an addictive personality; he's compulsive. In retrospect, I realize there was little I could have done, except maybe in the initial stages when everyone was assuring me he would outgrow it. (Today, of course, I'd receive different advice.) The truth is, Scott finally told me, he started smoking pot when he was eleven years old.

Slow to understand the dynamics of drugs and drug users, and believing in my son as I did, I plodded along year after year doing everything I knew of to help. When he showed an interest in backpacking, I happily went out that Christmas and bought him backpacking gear, including a beautiful down sleeping bag that cost a fortune.

Unaware that kids used backpacking as a means of getting away to enjoy their drugs, I watched my fifteen-year-old son unroll the sleeping bag on my king-size bed and crawl into it the way a kid does, checking it out. We started talking about drugs. I was my usual moralizing self, reminding him of the harmful effects of drugs and listing them in categories. Finally I got to heroin.

"Of course," I said, "I know you would never use heroin. I *know* that. I mean, you've seen pictures of all these down-and-out addicts. . . . Would you?"

Scott gave me a little smile. "Oh, I don't know."

Suddenly I felt such rage I could hardly control myself. I came as close as I ever had to striking him, and seriously injuring him.

But if he had fallen into a pattern, so had I. Still the father and not the police officer, I would bestow material things on him every time he seemed to be off drugs. I gave him anything I thought could possibly buy him out of this, could help him through: bicycles, four motorcycles, including one that Sam gave me as a present, three automobiles—or maybe it was four—clothes, skis, ski boots, fishing poles. All of which would disappear.

In high school his grades got worse and his lies more bold. One season he told me he had gone out for football and boasted of how well he was playing. But when I stopped by at practice, Scott wasn't there. "I decided," he said, "I didn't want to play football anymore." Later I learned he had not gone out for football at all that year.

I probably spent more time in school than Scott did, talking to counselors, principals, teachers. But the schools didn't know what to do with these kids, and neither did I. I continued to send Scott to a psychiatrist, to doctors, to counselors. But his grades only got worse, and now he wasn't going to graduate. Already, he'd had run-ins with the police and was arrested twice. Nothing came of either arrest. Then he was picked up for possession of codeine. He went to court and was put on probation.

The years blur, but little vignettes pop out. My wife, Sam, had a '65 Mustang, in mint condition. It was her first car and she just adored it. Scott was eighteen and going through an outpatient rehab program. We thought it would be good if he had a job and could bring some discipline into his life. So Sam gave him her beautiful little Mustang as encouragement.

Six months later we learned he'd sold it to a neighbor for the ridiculous price of $400, obviously zonked out of his mind when he did. When I asked him why, he said, " 'Cause there was this other car, a Volkswagen, that would get better mileage and the Mustang's always breaking down."

That made sense. But it was just another example of Scott's ability to con. In truth, he had an opportunity to buy some coke. He was then going to sell it for a lot of money. Only he got ripped off for the four hundred bucks. Here was this kid swimming in the delusions that come from drug use, and here I was blinded once again.

When I learned he had been getting codeine by visiting every dentist in town, complaining of a toothache—conning them, too—I decided I had to take drastic action.

Working with his probation officer, I had my son committed to Norwalk State Hospital for the mentally ill.

Just to say the name gave me cold chills.

To the public, Norwalk is considered a place for the hopelessly insane. But by then, drug addiction was being classified as a mental illness, and Norwalk had a good rehab program. We were at our wits' end. The outpatient programs we had tried hadn't worked. Perhaps this one would.

Six months later, I returned to Norwalk, twenty-five miles southeast of Los Angeles, to pick him up. I was going to take him home to live with me. He looked terrific, blond, tan, healthy. Our ride home was filled with all the hopeful phrases we had spoken to each other so many times before.

But once again, it was an illusion. Scott hadn't been cleaned out, only cleaned up. He had managed to mesmerize the entire hospital staff in about three minutes, including two nurses who couldn't do enough for him. Sweet-talking and romancing them, he finagled several unscheduled leaves. Scott, I'm convinced, is one of the greatest con men of all time. If he had an evil mind, or were out to make a buck using fraud or bunco, he'd have made a fortune by now. Instead, all he wanted was a hit. He found one the day he got home.

Again, I ignored the telltale signs, crawling into my usual state of denial. But when the subtle signs became obvious ones, Wanda and I put him into a private residential program run by a psychiatrist.

"You have to understand," I told the psychiatrist, "Scott is skilled at conning people and he will get you to believe anything. He will convince you he is cured. Now this is what you have to watch out for."

I explained how Scott had all the answers down pat. He had been counseled by me or other experts to such a degree that he would appear to be accepting what the doctor said and would probably parrot it back more articulately than the doctor. Scott would also weave quite an intricate web of why he had turned to drugs in the first place. "He'll tell you there was no father at home, that at age nine he was the man of the house and that awesome responsibility drove him to drugs." Finally, I warned, "You must never allow him out. If you do, notify me immediately."

At last, I thought, I was acting like a police officer who had become an expert in the field, rather than a father in a constant state of denial. The psychiatrist gave me all the right assurances and took Scott away.

As soon as he had, they routinely searched Scott's suitcase. In it they found a gallon and a half of liquor, which Scott had taken from my house, and which he had poured into every conceivable little container he could find.

Right away, Scott befriended a nurse, just as he had at Norwalk. He also made friends with a patient. He "borrowed" the patient's car and didn't come back. The patient complained to the nurse. But the nurse was having a romance with Scott and didn't want to report him. I mean, he had the whole place *under control*.

Once alerted, I went searching for him, found him, and took him back to the hospital. The car he had borrowed had a big dent in it, which I paid for. We kept him in the hospital another month; then, realizing the futility of it all, I yanked him out.

I drove him home again, wondering what the hell to do.

■

Evil returned to Los Angeles on September 9, 1977.

Partially stripped, sexually molested, and strangled, the body of twenty-six-year-old Laura Collins had been dumped near an off-ramp of the Ventura Freeway. Victim number one. Then, one after another they came. Two more bodies in October. Eight in November; three discovered in a single day. All were young females; all had been strangled to death.

I had their pictures tacked to a board in my office. Pictures of their smiling young faces taken when they were alive; pictures of their sprawled, mangled bodies after they were dead.

We didn't even realize, at first, that the deaths were connected. In a city that tabulated 631 murders that year, it's pretty easy to relate one homicide to another. You can probably take any half-dozen random homicides through shooting and find many similarities among them, even though they're not related at all. So it took long thought and careful analysis of three or four bodies before we concluded that we had a serial killer on the loose. And it was chilling.

I used to stare at the pictures over and over, hoping *something* would pop out. Serial murders are horrific enough, but when the victims are females who have been sexually assaulted, *then* killed, I can't help feeling even more horrified. Maybe because women are more defenseless than men, or maybe being of the old school, I am overly protective. A police officer gets used to murder, mutilated bodies, all the hideous things people do to one another. But you never get used to brutality against children—or, in my case, women.

Just looking at their faces played on my emotions. I would think, *My God, what's the next one going to look like? Are we going to have a next one?* And then I'd hear the call: "Homicide." And the location, and I would go to the scene and *damn*, there's another one. And it just kind of eats at you . . . constantly, constantly, constantly.

By mid-February, the toll had climbed to thirteen. I still recall all those bodies in their positions, and all their faces in life. I can see almost every one of them, even now.

■

"All right. This is what I want you to do."

Seated across from my desk were Bill Herrman, a retired LAPD lieutenant with a Ph.D. and a mind for computers, and Carl Holt, also a retired LAPD officer and computer whiz, both geniuses in their own right. As assistant chief of Operations, I had command of 85 percent of the department, so the Hillside Strangler investigation, as it was now being called, was conducted under my supervision.

It was early December and we had no leads. The two weeks previous had been brutal. On November 20, the bodies of twelve-year-old Dolores Cepeda and fourteen-year-old Sonja Johnson had been found, as well as the body of Kristina Weckler, twenty, an art student. Three days later, a Caltrans worker stumbled across the nude body of Jane King, a beautiful aspiring actress, sticking out of the bushes near an off-ramp. Victim number ten.

By now our Hillside Strangler Task Force had swelled to 162 officers and homicide detectives brought in from Robbery Homicide and the divisions where the bodies were found. But because the bodies were turning up in the northeast L.A., Glendale area, the investigation necessarily involved the Glendale police department and the sheriff's department, as well as LAPD. Trying to coordinate efforts was a task in itself.

Our organization chart looked like a major military unit. The man in charge of the investigation was Captain Eugene Rock, commander of Robbery Homicide division. His assistant was one of the very best, Lieutenant Ed Henderson; Lieutenant Ron Lewis was the task force night-watch commander. Given the weight of my normal duties, my participation was limited to that of an overseer. One of the things I tried to oversee was urging detectives to go home at night and get some sleep.

It wasn't easy. By late November the city was in a panic.

It became even more panicked on November 29, when victim number eleven hit the afternoon headlines. That morning, the nude body of Lauren Wagner, an eighteen-year-old business school student, had been discovered in the Mt. Washington area in brush beside a twisting, narrow roadway. Her legs were sticking out onto the pavement. She, too, had been strangled to death.

The night she died, Lauren had driven to her boyfriend's house for coffee about 7:30 and had watched TV with him until 9:45. Fifteen to thirty minutes later, Beulah Stofer, who lived on Lemona Street, just down the block from the house where Lauren lived with her parents, looked out her bedroom window. She noticed two cars moving side by side. The larger vehicle, a navy or black sedan with a white vinyl top, forced the smaller vehicle, a 1967 Mustang, to the curb.

Mrs. Stofer told Sergeant Bob Grogan, one of our homicide detectives, she heard a female voice say, "What do you want of me?"

Next, the dome light went on in the larger car and she

was able to see two men in the front seat. They got out, went over to the Mustang, and forcibly pulled the girl's hands from the steering wheel and hauled her out of the car. Mrs. Stofer watched as they shoved the girl into their car.

"You can't get away with this," the female voice said. Followed by a deep male voice saying, "Just come along quietly." And then they drove off.

Mrs. Stofer had not reported these events. Grogan, in canvassing the street, had knocked on her door. Over the next six months he would call on her repeatedly, hoping she could recall just one more detail. But what Mrs. Stofer told Grogan the day the body was found confirmed my suspicion that the murders were being committed by two men. It seemed to me from the way the bodies were left—never any drag marks, and always in some hard to reach, hilly location—that it would be physically impossible even for a large male to handle a body by himself.

Many in the department disagreed with me. I kept saying, "Chief, I'm almost positive that we've got two people involved." But Ed Davis stubbornly held to the single-killer theory. The detectives were uncertain. Even police officers could not make themselves believe there were *two* people this bad, working in concert. The single-killer advocates would say, "Why would two people join together and murder women? You mean, *two* guys raping a woman, *then* murdering her?" The mind just rejects that—impossible.

Only it's not. What is hardest to comprehend, even for us, is that people who perform these kinds of acts are not necessarily mentally unbalanced. That's what is scary. They know what they're doing; they understand right from wrong. They are just . . . evil. Law enforcement expert James Q. Wilson wrote, "Our habits of the heart have been subverted by the ambitions of the mind." Society flinches from the truth; we do our very best to find psychological and sociological reasons to excuse behavior that our minds won't accept for what it is. You walk into court and you have all these attorneys explaining away all of the things that you can sum up in one simple word: Evil.

In Los Angeles, we were dealing with the reality of two evil minds. I was sure of it.

■

Inside Parker Center we were in disarray, choking on tips, leads, and clues. We had, in time, more than 10,000 clues, 4,800 parolees to check out, and 120,000 fingerprint cards to run for comparison. Hundreds of witnesses and people close to the victims were interviewed. The usual allotment of "confessers" had to be interrogated. We arrested people, let them go. At one point we set up a four-line twenty-four-hour hotline, staffed by forty people; they took one thousand calls the first week alone. ("My boyfriend's been acting crazy lately. . . . Maybe you should check him out!")

Among the hundreds of leads we were checking out was something else Mrs. Stofer had told Detective Grogan. We had been bothered by how easily the murderer(s) had been able to coax the victims to go along with them. And now this witness confirmed our worst fears. Riding in what could be mistaken for an unmarked car, the two men had pulled Lauren over and acted like police officers.

Unlikely as it seemed that a couple of cops were committing the murders, we'd been around long enough to have seen police officers do almost everything, unfortunately. So we couldn't write that off. We began looking at certain officers. In fact, we looked at one without his knowledge for some time. Still, even though the murderers knew a lot about evidence and crime scenes, they didn't have to be cops. There's enough information in whodunits and on TV to give anyone a pretty good sense of what the police can do and what they can't, and to know what we look for. Armed with even this fictional insight, it isn't hard to stay one step ahead of the police.

■

"What I want you to do is study the locations where the victims were found," I told Herrman and Holt. "Get the exact time of death from the coroner and collate that, to the extent you can, with the time their bodies were dumped."

One of our numerous problems was that none of the victims had been murdered at the location where they were found. This left us with no crime scene, none of the usual shreds of material or bits of evidence you often pick up. All we had to go on were the ligature marks on their wrists and around their necks, and the signs of forced sexual activity.

"After you do that," I said, "see if you can find any people who heard a car drive up or something of that nature, to pinpoint when the bodies were dumped. And then try to calculate, however you can, a rough idea of the area where the murders could have occurred."

Somehow they did this. Their method wasn't very scientific, but they came up with a system of concentric circles. They would draw them according to the location of the body, the time of death, the last time they were sighted by a witness, and how long it would take to go from one point to another. When all the information was compiled, they had made a circle surrounding the approximate area where all the murders could have taken place.

It was a big circle, a mile in radius. But studying it after the case had been solved, I could see that almost right in the middle of the circle was the home and automobile upholstery shop of Angelo Buono, Jr.

We didn't know about Buono then. Or his adoptive cousin, Kenneth Bianchi. But armed with this map of concentric circles, I did something that was unprecedented. I went to the Glendale police chief and got his not very happy approval to flood his area with two hundred LAPD officers. The hope was that one of the officers would spot two men in a car—anyone moving who looked suspicious in any way. We did that for quite some time. But like so much else we tried, we came up empty.

If only—there were so many *if onlys*—we had started banging on doors, using all the officers and whatever time it would take, I think we could quite possibly have discovered the upholstery shop, which might have led us to the adjoining apartment where twelve of the thirteen women were strangled. Just maybe. But this was only one of the many frustrations that plagued us for sixteen agonizing months.

Despite all the manpower we had on the case, it became humanly impossible to manage the information we had effectively. A different team of detectives was assigned to each murder. They would come back to Parker Center and confer. They would list things on the blackboards, then list them in different ways, kind of play with the information.

But the human mind is able to comprehend only so much. At some point, the mind just shuts down. We had also placed all of the information in computers with a computer program that identifies comparative data. But computers need human manipulation, and our manipulators were not coming up with anything either.

On December 14, Kimberly Diane Martin, eighteen, was found strangled and nude, lying spread-eagled on a steep hillside lot off North Alvarado Street. The victim used an out-call service that specialized in modeling jobs and, it was believed, prostitution.

On December 13 the service had called her, saying a man had phoned, asking for a "young, blond, attractive modelish, cute-looking girl." At 9:00 P.M. Kimberly arrived at the address, a three-story apartment house on Tamarind Avenue in Hollywood. She was never seen alive again.

Bells should have gone off at this point, but in retrospect, they didn't ring loudly enough. The apartment Kimberly Ann Martin was sent to had been vacant for a long time. Since there were no signs advertising a rental, only someone familiar with the building would have known of its existence, it seemed to me. At this point we still had no connective bits of evidence, and thinking the Tamarind address might provide a connection, I asked detectives to check all the people who lived in the building and trace those who had since moved out. To what extent this was carried out, I never knew. But the name Kenneth Bianchi, or his description, should have turned up then and there.

He had lived in this building previously. But our detectives didn't catch that. Moreover, Bianchi had been interviewed by police officers on three separate occasions; once because someone told us they thought he carried a badge. (He had one, it turned out, a California Highway Patrol badge that he bought at a swap meet and which he flashed when stopping his victims.) The third time Bianchi was interviewed by the LAPD, a woman called to complain that the man her daughter was dating was "strange." (Another one of *those* tips.) But our computer software could not collate all the information fed into it, and Bianchi's name was spelled differently each time.

■

The problems continued to build, but not our evidence. Although Mrs. Stofer was able to help us tremendously at first, she began to grow fuzzy about details as the months went by. The more Sergeant Grogan went back to visit her, the less she was willing to say. It is a common syndrome. She was feeling guilt and her mind had started to withdraw. Her mind was saying, *Hey, I should have done something. I should have called the police. I didn't. Now my neighbor's daughter is dead. And I didn't do anything about it.*

The detectives were as delicate with her as possible, because they knew her testimony would be vital. At the time, it was all we had.

The media presented another major headache. Whenever a new body was found, we would block off the immediate area for our investigation and control that, but once we left, reporters swarmed in, banging on doors, stopping cars, talking to anyone who might know anything at all.

This drove the detectives crazy. When they went to conduct their own interviews, they had no way of knowing how much information was legitimate and how much had been distorted by the media. A reporter might say, "Did you see a red car?" planting that notion in a person's mind. We would say, "What did you see?"

Commander Bill Booth, our press relations officer, came to me and said, "We've got to get the media off our backs, off the detectives' backs, and there's only one way to do that."

"How?"

"You're gonna have to give regular briefings."

Reluctantly, I agreed. Mostly, I went to those briefings without an ounce of information that I could provide the media. Once a week I held lengthy press conferences and managed to say absolutely nothing. I found it was a kind of an art: to give the media something they could write about without giving them anything at all. For instance:

Q: Chief, everybody I've talked to on this case seems convinced that whoever is luring these women must be posing as something. Are you entertaining any other theories besides a police officer? Is there any evidence to indicate that he could be posing as a priest or a cab driver?

ME: We're entertaining many, many different theories. We're also entertaining the possibility that they have the ability to utilize immediate force in such a way that no one is going to argue with them. They go along without any kind of struggle. So that's a possibility also.

Q: Is the task force looking into the files of active duty policemen to see if you have any with histories of violence?

ME: We are not closing any options. We are keeping an open mind, examining a number of things.

Q: Is that yes?

ME: We are examining a number of things.

Q: Have you moved on to one single policeman, checking to see if he might possibly be involved?

ME: We have looked at not just one; we've looked at some police officers in connection with the case.

Q: Are they still under surveillance, those you have looked at?

ME: Well, we never had them under surveillance. Most of them we have cleared. I think there is one or two that we are still examining.

Q: Are they in a particular division?

ME: I wouldn't want to indicate that. Again, it's not to suggest that they *are* involved—it's simply to show you the great latitude that this investigation is taking. We're doing our utmost to look at everyone that might have a problem. . . . It might even be that we're looking at some of *you*.

That was on December 27. Since the word was out that a police officer might be the Hillside Strangler, we sent around a departmental memo emphasizing that officers must not chase after a female suspect, no matter what. If a woman runs from you, we said, don't chase her. Understand that she may be panicking, thinking that you're *him*.

Women throughout the city were understandably panicked, including my wife and two daughters. The bodies were turning up near our neighborhood—Highland Park,

Glendale, Eagle Rock. In fact, my wife often shopped at Eagle Rock Plaza, where the two little girls had been seen earlier on the day they were murdered. I tried to be reassuring. I went through the usual safety precautions. They each carried a whistle. I also gave each of them a little instrument you attach to your key ring. It's called a Kubla Khan, a small, hard, cylindrical object that you use in a jabbing motion to strike an attacker in the throat or the eye. I also tried to tell them that while they should be cautious, the odds of their becoming victims were remote. When you consider the number of females thirteen and older in Los Angeles, and you factor that with the number of possible contacts that any two individuals—the murderers—could have, it comes out like the lottery.

Similarly, we tried to reassure women throughout the city that their chances of encountering the Hillside Strangler were infinitesimal. Nobody listened.

As the turmoil inside and outside Parker Center only intensified, I finally went to see Ed Davis. "I want to be relieved of all my other responsibilities so I can head up the task force myself and spend all my time on it," I said.

Ed shook his head. "Sorry. You're going to have to let somebody else head the task force, because there's too much else to do running your part of the department. You can't neglect that, can't assign somebody else to it. *You've* gotta do it."

With 80 percent of the LAPD under my command, it was hard to argue Ed's point. But I came away feeling more frustrated than ever. Almost every day I was holding briefings, bringing in detectives, finding out what they were doing. Often, I would make suggestions—Have you tried this? Can you check out that?—the way any assistant chief would. And they'd say, "Sure, Chief, we're gonna do that," and they'd walk out of the room, and maybe they would, maybe they wouldn't, figuring they didn't need some assistant chief telling them what to investigate. Like the Tamarind address. I am certain the intensive checking was not done, and it continues to haunt me today that I didn't personally go over every detail.

Although it had been twenty-five years since I had been a patrol officer, the urge to jump in a car and do it myself never left me. No matter that my job was to assist and supervise, I couldn't help but think I could handle things better, faster, more thoroughly myself. But like any executive, I knew I wouldn't be an effective one if I didn't delegate. My job, I reminded myself, was not to single-handedly capture the Hillside Stranglers, though I wanted to, but to work diligently through the instrumentality of others. It was easier thought than done.

Unable to sleep, I kept others awake as well. I would call Gene Rock, the head of the task force, bothering that poor guy in the wee hours, keeping him on the phone, going over again and again certain elements of the case. I would get an idea and call him and say, "Tomorrow, I want you guys to do such and such. And get back to me." I never knew, when I told Gene I wanted certain things done, how often I was shined on. Or whether the effort was as intensive as I had hoped.

I was particularly bothered by a telephone call we seemed unable to check out. The day the two little girls disappeared, one of them phoned her boyfriend, possibly during the time frame she would have been with the killers. She had giggled playfully, not sounding distressed at all. Then she had hung up. I wanted to see if there was a way to trace that call.

"Look," I said to the detectives, "when a person makes a call out of zone, it shows up on their bill—the number and the charge. I want to see if the phone company can do the reverse with its computers: Go through every bill that had a call to the boy's phone number."

The detectives seemed reluctant, but finally they went. Sorry, said the phone company, we have no way to do what you want. Unconvinced, I sent the detectives back to the phone company three or four times. Each time they were told: "It's impossible to do that."

Maybe it was; maybe it wasn't. It became another *if only*. *If only* I'd had more time, I would have gone to the phone company myself.

■

Through January and February the pressure continued to build. In the movies you see the mayor picking up the phone and calling the police chief: "I want somebody in jail, Chief. Do something!" But that's not what happens in *this* city with *this* mayor. No, the pressure came from the public and from the media, but mainly it came from us. We are like a team that wants to win and most of the pressure we heap on ourselves.

Unfortunately, when this happens the tendency is to assign more detectives, which, I learned, is probably the worst thing you can do. You only end up losing continuity.

If only . . . I agonized, we had more sophisticated computer software. But detectives don't want to sit down and work at a computer. That's not what they do. As chief, I tried for years to hire paraprofessionals, people who don't carry a badge or a gun, but who can become as good as any detective who works the streets. People who can go through the massive data and sort out facts. I was never able to get the funds for it from the mayor.

Lacking computers, I gave in to the demands for more manpower. If homicide wanted detectives, I assigned more detectives. But I doubted it would help. Detectives are sometimes reluctant to share information. They might think, *Well, I got a lead here. It probably isn't anything, but I'm gonna look into it and not tell anybody till I know if I have something or not.* You can't ever know how much of that goes on. And here we had three police departments involved.

I never knew how much information was innocently lost.

■

March came and still we didn't have one solid lead. Then out of the blue we were handed what appeared to be the big break.

At Walpole prison in Massachusetts, a recaptured felon named George Shamshak, twenty-seven, came up with a story. Shamshak, who had escaped from prison in October 1977, and who had been on the loose for 107 days, told authorities that he hid out with his friend Peter Mark Jones, thirty-seven, a Beverly Hills handyman, in Los Angeles. He said he had driven Jones's van while Jones was in the back murdering two victims. We immediately dispatched Grogan and another detective to Boston.

There is a special jailhouse breed that possesses an uncanny ability to gather information, such as details in the media we have no idea are even published, and play it back in an utterly convincing manner. Shamshak had apparently done quite a bit of reading about the Hillside Strangler murders, and perhaps he guessed a little bit more, for he seemed to possess special knowledge of the two murders as he again "recounted" them to the detectives.

Hoping this was their man, the detectives allowed themselves to be led down the garden path. They should have been more discerning, but sometimes detectives go off to never-never land and it's hard to bring them back to real life. So eager are they to complete the puzzle, they overlook a number of pieces that simply don't fit. They rationalize the inconsistencies. They say, "Yes, but it is *possible,* and if it *is* possible, a hell of a big gap can be filled in." Or they avoid the gap, which is actually a cavern, completely. And you can't do that. You've got to look at that cavern and say, "Hey, how do I get from here to there, even in spite of all this?" And often, if you do that, you find out you can't, and you realize what you have is pure garbage. That's exactly what did not happen here. They flew Shamshak back to L.A.

There were some skeptics, Lieutenant Henderson in particular. He had the kind of mind needed to rope detectives back to reality. But they were deluging him with all this stuff and you can't simply dismiss detectives when they say, "This is something we need to follow through." You just can't do that.

So we put surveillance on Peter Mark Jones. And on March 30, we booked him on suspicion of the murders of Jill Barcomb, victim number five, and Kathleen Robinson, victim number eight. Shamshak was already in protective custody in San Diego.

Desperate to convey good news, I personally jumped in front of the microphone to announce our big break. But after searching Jones's apartment, and his van, we couldn't find enough evidence to file a formal complaint. Under California law we must charge a suspect within forty-eight normal working hours, or release him.

On Monday, April 3, 1978, we released Peter Mark

Jones. There was simply no evidence to support Shamshak's claim. It had become such an emotional case for the public, as well as the police that at the press conference I held to make the announcement, Jones's attorney, John Albert Johnson, graciously praised the LAPD officers, defending their arrest of Jones. "The Los Angeles police department, in my opinion," he said, "had reasonable cause to cause my client's arrest on suspicion that was brought about by the statements which implicated him in these murders by Mr. Shamshak."

I formally apologized to Jones and we all posed, smiling, for the cameras. But having to stand up at that press conference to admit our mistake, to have to apologize to an innocent man who unwittingly became a household name, was one of the most embarrassing moments of my career.

I wanted to give the back of my hand to Bob Grogan, who obviously had been led to never-never land. A fine investigator but, God, he got sidetracked. He was the one who got us into this mess, but taking the blame is part of being the boss. I said, "Okay, you made a mistake. We all made a mistake. Your job is to press on. Mine is to take the heat for it."

And I did.

12

Chief

As the hunt for the Hillside Stranglers intensified in the early months of 1978, so did LAPD's search for a new chief of police. After eight years in the job, Ed Davis concluded he wanted to run for governor, so he left the department in January. An interim chief, Assistant Chief Robert Rock, was named while the woods were combed for Ed's successor.

I was determined that the successor would be me.

People running the city had other ideas, however. When the City Charter was amended in 1938 to make the police chief an appointment of the Police Commission, not the mayor, the city was hoping to insure itself against political control of the LAPD. No system is perfect, however. Word spread that the political leadership, especially the mayor, who was now Tom Bradley, intended to go outside the department to seek its chief. They were tired, they said, of what they called "the LAPD mentality."

This "mentality" had been exemplified by Ed Davis, Tom Reddin, and Bill Parker, all strong, outspoken, free-thinking chiefs, who would not be bullied by politicians. But in the eyes of the city leadership, this "mentality" represented an independence that bordered on arrogance. "Let's get somebody that *we* can appoint," they said—meaning, of course, "control."

So the word went out across America that the LAPD was looking for a chief. Never before had the position been open to anyone outside the department. Now letters were being sent to big chiefs and little chiefs, begging them practically, "Come take this examination!" It was almost demeaning. But the political leadership just said, "Hey, all we're trying to do is make sure we get the *best* person available, okay?"

It was also the Bradley administration's first opportunity to choose a chief. Ed Davis had been selected in 1969 and Bradley had been elected in 1973. Still, no matter who applied, there was a testing process, and according to the City Charter, an "outsider" could not merely rank in the top three and be selected, as an LAPD candidate could; an outsider had to have the highest score overall.

This time I studied like crazy. There is no prescribed way to prepare, but I knew the areas that likely would be covered. I read up on the most recent court decisions, new evidentiary procedures, and as many books as I could on the latest administration and management techniques. Books on law and leadership lined my study area. President Jimmy Carter's zero-based budgeting was in vogue, so I immersed myself in that as well.

Then, as exam day approached, a rumor spread that an exercise called "in basket, out basket" might be included in the test. I remember that Mary, my secretary, mentioned there was a book on the subject, but somehow I never got around to looking at it.

The exam for chief of police cannot be manipulated, supposedly. Answers to written questions are sent to experts nationwide to grade. Oral answers are heard by a distinguished panel of generals, CEOs of large corporations, judges, law-enforcement officials, and legal scholars. But this examination proved to be a little bit *tilted*. One of the candidates was an ex-chief from Seattle whose wife hadn't liked the climate, and he was now serving as chief in Santa Monica. And this chief happened to be an expert on the in-basket exercise; he was, actually, the co-author of the in-basket book.

I knew *nothing* about the "in-basket." I looked at the test questions and I thought, *Oh, my God, what is this?* The premise was: you are a new chief and you have certain matters pending in your in-basket. In a written exposition, I had to explain how I would deal with each issue, in what order, and the logic behind it. For one third of the test score.

When the results were posted, the Santa Monica chief's combined oral and written scores were higher than mine. But after adding points for my seniority—an advantage given to LAPD candidates—I ended up number one on the list, substantially ahead of everyone else. Outscored, the Santa Monica chief was disqualified from further consideration. (He went on to become the chief of Anaheim, but after about four years he left with a stress pension . . . from *Anaheim.*) This left the Police Commission to choose among the top three scorers: Me, or one of the next two highest-ranking candidates, Robert Vernon or Charles Reese, both of whom were talented LAPD deputy chiefs.

Normally it takes two weeks to make a decision. This time the process took two months. The Commission was having difficulty coming to grips with what appeared obvious to everyone—that I, a dreaded Parker/Davis "clone," was, on merit, clearly the best choice. Hoping to find a flaw, each of the five commissioners summoned me for a lengthy private interview. I admit I behaved with a touch of arrogance. I was, in effect, daring them to select somebody else, then justify it.

One commissioner, Jim Fisk, a former deputy chief, took me aside and said, "Daryl, can't you be a little more flexible? The Commission sees you as this very inflexible person."

I smiled. "Okay. What issue do you want me to compromise on?"

"Just look at some of these issues and see if you can come up with a view closer to what the Commission wants done," Jim urged.

I considered his advice. Then I thought, *I am what I am, and it would be absolutely horrendous for me to make them believe I'm something I'm not. With me, what you see is what you get, and they might as well accept that.*

Unlike me, Bob Vernon went in with charts and did a magnificent job of showing the commissioners how he planned to eliminate top jobs in a stab at cutting costs. Then I was called in and asked if I, too, would eliminate some of the top brass.

"No."

"Why not?"

I noticed Fisk staring at me, silently willing me to *bend*.

"You know," I said, "you people are really amazing. On the one hand, you talk very strongly about affirmative action, about moving blacks and Hispanics and women up in the organization. At the same time you want to cut out all of these top jobs. How are you going to have vacancies to move people into when you've slashed all these positions from the top? I'm not adverse to reviewing each job and, where I think it's appropriate, cut it. But across-the-board cuts? I won't do it. And I think you're talking out of both sides of your mouths."

Well they didn't like that at all. So they stalled some more. This Police Commission, appointed by Bradley, clearly had Bradley's stamp, or the Democratic party's, all over it. In Los Angeles, elections for public office are nonpartisan, and party politics are not supposed to be a factor in running the government. Past mayors had appointed civic-minded persons to commission seats; some were engaged tangentially in party politics. But Bradley just reached right in and pulled out leading members of the Democratic party to fill his. Stephen Reinhardt, who is now a judge on the Ninth Circuit Court of Appeals, had orchestrated all the tactics for Bradley's election and he was deeply involved in the election of Governor Jerry Brown. Sam Williams, a black lawyer, was also heavily involved in the elections of Bradley and Brown. The president of the Commission, Mariana Pfaelzer, now a federal court judge, had been the treasurer of Brown's campaign, but she liked me and I believed I had her support. Sal Montenegro, who considered himself a political liberal, was inclined toward me too. He had come to know the police department and its officers by actually going out on the streets.

Still, it seemed imbedded in the city's history that conservative Republicans or Democrats tended to support the police department while those with liberal leanings instinctively viewed us with skepticism.

Although Bradley seemed to like me well enough, he was eager to break away from the "LAPD mentality" and not have this Parker/Davis clone. Had he wanted to, he could have pressured the commissioners not to vote for me by threatening to remove them from the Commission. In the end, perhaps he came to the same reluctant conclusion that his commissioners did: Gates is the best qualified. We have no choice.

On Wednesday night, March 22, 1978, I was attending a party at the home of David Gerber, a TV producer at MGM. At the time, he was producing the series *Police Story*. Steve Lawrence, who portrayed a sergeant from Internal Affairs with stunning veracity in one of the episodes, was telling me he had called his mother to ask how she'd liked it.

"What did she say?" I inquired.

"She said, 'Stevie, so why can't you play a doctor?' "

We were still chuckling when David Wolper, a legendary producer in his own right, came up to me and said, "Hey, congratulations."

"What for?"

"I know you're gonna be the chief," Wolper informed me. "They're going to make the announcement on Friday."

How he knew, I don't know, but it turned out he was right. They made the announcement on Good Friday. After being given the official word, I tried to call my wife to tell her the rumor was true, but I guess she wasn't on tenterhooks, because the line was always busy.

■

I was sworn in at the Police Academy auditorium before a thousand persons on March 28, 1978, the city's forty-ninth chief of police. As I nervously sat through the preliminary remarks I realized that the safety and welfare of 3 million people spread across 467 square miles would now fall directly to me. No other police chief in America had such a huge responsibility with such minimal resources. With a force of only 7,500 to patrol 467 square miles, we had fewer officers per population than any major city. New York City had less than three times as many people and more than

25,000 officers, with 301 square miles to cover. Chicago, with a similar population to ours, but only 228 square miles, had 13,000 officers. Most big-city departments averaged four-plus officers per 1,000 population. Washington, D.C., averaged six or seven. We averaged two. Our inadequate budget, $300 million, tested our ingenuity every day.

Sam, sitting beside me, had her own trepidations. She knew how badly I had wanted to be chief, but she also realized that now I would be in the public eye. I am a quiet type who cherishes my privacy. Not much of a socializer, I was happy to spend my occasional free evenings sprawled in front of the TV and my weekends reading on the beach. Sam knew this would all change.

As I walked up to the podium, I spotted my daughters Debby and Kathy, and my brother, Steve, an eighteen-year veteran and a captain with the LAPD. My parents had long since passed away. I kept scanning the audience, wondering if my son, Scott, would show up. And . . . *there he was*. He looked terrific and, at a glance, seemed to be in good shape. I felt thrilled that he had come.

It was several weeks later that an informant for the sheriff's department told me the truth. Earlier that morning, Scott had a guy shoot him up with heroin for the first time.

Under the influence of heroin, my son attended the ceremony. Swearing-in ceremonies for me, the Los Angeles chief of police.

■

Like my beginnings at the Academy nearly three decades before, my beginnings as chief were anything but auspicious. Each of the first three months had a major glitch in it.

On March 30, I held that press conference to announce that we had just arrested one of the Hillside Stranglers and had a possible accomplice in protective custody. On April 3, I publicly ate my words.

On May 3, determined to follow William Parker's concepts vigorously, I delivered a speech.

Like Parker, I had begun to build a base of support by speaking whenever I could. I went before every conceivable group. I talked morning, noon, and night. Because I had the advantage of TV, which he didn't, I accepted all requests for

interviews. In my efforts to build a strong power base, I also
had meetings with people in the community. I invited CEOs
from major corporations to Parker Center, offered them
coffee and gave them an insider's view of the department
(although not any inside information). It was never my
intention that people would say, "Boy, I really like that
guy." But I did want them to be able to say, "Well, he's
kind of an S.O.B., he is extremely outspoken, says things
he ought not to, but he's a hell of a fine chief."

I had set the same goals inside the department. If you
asked anybody about Parker, they would say, "Oh, he's a
miserable guy!" But every officer in that department respected Parker totally. Police officers don't respect a chief
who is wishy-washy. They want a chief who stands up.

I was determined to be like Parker, respected inside the
department and out. And for about a month I did okay. And
then I had to open my big mouth.

The Coalition of Mexicanos/Latinos Against Defamation
invited me to a luncheon to discuss career advancement in
the LAPD for Mexican-Americans and other Latino officers.
Sal Montenegro of the Police Commission advised me not to
go. "They're a bunch of flakes," Sal warned. "They'll do
everything in their power to put you in a compromising
position. You will not get a fair shake from them. Don't go."

I figured I could handle any group. Prejudice or racism
wasn't something I had to duck—I'm not a prejudiced man.
I admit I can be very prejudiced against individuals, but not
against whole racial groups or religions. I was always terribly conscious of this because my dad was a four-star bigot.
I used to cringe when he said "nigger." So I knew deep in
my heart that I was *not* a bigot, because I had so resented
my father's attitudes. I felt perfectly comfortable addressing
this group.

When my turn came, I was asked if a Mexican-American
officer would replace Captain Rudy De Leon as commander
of the Hollenbeck division on the city's east side, now that
Governor Brown had appointed him to the Community
Release Board. Rudy was one of the few Chicanos in the top
ranks of LAPD. I answered that his replacement would be
an Anglo and spoke of how sorely we needed more of our
Latino officers elevated. I explained LAPD's policy on

promotions: how it's a competitive process, how there weren't any shortcuts, only long diligent hours of study. And then I used an example.

A lieutenant named Bob Medina recently took the captain's exam, I told the group, and did poorly. He is a bright guy with a master's degree and I asked him: "Bob, where did you fall down?"

"I got a good oral," he replied, "but my written was bad."

"There's only way to pass that written," I emphasized. "You have to work at it. You can't just shine on the studying. You're a bright guy. So there's only one reason that you didn't pass that examination. You're lazy. You didn't work hard enough."

I then told the group about an interview I had done with the *L.A. Times* in which I had pointed out that black police officers were far better organized, far more committed to advancing themselves and working much harder at it than Latinos. Latino officers, I said, liked being detectives, were very good detectives, and seemed content to stay at that position rather than move up into administrative jobs.

My remarks angered just about everybody who heard them at the lunch, and those who hadn't were outraged by the *L.A. Times* story the next day, misrepresenting what I had said. GATES' 'LAZY' REMARK IRRITATES AUDIENCE: POLICE CHIEF CALLED INSENSITIVE IN REFERRING TO LATINO OFFICERS, the headline read.

"Los Angeles Police Chief Daryl Gates," the story began, "came under a barrage of criticism Wednesday when he told a Chicano audience that some Latino policemen do not advance in the ranks of the Police Department because they are 'lazy.' "

I hadn't said that at all. I had talked about Bob Medina only. I had said that as a group, Latino officers seemed less inclined to advance, satisfied as they were with being detectives. No matter. Suddenly I was labeled a bigot.

Stunned and upset, I thought about Charlie Guzman, the best partner I'd ever had, who'd left the force to work for the State Department. I remembered how Charlie used to have me over for dinner and how shocked I was when he told me his family couldn't join a certain club because they were Latino. If I had done anything wrong, it was to tell one Latino officer that he was being lazy, a word I chose hoping to prod him into forging ahead.

That my remarks were misreported should have taught me a lesson: You get no second chance to "explain." While everyone expects the media to be adversarial and to sniff out wrongdoing on the part of public officials, we who are their targets draw the line when they substitute creativity or misinformation for facts. The media determines what is important and what is not. People really don't have the freedom to know what is going on in the world, only the freedom to know what the media wants us to know. In determining what that is, in deciding how the American people are going to hear about it, the media can give a false impression that will never be erased. The media's selection of facts and its creativeness in choosing an angle would drive me right up the wall.

From that point on, I should have written down my remarks before delivering them. Somehow, it was a lesson I would never learn.

■

The "Latinos are lazy" controversy ate up most of May but dropped to second place after what awaited me in June. In June, the voters of California passed Proposition 13, which substantially lowered property taxes and meant less revenue for the cities. Governor Brown and Mayor Bradley had both strongly opposed Proposition 13 and it seemed almost overnight there was a desire by those in government to tell the people: "See, we told you so! Now look what's going to happen to *you*."

Right away, department managers received memos from Bradley ordering cuts. Mine was to cut $39 million out of our previously approved $300 million budget for the coming fiscal year. "Layoffs are what I propose," he wrote.

I seemed to have little choice. The police department is labor intensive, with 95 percent of our budget being spent for personnel costs. We were already short-handed; now, in order to conform with the mayor's demands, I would have to dismiss 1,100 of our 7,500 officers, and 500 of our 3,000 civilian employees.

The only way to go about this, I reasoned, was to lower people in rank and eliminate jobs from top to bottom. This would turn into a game of musical chairs. A lieutenant becomes a sergeant, and a sergeant is demoted to an officer, and those at the bottom—our big affirmative-action crop— would lose their jobs through layoffs.

The prospect truly upset me. *Here I am*, I thought, *a brand-new chief, and I'm being given a scalpel to slit my own throat.* We were already policing the city badly, too short-handed to respond to calls quickly, and now I was supposed to make matters worse. With grim misgivings, I drew up a plan in accordance with the mayor's wishes and sent it off to him.

A few days later, I left town for a three-day retreat with my top staff to plan our management strategy for the coming year. By the end of the first day it became obvious to me and our entire top staff that the layoffs were just ridiculous. They would cause a managerial nightmare. Morale would deteriorate and it would drastically affect overall efficiency. So, with my budget guy and a couple of others, including Police Commissioner Jim Fisk, we hammered out a plan that would save $39 million *without* any layoffs. Needing to get back for my meeting with the Finance Committee of the City Council, I grabbed the plan and rushed off to present it.

According to L.A.'s budget process, the mayor consults with each department's general manager, as he had with me, then presents his budget proposal to the City Council. The Council's various committees hold hearings with the general managers: Do you agree with the mayor's budget for your department? If not, you argue your points. The proposal may be altered and then presented for final approval before the whole City Council. The mayor can veto the budget; the Council can override his veto.

I arrived at Council chambers a few minutes late. I hadn't had time to consult with Bradley about my new plan and I probably should have called him for protocol's sake. But I did reach a second police commissioner, Sal Montenegro. Both Fisk, who had been with me on the retreat, and Montenegro were my bosses and they liked my proposal immensely. Attempting to sound statesmanlike, I told the Finance Committee:

"This is a time when the political leadership ought to get together with the general managers and the labor unions and see if we can't work out a better solution to Proposition 13 than layoffs. Since we really don't know what the fiscal impact is going to be, we should proceed cautiously, working together, and rather than lay people off, we should simply stop hiring."

I pointed out that in the police department, we lose 350 officers a year through attrition. If every department stopped hiring, I suggested, we could mark time and see what the savings were in relation to the reduction in revenues, which would become apparent when the new property-tax bills were sent out later in the year.

"Until we have a better fix on these things, it would be a far less destructive way to go."

I managed to convince both the Finance Committee and the Police, Fire and Public Safety Committee. But when the proposal reached the full Council, Bradley blew his stack.

The mayor stormed into the chambers and alleged that I was the one who had recommended the layoffs and now *I* was reneging. Furiously, he berated me for coming up with this attrition plan.

I was quite shocked; I had no idea I was stepping on his toes. I thought I was doing something significant—offering a plan that would save jobs, not erase them. Furthermore, I was angered by his statement that I had proposed the layoffs. I hadn't. I was only trying to conform to his stated order when I sent him my plan, and I had indicated that I didn't think this new budget was sound.

The chief engineer of the fire department joined me in support of my proposal. Bradley berated us both. Again, I was stunned by his outburst. I had worked with Tom for so many years, when he was a councilman and I was assistant chief, and I had always gotten along with him. But from the time he tried to vote down the Jacobs Plan, I sensed in him a lack of vision. Before he was sworn in as mayor, we spoke. I said, "Tom, one of the things you need to do is get all twenty-six departmental general managers together and build a team. Try to get everybody in a spirit of working together. As it is, everybody goes their own way." Now, in proposing my budget plan, I was trying to make this point again.

When Bradley finally ran out of steam, I took the floor and played another card. It had been bothering me that layoffs would undo our affirmative-action efforts. The first people to be laid off would be those last hired—the minorities. No one seemed to have thought of that. So the week before, I had cooked up my own scheme. I called Harry Caldwell, Houston's chief of police.

"I hear you're hiring down there. Is that right?"

"We sure are, Daryl. We're having a hard time too."

"Well, I'm being forced to lay people off here, if you can believe that," I said, "and they are good people—I mean really top-notch people."

"What if I put out a press notice that Houston will take anyone who is a Los Angeles police officer? Anyone who gets laid off can come here and not even take the exam."

"Would you do that?"

And Harry did. He put out the notice. My motive was to impress the City Council with how desirable LAPD officers were and to force them to think twice about laying any off. "I just want to mention," I said to the Council, "the chief in Houston says he found out we're laying people off and he's willing to take them all."

The City Council sat up straighter. "Tell us about your plan again?"

This made Bradley even angrier. Although he was now the mayor, he continued to regard the LAPD from the same limited viewpoint he'd had when he was on the force. He had served only in a lieutenant's capacity, as a watch commander. His duties were narrow. He oversaw the uniformed people in the Wilshire division during his watch, deploying officers, making sure calls were answered and service was provided where needed. It's an important police function, but it has little to do with the intricacies of managing a major organization. Time and again I would be confronted with fundamental decisions that any good manager would analyze and conclude, "Yeah, that makes sense. Do it." But some of the most basic kinds of things Bradley screwed up because he doesn't understand them.

This struck me when he was a councilman and did not change when he became mayor. For instance, one of the ways of better managing our budget, I thought, was to provide a contingency plan for replacing equipment. Since cars and helicopters have predictable life spans, I tried many times to get the City Council to approve a separate budget for replacing these items. Bradley always refused to. In 1982, I carefully prepared and followed a financial plan designed to save a substantial amount. At mid-year I appeared before the City Council and proudly announced we had already saved $3.5 million. "I would like to use that money for cars," I said.

At Bradley's urging, the City Council voted to take the money *back*.

At times like that, baffled by it all, I walked away shaking my head, thinking, *The guy doesn't understand what I'm talking about*.

His attitude has never changed. Whether out of ignorance or displeasure, he's never given the LAPD enough people. In the early eighties, when the city's chief administrative officer recommended that we cut back on community-based policing, because its decentralized nature represented an inefficient use of deploying officers, Bradley agreed and cut our budget. I maintained the operation as best as I could, believing in its value.

What increases in personnel we've ever gotten have come at election time. Suddenly Bradley would add one hundred police officers in the budget—only he wouldn't give me more money, so I couldn't hire them. Then, to show how much he loved the LAPD, Bradley would circulate this picture of himself in uniform. *It's 100 years old*. But just before an election, the picture runs in all the papers: Mayor Tom Bradley . . . *Lieutenant Tom Bradley!*

In June of 1978, I wasn't so amused. While the City Council was still debating my attrition plan, I was wondering if I would be chief long enough to implement it. I was on a one-year probation and I could be fired without a hearing. Led by the three commissioners who routinely sided with the mayor, the Police Commission reminded me of that. "If you were the general manager of General Motors," one commissioner declared, "you would be fired."

"Well, I'm not the general manager of General Motors," I shot back. "And you *can* fire me if you want to, but I have a charter responsibility to serve the people in the city of Los

Angeles, to manage the police department in the best possible way, and the layoffs being proposed by the mayor are *not* in the best interests of the people, nor the department, and I came up with a better plan.''

That is what really upset them. I *had* come up with a better plan and it made their pal the mayor look bad. I came very close, I think, to losing my job two months after I'd been given it.

In the end I prevailed, and so did my plan. The City Council not only approved attrition for the LAPD, but for all city departments. Not one person was laid off. The city did not go bankrupt.

Still, I always believed the forced reductions in the police department over the next two years were far greater than they had to be because of the mayor's continuing lack of good humor over what I'd done.

From that point on, there began a steady downturn in our relations. I have always had a chief's dislike for the mayor. I think he does a lousy job. And he has said the same of me.

■

Summer came and went; so did autumn. And there were no more strangled bodies. Since February 17, when twenty-year-old Cindy Lee Hudspeth was discovered stuffed in the trunk of her orange Datsun up in the Angeles National Forest, there had been no more bleak headlines: STRANGLER STRIKES AGAIN! Nor had there been any progress in solving the case. In time, the Hillside Strangler Task Force dwindled to a handful of determined detectives.

Then, on January 12, 1979, we got a call from a police officer in Bellingham, Washington. Two co-eds had been strangled and a suspect had been taken into custody. A Kenneth Bianchi. He'd come up to Washington from Glendale eight or nine months before. Did we know anything about him?

I thought, *Imagine that*. This little old burg up there does a job we should have done with all of our expertise, with all of our fabled skill as detectives, with this *huge* task force. A whole series of killings, and he goes up to a little burg like that and they capture the guy through good straightforward detective work. Even though Bianchi left them a lot more clues than he ever left us, I couldn't help but say, "Shit." Then I felt overwhelming relief and gratefulness to the police officers in Bellingham, and the fervent hope that yes, this is the guy, and that once again we were not going to be led down a blind alley.

We weren't. But the road to justice took some peculiar turns. Bianchi was tried and convicted for the two murders in Washington. He was charged with five of the Hillside Strangler killings. But when he was interviewed by a team of psychiatrists, he suddenly developed multiple personalities. Four, I think. One of them, "Steve Walker," admitted *he* had committed the murders, along with Bianchi's cousin Angelo Buono, Jr. Then another personality would recant, re-admit guilt, or change his story altogether. He acted as if he was schizophrenic, which was crap. He was a complete fraud. We turned our attention to Buono.

Right away, we ran into problems. There's such a thing as police evidence: A police officer *knows* a guy did it, but much of the evidence that led to his conclusion isn't ironclad and can't be used in court. Probably 99 percent of the time, when a detective is convinced he knows who did it, he's right. The question becomes, "How do we prove it?"

The first job is to figure out how to put together enough material and facts to convince a prosecutor that the case will hold together in court. Courts don't always deal in truth. They deal in what is admissible as evidence.

Our physical evidence was skimpy. All we had, mainly, were some fibers and hairs. As the preliminary hearing dragged on, week after week, and witness after witness testified, it became obvious the case would have to be carefully woven together, thread by thread, very skillfully.

Unfortunately, Deputy District Attorney Roger Kelly was not the man to do it. To my mind, Kelly wanted to go into court only with pat cases, sure things, with all the T's crossed and the I's dotted. Sometimes a prosecutor has to take a chance. If he's dealing with circumstantial evidence, he has to build his case carefully and it takes an aggressive, hardworking prosecutor to do that. It seemed unlikely Kelly would risk his reputation under the glare of the enormous media attention this trial was bound to attract.

Sure enough, Kelly wanted to try Buono on a rape charge brought by a woman in Arizona, just to get him off the street. Then maybe somewhere down the line, he reasoned, we'd come up with more substantial evidence to try Buono for murder.

I called in my detectives and asked if time would buy us more evidence. This time Grogan was clear in his analysis of the case. "Absolutely not," he said. If anything, time would lose us evidence. Time has a way of eroding the mortar that holds facts together. Memories fade. Mrs. Stofer would become even more skittish.

I phoned Kelly's boss, John Van de Kamp, the district attorney. I knew no one wanted to go forward with this case more than he, and I understood that, according to the information Kelly had given him, John feared he could not win it.

"John," I said, "I know you have confidence in your people, and it's right that you should, but I really think—and I'm giving this to you like a father and a friend—I *really* think you need to look at this much more deeply. I believe you need to go over this case yourself, because I think you're wrong not to try Buono for murder. The facts are there. But it's your judgment call."

Apparently, Van de Kamp remained unconvinced. During the pretrial motions, he moved to drop all murder counts against Buono, due to the flip-flopping testimony of the prosecution's star witness, Bianchi. Superior Court Judge Ronald M. George said he would take the matter under submission and would rule the following week.

That was bad news. Judges routinely accede to motions for dismissal from a prosecutor. If Judge George did this, Angelo Buono would never be tried for murder. The murder charges against Kenneth Bianchi for five of the Hillside Strangler slayings in California had already been dropped. Thirteen families of thirteen victims were never going to see justice done. And Buono would be back on the street in no time.

I was home brooding over this one night when I got a phone call from another judge. This was highly irregular. I don't believe what transpired was improper, it certainly wasn't illegal, but it definitely fell into a gray area. This judge wondered what I thought about the prospects of the murder charges' being dropped.

"It would be a terrible mistake," I replied. "The evidence is there to convict and there is no way we will ever come up with any more."

I told him I believed a case for murder against Buono could be made, but only by a much more aggressive prosecutor than Roger Kelly. I was careful not to criticize John Van de Kamp, but I reiterated that we absolutely, positively could win the case.

I have always assumed the judge in some fashion recounted this conversation to Ronald George, though I cannot prove it.

In any event, to everyone's astonishment, Judge George ruled there was enough evidence for the trial to proceed. The District Attorney withdrew from the case and it was turned over to the state for prosecution by two aggressive deputy attorneys general. Two years later, when the trial finally ended, justice was served. Angelo Buono, Jr., was convicted of nine counts of murder and was sentenced to life imprisonment without the possibility of parole. Kenneth Bianchi, who had been sentenced to life without parole for the two Washington murders, is serving time in Walla Walla Prison.

Once in a while, against all odds, the system actually works.

13

Eulia Love

My day-to-day job as chief shifted from football coach to top executive officer of a large corporation, with turns as dignitary, politician, and crime-solving detective sprinkled throughout.

As coach, I had to provide leadership to almost seven thousand sworn officers and three thousand civilian employees spread across a city fifty miles wide. I had to make sure they were well trained and focused, as any coach would, but what made this task particularly challenging was that police officers function like executives.

Facts are fed to them very quickly. They must determine what the facts mean and what actions those facts suggest they take. Then they must be willing to make those decisions and act on them, for officers can simply go through the motions and there is no way to discern if they have done what they are supposed to. So I not only had to make sure they were prepared to make these difficult decisions, I had to find ways to keep their morale high, making them *want* to do their job.

It was like keeping an army ready to invade every day.

One technique I used was to let my officers know: "I am one of you." For symbolic reasons, I immediately dispensed with the ridiculous dress uniform my predecessors had worn for ceremonial occasions. Instead of appearing in a blaze of brass, I wore a regular officer's uniform and let them know I considered myself a Los Angeles police officer—with a specialized job. Often, I went out into the field in uniform, accompanying officers on patrol, on drug busts, or showing up in Hollywood on Halloween night, when roving crowds often become rowdy.

I ran in departmental relay races and joined the LAPD team when it competed in races with other departments. On Christmas Eve, I visited divisions, took calls, and tried to show I was a working officer too. I wanted officers to know I was not some distant figure, that I was one of them and I cared about them. This gave me credibility, so that if there was a problem, I could talk to them directly. After battles between their union and me, I would drop by various divisions, restore relations, and give my side of the story. If I didn't have a rapport with them, I couldn't have done that.

I also turned up at roll calls, to the astonishment of many. One old sergeant came up to me after such a visit and shook my hand. "No chief has ever come to a roll call before," he said. "I've been on the department twenty-one years and I've never even *met* one before."

At the time, LAPD had this convoluted system for deciding when officers could wear short-sleeved shirts. Every morning we got a meteorological survey for the city, plus another for the San Fernando Valley, which is hotter. We would take the high mean temperature and if it rose to a certain level, we would proclaim: Short sleeves are okay today. Every morning, officers would have to call in to find out what they should wear.

One of the first things I did was to change that. I thought, police officers are grown up, responsible individuals who make dozens of important decisions every day. I realize the other decisions pale in comparison to this one, but it seems to me they ought to be able to decide what to wear.

I also served as personnel director and counselor. I sweated over top-level promotions, dealt with every grievance brought by an officer over a job-performance evaluation or a transfer he or she objected to. I changed policy so that any officer with a problem could write me a letter directly, rather than going through channels; previously, the letter had to be okayed by a sergeant, lieutenant, captain, and bureau chief. Others found, to their delight, that I had a seemingly open door, thanks to my secretary, Mary, who let more stray dogs into my office. It was pathetic.

"Mary—" I would plead.

"But, Chief, he *really* needs to see you."

I also installed a special phone number with an answering machine so that anyone could leave a message overnight, using his or her name or not, to express an opinion. Such as: "Yeah. Well, I think you're a lousy chief."

At the same time, I was operating as a CEO managing a $1 billion-a-year organization. With a budget that size (as it would be by 1990), I had to make sure we had no cost overruns, that we got the most out of our equipment, that we were properly organized, and that we carried out our main task: service to the people.

I had countless people to see. Visiting dignitaries from all over the world stopped in; so did consuls general based in L.A. I had groups like the Chamber of Commerce to call on and school functions that children would invite me to attend. As time went on, I began spending entire chunks of days in court or being deposed. Any citizen who felt he had been wronged by a police officer included my name on the suit. By the end of the decade there would be more than $1 billion in lawsuits at any one time against *me*.

Then there were politicians. Thirty percent of my time, or more, was devoted to politicians and commissions. However independent a character I've been perceived, I always made sure LAPD was responsive to the mayor's and the City Council members' needs. I understood they were elected by the people, and the people expected to be served. Anytime they had a problem, LAPD did everything it could to solve it. "Care and feeding of your local councilman" is how I put it.

I also, obviously, had to stay on top of crime. I was regularly briefed on important cases. I would meet with detectives, listen to their progress, and offer my brilliant suggestions—which, more often than not, I suspect they ignored.

And of course, there were the major disruptions. It was these that would throw a monkey wrench into the smooth running of the department, divert me from my day-to-day duties, grab the headlines, bring activists out of the woodwork, focus citywide attention on the LAPD, and shape the public's image of the department and me. That 6,900 officers might be doing their job very well would get lost in the furor. As I was about to learn.

■

The phone call came just as I was finishing dinner.

After nine months as chief, I had already learned to dread the voice on the other end of the line: Lieutenant Charles Higbie, Robbery Homicide. Sometimes Chuck's calls came in the middle of the night, and the hollow ringing of the telephone usually signaled one of two occurences: Either a police officer had been shot or a citizen had been shot, by a police officer. Chuck never wasted words.

"Chief, late this afternoon two patrol officers in South Central shot a black female. They both emptied their weapons. She's dead."

"They fired *twelve* shots?"

"Yes, sir. Eight of the bullets struck her."

"Oh, shit," I said.

That hardly covered it. But then, no words I knew could have. The terrible shooting of Eulia Love on January 3, 1979, would turn into a powder keg. For the next ten months the city of Los Angeles and the police department would be in utter turmoil, fomented by relentless newspaper stories that played up the facts selectively and turned a mentally unstable woman's death into a nightmare that continues to haunt the black community and the LAPD today.

■

Eulia Mae Love was a thirty-nine-year-old widow with three daughters, two of whom, aged twelve and fifteen, lived with her in a three-bedroom house on South Orchard Avenue, a well-tended street in south central L.A. Her husband had died of sickle-cell anemia six months before and she was paying the bills and the mortgage with a monthly Social Security check of $680.

On the morning of January 3, John Ramirez from the Southern California Gas Company showed up at Mrs. Love's door. She was six months and $69 overdue on her bill. Ramirez told her he would have to receive payment of at least $22, or he would disconnect the service. Immediately, Mrs. Love began yelling profanities at him, Ramirez said. He turned and walked to the gas meter, which was located around to the side of the house, stooped down, and reached for the valve.

Mrs. Love came up behind him with a large, long-handled shovel. When he looked up, she was standing above him with the metal part of the shovel raised above her head. Telling him she wasn't going to allow him to shut off her gas, she screamed several expletives and brought the shovel down. It struck Ramirez on his left forearm, causing a contusion. Mrs. Love raised the shovel, "frothing at the mouth," according to Ramirez, as she prepared to hit him again.

He fled. When he got back to his office, he reported to his boss. The LAPD was called and Ramirez filed an assault-with-a-deadly-weapon report. Meanwhile, Mrs. Love took her Social Security check around the corner to Boy's Market and used it to buy a money order for $22.09.

That afternoon, the gas company dispatched two more men. They arrived at South Orchard Avenue a little after 4:00 P.M., in two separate vehicles. One, a gas company truck, was driven by Robert Aubry, who stopped to call the police dispatcher from a pay phone and asked for an officer to accompany them. Parked several doors down the street, he waited. Mrs. Love, spotting the truck, came out and said to Aubry: "Gas man, are you here to turn my gas off?" Before he could reply, she said, "Those motherfuckers said that I owe them eighty dollars. I'm not paying them any motherfucking eighty dollars."

"I don't know anything about your gas bill," Aubry replied. "I'm just here taking a break."

Mrs. Love started to walk away, then turned. "You guys can suck on my ass. I'll give them twenty dollars, but I'm not going to give them no motherfucking eighty dollars—they can suck my ass." At which point she disappeared into her house.

Three minutes later out she came, clutching an eleven-inch serrated boning knife. Without a word, Mrs. Love began violently slashing branches of a tree on her front lawn. Several fell to the ground.

While this was going on, a call went out from police communications: "Any unit in the vicinity, 415 business dispute, meet the gas man, 11926 South Orchard Avenue, Code 2." Driving west on 120th Street, Officer Edward Hopson nodded to his partner. Lloyd O'Callaghan reached for his radio transmitter and acknowledged the call.

It was 4:15 when the patrol car rolled up beside the Chevy driven by the second gas company man, W. L. Jones.

Pointing across the street to Eulia Love's house, Jones said, "We want the lady to either pay her gas bill or we will cut it off." The officers turned and saw Mrs. Love pacing back and forth with the knife.

"One of our men was out here earlier and she hit him with a shovel when he tried to shut off the gas," Jones added. "A police report was made. Here it is."

While the officers read the report, Mrs. Love yelled, "You're not going to come down to my house and shut off my gas, motherfucking son of a bitch."

Hopson said, "What will you need from us?"

"We would like you stand by while we either collect the money or shut off the gas," Jones replied.

"Wait here."

Officer Hopson drove the car up to the house. Fifteen feet away stood Mrs. Love, five feet four, 175 pounds, flailing her knife. They observed froth coming out of her mouth. As they got out, Hopson, who is black, and O'Callaghan, who is white, both drew their service revolvers.

"You're not coming up on my lawn, motherfuckers," Mrs. Love screamed. "You're not going to shut off my gas."

As she continued to yell obscenities, the officers repeatedly shouted, "Police officers. Drop the knife, lady. We're not here to harm you."

Hopson and O'Callaghan pleaded with her for five minutes, but Mrs. Love wouldn't drop the knife. She began walking toward her house, which was set back along a walk. The officers followed, both with their guns pointed at the ground. They kept repeating, "We won't harm you. Drop the knife." She turned and began walking backward, yelling, "Fuck you! Ain't no motherfucker going to shut off my gas."

Then she stood still. Hopson stopped ten feet from her and raised his gun in both hands, arms outstretched, in a semi-crouched position. O'Callaghan, nearer, stopped too, baton in his left hand, gun in his right hand, pointed at Love. For several seconds they formed this tableau. Then O'Callaghan, using his baton, struck Mrs. Love on her right hand, forcing her to drop the knife. Before he could scramble for it, Mrs. Love swooped down and grabbed it. Holding the blade in her fingers now, she raised her arm and faced O'Callaghan. He was about six feet from her; Hopson, roughly eight. She reared back to throw the knife.

"Don't do it, lady, don't do it!" Hopson shouted.

Eulia Love threw the knife. And that's when they shot her.

I don't know how close the knife came to hitting O'Callaghan, but it sailed sixty-eight feet. I do know it took less than three seconds for the two officers to empty their weapons. Eight bullets struck her. When the ambulance arrived moments later, she was pronounced dead.

"It was not a medal of valor shooting," Chuck Higbie concluded.

And all I could say was "Oh, shit."

■

Most people are unaware that LAPD investigates officer-involved shootings as thoroughly as any homicide, probably more so. Each bullet spent from an officer's gun, no matter what the circumstances, is tracked. Within minutes of a shooting we have people from Robbery Homicide on scene. After the officers involved give the investigators a brief walk-through of what has occurred, they are immediately brought separately to headquarters and interrogated. Then the Officer-Involved Shooting Team, eight officers and a supervisor, goes to work.

No one could question Eulia Love. There was no way to learn what was going on in her head. Why, if she had the money for the gas bill, she didn't just hand over the check.

What made her come out brandishing a knife. Why she didn't turn over the knife to two patrolmen who repeatedly asked her to.

All the Officer-Involved Shooting Team could do was to collect evidence, get statements from five eyewitnesses, accounts from the two officers, and insight from the medical examiner. Once its report was completed, it was sent to the Shooting Review Board. The Board is made up of five deputy chiefs whose job it is to determine if the officers had acted properly or improperly, if the shooting was "in" policy or "out" of policy, according to the department's use-of-force guidelines.

In the case of Eulia Love, four of the Board's five members concluded the officers had fired their weapons in self-defense, which is permissible by law, and so ruled the shooting had been "in" policy.

Assistant Chief Robert Rock reported the decision to me.

Three months had passed since the woman's death and Los Angeles remained in an uproar. The black community in particular was outraged, as once again the trigger-happy LAPD had ridden into their streets, guns smoking. At one loud and emotional City Council meeting, a group of black ministers came forward and just blasted the department. I had been spending a lot of time developing friendships among the black leadership, speaking to black groups whenever I could. Now I sat there, terribly disheartened, listening to them call us racists. And I thought, from this one unfortunate incident, how could they generalize like that?

To me, it was another significant display of the lack of thoughtful black leadership that stretched back to Parker's day. Because Eulia Love was black, they had turned this terrible shooting into a racial issue, when if she had been white, the issue never would have been raised, even though one of the officers who shot her was black.

Racial sensitivities were high. Court-ordered school busing had sent many white families fleeing into the Valley. In an interview with James H. Cleaver, the executive editor of the L.A. Sentinel, a paper with a predominantly black readership, I said, "I only wish I could reach in and wave a wand and change all of the social injustices in the world and people's attitudes, but I can't do that. Nor can anyone except God.''

The media tried to. Moral indignation became editorial policy. Jim Bellows, the smart, aggressive editor of the *Los Angeles Herald Examiner*, the money-losing number-two paper in town, needed a way to boost sales and must have gone for what he saw as a real opportunity. All the pathos of the situation, all the horror was retold daily in the *Herald*. Virtually every story began with the same graphic picture of a poor widow who was down on her luck, couldn't afford to pay her gas bill, children were going to go hungry because they wouldn't be able to light the stove, and of course it was winter, so it was cold; there would be no heat. *Then,* right in front of her horrified daughters, the police charged up and killed her . . . *for failing to pay the gas bill.*

The *Los Angeles Times* pretty much avoided the story until mid-April. Among blacks especially, the feeling was that the paper's traditional attitude was to ignore most stories in the black community on the theory that *those* people didn't read the paper anyway and the rest of its readership couldn't have cared less. But when the national media picked up the scent, suddenly, the *Times* jumped on the story too. In its usual methodical way, the *Times* began to chronicle every nuance of the episode, enthusiastically adding to the furor.

In this charged atmosphere of angry politicians and crusading journalists, I agonized over the Shooting Review Board's ruling. As chief, I could overturn it. I sensed the enormous political opportunity, for to do so, I knew, would win me the support of the black leadership and perhaps the city—until the next crisis. But it would make me suspect as a leader to many in the LAPD. Police officers possess an uncanny instinct for sensing when leadership has ''rolled over,'' and they would see me as caving in to public sentiment. To lose the respect of my officers so early in the game would cripple me severely. Whatever I did, it would be a no-win situation. I could be a hero to the community or a leader to LAPD, but I couldn't be both.

Frame by frame, as if analyzing a film, I reviewed the facts. It was a terrible shooting. Prompted by the sight of this woman brandishing a knife, and knowing of her prior assault with a shovel, O'Callaghan had come out of the patrol car with his weapon drawn. That was his first *serious* mistake. He should never have used his weaker left hand to bat the knife away from the woman. A stronger whack, and he might have had a chance to recover the knife. LAPD training teaches you that if you are right-handed, you must always use that hand to wield a baton. O'Callaghan couldn't; his gun was in his right hand.

Having knocked the knife out of her hand, he didn't retrieve it. Both officers should have rushed her. Instead, they jumped back. Clearly, they had a woman who was frightening to behold, 175 pounds, snarling, screaming invective, menacing them with an eleven-inch knife. This was hardly the poor widow portrayed in the *Herald*, but an out-of-control woman with a history of mental problems, who was threatening to kill anybody who came near her.

O'Callaghan, six feet tall and two hundred pounds, was a karate expert. Both officers were perfectly capable of taking care of themselves and they should not have been cowed by this woman. Officers meet this kind of person all the time. Sometimes you just have to wade in, knowing you're likely to get cut, and hope it won't be fatal.

These officers did not. As she raised her arm to throw, O'Callaghan, six or eight feet away, and envisioning the boning knife embedded in his chest, turned sideways to avoid it. He fired without looking at her. Hopson, seeing his partner shoot, emptied his gun too.

The emptying of the guns, known as rapid-fire syndrome, was not uncommon, and in fact was the method we taught for close-encounter situations. Rapid-fire is almost an instinctive reaction, especially in a stress situation. Often, I've asked an officer: "How many times did you shoot?" And he would reply, "Twice." When I'd check his gun, it would be empty. The brain, under stress, keeps no accurate diary of what has transpired.

Because of Eulia Love, LAPD now teaches shot assessment instead. Officers learn to shoot a couple of bullets, then assess those shots before firing again.

But reviewing the case that April, I was convinced the situation was so tense, the action so fast, that neither one was concentrating on his fire. Their shots were all over the place—and they'd been *trained*. At that range, their shots should have been bull's-eyes. Instead, twelve shots, only one striking her in the chest, the fatal one.

Any way you viewed it, it was a bad shooting. Everyone in the department knew it was. To themselves, officers were saying, "Hell, had it been *me*, I wouldn't have shot her. No woman with a knife is gonna cause *me* to shoot. I'd somehow take that damn knife away from her. Thought of something else."

Police officers *are* flexible, but that flexibility comes from continuous training. Each division has a training coordinator who devises a series of training sessions taught monthly at roll call. Officers learn, or are reminded of, self-defense procedures, use-of-force policies, how to approach different situations, changes in the laws—such as search and seizure. In addition, we run "schools" for vice, detectives, tactical training, homicide, gangs, robbery, check forging, traffic enforcement, traffic investigations, and night shooting, to name but a few. There are seminars run by POST—Peace Officers Standards & Training—which sets training standards for the state of California. Other law-enforcement groups run seminars or schools, too.

Each time an officer is promoted he studies hard for the test, which is designed to be used as another training tool. Once promoted, he goes back to the Academy for sergeant's school, lieutenant's school, and so on. The schools last one to three weeks. Most officers who want to advance within the department attend night school as well, working toward advanced degrees, perhaps in business or law. LAPD officers never stop receiving instruction. We are not, despite what some people may believe, a bunch of Neanderthals taught only to shoot and bash heads.

So O'Callaghan and Hopson should have been able to come up with a better course of action. Or so most of their fellow officers thought. Yet once they had gotten themselves into that situation, confronted by a woman rearing back to throw a knife, the law clearly stated they could shoot in self-defense.

I went to the scene and walked off the action. I staged a demonstration with female civilian employees to see if any could hurl a knife sixty-eight feet. They all did. I then stood six feet in front of one of them, trying to envision how O'Callaghan might have felt. I had the woman throw a stick at me. Even though I knew it was coming, and tried to move out of the way, it still hit me dead-center in the chest just as I simulated getting off my shots.

Still agonizing over what to do, I went to see Assistant Chief Robert Rock, to whom the Shooting Review Board had reported.

"Look," he said, "I know this is going to put you in an awful situation, and if you want to change our decision, go right ahead. But when you get right down to the shooting, O'Callaghan and Hopson conformed to both the law and the policy of this department. They shot in self-defense."

I left his office torn. Either I could follow the rules as the LAPD set them down, an inner voice prompted, or I could not; either I was a person of principle or I was not.

But it was not that simple. It was not just determining the shooting "out of policy." The community, which I served, was demanding the officers be punished. The community had already convicted the officers. Next would come the lynching. The LAPD, which I ran, was critical of the shooting, too, and probably would not have objected had I overruled the Shooting Review Board. But I was trapped inside my own dilemma: My moral judgment and my political judgment were diametrically opposed. My moral judgment—that I uphold the rules of the LAPD—was further complicated by the fact that it was a bad shooting.

Then a second voice began to nag: "Hey, I'm the new chief of police and what an opportunity. I can step forward right now and be a hero. Why, overnight, the media would shine down upon me and say, 'By golly, there's an extraordinary chief with a lot of strength.' "

But the truth is, I wouldn't have been. I'd have started on the road to compromise—glory for me, oblivion for those officers. Besides, what if the knife had torn into O'Callaghan's chest? Would the *Herald* and the *Times* have been up in arms over that? One paragraph maybe. Another cop killed in the line of duty.

I thought: *Let the politicians go out and appease their interest groups*. I had to follow my own imperatives. As a disciple of Bill Parker, I knew that all other considerations were extraneous. My job was not to make friends but to run a police department. Parker used to say, "If I have a friend as chief, it's purely accidental."

I knew in the end I had to follow the principles and the values of the LAPD. I wouldn't have been able to live with myself otherwise.

◾

"We found the shootings to be 'in' policy," I announced. "None of us thinks it's a wonderful shooting. We will change our training; we will do everything in our power to make sure it never happens again. But the shooting *is* 'in' policy."

The announcement rang like a call to arms throughout the city. Once again, the community jumped all over my back and the media rockets went off anew.

A newspaper war broke out, with both the *Herald* and the *Times* harping on the emotional aspects rather than the factual ones. The story, gripping to begin with, was made all the juicier by this bloodthirsty chief of police defending his brutal officers who were out there needlessly taking this poor woman's life. Both papers, in their game of one-upsmanship, lost control and became hysterical. Instead of dutifully reporting a story to the public, they charged off on a frenzied crusade.

A cartoon by the *Herald*'s Bill Schorr summed it up. A little black girl hails a passing squad car. "Quick, officer, get my kitty outta that tree!" Next panel: "Blam! Blam!" The officer shoots the cat.

◾

Within weeks of my announcement, the district attorney made one of his own. After a careful investigation by his office into the shooting, no criminal charges would be filed against the two police officers, he said.

Even this did not quell the tempest. Dissatisfied with both our decisions, the Police Commission declared it would conduct an investigation of its own. Then the mayor jumped in. "The officers who killed Mrs. Love could have avoided the shooting," he pronounced. "Such incidents could lead to another Watts riot."

Was he serious? "Such incidents could lead to another

Watts riot"? How could the mayor of Los Angeles do something so potentially dangerous as even to suggest violence? I was dumbfounded.

The attacks continued, as the city figuratively stormed the LAPD, hurling anger and accusations. Instinctively, my defense of the officers became more strident, and the more strident I became, the more strident the opposition became.

I had little going for me. *I* didn't have a newspaper, or a television station. I had no one outside the department to support me, and few within it did so vigorously. I don't know anyone except my wife and my office staff who defended me, and I think sometimes even Sam questioned what I'd done. The top LAPD brass *said* it supported me, but some of them sounded a little bit squishy.

Ultimately, it became another discouraging episode of Us Against Them. It's human nature; you cannot batter the psyche of an organization without its rearing on its hind legs. Confronted by growing criticism, officers who had started out saying "*I* wouldn't have shot her" were now saying "Why, those officers did exactly what they had to do, and if I were there, I'd have shot her too!"

So out the window went our plan to use the Eulia Love incident as a classic training example of how never to get involved in a shooting like that again. Any officer who was here at the time will tell you: "Hell, yes, Eulia Love deserved to be shot"—which was terrible. It turned into a total reversal of what the attitude had been at the outset.

I was just as bad. Because of all the attacks on me, I went on the attack myself.

■

On October 3, the Police Commission announced its findings. The shooting of Eulia Love, it declared, *did* violate LAPD policies on the use of firearms and deadly force and it was the result of serious errors in judgment and tactics by the officers involved. But, it concluded, since I had already ruled that no disciplinary action would be taken, any action now would violate the officers' rights of due process.

Some in the city were astonished. For decades the Police Commission had been accused by editorial writers and community activists of being a rubber stamp for the police

Lowell, Steve and me with our mom, around 1940

With Lowell and Steve, 1943.

"The Bear," 1949, the year I joined the LAPD

My mother, Arvilla, during a trip to Hawaii in 1955 to see Steve, who was stationed there by the navy

My dad, Paul, with my son, Scott

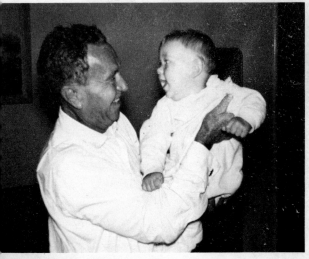

The day I was appointed captain of police. The uniform is a joke, of course.

President John F. Kennedy with Chief Parker (center) and Jim Hamilton, captain of the Intelligence Division just before I succeeded to that post.

One of the many press conferences I held on the
Hillside Strangler, December 22, 1977

With Sam at my swearing-in
as chief, March 28, 1979

THE OLYMPICS, 1984

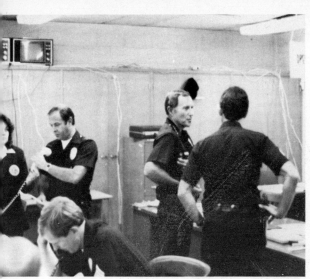

Inside the Emergency Operations Center

The smiling, friendly face of the LAPD

Parker Center

SID Photo Lab, LAPD

With Vice President Bush, 1988

Frank Giles, LAPD

Going out on a drug bust with First Lady Nancy Reagan

With a bunch of DARE kids

At the LAPD party marking my forty years of service, September 1989. The man with the cigar is retired commander Ken McCauley, who first interviewed me for admission to the Police Academy.

Presenting Officer Randy Marshall's badge to his daughters after he was killed in the line of duty

Daughter Kathy
and her husband,
Sam Perricone, Jr.

Daughter Debby
and her husband,
Danny Ladesma

Son, Scott

A recent picture with my "little" brother Steve, who has over thirty years in the LAPD

With Mayor T. Bradley at an Operation Hammer roll call

One of the more flattering portraits of me in the *Los Angeles Times*

department—its fan club rather than its overseer. This was never true. But under the manipulations of Tom Bradley, the Commission began wielding a big stick. Even the *L.A. Times* took note, pointing out that the five Commission members were staunch Bradley supporters and that the commissioners "have been more liberal, more questioning and more critical. They also are more political."

Former Chief Ed Davis was, typically, even more blunt. The Commission, he noted, "has just been one of suspicion and hostility, faithful to the cold, critical attitude of the mayor."

At its next meeting, the Commission's rhetoric escalated. Lieutenant George Aliano, as head of the Police Protective League, the union for most of the LAPD's sworn officers, presented a petition signed by 4,363 officers, declaring no confidence in the Police Commission. Before he could sit down, Commissioner Jim Fisk grabbed the floor and called me two-faced.

"The real issue here," declared Fisk, "is that the chief of police has failed to say publicly what he has said privately. From the very first statement made by the chief in executive session, his feelings were strong about it being a poor shooting. The Commission's findings, in essence, are consistent with the position taken by the chief of police from the very beginning. Why not say publicly what he has said privately?"

Then, before I could respond, out lashed Reva Tooley, the newest commissioner. "Daryl, you have said to me privately, in the presence of others, that you thought Eulia Love was a bad shooting. Privately you said this shooting did not have the stamp of approval of the Los Angeles police department. Yet publicly you have given it the stamp of approval."

I could not believe this. Yes, I had told the Commission, *privately*, that it was not a model shooting, and that had it been me, I would not have shot Eulia Love. But I also said that without question, this shooting was within the law. Even the district attorney had agreed.

All I'd been trying to do, *privately*, was express my feelings as a human being. To take those private remarks and misconstrue them in public was one of the lowest blows

I'd seen. I vowed I would never tell this Commission another thing in private session, would never level with them again. They had revoked my trust.

"I think we ought to end debate on this Eulia Love issue," I finally said. "I'd like to see it stop—let's get over it. If you want to do it with another chief of police, then why don't you tell me?"

There was a stunned silence. Then—shockingly—a burst of applause. I turned. The several dozen police officers who'd come to support Aliano's petition had jumped to their feet.

"Way to go, Chief!" one of them called as I walked out.

∎

No heroes emerge from this story, only victims. O'Callaghan wound up getting a stress pension. He'll never be the same. After talking to him I understood how this big, tough karate expert got himself into such a mess. He was a devout Catholic who wouldn't hurt a fly. He had no aggressive nature at all. Because he was so inwardly concerned about the welfare of people and fearful of hurting people, I think he didn't use his baton as forcefully as he should have; he didn't want to hurt her. The shooting, the publicity, and the lynch-mob mentality just ate at him, tore at him. He spent his own money to write a book to give his side of the story. But nobody bought it—the book or his story.

Apparently, Hopson wasn't as shaken. He stayed on the force and only recently retired. Perhaps because he is black, like Eulia Love, he didn't have to torment himself over whether he was guilty of racism and this allowed him to assess the situation correctly. "Hey, this woman's gonna kill my partner, so I shot her."

When he retired recently, he sent me a note. I probably didn't remember him, he wrote, but he would always remember me. I was the only person in the city who had supported his action.

Time did not erase the scars on the department either. The next September, 1980, in anticipation of an upcoming

Dallas episode that would reveal who shot J. R. Ewing, the *Herald* ran a now-famous Bill Schorr cartoon. It featured three likenesses. Sue Ellen, Cliff Barnes, and a Los Angeles police officer.

The caption read: WHO SHOT J. R.?

14

Internal Affairs

On Sunday, December 6, 1981, I fell asleep expecting that sometime in the night my phone would ring. If it did, it would mean that our sting operation had been a success. If it failed, they would probably be nice to me and wait till 6:30 A.M. to deliver the news. For once, I hoped our mission would fail.

This was no ordinary sting.

The plot was common enough: Cops hoping to trap a pair of bad guys, in this case burglars, who preyed upon video stores in Hollywood. For nearly three months we had been gathering information, but we still lacked strong, irrefutable evidence. The only way to get it was to catch the burglars in the act. If our setup worked, the suspects would be arrested holding the loot.

What made this operation unusual is that the bad guys, Jack Myers and Ronald Venegas, were LAPD officers working the morning watch out of Hollywood division. The sting was being run by Internal Affairs.

As chief, I am responsible for the actions of my officers. But with a roster that ranged from 6,800 to 8,400 during my tenure, I could not, obviously, check up on each. I didn't even know most. In an organization this big, drawn from the population at large—and not from a perfect planet in outer space—some officers are going to have trouble; others are going to cause it. The best I could do was assign talented people to the ranks of captain and commander and hope the deputy chiefs they answered to would be alert. The deputy chiefs reported to me. So did Internal Affairs.

Internal Affairs is the division that polices the police. Various characterizations of it have been depicted on TV and in the movies, but rarely with a whole lot of accuracy. We aren't secretive about who's working in Internal Affairs, nor do we spy on one another without damn good reason. And unlike Richard Gere in that deplorable movie *Internal Affairs*, we don't beat each other up. The boring truth is, Internal Affairs people are very professional, exceedingly polite—and have absolutely no sense of humor. They come from the Jack Webb-*Dragnet* school of "Just the facts, ma'am" . . . *boom,* boom, boom, boom. They are courteous to a fault.

Still, it is a worrisome thing to be contacted by Internal Affairs division, as almost every police officer is at least once in his or her career. IAD must check out every complaint against a police officer, whether from an angry citizen or an officer suspicious of his partner. When it happens to you, you feel the same way a motorist does when he sees the black-and-white loom up behind him, red lights flashing. *Oh, my God, what'd I do?* Suddenly you are overwhelmed with guilt. *Well, I must have done* something.

An IAD investigation into a complaint can be resolved in four ways. "Unfounded"—meaning there was absolutely no substance to the complaint at all. "Exonerated"—the officer's actions were proper and legal. "Not sustained"—it can't be proved either way. And "Sustained"—the preponderance of evidence supports the complaint. Of the thousand complaints IAD investigates in an average year, usually fewer than half are sustained. Disciplinary actions range from admonishment to suspension for days, weeks, or months, without pay. Some officers I fire, roughly fifteen to thirty a year.

Most of the complaints are routine. When they're not,

they attract huge attention; the police are supposed to uphold the law, not break it—and the whole department is unfairly branded along with the errant officer. But like the average citizen, some police officers will try to get away with things that they shouldn't. Sometimes they try to get away with murder.

There was a case, some years ago, concerning a patrol officer who responded to a domestic dispute call. After the problem had been settled, the man involved in the dispute told Officer Keith Moser about the pressure he'd been under lately, how angry he was at his partner, something about a lot of money figuring in. Moser listened sympathetically and left. Later he phoned the man.

"Look, I've been thinking about your trouble and if there's any way I can help . . . on the side I do some private investigating . . . so maybe I can help you in some fashion."

"Yeah, well, if you'd get rid of my partner, that'd be the easiest thing and save me a lot of money," the man grumbled.

There was a pause. "It's possible," Moser said.

After he hung up, the man thought, *Christ, I was just kidding. What's that cop talking about?*

Officer Moser then returned to the man's house and said, "You're thinking about getting rid of your partner? It can be arranged, but it'll cost a few bucks."

Now the man was concerned, so he got in touch with Internal Affairs. They didn't like the story either, but they suggested the man play along with the officer.

Ensuing phone calls between the man and Moser established a price of $80,000 to get rid of the partner. Internal Affairs put together a bundle of bills and gave it to the man in a suitcase.

The sting operation was set. Moser, who worked out of Wilshire division, told the man to meet him in a parking lot in Hollywood. And I swear, this officer showed up in a black-and-white, *in uniform*. He slipped into the man's car.

The man was wired. But—and this is the stuff you don't see on TV—the wire didn't work very well. In fact, wires almost never work. But we were videotaping the whole thing too. The man had been coached what to say.

"What're you gonna do with my partner?"

"Don't have to worry about it—you'll never see him again."

This was followed by a little discussion, the guy expressing anger at the partner. And Moser saying, "Don't worry, he won't go easily," even hinting at some torture.

Finally, Moser got out of the car, taking the suitcase of money. Internal Affairs was on him in a flash. Right out in public they spread-eagled this uniformed officer on the ground, like a common suspect, handcuffed him, and hauled him away.

At his criminal trial, Keith Moser was convicted of grand theft, but not conspiracy to commit murder. The jury believed his defense that he was only playing along with the man in an effort to implicate *him*. Before we could ask a Board of Rights to recommend removal, Moser resigned.

■

Such episodes are rare. More typically, police officers will be caught in lapses of conduct. Many of those lapses come during morning watch, the 11:00 P.M. to 7:00 A.M. shift, and after 2:00 A.M. in particular. By then the streets have died down and the bars are closed. By 3:00, the people running the nightspots are on their way home. Traffic becomes sparse. The police have the run of the streets.

Police departments across the country have experienced a variety of problems on morning watch. It seems to be a time, universally, when police officers can get themselves into trouble. With little demand for their services, they can slip away to visit a girlfriend, or go to sleep. The clever gambits that officers think up to fool their supervisors are amazing. When I was working Juvenile, I had a partner, the damnedest guy I ever saw. He had four kids and two off-duty jobs. He was really a fine police officer—never missed a call—but he didn't want to go on patrol. Understandably, he wanted to sleep.

He'd say, "Gee, I'm really tired tonight," and I would make a deal with him. I'd say, "Okay, I'll drive, and you can sit there and look like you're observing and close your eyes and I'll do the patrolling. I'll wake you when we have a call." Some of his other partners, I knew, would pull off somewhere and sleep right along with him.

Like opponents in a chess game, supervisors try to match officers, gambit for gambit. They check the mileage when officers go out and again when they come in. It's a good indication of whether they've been working or not. One story circulated about a guy whose friend had a lube rack, and he would raise the car up on the rack, or just jack up the wheels, switch the motor on, and put the car into gear. The officer dozed and the odometer ran. Problem is, you can't make the wheels go fast enough to put on enough miles, plus you run the risk of getting asphyxiated. Many such stories have been picked up by Joseph Wambaugh in his novels, and whether they're true or myths, who can say?

What is true is that morning watch will attract those officers who don't want to do much work. They might be people who have other jobs during the day and police work takes a back seat to that. Most of the command staff works daytime hours, so there's only a skeletal supervisory staff of one lieutenant at every division and a few sergeants. Mostly the sergeants are catching up on paperwork and not backing up calls on the street. Off-hours inspections by captains are made with frequency, but not frequent enough to get the feel of the watch.

■

In 1981, supervision of the morning watch in Hollywood division was nonexistent. Police work was simply not being conducted. On the morning watch, it had come to a screeching halt.

The geographical Hollywood is a section of Los Angeles, northwest of downtown, where, in the early 1900s, the first movie studios were born. Most have since moved—to Burbank, Culver City, Century City—or were never located there to begin with, but the name Hollywood still signifies America's movie capital to much of the world.

The area had its heyday in the thirties and forties, when the studios were churning out glamorous stars and movies that somehow seemed magical. The streets reflected that magic. All along Hollywood Boulevard were elegant theaters: Grauman's Chinese, with its legendary footprints, and the Egyptian, where on any night of the week the klieg lights might have signaled a star-studded premiere of a new film.

There were restaurants like the Brown Derby, and night-clubs with big-band music, where celebrities dropped in to be noticed. But that Hollywood began to disappear in the fifties.

In time, the area deteriorated into one of the sleaziest, slimiest parts of the city. The theaters and businesses had slipped, replaced by porn palaces and prostitutes—male and female—and the people on the streets were largely thieves, robbers, con artists, weirdos, drug dealers, and tourists who didn't know any better. Car thefts were among the highest in the city. No woman could walk Hollywood Boulevard without being accosted. A woman fifty-five years old with grocery bags would be hustled, since it was automatically assumed that any female on the street was a hooker.

As we moved into the eighties, an effort was begun to revitalize the area and drive the bad elements out. The main bad elements were still the massage parlors—a fancy name for houses of prostitution.

Several years before, Ed Davis and I had taken a crack at doing something about that.

Right in front of a massage parlor, a squad car would be parked. The uniformed officer would walk a foot beat—back and forth, back and forth—from one end of the massage parlor doorway to the other. Some guy would walk up and the officer would say, "Hi, how are you?" Then, friendly soul that he was: "Say, what's your name?" It was amazing how many customers suddenly remembered they had to be elsewhere and scrammed.

The city attorney informed me that this ploy was clearly an act of harassment.

"Right," I said. "And I don't care."

To some, it became another example of the LAPD's bordering on civilly improper practices, if not restraint of trade—things we could clearly be sued over. I refused to back down. And the job got done. By the early eighties, Western Avenue, Vermont, up along Sunset and Hollywood Boulevards, areas that had been rife with massage parlors, didn't have them anymore.

We were not entirely successful in Hollywood. Prostitution is still rampant, though less pervasive than it was (the ACLU never tires of accusing us of sex discrimination, claiming we arrest more women than men, no matter how many tricks we pick up) and the area continues to attract fringe people like a magnet. All the kooks in the world pass through Hollywood, and seeing what walks up and down the sidewalks is a sight to behold. Somehow even the sight becomes part of the magnetism.

And the magnetism affects police officers.

If you were to look at the number of officers who have gotten in trouble, either domestically or with the department, Hollywood division would be way up at the top. There is something about the place—an almost carnival atmosphere that suggests "here, anything goes"—that causes good people to deviate from their normal conduct and their values. So you've got to have officers out there with a great deal of moral conviction and strength, willing to stay on the right track and keep others on the right track.

Jack Myers and Ronald Venegas were two who got sidetracked.

Veteran officers, they worked the morning watch, assigned to a Code 30 car. "Code 30" means a burglar alarm has gone off. At one time burglar alarm was a Code 2, which meant "Get there right away because there's a burglar." But we learned from experience that when a burglar alarm goes off, 97 percent of the time it's a false alarm. So we invented Code 30—"We'll get there when we can."

Myers and Venegas, patrolling the empty streets, would get a Code 30 over the radio and respond. A store had been broken into. They would enter, and before calling the owner with the bad news, they would pick up some merchandise— not much, just a little—and put it in the trunk of their patrol car; maybe find some loose cash lying around, take that too.

Some of the burglarized stores carried merchandise that didn't interest the officers. So they came up with the idea of setting off alarms themselves. They would fire marbles from a slingshot, hitting the store window and jarring the glass, which set off the alarm. Then they would jump back in the car and drive around until the call came over the radio: "Code 30."

Back to the store they would go. Wanting to simulate a burglary, they would smash a window or use a pry bar to open the door. One of them would do what he was supposed to do, call the owner, call the alarm company, wait for the owner to show up. Meantime, working very quickly, the partner would load up the trunk with merchandise and drive over to Hollywood station, where he would transfer the goods to the trunk of his own car. Then he would race back to the store and commiserate with the poor owner.

Their specialty became video stores. They never took expensive electronic equipment, only cassettes. They both built up libraries of several hundred films.

Through an FBI informant, Internal Affairs got word that Myers and Venegas were staging these video store robberies. When I was told, I took it with a grain of salt. You get this kind of information periodically, stories of police officers engaged in some nefarious activity, and most of the time there's nothing to it. I thought, "Nah, nothing like that would happen here."

■

The sting was set for 1:00 A.M.

A store called Audio-Video Craft on Melrose was the planned target. With the owner's consent the store was made to look as though a burglary had just occurred. To tempt Myers and Venegas even more, $673 in marked bills and money dusted with ultraviolet powder was left conspicuously lying around.

Outside, we had our lookout post in a van outfitted with listening devices, parked at a vantage point where the officers could look through binoculars and see into the store. Several patrol cars and a dozen officers were in the area ready to pounce. A helicopter patrolled overhead. Elsewhere in the city, police officers had been alerted to be ready to go to work.

At 1:00, Myers and Venegas heard a "Code 30" over their radio, assigned to Unit 6Z5—them.

They appeared nervous. Maybe they were worried that over time someone had become aware of their activities. Or maybe some sixth sense on that night made them wary. For a while it did not appear they were going to do anything but go into the store, conduct their preliminary investigation, and leave.

But their innate greed got the best of them. Our guys

were smart to leave the money out in the open. It was just too much for them. They *had* to pick up that money. And finally, they could not resist the video tapes.

Over the next two hours of surveillance, Myers and Venegas were seen putting several video cassettes in the trunk of their car and under the front seat. On one trip, however, one of them spotted the van in the alley and he went over to take a look. He tried to see inside, but the van had no windows in the back and the doors were locked.

At 3:30 A.M., after saying good-night to the store owner, they left.

But before they could reach their patrol car, a plain-clothes sergeant from Internal Affairs jumped out, flashed his badge, and shouted, "Police! Internal Affairs! Keep your hands away from your weapons. You're under arrest."

∎

At four o'clock the phone rang.

I have a unique ability to wake up from a very sound sleep, almost on the first ring. And I can get all the details and fall right back to sleep.

Sam can't. Once awakened, she never goes back to sleep. So when the phone rang, out would come all this terrible language. I never learned to swear quite the way Sam does (though she has reformed *considerably*). Finally, I moved the phone into another room, so whoever called wouldn't have to hear all this cussing in the background.

This time, after hanging up I couldn't go back to sleep. I felt as if my blood had literally started to boil. For me, something I hoped never would be true *was* true, and I found myself going through this whole process of terrible anger and wanting vengeance and finally sadness—the mixture of emotions I feel when I find a police officer has done something seriously wrong.

And those emotions continued to surge. The arrests of Myers and Venegas were only the tip of the iceberg. As they were interrogated into the night at Parker Center, they began to implicate other officers who were involved in similar thefts and robberies. By breakfast time, Internal Affairs was already knocking on doors with search warrants in hand. They hauled in eight or nine more officers.

By the time the eleven-month investigation was completed, we had turned up a rat's nest of wrongdoing in Hollywood. It wasn't just stealing. All kinds of things were going on that indicated a total breakdown in discipline and a loosening of values, the very safeguards intended to keep the seeds of corruption out.

In Hollywood the seeds had been planted and we were growing a real lush crop.

One group of officers caught met after work at a location they called "The Tree." The British have pubs next to their station houses, but we don't in L.A. So these officers manufactured their own. It was nothing more than a parking lot up in Griffith Park, part of which extends into Hollywood. Kind of dumb, I always thought, to stand around in the cold and drink beer at seven-thirty in the morning. For company, they brought up prostitutes who entertained them with sex acts.

One guy, Sergeant Roger Gibson, *on duty,* had gone to a house in the Hollywood Hills where a party was in progress. He parked his patrol car, took off his uniform, and jumped into the hot tub with naked women. When a call came out for a supervisor, he didn't respond, because he was in the hot tub. He was charged with eighteen counts of misconduct and found guilty on thirteen counts. We fired him.

Myers and Venegas continued to talk into 1982. On May 11, Jack Myers struck a deal with LAPD and the L.A. County district attorney's office to identify all other officers in the on-duty burglary ring. In return, he would plead no contest to one count of burglary and receive no more than a year in the county jail. In a similar plea bargain Venegas pleaded guilty to burglary and was given probation. Both resigned from the department.

Around five the next morning, Myers was driving on the Simi Valley Freeway, en route to a truck driver's school he was attending, when his Chevy Blazer careened off the road at fifty-five miles an hour and flipped over. Myers was hurled out of the truck and thrown fifty feet, landing on his head. He was killed instantly.

As suspicious as the accident appeared, nobody could prove wrongdoing. No other vehicles were involved and nothing was the matter with the truck. An autopsy did reveal that Myers had ingested lethal levels of Darvon, toxic levels of an antidepressant called Doxepin, and trace levels of codeine. Even without the accident, the autopsy report said, the drugs might have killed him.

In the end, we fired or accepted the resignations of twelve officers for burglary, theft, receiving stolen property, sexual relationships with prostitutes, and other serious neglects of duty. Another fifteen officers were charged with various allegations of neglect of duty or unbecoming conduct and were punished.

The commander of Hollywood division took early retirement rather than accept a demotion. I brought in an iron disciplinarian, Robert Smitson, and two no-nonsense captains. Internal Affairs interviewed every one of the 250 officers in the division. Some were transferred out; new blood was shipped in. I reviewed our internal processes and tried to strengthen them.

■

In any other police department, the Hollywood burglary scandal might have been regarded as no big deal; it involved only twelve officers and there were no large payoffs, just small-time stuff.

I saw it differently. The big deal here was the tremendous loss of trust and faith from the public. That the very people they counted on to protect them from burglars *were* burglars. No matter how anyone looked at it, the running of Hollywood division had been my responsibility. Vague reports of laxness had come to my attention, and I had begun to move people in to take a look. But I hadn't responded fast enough, nor sensed the extent of the trouble.

For a long time I stuck pins in myself—"How come I allowed this? How come I didn't know?" I could come up with no answers. But from then on, I learned to be more cautious in trusting the ranking officers I had previously assumed I could trust.

The episode produced the predictable humor. "What does your father do?" "Oh, he's a burglar for the LAPD."

Every time Johnny Carson told a joke like that, I winced.

15

Take This Badge and Shove It

I had been on the job four years now, four of the five I had set out for myself when I took it. But with the 1984 Olympics slated for Los Angeles, I adjusted my timetable to see them through. After that I would find something else to do. I was acutely aware that you could become very ill being chief of police.

So far, I had managed the pressures. I did not bring war stories home to Sam. I worked out with weights every other day, I ran six miles almost every night, and fortunately, I was always able to sleep. But the pressures never relented. Although I functioned like a chief executive officer, many times I wished I functioned like one in the corporate world. In business, things get settled and conflicts get resolved: The new product gets the go-ahead or it doesn't; the marketing plan is approved, amended or shot down; the public either buys the product or ignores it.

In society there is no such closure. Conflicts go on and on until something in society changes. The pace is glacial, and in the meantime the chief has to deal with them. It's like walking a tightrope, buffeted by unpredictable gusts from unexpected quarters.

During the next two years, 1982 and 1983, the gusts would become gale force.

■

Inside Parker Center we had been reviewing for some time methods of subduing violent citizens. Always on the lookout for better tactics, LAPD does considerable research and development on its own, as well as studying what the military and private industry are doing. Still, the perfect method had not been found. In a country that historically has been at the forefront of designing weapons that kill, little effort is made to find safe ways to subdue.

The tactic of choice among police departments at the time—upper-body control holds, dubbed "chokeholds"—had always been a problematic tool. One version, the modified carotid, was most effective. Applied correctly, from behind, a police officer places his bicep and forearm on either side of the suspect's neck, pressing the carotid arteries and cutting off the flow of blood to the brain for a split second. The individual goes limp. You handcuff him and cart him off to jail. We felt this control hold was far superior to banging someone over the head with a PR-42 baton.

But there was a second version of the chokehold, called the bar-arm control hold. An officer places his forearm across the trachea, cutting off the supply of oxygen to the lungs. The problem with this hold is that a person instinctively fights harder when deprived of air. The police officer uses more pressure and, if not careful, can break the hyoid bone, causing death.

I never liked the bar-arm hold and neither did Ed Davis before me. But a police board of inquiry in the seventies, after reviewing the procedure and consulting with medical experts, said, yes, if applied correctly it is very effective and not dangerous. I disagreed.

Because we had been encountering more and more use of PCP and cocaine, drugs that can cause violent behavior, we found it necessary to use both chokeholds more often. Over the past few years we'd had several situations when, during a violent encounter with a police officer, one of the chokeholds was applied and the person died a short time later.

In April 1982, James Mincey, a twenty-year-old black man with a history of violence and drug use, went into a coma after an LAPD officer used a modified carotid hold to subdue him. He died two weeks later.

Once again, debate raged over use of the chokehold. The papers kept running figures, saying that between 1975 and 1982, sixteen people had died from one type of hold or the other and it was mainly black people and obviously LAPD was racist and was systematically trying to kill off blacks.

In truth, we did not know how many people died specifically from the chokehold. The coroner would always include blunt-force trauma—the chokehold—as part of the cause, though not the primary one. The person might actually have died of a heart attack, brought on by overexertion while in a drug-induced state. Eighty-five percent of all suspects we arrested had drugs in their systems, and most of those who died had ingested narcotics. Cocaine and PCP make the heart beat faster and often cause violent behavior. Any number of factors could have accounted for these sixteen deaths.

The point nobody was making, the question *nobody* ever bothered to ask, was why did this person get into a violent struggle with the police in the first place? To me, the real cause of death was that some guy ingested all these narcotics and, stimulated by them, got into a fight with the police. Furthermore, we had any number of cases where there was no blunt-force trauma, no upper-body holds placed on an individual, and he still died after he was put into restraints.

In addition, our numbers showed that in the first quarter of 1982, we had used upper-body chokeholds on forty-seven whites, forty-four blacks and forty-six Hispanics. The only serious injury was Mincey's.

After his death, public anger brought on a series of discussions involving the mayor, the City Council, the police department, and the Police Commission. Deciding I didn't care what the LAPD brass thought, I told the Police Commission I was going to eliminate the bar-arm control.

Privately, some officers came to me and argued to keep it. To comply with a court consent degree that LAPD hire more women, blacks and Latinos, I had reduced the height requirement to five feet. Despite new training techniques at the Academy to help our shorter officers cope, some of them felt vulnerable. I remember in particular a female sergeant who said, "Because of my height, Chief, it's the only hold that works for me in subduing a suspect."

I understood. But I felt queasy about the bar-arm hold nevertheless.

Days later at a staff meeting, Dave Dotson, the deputy chief in charge of Personnel and Training Bureau, who had been extensively researching the physical impact of the control holds, wondered aloud if some blacks, due to various physical problems, might be more vulnerable to injury when a carotid hold was applied. His thinking, which I shared, was that some groups of people are more susceptible to some diseases. Ashkenazi Jews, for example, are susceptible to Tay-Sachs disease. Blacks are vulnerable to sickle-cell anemia. They have a high level of hypertension and a high risk of heart failure. There is also a sudden death syndrome, which is far greater in blacks than in other groups. The military has done research into this, and while nobody has yet to explain it, some blacks have been known to die a sudden death without discernible cause.

By early May we had talked about all these possibilities exhaustively. Convinced the bar-arm hold was too risky, I still planned to announce a ban on it. At the same time, I wanted to explain publicly how the carotid hold should be judged from the standpoint of the number of police officers it saved and the number of people it also saved from serious injury. I wanted to stress that we were not an intractable organization, that we *were* flexible, that we were looking at everyone's welfare, and that perhaps the numbers being attributed to deaths from the chokehold should be open to question.

On May 6, into my office waltzed a reporter from the *L.A. Times*. I thought, *Aha, here's my chance.*

The interview lasted an hour and a half, and near the end I mentioned our concerns that possibly something happens in blacks when the modified chokehold is applied. I remember using the phrase "normal people," referring to healthy people, white *or* black, as distinct from those blacks who might have problems with their circulatory systems.

That was on Thursday.

On Friday this same reporter returned. He wanted to go through it again. So we did. However I phrased it this time, I did not use the word *normal,* as I had the day before. So he supplied it.

"Do you mean like in normal people?" the reporter said. And I said, "Yeah, *functioning* normally." As in healthy.

"You mean normal?" he persisted.

"Yes."

Saturday morning I picked up the *L.A. Times* and there was the story. It hit me right in the face.

> Los Angeles Police Chief Daryl F. Gates has asked his department's personnel and training division to determine if blacks are more vulnerable to injury from chokeholds than white people.
>
> In a move likely to generate renewed controversy about the disputed holds, Gates said he has "a hunch" that blacks are more susceptible to neck injury because more blacks are injured with the holds than other people.
>
> "We may be finding that in some blacks when it is applied the veins or the arteries do not open as fast as they do in normal people. . . . There may be something arresting the ability of the blood to flow again (after the hold is applied). We're going to look at that very carefully."

"Oh, God," I said and stopped reading right there.

"You didn't really *say* that, did you?" Sam said.

"Yeah. But I said it in terms of a person being healthy and that's all I was talking about. Wasn't talking about blacks being different from other people, or that other people are normal and blacks are not. My God."

"Well, I can't believe you'd even say *that,*" Sam chided.

"But that's not what I *meant.*"

Too bad. Too late. Monday morning, by the time I arrived at the mayor's office for a budget meeting, he had already been deluged with people asking for my head.

"What's this all about, Chief?" Tom Bradley said.

"There was nothing racial intended in my remarks," I answered. "I was trying to express my concern about an upper-body hold. I'm concerned about people and concerned about officers. I was just trying to describe something I thought needed further research. And now I'm a bigot? *A racist*?"

The mayor should have understood; being misquoted comes with the territory. But Bradley simply stared at me, stone-faced, and left me to fend for myself. Already that morning three members of the City Council, *all* of the black leadership, and of course the ACLU, had demanded my resignation. The story stirred up such controversy that the *L.A. Times* released a transcription of the tape recording of the first interview. That is, they released a small portion of it. But they refused to release the second interview, the one in which the reporter put the words "You mean like in normal people?" into my mouth.

When the Police Commission asked the *Times* for that tape, they said their lawyers advised against it. The stated reason was California's shield law, but I always figured the real reason was the tape would show the *Times*' reporter had put words in my mouth.

From this point on, it hardly mattered what I thought or said, or intended to say. Again, the lynch mob mentality had taken over and this time it worried me. I began to get a sense of how people felt when actual lynch mobs came after them. To experience that kind of anger, and venom, coming from supposedly respectable people just chilled me. I remember the Urban League in particular denouncing me as it demanded that I resign. I phoned John Mack, president of the local branch.

"John," I said, "what's going on? The Urban League board made this decision to call for my resignation and never even heard from me? Don't you think a guy like me, even though I'm chief of police, has a right to be heard? I mean, your board is espousing civil rights and due process for people all the time. That's what the Urban League is all about, I thought."

He said, "I'll get back to you."

The next day, John called, and so help me, he said, "The board doesn't want to hear from you."

I guess it's my nature to fight and I became more and more defiant. I lashed out at a lot of people. Given the context of the entire story, those who read it to the end, and with any objectivity, would have understood my seemingly insensitive remark was not racially motivated. But the "Get Gates" momentum was strong and a lot of people were jumping on the bandwagon.

Then came the worst snub of all. The children from a grade school in south central L.A. had invited me to attend a ceremony. While many public officials write polite notes of regret, I never did. A real softie for children, I loved visiting schools and tried always to oblige—to the delight of the teacher and, most of all, the kids.

A day or two before this particular event, a letter arrived from the principal. "In view of the ongoing controversy," he wrote, "we think it would be best if you didn't come to the school." More than anything, that really got to me. I doubted the children even knew what the controversy was about; they were fifth-graders. If it wasn't for the self-righteous adults, who *also* didn't know what the controversy was about, I can't imagine one child who would have looked at me as a bigot. It hurt.

The attacks grew worse. Far worse than anything I had experienced, and in some ways worse even than Rodney King would prove to be—or maybe the vehemence of the public outcry no longer shocks me. But I don't believe *any* chief of police in modern history anywhere in the United States ever went through anything like this. Even if he was involved in wholesale corruption, public anger rarely reached this proportion or would endure for so long.

On May 12, the Police Commission held a public hearing. Regular Commission meetings are open to the public, but few people ever come. By advertising the meeting as a public hearing, and holding it in the four-hundred-seat auditorium rather than the board room, the Commission was inviting anyone to come in and make a speech. More than four hundred came, and mostly made speeches about how much they hated me.

The overflow spilled out into the halls.

Along with members of the Police Commission, I sat on the stage and listened as one person after another denounced me as a racist. Bishop H. H. Brookins, the esteemed religious leader and Bradley's trusted political adviser—the same Bishop Brookins who the *Los Angeles Times* later reported had used a federally funded interest-free loan awarded by the city to renovate an office complex that he secretly owned—stood up and declared, "I at one time had hope for this chief, but he's nothing more than a clone of Bill Parker. Another racist chief of police."

I recognized very few people in the audience as plain old folks. Mainly I saw outspoken black activists and a few white liberals trying to curry favor with the blacks.

One, Zev Yaroslavsky, a councilman, was a good example. Actually, a bad example—he made me want to throw up. Zev played to the crowd, whatever it was. With his politics all over the map, he was a top-notch S.O.B. He's still a councilman, and, in my book, still an S.O.B.

Zev was chairman of the Police, Fire and Public Safety Committee and he had been working with Deputy Chief Dotson on clarifying regulations dictating when the modified chokehold could be used. One of my staff bumped into Zev as he made his way into the auditorium.

"You're not going to testify, Councilman, are you?"

"I sure am," Zev replied.

"Come on. The chief's been working with your committee. You know how concerned he is over this."

"Fuck him," said Yaroslavsky and walked away.

Zev stood up and condemned me. He withdrew his support for the restricted use of the carotid hold, having decided, he said, I was "not a man whose word could be trusted." The crowd applauded. Councilman Dave Cunningham attacked me too. Others, who I thought were my friends, grabbed the microphone and shouted that I was a bigot.

I was reminded then how little had changed since Watts. For a while, prospects had looked promising. The McCone Commission had listed several causes ahead of LAPD for the uprising, but we had taken their recommendations to heart. We assigned a Community Relations Officer to each division. We had the neighborhood-watch groups. We had police officers teaching a course in high schools about government. All these programs met with success. Bradley, of all people, came along and recommended eliminating Community Relations Officers, the Police Role in Government program and, years later, nixed overtime money for foot beats.

As a result, a joint task force of the National Conference of Christians and Jews, the American Jewish Committee, and the Urban League issued a report on south central Los Angeles fifteen years after Watts, and strongly urged that these same programs, or ones like them, be resurrected. That's what I was trying to do now. But in almost every case I had to find ways to circumvent Bradley's budgetary roadblocks. I expanded Police Academy training from four months to six. I got professors to write a human relations handbook. I demanded we hire more black officers. I begged for more officers, period, every single year. But always my demands were met by Bradley's deaf ears and stone face.

Now, because one person out of 137 who had been put in a chokehold in 1982 had died—a person who was black—I was the target of a community's rage.

They raged for three hours.

Finally, I was allowed to read a four-page statement that I hoped would explain my position. The first two and a half pages spoke of my efforts to constantly review and revise LAPD policy on upper-body control holds. How nothing had consumed as much of my time or thoughts or had been of greater concern to me. How I had been seeking the advice of medical experts and high-technology companies to assist us in developing sophisticated new devices that would be effective, without danger of permanent injury to suspects. The difficulty of balancing the safety of suspects with that of police officers.

I told of my very real concern that, even though I had no medical training, possibly there was a problem in some blacks that we were unaware of. And then I said the following:

> "My reference to 'normal people' was clearly unfortunate. I had no thought in mind that in referencing normal people I was referencing anything other than the normal functioning of the arteries that carry blood to the brain. . . .

"Clearly, the words that I've used have offended a great many people and for that I am deeply sorry. As chief of police, I recognize the great responsibility I have for being as sensitive to these kinds of statements as possible. My only defense is that I was pursuing what I believed to be a responsible course. I was pursuing what I believed to be a compassionate course. I was pursuing what I believed to be a concerned course, and in my heart I know that I made absolutely no distinction between races in the statement that I made. . . .

"Again, I must restate that obviously people have been offended by my statement. My statement was not meant to offend them; there was no intent to cause anyone any hurt or injury, only to achieve my objective of reducing tensions within the community and doing my utmost to reduce the loss of life.

"I have no apology to make at all *for what I was thinking,* but I very deeply want to apologize for the manner in which I expressed myself."

I could have saved myself the trouble. My statement didn't get even one person in that auditorium to shut up. All the time I spoke, they heckled me, shouting that I was a racist. One guy yelled, "You hate us. You hate us like a dog." They were whipped up into—*yes*—a frenzy. That is the only way to describe it. Some of my officers became concerned for my safety, that some guy would pull out a gun and shoot me, such was the intensity of the hostility in that room.

Outside that room, and in the days and weeks to come, I found tremendous support from blacks and whites. The *Herald* conducted a poll: How do you feel about Chief Daryl Gates? And the results showed that of 28,027 people who called in, two thirds said they supported me.

But inside that room, all I felt was tremendous anger, or maybe it was hurt. I felt as if somebody had punched me right in the solar plexus. I had worked for thirty years trying to do something worthwhile for people. I had worked in the black community since Watts, building good relationships and friendships with so many people there. I'd spent my whole life preaching fairness and equality to my family: from the time I was a kid, and would argue with my father and mother, until, as a parent, I tried to instill the same values in my kids.

I thought, *Did I really let myself in for this?*

To some extent, yeah. The failure to choose my words more carefully made me realize why politicians have all their speeches written for them. I'd always thought that was an insincere way to communicate with people, that you communicate through your sincerity, not simply by words. That if you must worry about the meaning and the context of every single syllable of every word, worry about how they might be misinterpreted, you lose a great deal of the ability to make a real connection with people.

Inside that room, I sorely wanted to quit. Like Gary Cooper in *High Noon,* I wanted to take my badge and shove it right in the faces of some of those sons of bitches who stood in front of that microphone. After decades of hard work, and saving *their* asses on a whole variety of things, I just wanted to take my badge and shove it.

I toyed with the idea.

Then I thought, *Nah. I'll do that and get fifteen minutes on prime time, and that'll be it. I'll spend the rest of my life saying "They ran me out."*

That was the moment when it became firmly implanted in my mind that no one was going to run me out of this office.

■

In 1983 the cross currents blew mightily once again. According to the media, the Los Angeles police department was conducting a massive spy operation on local politicians, civil rights activists, judges, City Councilmen, the mayor, and, quite possibly, the doddering lady with the dog next door. We had a vast army of undercover agents whose job it was to gather damaging information on citizens and add it to our bulging files secreted away in Parker Center.

My real name wasn't Daryl Gates. It was J. Edgar Hoover.

These were the allegations that I read over my morning coffee for most of that year. In the age-old battle between

the watchdog media and the always suspect police, anything
we did that appeared questionable to reporters was routinely
blown out of proportion; our explanations, if sought, summarily dismissed. Reporters, seizing an angle and running
for broke, shaped a city's thinking. Editorial writers were
even worse. They read their own front pages and sounded
off. Not once while I was chief did an editorial writer ever
phone me or seem to do any independent checking. The
public read the headlines and heard the TV sound bites
and whatever the LAPD had to say was branded part of a
cover-up.

And so it was in the case of our Public Disorder Intelligence division.

Started by Ed Davis in 1970, PDID had the job of
monitoring subversive organizations and, as its name im-
plies, those people and organizations that planned to seriously disrupt public order illegally.

In the past, LAPD's subversive intelligence operation
had been kept so secret that it did not show up on its
organizational chart, and most officers were unaware it
existed. This was the group that had operated out of a room
in Wilshire division when I was captain of Intelligence, and
its main focus was the Communist party. But by 1970, when
civil disruptions were occurring all over the city, Ed Davis
said, "We don't need a secret organization anymore. We
need to be up front."

The newly created PDID was staffed with sixty or seventy officers and formally listed on the organizational chart.
It kept busy. Numerous subversive groups had sprung up—
such as the Weather Underground, the Black Panthers,
SDS—some of whose members were sought for bombings.
Offshoots of terrorist bands operating out of foreign countries had appeared on the scene too. Many had bombs and
blueprints for overthrowing the government of the United
States. The FBI, America's federal investigative agency,
does look into domestic and foreign espionage, terrorism,
and public disorder. But due to the FBI's small size, it falls
to local law enforcement to keep tabs on subversive groups.
So LAPD, like other major city police departments, tried to
stay abreast of who these people were and what, exactly,
they might be up to. Some were up to murder.

In 1982, for instance, the Turkish consul general was assassinated in west Los Angeles by members of the Justice Commandos of the Armenian Genocide. Through PDID surveillance operations, we were able to arrest Hampartzoun Sassounian, who was convicted of murder.

Two weeks later his brother was arrested for an earlier firebombing of the residence of the Turkish consul general. Then, working with the FBI and the sheriff's department, we arrested three Armenian terrorists after they placed a bomb at the LAX Air Canada cargo facility. They were hoping to retaliate for the arrest of four of their colleagues in Canada. We dismantled the bomb.

Doing surveillance on terrorist or subversive groups was extremely dangerous and required utmost secrecy. So in addition to the sixty or seventy PDID officers who were known to the department, we had thirty-five undercover agents who were not. If they showed up on the official roster at all, they were listed as having phony duties, such was the danger these officers faced.

To gain access to subversive groups took months of laying meticulous groundwork. Because the groups were composed of tiny cells, each member knowing the others, a direct approach could not be made. Some seemingly harmless groups, such as SDS, might have within it a cell of people with dangerous ideas which even the general membership was unaware of. In stalking their targets, undercover officers would first infiltrate feeder groups—say, an SDS campus group—and move cautiously toward the inner circle.

This required not only an identity change but also learning the ideology and lingo of that particular organization. They had to take extreme care never to misspeak or act out of character. Since they could not participate in anything unlawful, it took a fast-stepping, fast-talking officer to demur without raising suspicions. Frequently, the officer had to move into another area of the city and take up residence in a seedy neighborhood. But LAPD had only two choices really: Do nothing and react to a disruption or a bombing; or be pro-active and try to stop one from happening. Ed Davis chose the latter.

In 1978, I inherited PDID. Along with it I inherited a

lawsuit. A coalition of activist groups, convinced that PDID was using its license to spy on the public at random, had filed it, and even though the transgressions they alleged occurred before I became chief, they cited me as a responsible party. Later they amended their complaint to include transgressions by PDID that allegedly occurred after I became chief.

The lawsuit—and the accusatory news stories condemning us as spies—put LAPD in an awkward situation. So sensitive was some of PDID's work that we could not publicly reveal it. Moreover, some of our undercover operations were based on information given us by the FBI and CIA. If they couldn't trust us to keep that information secret, they warned, they would drop us in a minute.

The City Attorney at that time was Burt Pines, a civil rights lawyer who had been elected on a strong liberal platform. I liked Burt, but I always thought his pro-civil rights sympathies caused him to drag his feet, though maybe it was just standard defense tactics. He would assign a lawyer, a while later he or she would be transferred, and then came another lawyer, and all they did for four and a half years was shuffle papers. They never once took a deposition.

The plaintiffs, meanwhile, were attacking the suit aggressively, going through the discovery process, demanding every document they had the slightest legal basis for discovering. The Superior Court generously allowed them access to thousands of pages of sensitive PDID information, which in our judgment could have proved harmful if it fell into the public domain. We pleaded with the court for a protective order on all information released. By the time the court granted us one, it was too late.

Though we could never prove it, we believed the plaintiffs ignored the order. Somehow almost all the information leaked to the media. Reporters grabbed these bits and pieces and, with a bit of imagination, wrote eye-catching stories about this cache of secret files LAPD was greedily hoarding.

Everybody had read too many espionage stories. Images of police officers looking through a telescope, peeking into a bedroom window, following people, checking to see whom they met for political reasons, were conjured up by politicians and reported by the media. *None* of those things was being done, except as they had to do with our objective of moving in to thwart illegal acts disruptive of the public order.

Much of what PDID was hoarding in its files were newspaper articles. Gathering information is what an intelligence organization does. Tons of it may be gathered before any sense can be made of it. The information must be skillfully sorted and filed and—most important of all—intelligently evaluated. For instance, an undercover officer with an eye on a particular group member—let's call him Mr. A—may report back on everyone who attended meetings that Mr. A went to. Those names will be filed and may never be looked at again. As time goes on, newspaper articles mentioning various people who attended other meetings at which Mr. A was present will be clipped and filed as well. A specialist combing the files may notice that Ms. B, who was not the initial target, was seen time and time again with Mr. A, suggesting a possible connection between them. What action will be taken on the basis of that information about Ms. B will depend on the individual case. However, only when you can weave pieces of information together in a meaningful way do you have real "intelligence."

Not trained as intelligence specialists, our undercover officers simply reported everything they learned without having the skills to refine the information. There was not enough trained staff to evaluate it, either. So the files just kept building—to no useful end. Most contained nothing more than a couple of news articles. In one case, we kept a file on a councilman because he had been threatened, and we were gathering information on who might be threatening him and why. When this was leaked, the media accused us of spying on political leaders, and we got nailed with that over and over again.

Yet, countless groups were posing a real threat. Schooled in sophisticated tactics, they seized on a favorite ploy. They would select a prominent public figure who moved freely in legitimate circles, then penetrate one of those circles. Our intelligence would lead us to the circle, and then these revolutionaries would circulate the rumor that this pillar of the community was being spied on by the police.

Mayor Bradley was a favorite target. He may have gone
to a function attended by an individual we were interested
in. A newspaper article about this event would appear and
someone would have underlined the mayor's name and put
the article in a file. There would be a leak and . . . now we
were spying on the *mayor*!

It didn't help our case that few people outside PDID
were privy to what PDID was doing. Not LAPD officers,
political leaders, or even Tom Bradley could be briefed on
some of the sensitive matters we were exploring. The Police
Commission, given Bradley's mandate to keep the department in check, turned a jaundiced eye on everything we did.
That any newspaper morgue contains far more information
in its files than PDID did was irrelevant.

"You can't justify keeping all this stuff," the Commission railed. "Newspapers can, but a police department
can't!" Interesting.

In 1975, the Police Commission had ordered a big file-
burning program in which, it was publicized, 2 million
"secret files" were to be destroyed. Many of those "files"
were 3×5 index cards used to reference files, 95 percent of
which contained only newspaper clippings. The other 5
percent contained highly sensitive information about subversives.

So blinded by this witch hunt was everyone that nobody
stopped to think clearly. It seemed to escape the witch
hunters that information-gathering runs America. Big business collects volumes of data on consumers; political parties
collect their demographic data. That newspaper morgues
and businesses hold far more information than we did mattered to nobody. Our files had to be destroyed.

Sorting through them took years. The lieutenant in
charge would ask detectives, "Do you need this stuff on
busing?" and everyone would say no. So it would be put
into cartons and hauled away. What we didn't realize was
that one PDID officer was hauling some of it home.

Jay Paul was a detective with a pack-rat mentality.
Seeing that nobody wanted this stuff, he grabbed cartons
full and stacked them in his garage. Some of it he transferred
to a computer he said belonged to his wife.

When we found out, in January 1983, we went to his

house with a search warrant and confiscated fifty cartons from his garage. I went through them myself. Most of it was crap, yellowed newspaper clippings—old copies of the *Daily Worker* in particular—pamphlets and magazines, but Jay Paul did possess a few items he absolutely should not have had. Nothing major, but he had no business taking it anyway. Moreover, we believed his computer had been bought with funds supplied by a right-wing, anticommunist group headed by a member of Congress. We also believed Jay Paul was moonlighting for this group and possibly supplying it with information from PDID.

We charged Jay Paul administratively and made public the actions we had taken. We were trying to be so pure, saying, "Hey, we don't allow our employees to do these things, and we are going to punish him."

"Hidden files," the newspapers wrote, "that must contain the *real* 'spying' that was being conducted by LAPD!"

Nobody wanted to believe us. And nobody did.

∎

Increasingly, I was being ripped apart for continuing these undercover operations. Publicly, I defended Ed Davis and PDID, but behind the scenes I was trying to tidy up the mess he had created. Realizing that most of the PDID files were junk, I had given the order, right after becoming chief, to stop clipping newspapers. Instead, we hooked up with Lexus/Nexus, the computer research service, that provided us—in the same way it provided libraries, law firms and news organizations—with articles we might need.

At the same time I was eliminating undercover PDID personnel as fast as I could. Of the thirty-five officers we had undercover, I got rid of all but two. The barrage of media attention was proving a real danger to them and several agents had received death threats. Fearing our phase-out would present a terrible security risk, I did not announce it. But I did inform the Police Commission that I had made substantial reductions. "My God," they cried, "don't tell anyone. We want those people engaged in terrorist activity to think the police are undercover everywhere, and to watch out."

By 1983, when the ACLU leapt in to represent the

Coalition Against Police Abuse (CAPA), the group that was suing us for illegal spying activities, we seemed pinned down from every direction. The leaks to the media of thousands of pages of information presented one half-baked side of the story, and we, conscious of security risks, were unable to present our own.

■

As the spying allegations continued to spill forth, we still had no representation. No defense team, no depositions, no discovery. The suit was like a hot potato in the city attorney's office. Every six months a new lawyer showed up—and quickly disappeared. Then Ira Reiner, the newly elected city attorney, who since has become L.A. County district attorney, made a startling announcement.

Appearing before the City Council, Reiner astonishingly proclaimed that PDID was clearly trampling on people's rights, that certain "zealots" in PDID believed it is "completely appropriate . . . to abuse every single moral or ethical precept that's involved in what we understand is a free society." And that he, as an officer of the court, could not abide by that.

Which really took the cake.

I mean, here was *my* attorney, the attorney for all these officers, for the city of Los Angeles, all of whom were being sued, and this unscrupulous idiot was announcing that those he was defending were guilty!

Over lunch, and trying to hold my temper, I said, "Ira, you can't do that. You're *our* attorney. You've got to make a public statement—I can't imagine what—but you've got to admit your first statement was erroneous. Or get us private counsel."

"I won't do either," said Reiner dismissively. "You fail to understand that city attorneys are not a public relations firm for your PDID."

"Then screw you."

Seething, I took my case to the City Council. I demanded private counsel for the officers, the city, and myself. A complaint was registered with the State Bar Association against Reiner, who, I thought, should have been disbarred.

As usual, Reiner had been surveying the political landscape. Less a man for the people than for himself, he must have figured: *I'd better remove myself from this mess. I'll make this public statement and I will be a big hero when it all hits.*

Only it backfired. Superior Court Judge Lester Olson removed Reiner as defense counsel for the eleven officers accused of improper intelligence-gathering, and ordered the hiring of private counsel.

Reiner's self-serving remark would cost the taxpayers in excess of $2 million in attorney's fees.

■

The firm we hired was Gibson, Dunn & Crutcher. The attorneys assigned, Tom Holliday, Nancy McClelland and Willard Carr, immediately started doing what our city attorney should have done five years before, which was to start discovery motions and take depositions. Finally we had competent representation. Once this was done, the City Council asked to meet with them in executive session. The Council, which would have to decide whether to pay any damages incurred against the police officers, the city, or me, wanted to know the score. "We're going to tell them exactly what we've found," the lawyers informed me.

"Right. I want you to."

Frankly, I gulped. Some of what had gone on during Ed Davis's reign could be damaging, I realized, and I would have to take the heat.

Inside the Council chambers, the lawyers Tom Holliday and Willard Carr laid it all out. In infiltrating subversive groups, PDID had, in the strictest sense, possibly violated several citizens' rights, simply by reporting that they had been present. The lawyers estimated what the city's liability would be. When they were finished, one of the Council members blinked. "Is that all?"

"Yeah," I agreed, "that's it."

And it was a hushed City Council. For, as set forth by Gibson, Dunn & Crutcher, there were two cases of questionable abuse, maybe three.

"It's possible," the lawyers said, "there are some situations for which the city will have to pay a modest amount.

In some cases we think undercover officers did violate someone's rights, but we don't think it's going to be major.''

The Council said, "What do you recommend doing?''

"We recommend you fight the suit. We think we can defend the city very well.''

You could have heard a pin drop. Councilman Joel Wachs, who is very sensitive about people's rights, and who was really angered by some of the allegations he had read, kept repeating, "What? That's *it*?''

Zev Yaroslavsky, who had been an ardent supporter of the plaintiffs, was back-pedaling all over the place. Saying, "I can't buy it. There's gotta be *something* more to this. I don't *understand*.''

Buoyed by the lawyers' words, the Council voted, eleven to three, to defend the case rather than settle. And I walked out of there about two feet taller. Only when the lawyers told the Council the true scope of the charges did it agree to fight them. But they had to hear it from lawyers. They hadn't believed me.

The trial was set for January 1984. On the one hand, I wanted a gold medal just to jam this case right down the ACLU's throat. At one time I had great respect for them, particularly their legal staff. Today, I have no respect for them. I believe they have become self-serving hypocrites. I can't point to one constructive thing they've done in L.A. in the last twenty-five years. Still, to be publicly revealing our intelligence operations in a court fight months before the Olympics worried me greatly.

Already, various law enforcement organizations, including the FBI, had begun backing away from us. Yaroslavsky was trying to pass an insane proposal for a Freedom of Information Ordinance specifically for the city of Los Angeles that would have put us out of business. Fortunately, we were able to modify the ordinance. But in the intelligence community it was already as if we had a terrible case of halitosis. Nobody wanted to play with us, scared to death that anything they might reveal would wind up in the columns of the *L.A. Times*.

In the end, the trial never took place. Councilman Marvin Braude came to me and inquired if we might settle out of court. "The ACLU's going broke,'' he explained.

I chuckled. Actually, I laughed.
I laughed out loud.

■

The settlement cost the city $640,000, to be paid to parties we agreed were legitimately injured by our surveillance. It also crammed down our throats the most restrictive guidelines of any police department in the nation. The guidelines state we can gather intelligence only on people suspected of criminal activities, and before we can proceed we must create a paper trail from here to the moon, explaining who was being surveilled and why. The Police Commission formally disbanded PDID and replaced it with ATD—Anti-Terrorist division. And wished us good luck with the impending Olympics.

My own reputation went unchanged. J. Edgar Hoover was still my name. Political blackmail was undoubtedly my game.

■

Not that I don't *know* things.

As chief of police, I know plenty. Police officers are the world's greatest gossips and they hear *everything*. Sometimes it filters up to me. As a result, I know far more than I care to about people's personal lives.

An officer stops a speeding motorist, and the motorist just happens to be an esteemed judge, and with this esteemed judge is a scantily dressed woman who is not this esteemed personage's wife.

Police officers raid a house of prostitution. Get their hands on their records. Names of important men in this town filter back to me. Prostitutes on the street tell police officers names of men whom they have entertained. Bookmakers brag: Guess who dropped a grand on the Super Bowl?

I know about major politicians who are having affairs—even one whose wife is having an affair. I know about the peccadilloes of various political "leaders." Usually, this information comes to me from our best source—the average citizen. I'll be at a business luncheon and someone will come up to me and, trying to act in the know, will say, "So,

Chief, what do you think about So-and-So's affair with Ms. X?"

And, of course, I didn't know about it at all.

Information came to me in other ways. Through our helpful contacts at airports and hotels, we knew the movements not only of Mafia figures but also of those they might potentially try to muscle. Recently, over lunch with Lew Wasserman, the longtime chairman of MCA, the parent company of Universal Studios, I told him, "We knew every time you boarded a plane for Las Vegas."

Lew was stunned. "But why?" he asked.

"You're a major figure in Los Angeles and you're in a business that's highly attractive to organized crime. Many people get mixed up in organized crime, not because they want to, but because they become victims. We tried to make sure important people, good people like yourself, were protected and not preyed upon by the Mafia. We wanted to know who was running with whom."

Through mutual contacts, I also came to know a lot about the mayor. And quite a bit about the people around him. Many are good people; some are outstanding. Others, I think, have shut their eyes to some of what goes on in his office.

Collection of political funds—unquestionably there's been wrongdoing. But it's nearly impossible to prove. The ability to cover up campaign contributions has become an art: where the money comes from, who may be skimming off the top, which commissioner is leaning on someone with official business before him. LAPD's Bunco-Forgery people have been investigating the mayor and some of his associates for some time, because of allegations made in the press. Because of my known dislike of Bradley, I've kept them at arm's length. They report to me periodically, mostly in writing, but I rarely debrief them, because I don't want to be accused of influencing the investigation.

I know of individuals who wanted to get Bradley in the worst way, who tried their damnedest to get into his LAPD personnel file. I was the one who prevented them. It contains little of importance. But that they wanted to get it, hoping to destroy him, offended me.

Over the years I've come to know a lot about many

prominent people. From time to time I've written things down. Not in a secret file—just notes I scribble on scraps of paper. I've done this because the incidents are so connected with my growing up in the department, and I record them as a kind of unofficial diary. I suppose I—and Bill Parker and Tom Reddin and Ed Davis—could have crafted some system to use this information. But that's not what the LAPD is all about. It would be violating principles that we grew up with and believe in.

People say, "That's bullshit."

Only it's not. It's the way we look at things. And I'm very proud of that fact; it allows me to sleep at night.

16

Games Within the Games

Once we settled the PDID affair, the Olympics were only eight months away and I was forced daily to come to grips with the fact of them.

Like a lot of people in Los Angeles, I couldn't imagine a worse idea than holding the Summer Games here. With our ever-shrinking police force now down to 6,850 officers, we were already providing lousy enough service to the city. Add to that our everyday traffic snarls on the freeways. If one were to look at the city from the observation tower at City Hall . . .

> . . . you would be privileged to view a scene unparalleled in all the world. You would see one-half million automobiles, a stream of steel and rubber massed on the roadways as far as your eyes can travel. Over most of the scene you would see them packed one against the other so closely that movement can hardly be discerned. You would see great six-lane freeways like swollen rivers, as sluggish as the smaller streams.

And if it appeared to you that Los Angeles lay inundated by some catastrophic flood, you would be near the truth.

The eloquence of that description comes not from me but from William Parker. The year was 1953. Thirty years later, the flood had only spread farther, in all directions. Then there was the sheer size of the area the Olympics would encompass. The twenty-three sporting venues would stretch over ten thousand square miles, through *six* counties, from Santa Barbara to San Diego, a distance of more than two hundred miles. It would require the services of fifty law-enforcement agencies.

The Olympics, I thought, was a nice event . . . for Greece.

■

Nevertheless, knowing that I would have to play ball, I decided from the start to play hardball. With the nightmare of Munich still in mind, and terrorism a distinct possibility, I was determined that no Olympic committee, however prestigious, was going to wrest control of security from me. So in 1979, I appointed a young commander, Bill Rathburn, to head up our Olympic planning committee. Bill, I knew, had ambitions of becoming chief of police (and in 1991 he became one, in Dallas), so I told him:

"You must follow my directions implicitly. There will be *no compromise on anything*. You will be dealing with very high-powered people and it's gonna be tough for a guy who wants to be chief of police someday to face up to some of these people if you promise them we will meet certain demands when in fact we're not going to. So whenever I tell you to do something specifically, I expect you to carry it out and not back off in any way, shape, or form. Or," I added, "you will be gone the next day."

Bill never wobbled, not once. Often, he would become upset with me and get red-faced over positions I would take, but he stuck to his guns. And so the stage was set for some terrific battles with the Los Angeles Olympic Organizing Committee. Most of those battles were with Peter Ueberroth, the head of it.

When I met him, I was impressed. Peter is a bright guy and I liked his candor. He invited me to lunch and, without pulling any punches, said, "You know, Daryl, if I or we are successful in these Olympics, it'll look good on the résumés. If we're not, our résumés won't mean much."

He was really talking about himself to a large degree, which I thought was pretty frank. He seemed very straightforward. But as time went on, I lost my feeling that he was candid; I felt he was anything *but* candid. There always seemed to be a second agenda that I wasn't quite privy to, looming over every discussion. I kept wanting to say, "Peter, you're not exactly telling me everything." Police officers are, I suppose, hypercritical. But we're pretty good at judging people's sincerity. And I couldn't find his. In the world of big deals, sincerity has no place, I guess.

He was, for instance, supposed to be part of a law-enforcement policy committee. He never attended. Occasionally he would speak to us in other settings. Kind of like Moses coming down from the Mount to address the masses. Those of us in law enforcement got the impression he was condescending to us. He would say all the right things and try to show his pride in law enforcement, but you never got the strong feeling that he meant it.

We always left him muttering to ourselves.

■

"Okay," I said to Bill Rathburn, "this is what we have to do. When you negotiate our contract with the LAOOC, one of the things I insist on is that we have oversight of all security, including all sporting venues within the city of Los Angeles. *We* ultimately will decide how the security is going to be done and whether the security is adequate or not."

To get this kind of control would be a major departure. In past Olympics, the organizing committee policed inside the venues, while local agencies policed the streets. But already, from what I could tell, the security they planned for the venues would not be adequate. If anything happened, I thought, no one would point the finger at the Olympic Organizing Committee and *their* security; they'd point at the LAPD and scream, *"How did that happen?"*

So I intended to insist that we would add whatever *we*

thought was necessary for venue security and *they* could pay for it. And that got into the really big head-knocking between Peter Ueberroth and myself.

The contract talks dragged on well into 1982. Although Peter is probably one of the toughest negotiators in the world, and one of the canniest, we finally managed to slip our key clause—giving us final approval over level of staffing within the Olympic villages and the venues, *at their expense*—through the sharp negotiation process of Peter and his staff. As he would later put it, "Our agreement with the City of Los Angeles had a loophole large enough to drive an eighteen-wheeler through it and Daryl Gates was an expert driver."

I would have to keep driving right up until the eve of the Olympics.

■

In the meantime, in an effort to get into the spirit of the thing, I decided to attempt some positive public relations with the media. I should have known better.

Having often been invited to the *L.A. Times* and other news organizations for informal background sessions with editors and executives, I asked Commander William Booth, LAPD's press relations officer, to organize one of our own, in January 1982. During this luncheon, to be held at the Police Academy, we would share some of the little-known facts and intelligence reports we thought might have an impact on the Summer Games.

One of the reports indicated that the Soviet Union was sending out KGB agents and criminals, in the guise of emigrating Jews. This we knew to be a fact; we speculated that their coming to Los Angeles could foment trouble during the Olympics. Although the briefing was off the record, Bill Booth announced that if any of the editors and news executives present wanted to do a story based on the information presented, to please get in touch with him. He could provide more substantial background.

One reporter did not. This snake simply went ahead and wrote that I said Soviet Jews were being sent to Los Angeles to disrupt the Olympics. The fact that I never said anything of the sort and that the story was misreported did not get me off the hook; I was an *anti-Semite!*

The Jewish community, which had always been strong supporters of the department, wanted to strangle me. A huge delegation arrived at my office to tell me so.

"Listen," they said, "we've got these people coming out of the Soviet Union and they're having a hard time adapting to America. It's very difficult for them and their children, and now you come out with this statement that only fans the flames of prejudice by calling them criminals."

I assured them that was the last thing I ever wanted to do, and that I had been misquoted. "But I must tell you this report is very specific," I emphasized. "The Russians are sending criminals to the United States—here and to Brighton Beach in New York—some of whom have been involved in counterfeiting schemes, extortion, even murder. These are not Jews, but people who are arriving here under the immigration quotas for Soviet Jews. I can prove this if you want me to. But I don't want to make things worse. If you'd like to draw up a mutual statement for the media that will put this to rest, I will do that."

They accepted my offer and were most gracious. But the impression that I had said something anti-Semitic exists to this day.

■

Some weeks before, in early December, Peter told me that he wanted to hire someone to be head of security for the Olympic Committee. He said that ex-Chief Tom Reddin wanted the job badly, but he didn't want Reddin. He said Peter Pitchess, then the sheriff of L.A. County, also wanted the job, and that he *absolutely* did not want him.

"Why don't you hire somebody from LAPD?" I suggested. "We'll keep him on the force, but he will be the head of security for the Games. That way we can fuse the plans for inside and outside the venues and he'll be a highly competent, skilled LAPD top executive."

"Oh, I don't think that's feasible," Ueberroth said.

It seemed like a perfect solution to me, but I suspect Peter didn't like the idea that the guy wouldn't be working for him, and he definitely wanted someone he could control.

We had a number of discussions about this and just before Christmas he invited me to lunch.

"Why don't you take the job?" he said.

To my amazement, he made a strong pitch and offered me a substantial amount of money. Enough—ten or twelve thousand dollars a month—so that I really had to give it serious consideration.

"Let me think about it over the holidays, Peter. I'll have an answer after the first of the year."

"Oh, good. Great!" Ueberroth said.

We spoke about the offer several more times, even to the extent of who I might hire to come with me, and I spent the holidays agonizing over what to do. I didn't really want to leave the police department. On the other hand, Peter kind of sold me on it. "This will be a crowning exit to your leaving law enforcement," he had said, "and after, there will be opportunities for many things. You could even run for mayor."

Plus, I had been through hell. Being chief had not always been fun. The job had been a pain from the word go. With not even four years served, I was already considered anti-Latino and anti-black. I ran a department that shoots women who don't pay their gas bills and was rife with burglars and spies. And here was a chance to make a lot of money, do something very special, and maybe even be seen as a good guy.

Backward and forward I discussed it with Sam. I told her that while I didn't want to leave LAPD, I was fed up with the constant criticism, not to mention the pitched battles with the Police Commission. Sam agreed. So after all this agonizing, I finally decided: "Okay. When he calls me, I'll tell him yes."

But Ueberroth didn't call me.

Days passed. Weeks. I thought, *Aw, he's probably busy.* Or, *Maybe he thinks I should call him.* But . . . *Naw, if he wants me, he'll call me.* Then I got the word: One of my assistant chiefs, Marvin Iannone, told me that Ueberroth had offered *him* the job. Could he take a leave of absence? I said I doubted we could afford to do that, but if he wanted the job, why not retire from the department and take it?

While this assistant chief was mulling that over, Ueber-

roth invited me to the Bel-Air Country Club to go over some
security matters.

"By the way," he said, "I wonder if we couldn't work
something out with one of your assistant chiefs, get him a
leave of absence, because without one he doesn't seem to
want to come."

"To be honest," I responded, "something is bothering
me. You asked me if I wanted this job, and frankly, I went
through absolute misery trying to make a decision over
Christmas. It interfered, really, with a decent holiday because I was so torn between taking this thing and staying
with the police department. But I thought it might be worthwhile and I made the decision to go."

"You did?" said Ueberroth.

"Yeah."

"I didn't think you'd ever agree to."

"You didn't ask me, and now you're talking to one of
my assistants. What's going on?"

Peter gave me this little smile. "Things kind of changed,
Daryl, when you made that remark about Soviet Jews. That
was reported *worldwide*. After that, there was no way I
could have you as head of my security, my goodness.
Already, the Soviets are trying to find excuses not to come.
Hiring you would give them one."

"Except I didn't make that remark," I broke in. "It was
taken from an intelligence report. Secondly, it was truth,
and thirdly, I can't imagine the Soviet Union is going to
come to the Games *anyway*. But you didn't even call to ask
if I'd made a decision, or ask for a clarification. I wouldn't
want to work for somebody who was that shallow in their
assessment of someone he was trying to hire."

"Gee, I didn't understand all of that," Peter said.
"Would you take the job?"

I almost choked. "Are you *kidding*? There is *no way* I
would ever take that job. There isn't anything you could
offer me—not now."

"Well," he said, "I'm sorry we didn't get together on
that."

Ueberroth eventually hired Edgar N. Best, formerly the
FBI agent in charge of the Los Angeles office. Ed was a
nice man and totally loyal.

He was the perfect choice for a Peter Ueberroth.

■

As the Olympics became a fact of life, I started to prepare for them.

Not only was the public down on the Games, so was the LAPD. Something had to be done, I thought, to turn this attitude around. So I prepared a little pep talk for the troops, attending every roll call at every division.

"You're going to handle this as we've handled so many things," I told my officers encouragingly. "We will rise to the occasion. You'll work your tails off and you'll be very tired when it's all over, but you will have a tremendous sense of self-worth and satisfaction because we will have shown the world what kind of police department we are."

All I would see was this dour, sour group staring glassy-eyed at me. I knew I had to build up their confidence, for I understood they saw the Olympics as something that might defeat them, might disgrace the department and stamp Los Angeles as the city that couldn't police the Olympics. At the end of my talk, I borrowed shamelessly from George Patton, exhorting, "Years from now, when your grandson is sitting on your lap and he asks you what were you doing during the 1984 Olympics, you can look him in the eye and say you weren't out shoveling shit in Ohio or Omaha. You were right here, proudly being a part of it."

We even had bumper stickers made up: LAPD—WORLD CLASS, with the Olympic logo and the LAPD badge . . . hoping to drum up a little enthusiasm.

■

As part of my own Olympic gearing-up process, I flew to Munich and met with the chief of police. I had read all I could about the massacre of the eleven Israeli athletes in 1972, and when I got there, they walked me through what had been the Olympic village to the apartments where the athletes had been held hostage. It wasn't that I thought we would have the same type of situation, but I wanted to get a feel for what had gone on and how the terrorists had entered the village. Later, I had the police chief drive me along the same route the terrorists took to the airport, where the murders occurred. In retrospect, I could see that because the Germans desperately wanted to keep the appearance of the police to a minimum, hoping to erase their storm-trooper image, there were little things that should have been done that weren't.

The main lesson I took away, though, was the need to guard against complacency. The attack on the Israelis came ten days into the Olympics. Everything was going extremely well, people were having a good time, the police were looked upon as doing a great job, friendly as could be—and that's when the whole thing fell apart. As we planned for the Olympics, I kept that firmly in mind.

■

Trying to secure a city as open as Los Angeles seemed an overwhelming task. It was our belief that if any terrorist group anywhere in the world cared to make a statement, they would make it in Los Angeles. I mean, where else, besides New York, could you count on the worldwide media attention that would be right here during the Olympics? And perhaps even more than New York, we had all the players in place. As Bill Rathburn said, "Every conflict that exists anywhere in the world is represented on both sides somewhere in southern California."

Indeed, we have everybody. The Serbians and the Croatians. The Hungarian Mafia and the Israeli Mafia. When the Shah of Iran's family lived in Beverly Hills, those who opposed the Shah rioted. We have people protesting Soviet Jews, and the Jewish Defense League, which protests Arabs of *all* kinds. We have a large Arab community, a large Japanese one, and the largest population of Koreans outside of Seoul. We also have the Chinese: the pro-Taiwanese, who object to the People's Republic of China, which, in turn, has its faction. Mexicans and Central Americans have settled in with their causes too.

So terrorism was a real threat. And given the wide-open geography of the city, it would not be that hard to bring fanatics in. Already we had thousands of undocumented aliens who had no trouble slipping across the border. Anytime they wanted to, a contingent of terrorists could enter Los Angeles and lie low until the Games began. With seventy-eight independent cities in L.A. County alone, and a population of 9 million, it's extremely difficult to identify individuals and keep track of them.

We also had the gang problem. Privately, I have always worried that gangs present a grave potential for terrorism. If some group really wanted to disrupt the Games, all it had to do was recruit from the gangs, which already possessed enormous firepower and could, if necessary, go to the local gun shop and buy some more, including an arsenal of semiautomatic weapons. All the recruiter needed to do was pay gang members to commit a mindless act of violence— which is what gang members do on a regular basis anyway.

So we built the "street thug factor" into our plan. Six weeks before the Olympics, we would send our gang details out to clean up the streets around the Coliseum. We would run the gangs right out of the area with a few well-chosen words, and post enough police officers to discourage them from returning too soon.

Hoping to get additional advice, I flew to the Winter Olympics in Sarajevo and asked the minister of police how he had dealt with criminals.

"We put the word out that it was time to leave town, that *no one* was to commit a crime during the Olympics," he said.

"How do you get the word out?" I asked, intrigued.

"We have ways."

"What did you do with the people who maybe had a disagreement with the government?"

"Oh, we've put them all in jail."

"What—you just took them off the street?"

"*All* of them. Any criminal who wouldn't listen to reason went to jail." He looked at me. "And you have to do that too."

"Um, I don't think we can."

"You *have* to. There's no way you can put on the Olympics and be safe unless you do that."

"Well, we have a thing called the Constitution," I said. "And the Bill of Rights. Besides, I don't have a place big enough to hold all the agitators, criminals, and sympathizers of strange causes that you want me to lock up."

"No, you have to," he insisted. "You must!"

More intriguing to me was the effort his country made. I watched citizens graciously jump off a crowded trolley so tourists could climb on. I noticed how everything was spotless. Most of all, I was taken with the opening ceremonies. Yugoslavia is not a rich country and it could not display the wonders of Disneyland and Hollywood, as we would. But they put on this splendid pageantry, dancing and singing, *their* way, and the heartfelt enthusiasm and pride made a deep impression.

I was sitting with local policemen, watching athletes from all the competing nations parade around the stadium. And I'll never forget how our delegation appeared, right after some country in crisp uniforms came lock-stepping in. Typical Americans—nobody in step, lots of swagger, kind of wandering along, waving, having a good time. I found myself grinning.

"You can always tell the Americans," one of the police officers grumbled.

Five minutes later, in trooped the Yugoslavians. They were so much like the Americans, I began to laugh. I said, "Yeah, you guys are just like us." And he laughed. "You're right. We feel the same way about these things."

Buoyed by my visit, I returned to Los Angeles with a whole new attitude.

But I'm getting ahead of myself here.

■

The big question that loomed over the Olympics from day one was, who would have jurisdictional charge if there was a terrorist attack?

The FBI, thinking it would, had formed its own anti-terrorist team, called HRT, for Hostage Rescue Team. It was a group of highly trained, skillful people, patterned in large part on the LAPD's SWAT. The thinking was that if we had a Munich-type incident, the FBI would deal with it. The FBI was also of the opinion that if there was a terrorist attack of any kind, it would automatically be considered a federal crime and it would come under federal jurisdiction.

I had no problem with some of that thinking. If terrorists demanded a release of political prisoners somewhere in the world, fine, let the feds handle it. But I tried to be very clear that the majority of the Olympic events would take place in Los Angeles. If there was a hostage-taking, say, or a murder, that would be the responsibility of the LAPD. I was not about to blindly turn over the Olympics to the FBI, or anyone, because if it went sour, the FBI would leave town and you know who would be holding the pot that had turned black.

The FBI, not caring what I thought, sent out a memorandum of understanding (or M.O.U.) that all local agencies were expected to sign, ceding control to it. It stated that in the event of a terrorist attack of some sort, they would dispatch a supervising special agent who would decide whether the FBI would assume jurisdictional control.

I chuckled when I read it and threw it out.

You mean to tell me some supervising special agent from Washington *is going to make a decision that may impact on me and the city of Los Angeles for a long time?* I thought. *No way! We don't do things that way here.* I'll *make that decision. Period.*

So they tried again. This time the M.O.U. came back saying the *local* agent-in-charge would make that decision.

I said, "Nobody understands. I am the chief of police in the city of Los Angeles. *We* are going to be there first. We will make an assessment. We will work with HRT, but I'm not about to blindly turn the jurisdiction over ahead of time. I might not *ever* turn it over. So take your M.O.U. and shove it."

Their next ploy was to fly me to Washington, D.C.

The FBI called and said it wanted the newly elected sheriff, Sherman Block, myself, and the chief from Long Beach to meet with the FBI, CIA, and military intelligence for the latest briefing on world intelligence. That sounded good to me. But no sooner was I on the plane than the FBI agent-in-charge of Los Angeles pulled out the M.O.U. and wondered if I wouldn't sign it.

Of course not, I said.

The briefing turned out to be more or less of a fraud. They didn't tell us much that we didn't know already. Afterward, Sherman Block grumbled, "The whole reason for this damn trip is you and the M.O.U."

Sure enough, we were having breakfast at FBI headquarters the next day when Director William Webster said, "Daryl, could I talk to you for a little while?"

I followed him into his office. "I don't quite understand, and the President doesn't understand," he said, invoking the President's name—"why you won't sign this."

So I went through my little number again. "If you think because this agent-in-charge of Los Angeles says there's a national policy interest, and no one's even going to tell me what the national policy interest is . . . forget it, Bill. I'm not going to sign it."

"The President's really concerned."

"I understand. And I know he ultimately will make some of the decisions if we are attacked by terrorists. I'm not dumb. But *you* have to understand that I have responsibility for keeping the Olympics safe. If it's a success, then I will take the plaudits. If it's a failure, everyone will heap condemnation on me. And because I know I'm going to be accountable, I'm not about to be shut out when the decisions are made."

I paused. "So if something comes up that's a matter of national importance, just tell the President to call me."

"Er . . ."

"Look, I'll tell you what. If the President doesn't want to call me, you call. I will be glad to listen to you. But you're going to have to explain what the reasons are, and if you do that, or the President does, and I think it's appropriate, I'll be happy to turn over the operation to you."

"We have to call you, right?"

"You've got it," I said. "And listen. I don't know anything about international politics or national issues and I don't expect to. I'm not about to interfere with those. I *am* going to run things in Los Angeles."

"And you won't sign?"

"Nope."

Actually, I did sign something, as I recall. A revised document so that it wasn't a total loss for the FBI. But the outcome was the same: The LAPD was the lead agency in the city of Los Angeles.

I was in charge, as I intended to be.

■

The media weren't helping matters. Reporters harped on terrorism, harped on the prospect of somebody waltzing in with a nuclear bomb, harped forever on the smog and the gridlock, and of course I was the villain for not cooperating with the FBI. I got so tired of hearing this that I popped off and said, "My people are so far superior . . ." and naturally that made everybody love me even more.

The fact was, we were cooperating. Early on, LAPD had orchestrated a joint planning operation that brought in all other agencies to one location, a fortress-like warehouse on the edge of downtown called Piper Technical Center. Working out of this state-of-the-art command post, built by the Department of Defense, were some sixty agency representatives, all with telephones and computer screens. We staged drills, calling up every imaginable crisis, from a lost tourist to a nuclear attack. Each law-enforcement person could call up anything needed from any agency and coordinate it. If the FBI needed something from the Secret Service, or the Coast Guard needed something from the sheriff's department, they could either ask a guy, *right there,* or get it off the computer. This coordination staff allowed us to police the Olympics the way they ought to be policed—without having a someone in charge.

We didn't need Big Brother running the show.

■

As 1984 rushed headlong into spring, my battles shifted from the FBI back to the LAOOC.

Throughout the six-county area, local law enforcement was drawing up security plans for outside the venues, while the LAOOC was drawing up plans for inside the venues. According to my disputed clause, if I found their security to be inadequate, I could insert my own troops and *make* it adequate. Naturally, I needed their plans. One of the damnedest things I ever saw—to this day I can't fathom it— going into March *1984,* Ed Best refused to turn over their plans for venue security.

Whenever we would ask, Best retorted, "I'm under orders not to provide them."

So I now had to go to the mat with Harry Usher, Ueberroth's second in command. Over and over I tried to explain that I had the responsibility for policing in the city of Los Angeles. Ueberroth had conveyed the strange idea that somehow the LAOOC could assume those duties, refusing to believe that LAPD can't simply turn over responsibilities that are given us under state law.

Perhaps worried about the expense of what I might add to their plans, the LAOOC tried to bully us into policing their way. And we would say, "You *can't* make those decisions. *We* make them. *You* just pay the bill."

At which point, talks broke off completely.

So I did what any good chief of police would do. I said, "Screw 'em. Forget they even have a plan. We'll police the whole thing ourselves."

Finally, the LAOOC grudgingly turned over its plan. In *April*. It was as expected, inadequate.

So with three months to go, off to a battle we trotted once more. On the advice of Bill Rathburn, I insisted fences be built around the perimeters of the two Olympic villages, at UCLA and the University of Southern California. Large and sprawling—USC's perimeter is three and a half miles; UCLA's, two—each university had more than 20,000 students. People wander in and out. USC bordered on South Central Los Angeles, a part of the city rife with crime.

At Bill's urging, army engineers had worked out a plan to build fences with sophisticated sensors. If someone merely touched the fence, the actual location would show up on a screen. Moreover, since it was possible to land a helicopter on either campus, I wanted interior fences placed around the dorms.

Naturally, the LAOOC didn't want to pay for any of it. "It's gonna look too hostile. The athletes will feel like they're being penned in."

"Yes," we countered, "but they're going to feel that we care about them. They're going to feel that much safer."

In fact, our plans were to encourage an atmosphere of freedom by providing plenty of friendly uniformed officers— short-sleeved shirts, open collars, big smiles on their faces— not oppressive Gestapo with automatic weapons slung over their shoulders. I stressed this repeatedly.

"We want to portray the image of free movement, all the freedoms that we try to tell the world we represent," I told the LAOOC.

No, no, *no*.

"We *will* have a fence, period," I said.

That's what I had to do. Anytime we knocked heads, it took that kind of intractable, no-negotiation, no-nonsense attitude on my part to get what we needed. It was not very pleasant. I was always under great pressure from some on the Police Commission to relent, and when I wouldn't, people moped. Here was this unrelenting, uncompromising, miserable, hard-nosed, opinionated son of a bitch—me.

And I wasn't finished. Another battle broke out over the number of officers assigned to the two Olympic villages. We wanted one hundred and fifty per village per shift. They came back and said fifty seemed about right. Fifty was preposterous. On a huge sprawling campus, even spotting one of fifty officers would have been a major event. Worse, they wanted to use volunteers, slap berets on their heads and train them to provide security—unarmed. And that's when negotiations came to a screeching halt.

I'll never be sure whether it was a money issue or a power issue with the LAOOC. It probably was a little of both. I think Peter Ueberroth, a tough and successful businessman, wanted to show a grand profit, which he did. So he was, understandably, counting his pennies. But when he accused us of trying to jack up expenses, that we were looking at the Olympics as a gravy train, I bristled. Certain costs were simply inherent in providing Olympic security and some of those costs we have never been compensated for. On the other hand, it was a power trip too. It just irritated him no end that he could not make decisions affecting LAPD.

Some of my loyal bosses on the Police Commission—reacting to pressure from Mayor Bradley, who reacted to pressure from Paul Ziffren, the LAOOC's chairman of the board—took Ueberroth's side. "Why are you doing this?" they cried.

"Because," I answered, "this is the security that we very carefully developed and planned. We are not *doing* anything to anyone."

To show good faith, I walked every single venue and village. I checked how every officer was going to be deployed. I took flights over the villages by helicopter and studied our staffing from that perspective. And I did find some places where we could cut back.

I also demanded that all of my people rework, remodel, and refine their system of security so that it was sleek but effective. Finally I said 125 officers per shift per village would be okay.

Still not talking to each other, we presented the LAOOC with an estimate of what our bill would be. The city had agreed to pay somewhere in the neighborhood of $15 million, using proceeds from a 6 percent bed tax and a tax on Olympic tickets. Anything more would have to come from the LAOOC. That came to $11 million, we said.

Dream on, the LAOOC said.

While we were deadlocked, Peter and I were invited to be head-table guests at a local business dinner. It was to be held at a hotel near the airport, and the day before, he phoned and asked me to arrive early and meet him in a room he had set aside.

"Daryl," he began, "we have to do something about your security costs. They're too high. We can't afford them."

"I have looked at them carefully, Peter. I'll cut wherever I can. But it's going to cost you somewhere around ten, eleven million."

"If it were a million dollars"—I'll never forget him saying this—"if it were a million dollars, we *don't have it*."

"Peter, if you don't pay, I'll tell everyone who will listen that the Soviet Union is absolutely correct. The security is lousy. I'm not going to allow the security to be lousy, so you're going to have to find eleven million dollars."

While I didn't have access to his books, I did know the numbers on some of the contracts he had signed. I knew that Coca-Cola was paying $12.6 million to be a sponsor, and what some of the other corporations were paying, including ABC's $225 million for the television rights. He had the money.

Ueberroth just shook his head and we went on to the dinner.

If an election had been held at that moment between Peter and me, he would have won it by a landslide. But Peter made one serious mistake. He miscalculated the City Council. Apparently unimpressed with the Council members, he did little to cultivate them. I did. I went to them and explained my position. I made them realize our contract with the LAOOC was clear and that Ueberroth had to pay up. They agreed and told Peter so. And that's when the check arrived—for $11 million. It was now May.

In May, the Soviets announced their boycott, citing the prospect of poor security. But since no Russian had ever asked to see our plans, I took the snub for the political grandstanding it was.

Then I fell into the headlines again.

On Sunday, June 24, I was sitting on my patio, drinking up the sun and reading Bella Stumbo's lengthy profile of Peter Ueberroth in the *L.A. Times*.

Peter, having seen an advance copy, had called me the day before. "By the way," he said, "there's an unfavorable comment about you in the piece." He hadn't said what. And I, having been profiled by Bella two years before, was sympathetic. "Well, I know Bella," I said.

Now, reading the piece, the "unfavorable comment" jumped out at me.

". . . On affable impulse, he [Ueberroth] wonders aloud about Los Angeles Police Chief Daryl Gates—'some of the things he says . . . Tell me, is he really a Nazi at heart?' "

I must admit, I chuckled. I could envision Peter coming back from someplace, Bella on the airplane with him, and probably he'd had a glass of wine or two, and out popped this thing in the form of a question, him saying, "Do you think Gates is a Nazi?"

Then it sunk in. A Nazi? I didn't like that connotation one bit. Not only had I been a student of World War II and Naziism, but I had just finished James Michener's *Poland*, which brought vividly to mind again all the atrocities the Nazis had committed. Sam had read the book, too, and now, seeing the article, she uncharacteristically broke into tears. "I can't believe anybody would think you were a Nazi," she said, "or even suggest it."

When I saw how she reacted, I really got upset. And then the rest of my family began calling, sounding even more hurt. I began wondering where Peter might have come up with this. I remembered the Soviet Jews comments that were attributed to me and how he had come away thinking I had been critical of Jews, and I thought, *That son of a bitch. I'll bet that's what stuck in his mind.* Plus the fact that I was being so hard-nosed about security, maybe he just figured I was a real storm trooper.

By Tuesday, my attorneys were sending Ueberroth a letter asking that he either apologize publicly or renounce what he'd said.

Ueberroth refused. He insisted he was merely repeating a reporter's question and he declined to say anything further.

Then Bella called and invited me to lunch. "As God is my judge," she swore, "he did say it. He said he didn't, but he *did* say it."

I was surprised. Reporters rarely are given to explaining anything. I think she talked to me without her editor's knowledge. I believed her.

A few days later Ueberroth met with me over the remark. "Okay, Daryl, what is it that you want?"

As if I were going to demand a million dollars or something.

"I want you to apologize, that's all."

"I'll be glad to do that," Ueberroth said, with obvious relief.

And he did.

■

The countdown to the Olympics continued on two parallel tracks. There was the public me, going out like a high school cheerleader and rallying support for the impending Games. I made dozens of speeches all over the city, stressing what a great moment for L.A. this would be. In doing so, I must have deflected questions on terrorism a million times. "Chief, do you think the potential for terrorism is great?"

"No," I would say, crossing my fingers. "Our security is so tight that if any terrorists do attack, they'll be dead terrorists." Then, crossing my fingers again: "And we are *not* going to have gridlock, either. It's going to be a *fun* time."

Ten days before the Games began, a gunman walked into

a McDonald's in San Ysidro, 130 miles south of Los Angeles, and shot twenty-one people to death, wounding nineteen more.

The night before the opening ceremonies, a man drove his car onto the sidewalk in Westwood, not a mile from the Olympic Village at UCLA, and mowed down forty-eight pedestrians, who were injured, and one who was killed.

As soon as I heard, I jumped in my car and was in Westwood before they finished picking up the bodies. I thought, *My God, is this the first of a series of attacks on Olympic athletes?*

The driver, it turned out, was not a terrorist but a psycho with a grudge. Having spotted two patrolmen on the sidewalk, and remembering some long-held grievance against uniformed officers, he aimed his car at them and tried to take them out.

Meanwhile, two rumors captured our attention. One, that a Libyan terrorist, supposedly part of a well-trained hit squad, was en route to the Games; he was detained at the Montreal airport. Next we heard that terrorists trained in Mexico were headed for Los Angeles. Efforts intensified to closely identify people coming across both the Canadian and Mexican borders. It was the best we could do. The countdown was over.

■

Saturday, July 28, 1984. Opening Ceremonies. More than 90,000 people filling the Coliseum, President and Mrs. Reagan among them, and the eyes of the world glued to their TVs. I arrived with friends and family members as a spectator, but my nerves were those of a chief of police.

The first two potential crises didn't wait long. Around 3:30, an hour before David Wolper's extravaganza would begin, I got word that somebody had placed a bomb where the torch was to be lit by former Olympian Rafer Johnson.

Johnson was supposed to run up a long flight of steps to the top of the Coliseum and light a gas line, which in turn would ignite the torch. Our information indicated there had been some tampering with the gas line and that it was going to explode. Within minutes we had our best bomb expert, Arleigh McCree, checking that gas line.

No bomb. An ABC technician had opened an electrical control box to make last-minute changes in the wiring, and in the process he'd severed one line and added another. When a second technician spotted the rewiring, he alerted security. My stomach muscles unknotted—though not for long.

President Reagan's appearance had presented all kinds of security problems. That morning he had gone over to USC to rally the American athletes with a kind of "Rah-rah, let's win one for the Gipper" exhortation. And that was okay. But there had been protracted debate over whether the President should officially pronounce the Games "open" from the floor of the Coliseum or from the steel-plated press box.

Peter Ueberroth had asked what I thought.

I said I would be happy to tell John Simpson, the head of the Secret Service, that in my judgment it was safe for the President to come down to the field. And it would have been. Although the President might seem an inviting target out there in the open, in fact it would take an expert marksman with a high-powered rifle and a hell of a lucky shot to strike him. With enough officers sprinkled throughout the Coliseum, it would be nearly impossible for somebody to rise up from the stands and get one off. And nobody had a prayer of sneaking onto the roof.

At the last moment, Ueberroth decided the President should stay in the press box, which would be heavily protected. What came as an unwelcome surprise to me was just how heavily.

Having seen the gridlock in Sarajevo caused by the magnetometers installed at the entrances to the stadium, Bill Rathburn and I had ruled them out. I saw no reason why we couldn't have a free flow of foot traffic coming into the Coliseum. Only now we realized there was *no* free flow. There was a huge jam.

The Secret Service, instead of letting people enter through the two tunnels nearest the press box, was sending them all the way around the Coliseum so they could enter through a tunnel only a few feet away, forcing them to walk a long and needless distance. Then, after arriving at the mid-level seats, people were stopped—including my wife and me—and made to go through magnetometers, installed by the Secret Service unbeknownst to me.

The crush of people backing up at the magnetometers was causing feelings of claustrophobia and near panic. Sheriff Sherman Block and his wife were caught in the crunch and she almost fainted. I had visions of what goes on at soccer games in other countries, where people have been literally crushed to death.

Barely able to move my arms, I flicked on my radio and told my security people to get the magnetometers down, now. They conveyed this message to the Secret Service, which took its orders only from John Simpson. Nobody was responding, and I, packed in like a sardine, couldn't move either. I could see the panic on faces all around me.

I got back on the radio and started yelling, something I rarely do, for somebody to get those damn magnetometers out, "before I tear them down myself." As near disaster hung in the balance, the magnetometers at last came down.

The next day, I chewed out the Secret Service for half an hour on their blatant disregard for people in this city. "If you try that again," I warned, "I will have the Los Angeles police department throw those magnetometers out. I would have torn them down myself but *I* couldn't move."

By 4:30, when the ceremonies began, I was a wreck. And the last thing I needed was the fireworks. I knew they were going to use fireworks, but it never dawned on me what the overall impact would be. It was an enormous display, and I sat there worrying every time one of those damn things went off: *My God, how are we going to distinguish between one of these and a bomb?* With each thundering explosion, I would tense up. By the end, I was almost sick.

Still to come was the helicopter headache. As daylight faded, a large industrial helicopter was going to appear over the Coliseum. Through clever lighting, no one would actually see the helicopter, only the spaceship with blinking lights that it would be hoisting. David Wolper wanted the spaceship to appear to hover over the playing field. We and the fire department said, "Absolutely not." The last thing we needed was for the spaceship to break loose from the helicopter and fall onto the spectators. Show biz can go only so far. So they agreed to bring the helicopter only to the peristyle edge of the Coliseum and we cleared a huge area behind it, just in case. The moment worked beautifully. The sight of that spaceship hovering at dusk, and the spaceman jettisoning out into the Coliseum, was spectacular.

Afterward, I went out to dinner, greatly relieved. In spite of the fireworks, the helicopter, the bomb scare, the Secret Service, and the panic, Opening Ceremonies generally had gone very well.

■

Like a Greek chorus throughout the city came the words: *Who are those guys?* Them, in the dark blue uniforms, big grins, posing for pictures with little kids, trading Olympic buttons, cheerfully giving directions . . . *not the cops!*

Los Angelenos were astonished. That's the LAPD? Even though we joke that our motto is "To know us is to love us," most citizens know us only as the scowling, mean-spirited bullies who write tickets and screw up a perfectly fine day. While Peter Ueberroth, the athletes, and the events were roundly and deservedly credited as the heroes of the 1984 Olympics, it was LAPD's finest hour too.

Even Ueberroth was impressed. He actually asked for additional security at the Coliseum and other locations—*asked* for it, knowing full well he was going to have to pay for it.

With mirrors and smoke and a mere 2,200 officers perfectly placed, we kept the L.A. portion of the Olympics running like Disneyland. Through meticulous deployment, LAPD gave the appearance of being everywhere, yet we were not. Due to our tough-talking chats with gang members prior to the Games, they disappeared completely from view. As people left the Coliseum we went with them in waves, escorted them to their cars and made everybody feel safe. It was a glorious thing: families strolling through these otherwise rough-and-tumble streets, the way people should be able to in a big metropolitan city.

Traffic seemed to vanish with the smog. Pulling that off took the concerted efforts of the city Department of Transportation, the California Department of Transportation, the local Cal Trans, the Highway Patrol, and LAPD. Whatever credit Ueberroth chose to take, the fact is the LAOOC did nothing but tell us when the events were scheduled. In addition to urging motorists not to drive, and encouraging businesses to stagger their work hours, we preset traffic signals so that traffic would move. We had helicopters watching traffic patterns constantly. We had tow services ready to move cars instantly. And while it was true that many people left town, the car count during the Olympics was actually greater than during a normal day of gridlock.

The feeling of joy was infectious. Everyone was courteous, people waited patiently in line, there was no pushing, and everyone seemed to be *smiling*.

Even me. Every day, wearing my uniform, I visited venues, stopped into our Emergency Operations Center, occasionally took a helicopter trip, and kept my fingers crossed. It became so idyllic that we actually had to drum up news to keep a very bored national and international press corps occupied so they wouldn't invent things. One of the "stories" we gave them was the arrests we had made of Olympic security people (the ones in the berets) stealing items from the villages. "We are very appreciative," I said, "of the Olympic Organizing Committee hiring these thieves. We don't have to go looking for them—they're right here."

Closing Ceremonies produced, once again, the knots in my stomach due to another idiotic barrage of fireworks. I never tense up, ever, but those continual booming explosions did it. The next day I had an upset stomach and was not feeling well at all.

Which is when we had the big bomb scare.

Late in the day, as athletes were packing their bags and heading for the airport a call came into our command post that a bomb had been found on a bus at LAX and that our bomb squad was on the way.

My security guy and I jumped in the car and took off. It was late afternoon and we got snarled in traffic. When we finally arrived, we drove through the gate at the north side of the field and onto the tarmac where the bus was parked.

"What happened?" I asked an officer.

The bus, carrying Turkish athletes, had pulled up to the service staircase at the gate, and as the athletes were getting off, Jim Pearson of Metro division noticed a bomb located in the wheel well of the bus. He had been able to remove it and nobody was hurt.

Pearson was pointed out to me and I went over to him. "Tell me what happened."

"Well, I was unloading the bus and I happened to notice something and I looked more closely and recognized it immediately because I've had some training in bombs," he explained. "I pulled the right wires, grabbed it, and threw it onto the tarmac. The minute I saw it, I yelled for Sergeant Matheny."

I thought, *Doesn't sound like any police officer I know.* Calling for a sergeant in the manner he described somehow struck an odd note. Plus, he had called his sergeant by name. As I walked away I noticed a tote bag on top of a car. "Who's that belong to?"

"That's Pearson's bag," an officer replied. "He's been our official photographer—it's a camera bag."

I turned back to Pearson. "That's a fantastic thing you did. You probably saved some lives. Very brave."

By then the media was clamoring all over the place, so I went to speak to them. I described this wonderful, heroic act of Jimmy Pearson's, told how he had some background in explosives, that the bomb squad people said it was a real bomb, and so on.

But the mystery of how the bomb could have been placed on the bus bothered me. At the airport I talked to some of my people and we went through the whole thing step by step. We'd had an elaborate plan to insure this could not happen. Busses were guarded around the clock. They were checked for bombs before they were loaded. A caravan of officers accompanied each bus along its route. "Chief, I can tell you that everything was done by the book, *everything,*" Commander George Morrison swore. "Just no way could that bomb get on there."

Unless it happened at the airport.

I noticed again the camera bag. I called the captain of Metro over, along with the bomb squad. "I know you're going to hate what I'm about to say," I told them, "but please don't question me. I want you to *do* it. I want you to get a bomb-sniffing dog and sniff Jimmy Pearson's camera case."

And it was: "Oh, Chief, it couldn't be!"

"Maybe," I said. "But I want it done."

The airport was in chaos. It had been entirely shut down. No planes were taking off and athletes were sleeping on the floor. Not knowing what we had, we weren't going to take any chances.

It was after 10:00 P.M. when I finally got away, and the more I thought about it, the more convinced I was that Jimmy Pearson had been involved. At midnight the captain of Metro phoned.

"You're right, Chief. Pearson admits he planted the bomb and we're now going through the process of searching his home and putting evidence together."

"But why," I inquired, "did he do it?"

"He felt he has not been getting recognition at Metro and he just wanted his sergeant to recognize his good work."

I couldn't believe it. But then it came back to me, how he pointedly said he had called for his sergeant. This guy was starved for love from his sergeant. So he planted the bomb at the airport, then turned around, "sighted" it, rescued all those people—just to get attention, like a little kid.

The next day more media people than I'd ever seen in my life showed up for the news conference. I was so embarrassed. I mean, we had just concluded an absolutely spotless Olympics, nothing could have been improved upon, and to top it off, here's this heroic act from a Los Angeles police officer.

"Except for the excitement created by our own Olympic athletes, the Olympics were so boring we had to create our own excitement, so we got one of our officers to plant a bomb," I said.

As with so many things involved in police work, you can cry or you can joke.

■

While I don't believe Peter Ueberroth gave LAPD proper credit publicly, he did, during the Games, tell me over and over how great our people were. As for the money, when we were adding up our bills I took issue with some of the expenses my people were putting in for. And Peter actually said, "Hey, you guys did a great job. Go ahead and pay their expenses, whatever they put in, they earned it." He gave me a torch as a memento, and I treasure it.

But the real memento will always be the memory of the spirit of the Olympics; it was infectious. And I'm confident the LAPD was a major, if not *the* major contributor to that. The way they looked, acted, responded. And while I believe Peter Ueberroth deserves all the credit he's received, in spite of our differences, in my mind a major part of the success of the Olympics has to go to the men and women of LAPD.

I really believe that. I always will.

17

To Kill a Cop

Sam had been wanting to try a restaurant in Pasadena called the Italian Fisherman, so that's where we were headed on Halloween night, 1985.

True to my word, I had taken several days off after the Olympics to relax and figure out what to do with the rest of my life. I sat on the sand in San Clemente, where Sam and I have a beachfront condo that we escape to when we can, and stared at the sun, the ocean, and my navel. We could take a cruise, I thought; we had never done that. And then I could retire.

Suddenly, I felt cold chills shoot up my spine. "You don't want to retire, do you?" I said to myself.

Myself said, "Uh-uh."

Right. I would stay on for another year, bask in the glow of the Olympics and have this discussion with myself some other time.

Going out to dinner remained a special occasion. With my schedule, and Sam's—she was still a flight attendant for United Air Lines—we ate out only about twice a year. We had waited for a few of the neighborhood kids to come by trick-or-treating, and then, as we were walking out, the phone rang. Assistant Chief Bob Vernon was on the line. "Off-duty officer's been shot out in the Valley, Chief. We don't know the details, if it was a suicide or what."

Normally, I would have jumped in my car and gone right to the scene. When a police officer gets shot, I want to be there. But after one look at Sam, I told Bob where I'd be and to keep me informed.

We had just finished our drinks, and the waiter was putting our plates down, when in walked Vernon.

"I've got a helicopter waiting," he said.

I stood up. Left my clams linguini, left a bottle of wine, left my wife—walked out.

It wasn't till I was airborne that I realized what I hadn't left; money or a credit card for Sam to pay the bill.

■

Detective Tom Williams, forty-two, was shot at 5:40 P.M. and he was still half-leaning against his orange Datsun pickup truck when I arrived.

Under the glare of high-powered lights, some one hundred officers and civilian employees were milling about. Many were part of the usual crime-scene crew: the lab technicians, the coroner, teams of detectives, fingerprint experts, ballistics people, traffic officers, a police photographer, and others. But many of the onlookers were LAPD brass. A police officer goes down, blood boils and everybody shows up.

Tom's truck was parked on the south side of a broad boulevard in Canoga Park in the northwest Valley, just a few yards down from the Faith Baptist Church day-care center. As was his habit, he had come to pick up his six-year-old son, Ryan. The boy was getting into the passenger side, and Tom the driver's side, when the detective noticed a two-door, light-colored Chevrolet, either parked across the street or slowly moving northbound. He must have seen the automatic weapon, or maybe he was alerted by a sixth sense, because witnesses said they heard him cry, "Duck!"

Ryan got down and was not hurt. But as dozens of costumed children stared in horror, the man in the car opened fire, hitting Tom four times, spraying his truck with bullets, and riddling the walls of the day-care center as well. Fourteen spent cartridges now lay on the sidewalk.

My heart sank. Every time an officer goes down, you feel it right in the gut. I remembered an officer named Charlie Monaghan, an ex-driver of Parker's, who was working out of Wilshire division. Sears Roebuck was right across the street, and they got a call that a guy had just written a check and the clerk thought he might be a forger. Charlie and his partner, Robert Endler, went over and were about to question the guy when he pulled out a gun and shot them both dead.

Eighty-six officers have been killed during my years with the department, twenty-nine while I served as chief. I grieved for each dead officer, but I didn't really feel the impact until I became chief. Jim Choquette, the first officer who died on my watch, was killed during a high-speed chase. He was attempting to apprehend a man who had just committed an armed 211 robbery when a motorist sideswiped his car.

David Kubly was the second. After seeing a man commit a robbery, David made a U-turn on Wilshire, jumped out, and confronted the guy. "Drop your gun," he warned. The guy shot him. David was a newlywed, just married to his high school sweetheart. It was then that it really began to hit home, this awesome feeling of responsibility that I felt for those officers and their families. At times, that responsibility would weigh more heavily on me than any others I had as chief.

Although 179 officers have died in the line of duty since 1915, when our record-keeping began, almost always they died while trying to prevent a crime. In 1984, Officers Duane Johnson and Archie Nagao had come upon a robbery in progress in Chinatown. An incredibly hair-raising shootout occurred. Three suspects were killed; one escaped. Both officers were hit. Johnson, riddled with bullets, died.

On rare occasions, officers are set up. A call will go out that a police officer is needed, and when the car pulls up, the officers are deliberately ambushed. But a specific officer had never before been targeted. Criminals are always warning: "Man, I'm gonna get you." However, no criminal yet had ever carried out his threat. No officer in LAPD history

had ever been killed like this: the stalked target of what
appeared to be a painstakingly planned hit. Tom Williams
had been assassinated.

I walked over to the truck and stared down at him. I
knew he'd been with the department thirteen years and was
a talented detective. He wasn't somebody who aspired to be
chief, or even a captain or lieutenant. Probably, he would
have remained a detective and would have achieved the
highest level for that rank. He seemed comfortable in his
work and his competence was unquestioned.

I had met him only once. There had been a fifty-mile
relay race in Newport Beach one Sunday afternoon among
a number of local police departments. Each officer had run
ten miles, including me. Afterward, as officers gathered at
their cars and campers, having picnics and barbecuing, I
remember chatting with Tom and his wife, Norma. He was
a good-looking man, tall, strong, and athletic. Now he was
slumped against the car, partially sitting up, the asphalt wet
with his blood. He was wearing dark-brown pants, a tan
shirt with a bullet hole in it, brown plaid tie, and a brown
herringbone coat. Brown loafers and socks. On his belt he
wore a badge—and a gun he hadn't had time to draw.

Hit in the left forearm, the right forearm, behind the
right ear, and in the lower abdomen, he'd lost most of his
blood. His face, as a result, had lost all its color. I suppose
in the back of every police officer's mind is the unwelcome
thought that if he goes down, he will be exposed out there
in the contortion and ugliness of death for a long time. It
was now after ten o'clock.

Hours before, Tom Williams had been a handsome, vital
person, and now he was a rag, filled with holes, totally
drained of everything.

I turned away and asked someone to drive me to his
house.

■

We have a system for comforting families. We are not so
cold as to have some factotum notify the wife by phone:
"Widow Brown? Your husband's just been shot."

The officer's captain responds first, going to the house—
if possible with a close family friend—to break the news,

make sure the children are cared for, and to drive the wife to the hospital or stay with her until others arrive. I am often the second to come by.

It's hard to describe the shock. Wives don't break down and cry on the spot. One time a wife went into a terrible rage. She climbed all over me, screaming that it was my fault her husband had been shot by a robbery suspect. But I've only seen that once. Usually, the women seem wooden, as if they simply don't have the capacity to take it in. And then comes the indelible sadness—it's just always written in their faces. Months, even years afterward, I can still see the profound sadness in their eyes, a haunted look that's somehow different from what you see in the faces of other people who lose family members. Maybe it has to do with the sudden and tragic circumstances of the officer's death, the feeling that this was so unnecessary. I can't really capture what I see in those faces, but it's there. It seems never to fade away completely.

For several months, other officers and their wives keep company with the widow, helping her with the children, comforting her, seeing if there is anything she needs. Then one day the widow notices nobody comes around anymore. Not only has she lost her husband, she's lost her social life as well; the picnics, the Christmas parties, the closely knit community of police families.

This ate at me. I thought, *This is ridiculous. We need these women. They're part of this family and I'm not going to let them go.*

So I initiated a number of programs to beef up departmental support. If an officer was ill, seriously wounded in the line of duty, or killed, I made sure the department went all out. Was the officer getting proper care at the hospital? If not, we hired a specialist. We hired babysitters. Once, when an officer was shot in the abdomen, I learned his wife was driving an old car with bald tires. Through our police memorial fund, we reconditioned the car. Another widow, with two hyperactive kids, was pregnant when her husband was killed. She was on a health plan, which allows for only a one-day stay in the hospital after birth. We paid for additional days and hired a home helper for two months, or longer if she felt it was necessary. Other times, if families needed to be flown in, the memorial fund paid for their tickets. I always stopped by the hospital to see the officer; if he was undergoing a long recuperation at home, I sent cards with cheerful messages.

Soon I found I was unable to keep track of everyone's needs, so I assigned a chaplain to take over. But after a while it began to take an emotional toll on him and he transferred to another position. Now a sergeant, Frank Virgallito, is assigned full-time to attend to the needs of all the families of the sick, injured, and deceased. I call him the Italian mother.

I also organized a family support group, which is one of my proudest achievements. Wives or husbands of slain officers, or officers who have died on active duty, can join if they wish. We give them an identification card, and they are invited to all social functions. Occasionally they come to roll calls, to lecture officers on how they can make things easier for the loved one left behind. Keeping their affairs in order, for instance, and keeping their spouses apprised of those matters. When an officer is killed, they are also there to offer support to the new widow or widower. They'll watch the kids, help the wife or husband through the mourning. Best of all, they seem instinctively to know the right things to say.

Comforting Norma Williams, her teenage daughter, Susan, and Ryan that night, I did not. So used to internalizing my emotions, I have trouble getting them out. My words stuck in my throat and I felt as if I had forty thumbs on each hand. As always, I just kind of sputtered and tried not to trip over the furniture. And then, in walked two women from the support group. They just swept in and smoothly took over. Grateful, I returned to the crime scene.

■

Eyewitnesses gave us this information.

The man in the car had been seen some minutes earlier driving south. He was light-complected, either Caucasian or Hispanic, short-haired, possibly with a mustache. But when he came back, driving north, and fired at Tom Williams, he was wearing a ski mask. Perhaps that's what had tipped Tom off: a man in a ski mask.

The first thing the detectives checked were the cases Tom had been working on. That afternoon, he'd given testimony in court. He'd been the investigating officer on the robbery of a movie theater manager in North Hollywood a year before. A suspect named Daniel Jenkins had been charged and released on bail. Three months ago, this same manager, George Carpenter, had been shot numerous times in an apparent assassination attempt while on a dinner break at a bar down the street from the movie theater.

He survived. Carpenter told us he couldn't identify the gunman, but detectives on the case suspected it was Jenkins, who was still out on bail awaiting trial.

That trial had finally begun only six days before, on October 25. Carpenter testified that it was Jenkins who had robbed him at the movie theater. Tom Williams, sitting with the prosecuting attorney during most of the trial, had testified that afternoon, October 31. The case then went to the jury. Jenkins, still out on bail, left the courthouse when the session adjourned.

Given that Jenkins may have already tried to assassinate one man who would testify against him—Carpenter—it was a distinct possibility that he would try to assassinate another. It's one of those things a detective can't overlook. But there were two problems with this theory: One, Tom had already given his damaging testimony against Jenkins, and two, unlike the man seen driving the car, Jenkins was black.

Going by the eyewitness accounts, our artist, Fernando Ponce, drew up a composite, which we gave to the media the next morning. The same day, Jenkins was found guilty of robbing the theater manager and was dispatched to the L.A. County jail.

Meanwhile, a woman came forward claiming she had information. She told detectives she knew of someone who had a contract to kill a private security guard who was scheduled to testify against Daniel Jenkins. This led detectives to a man named Voltaire Williams. He stated that on October 16, Jenkins offered to pay him $10,000 to kill a man who was going to testify against him in court. Jenkins, knowing he would have trouble enlisting an assassin to kill a police officer, had lied, describing his target as a security guard. That afternoon, Jenkins drove Voltaire Williams to the day-care center and pointed Tom out.

On October 17, Voltaire Williams was given a gun by a man named Ruben Moss. Moss instructed him to wait at a phone booth down the street from the day-care center and that Moss would let him know if Tom was coming. Moss phoned and said Tom wasn't coming. Voltaire returned the gun and refused to have anything more to do with the plot. Moss and Williams were arrested on November 2.

Jenkins found a new recruit. Alexander Xavier Hunter claimed that he, too, was offered $10,000 to ambush Tom at the Faith Baptist Church school. On October 25, Voltaire Williams provided him with a gun and a car, but once Hunter got to the school, he could not go through with it, he said. Arrest number three.

A fourth suspect in the conspiracy was Duane Moody, who admitted supplying a fully automatic assault weapon to Jenkins a few days before Tom's murder. Fed up with the bungled attempts, Jenkins decided to take care of Tom himself. Duane Moody said Jenkins told him why he wanted the gun, and that several hours after the shooting he was at Jenkins's house and heard him say he had shot Tom. Duane Moody was arrested too.

On the Monday after the murder, as the detectives were putting their case together piece by piece, Bob Vernon and I kept talking about how Jenkins clearly seemed to be the assassin, yet at least a dozen eyewitnesses identified the gunman either as white, or as wearing a ski mask. I don't know whether the detectives were ahead of us or we were ahead of them, but it flashed into our minds that Tom had been killed on Halloween, and on Halloween people wore disguises. "What if this guy, instead of blackface, put on whiteface?" we said.

So we immediately sent lab people to the jail to swab Jenkins's face. Makeup is hard to get off. Even though you wash your face very carefully, the chances of some adhering somewhere on your skin, maybe along the hairline, is very good. Most women are meticulous in cleansing their skin. But a pig like Jenkins, who probably couldn't even take a good bath, would surely miss some of the makeup, if he had used it.

Sure enough, the lab people found signs of makeup.

Still, this was not proof enough. In court, Jenkins's lawyer could plead: Well, he had this skin condition, needed to put some stuff on. And though we had four suspects under arrest, none of them very credible, we lacked, quite literally, the smoking gun. Therefore, we revealed nothing, not even that we had made some arrests. Such news could have tipped off whoever did have the gun and he could have driven out to the desert and buried it, or dropped it in the ocean. Without a gun, we had no case.

■

Tom's funeral took place Tuesday morning. Our Lady of the Valley Catholic Church in Canoga Park was packed with nearly two thousand people. Half of them were police officers who wore black bands of mourning across their badges. Afterward, we formed a motorcade to drive to the cemetery. Led by a mounted horse patrol, the caravan consisted of the hearse, the family, then me, followed by five hundred cars. This kind of outpouring for the death of a police officer was typical. And though we tend to snarl up traffic terribly, never once has a citizen complained.

It was while I was in the motorcade that my car phone rang.

The gun had been found. A man came forward claiming he had been given a satchel for safekeeping by an acquaintance. When he looked inside and saw the gun, he hid it under the hood of his car. But when he realized this gun had probably been used to kill a police officer, he called us right away.

It was a .9mm MAC-10 that had been converted to fully automatic. Ballistics was now trying to match the weapon to the slugs removed from Tom and the shell casings recovered at the scene.

The elation I felt drained as soon as I reached the cemetery. Our graveside services are emotional and dramatic. First, the traditional riderless horse walks by, with one boot propped in the stirrup. Then a bagpipe player leads the pallbearers. After comments by the clergyman, there is a seven-gun salute, followed by "Taps," which is when the tears really start. This is followed by the fly-by. Helicopters in formation fly over low, and one of them, as it reaches the graveside, drops off, representing the "wounded bird," which is what chokes me up more than anything.

I stepped forward. Sadly, I took from the color guard the American flag that had been draped over Tom's coffin, and walked over to Norma, Susan, and Ryan.

I have always said I marked my tenure as chief not by the number of years I served but by the number of times I've had to present that flag to an officer's family. You don't really feel the burden of a police officer's death until you become chief. I would get this terrible feeling of responsibility for every child and every wife. At once, I have this overwhelming desire to be a father, a husband, a grandfather to them all. I knew that if there was one single thing that would cause me to retire, it would be the funeral at which I would finally say, "I can't do this again. That's it."

Kneeling, I handed the flag to Ryan.

"I give you this, Ryan," I said, "not in any way to replace what you've lost. It's the flag of our country and it's symbolic. It's symbolic of courage and bravery and the things that your father represents, and it represents what he believed in. Every once in a while, take this flag out and maybe unfurl it and take a good look at it. It's a way of remembering what your father stood for. As time goes on, the memory of your dad is going to fade to some degree and you need every once in a while to pull this out and remind yourself what a wonderfully brave person he was, what he contributed. It's important that you do that."

I told him, too, that his father's last word—"Duck!"—meant to save Ryan's life, had earned him the Medal of Valor posthumously.

Six years old, a couple of tears trailing down his cheeks.

I have no idea if he heard a single word I said, or understood any of it.

■

By the time I arrived at Parker Center, ballistics was able to confirm that the MAC-10 had fired the bullets that killed Tom Williams.

Two and a half years later, Jenkins was convicted of murder and conspiracy to commit murder, as well as attempted murder on the theater manager, George Carpenter. He was sentenced to life without the possibility of parole. Williams and Moss were also convicted of conspiracy to commit murder. Moody was found not guilty of conspiracy and Hunter, who testified for the prosecution, was not charged.

But Tom's death lingered in my mind. He had been hit four times with an automatic weapon. Had Jenkins not had an automatic weapon, maybe he could have got off one shot, or two, and Tom might have lived.

It was the beginning of my crusade against assault-type weapons. The crusade would last until 1989.

18

"Casual Drug Users Should Be Shot"

On a Tuesday in July 1985, I was attending the weekly meeting of the Police Commission. I have no memory of the particular agenda, only the phone call that interrupted the meeting. Summoned by a secretary, I walked down the hall, into an office, and picked up the receiver.

"Chief," said Mary Miller, "the Huntington Beach police just called." She hesitated. "Scott's been arrested for armed robbery."

Mary gave me what scant details she had, and I, with a knot in my stomach the size of a bowling ball, returned to the meeting and woodenly reported the news. It was greeted with words of sympathy. Shortly thereafter, the Commission adjourned.

As I stepped into the lobby and walked toward the elevator, I was ambushed by a herd of reporters. Pushing a mike in my face, one TV newsman cried, "Your son's been arrested—how does it feel!"

Feel? Where did they get these questions, feel? Politely, I edged my way through the mob, saying as little as possible. One thing I knew for certain: It couldn't have been *armed* robbery. Scott was far too gentle ever to put someone in jeopardy by arming himself. I sidestepped another reporter, ducked into the elevator, and rode up to my office to learn the details firsthand, feeling numb. Feeling this terrible loss. As if my son were dead.

■

Desperate for a fix, Scott had walked into a pharmacy not far from his mother's house in Huntington Beach and, pretending he had a gun in his pocket, demanded not money, but drugs. Later, he told me he intended to swallow the pills and kill himself, but his tragic mission instead turned into a comedy of errors. The frightened pharmacist gave Scott everything he had, far more than Scott could carry. The alarm went off and Scott ran, dropping drugs all the way back to Wanda's house.

Because the pharmacist recognized Scott, and because he had left a trail a mile wide, the local police soon had the house surrounded. They ordered Scott to come out, but he was too scared and wouldn't. Eventually, his stepfather arrived and persuaded him to surrender.

So the nightmare began again—with a whole new twist.

■

At times it seemed as if all of Los Angeles were drowning in drugs. Tons of cocaine flowed into the area freely. Rock houses—single-residence structures, stark and choked with filth, where rock cocaine, also known as crack, is sold and smoked—were springing up like weeds on otherwise nice neighborhood streets. Drug arrests were up, but so was usage. Every day, people were being robbed or murdered in the name of drugs. And Hollywood, convinced that drugs were cool, was mindlessly splicing drug scenes into their feature films and television shows.

The stories filtering out of the schools were particularly horrifying. At Hollywood High, kids would sprawl in the middle of the football field at lunchtime and smoke dope. By doing it out in the open, they could spot an outsider approaching and dispose of their roaches. At Wilson High, near my home in Highland Park, a kid would walk into the main administration building every morning carrying a shop-

ping bag filled with drugs that bore a sign: FOR SALE—
ANYTHING YOU WANT. At some schools, children were
reluctant to use the restrooms, so dense was the smoke from
reefers. Teachers, intimidated by parents' taking them to
court for harassing their kids over dress and conduct codes,
walked in and ignored it.

Inundated with these stories since the early 1970s, we
began putting undercover police officers into the high
schools in 1973. Now, as drug use grew more widespread,
we increased their numbers. Outraged that the police were
spying on children, the ACLU took me to court. It was the
one time I ever agreed with the ACLU: It *was* a terrible
thing to do. But as I had learned through my experiences
with Scott, neither teachers, principals, nor parents had the
least idea what to do; I feared we were losing a whole
generation of kids. The ACLU suit was struck down by a
fine Superior Court judge whose decision I called a breath
of fresh judicial air.

With young undercover officers posing as students, the
arrests for drug sellers rose. Unfortunately, drug use didn't
go down one bit. So I began to think of other ways we could
attack the problem. Only one approach made sense: to try
to stop kids from taking up drugs in the first place.

In the spring of 1983, I went before the School Board
and laid out the problem. Something had to be done, I
urged. "What if we developed a drug education program
that would be taught by police officers? Not just a single
lecture, but one class a week for a whole semester?"

School Superintendent Harry Handler admitted it was
worth a try and he asked Dr. Ruth Rich, a curriculum
expert, to work with us on writing a program. Ruth said she
thought my idea had merit, but that I was completely nuts
to think a program could be developed overnight. Nevertheless, in three months she had one, in time for the fall
semester. It was designed with several thoughts in mind. It
had to be an honest portrayal of what drugs did. "The kids
must never be lied to," I insisted. They had to be told that
yes, drugs can make you feel good, but then, hey, this is the
result. Second, the program had to offer realistic scenarios
that kids could use to resist peer pressure. Finally, the
program would be presented by experienced police officers

who would have immediate credibility with students. Teachers did not. Many were not educated about drugs, and some, unfortunately, went home and used them.

I volunteered ten officers to initiate the program at fifty elementary schools, each officer teaching one fifth- or sixth-grade class at one school per day. We named the program D.A.R.E.—Drug Abuse Resistance Education—and began to talk it up.

I had practically no support for D.A.R.E. Some politicians and civil libertarians questioned the wisdom of putting police officers in the classroom, fearing we might turn L.A. into a police state, and pointing out that police officers were desperately needed on the streets. I tried to get additional budget money for D.A.R.E., but Tom Bradley refused.

"When the chief wants to start a new program," he told Assistant Chief Barry Wade, "tell him to talk to me."

I hadn't, because I sensed the futility. When Ed Davis was chief, he started a program to put police officers in high schools in an effort to keep gangs out. They taught a one-semester course called "The Police Role in Government." Kids really warmed up to the officers, we found, but Bradley eliminated the program, saying the police should be used for other things.

Furthermore, there was our experience with Community Relations Officers, the community-police relations program recommended by the McCone Commission after Watts. Despite the good results we were seeing, Bradley ordered me to cut the CROs from the first budget I presented him as chief. In an effort to get off on the right foot with him, I did. But even when the Urban League criticized the LAPD for taking away the CROs, Bradley would not reinstate them. Even given his concern for the cost, I found his lack of foresight appalling.

Fearing I would again be rebuffed, I wanted to gather as much support for D.A.R.E. as I could before making it a major budget issue. The Police Commission approved the concept but could not authorize funds. As a result, I began to divert, without any authority to do so, a great deal of taxpayers' money to the program—up to $5 million a year. I did this by reassigning officers to the D.A.R.E. program. I'd pull them from narcotics, or wherever I thought we could lose an officer or two. In addition to those who would teach the program, we needed a support staff and supervisors. Eventually, I convinced the City Council to pass a resolution supporting D.A.R.E., which took me off the hook, somewhat. But I still had no budget authority for the money I was using to pay for it. As a last resort, we began raising money from the private sector.

The program was a hit from day one and it was hard to tell who enjoyed it more, the officers, the kids, the teachers (who remained in the classroom), or the frightened parents. The officers, spinning tales of the streets, enthralled the children, who discovered they actually liked these guys. The officers would spend their day at the school, getting to know the kids, joking, playing with them, showing they were regular people too.

The officers, to their amazement, often discovered that they were the first people to teach values to some children whose parents had never done so. One officer told me: "The strangest thing, Chief. I've had kids tell me they didn't *know* it was wrong to steal somebody's lunch money. *In the fifth grade.*"

One officer, on his first day, scrawled his name on the blackboard, then went around the room asking the children their names. One kid stood up and boldly declared, "I'm a gang member and I don't like the cops, and I don't wanna be here."

The officer said, "Okay," and went on. The kid was twelve, a sixth-grade troublemaker, and lesson after lesson, he just sulked. Then one day he approached the officer. "Can I talk to you?" he said.

"About what?"

"I'm not really a gang member and I don't want to join a gang."

"Then don't."

"Except my dad was in a gang, and my brother's in a gang, and I'm gonna have to join one too."

"If you don't want to join, don't," the officer said. "I'll help you."

Eventually, the officer went to see the kid's parents. The dad said, "I am an ex-gang member, and my other boy's in one, but I don't really want any of my kids in gangs." Or so he said.

The officer urged the father to encourage the child to stay out of the gang and he continued to build his relationship with the boy—taking him to baseball games, giving him a bat, for instance. And before the semester was over, that kid had turned completely around. He became the officer's assistant in teaching the D.A.R.E. program. His school attendance improved and so did his grades. He became a model kid.

Another story took a different turn. One father showed up at school and told an officer, "Look, I know my kid's using pot."

"How do you know?"

"I just know. What do I do about it?"

The officer rattled off pointers on telltale signs of drug usage. The father was a doctor, by the way, and genuinely concerned. A week or so later, the doctor returned. "I now know my son is smoking marijuana."

"Well, how did you determine that?" the officer asked.

And the father said, *"Because he stole my bong."*

In time we found that D.A.R.E. made such an impact on some kids that they actually approached the undercover agents who were posing as students, and gravely warned, "Listen, you've got to stay away from that group you're always with. They use drugs!"

Seeing a glimmer of hope, I met with some of Vice President George Bush's people on the eve of the 1984 elections. I wanted to push the subject of drug education. Sheriff Sherman Block was with me. We explained we had recently started D.A.R.E., and while we hadn't had time to evaluate it fully, we were seeing early signs of great success.

Education, Bush's people responded, was a politically touchy topic. They told us that many parents did not want their kids to know about drugs, believing that knowledge alone would lead them into a life of depravity. Instead, the prevailing wisdom was to use scare tactics. It reminded me of the days when kids were told masturbation would make them blind. When it didn't, they kept on doing it. Drug users, we argued, would come to the same conclusion. "Drug education," the Bush people reiterated, "is just too sensitive to touch."

"That's the biggest bunch of nonsense I've ever heard,"

I came right out and said, "and I don't give a damn if it's politically sensitive or not. It's the *right* thing to do and you ought to *insist* that it be part of the Reagan/Bush administration." Not mincing words either, Sherm took them to task as well.

Several years later, Nancy Reagan attended one of our D.A.R.E. classes. She did a beautiful job of role-playing, acting the part of a sixth-grader, and her interest gave our program immediate credibility. Why, I'm not sure. But suddenly, some of the federal agencies came through with money so we could begin regional centers to train D.A.R.E. officers around the country. By then, our classes were so overloaded with visiting officers, we couldn't take care of the demand.

In time, D.A.R.E. would be taught in all fifty states. It's taught in other countries as well—Brazil, Argentina, Chile, in Central America, Puerto Rico, Germany, and England. The Department of Defense adopted it and it is taught in all the military-dependent schools. Taking it a step further, we started STAND, an outreach program for private industry. Officers who are experts in the field teach it to management, human resources people, and employees on an off-duty basis. We charge the company only for the officer's time and ask that it make a contribution to D.A.R.E. Companies cannot believe how cheap STAND is, compared to the cost of other commercial training seminars.

Still, I wouldn't let up. I wrote to President Reagan, urging more attention be paid to the nation's devastating drug problem. But all I got back was a letter from a doctor on his staff, who mainly gave lip service to the problem. Silly as it sounds, Nancy Reagan's slogan, "Just Say No," did more for raising the consciousness of the American people than anything her husband did. But it wasn't enough. I began speaking out, taking on the federal government, chastising its complete ineptness in dealing with the drug problem. I made so much noise that finally, Vice President George Bush's people requested a meeting with me. In May of 1988, when Bush came through L.A. on a campaign swing, we arranged to spend some time together. The first day, we picked him up at the airport and took him first to a rock house in South Central Los Angeles, then to a

D.A.R.E. classroom. The second day, before attending a roll call of officers going out on gang patrol, we would meet at Parker Center.

That morning, when I got to work I hardly recognized my office. Having learned that Bush liked rolls and coffee, Mary Miller had swept the usual mess of papers out of sight, set the conference table with dishes I didn't know we had, and put out the coffeepot and a big plate of rolls.

Bush arrived and I began laying out my thoughts on how the United States should prosecute its war against narcotics and dangerous drugs. Actually, what I did was lecture the poor man for two solid hours.

"The Reagans have done a wonderful job of raising the level of consciousness," I said, "but there's been no real follow-through. I understand you're very loyal to the President, but if you're going to be President, you'll have to break away and go your own direction."

I then recited what I thought needed to be done to fight the war on drugs. I talked about our unprotected borders, the need to establish priorities within the entire Executive branch, and how the American public had to play a big role too. "You know my theme in fighting the war against gangs and drugs in Los Angeles?" I said. "Whatever it takes for however long it takes—no retreat, no surrender."

I hammered him with ideas on how to get people involved. "You've got to sell the drug problem as something that is bad for kids," I said. "Remember when we were in school and the teacher passed around a jar or a tin can for polio? Every kid would put in a few cents. The point wasn't the money. It was to teach kids about polio, that it was bad, that it attacked kids. Their pennies were helping to get rid of a plague on society. I think this is one of the things we could be doing about drugs."

I harangued Bush some more. He listened—really listened, not like most politicians, whose minds are somewhere else. I felt I had his full attention and he said he couldn't agree more with what I had said. His responses cheered me and I considered the meeting a success. I came away very impressed.

A week later, the LAPD photographer handed me a batch of pictures he had taken during the meeting. Proudly, I took them home to show my wife.

"My God," said Sam, thumbing through them. "This is embarrassing, Daryl. Did you look at them?"

"Why, no. What's wrong?"

"Every single picture, the Vice President's sitting there with his hands folded and there you are, jabbing your finger in his face."

■

The drug problem I railed against publicly continued to dog me privately. Scott was booked for robbery—the *armed* part of the charge was dropped—and taken to jail. By now, he knew better than to call me. Four times before he had been picked up for possession; the first three charges were dropped. Each time, I had bailed him out. Always there was the pain of watching my son walk into a courtroom dressed in jail clothes. And always the media were there to record the event. Then, in November 1979, he was arrested a fourth time, for possession and driving under the influence.

Once again he called and begged me to bail him out. This time I said, "I won't."

Never before had I said no to my son and it was probably the hardest thing I've ever done. But by then, I was as desperate in my own way as he was in his. After one failed attempt at rehabilitation after another, after seeing him steal from his own family to support his habit, I had reluctantly gone over to the "tough love" school of dealing with addicts.

Tough love goes against every parental instinct. A parent's normal reaction is "Oh, God, there's my child living in filth. I must clean him up, dress him, and give him money." This does not help the child at all. It is enabling him to continue his behavior and you can't give him a single crutch. Tough love means that if you really love your child, you are willing to give up that natural instinct to reach out and give him an assist.

I memorized the words they advise you to say: "I love you enough to allow you to reach way below the bottom until you decide to cure yourself. And once that happens, I'm here; you'll have all my moral strength and we'll take it one day at a time for the rest of your life."

I said those words to Scott. And I added a few of my

own. "If you clean yourself up, I'll do anything in the world for you. But I won't lift a finger to help you while you're on drugs. Don't even call me. You're on your own."

Now that he was in jail, surrounded by criminals and addicts, my hope was that he would finally hit bottom and jolt himself into the iron commitment that drug rehabilitation requires.

It was a desperate gamble, I knew. For by then I understood that addicts are controlled not by their devoted family or good intentions, but only by the drugs their bodies cry out for. Rehabilitation had become, for me, an act of faith. Despite the number of people lined up to get into clinics, most want only to get cleaned up. Once out, they go right back to narcotics. Looking for a magic cure, they and their families learn that no addict is ever cured. All they can do is maintain themselves in a sober state each day as it comes. I shut my mind to the heavy numbers that spoke of failure, and geared my faith to the success factor—long shot that it was.

But my slim hopes for the shock of jail life to jolt Scott into a desire for sobriety were quickly dashed. The sheriff of L.A. County at the time was Peter Pitchess, a good friend, who refused to put Scott into a regular cell. He feared that other inmates would learn his identity and harm or even kill him. So Peter put Scott in isolation in a district jail in Sierra Madre.

Being the charmer that he is, Scott soon had all the deputies fathering him and practically ran the jail. Polite and respectful of authority, he was always agreeable and could converse with them intelligently. He washed their cars and they gave him tips. The money he earned, he later confessed, he immediately spent on drugs. "While I was in jail," he told me, "I got all the dope I wanted. Everyone did. Visitors and deliverymen would bring it in."

It was not the first time I had heard that drugs made their way into the jails. But it was the first time it became personal.

■

The failure of America to deal with the drug problem is indelibly written on its streets. The results spill over into our ledger books. Most crimes committed in America today are the result of someone needing money for drugs.

Some 60 to 70 percent of all burglaries and thefts are drug-related, and so are 65 percent of all homicides. Each year in the mid-to-late eighties, LAPD would confiscate seven-and-a-half tons of cocaine off the streets. In the last few years, due to crackdowns in Colombia, Peru, and Bolivia, and the shoring up of our own border patrols, drug seizures have fallen off probably by half. As President, Bush added substance to Reagan's mere platitudes. He appointed a tough drug czar in Bill Bennett. He authorized the money to bring the Coast Guard and other agencies to bear on the borders and coastline. In addition, due to drug education perhaps, cocaine usage is down by as much as 20 percent, particularly with kids. Oddly, this turn of events made our job of going after drug users and pushers all the more difficult.

LAPD has the largest narcotics division in the country, outside of the NYPD's (which is twice as large, but we make about the same number of arrests). While not all officers work undercover, they have to be able to blend into any part of the drug culture. They operate at all levels, from a guy on the street looking for a little dope, to officers posing as bigtime drug dealers. The job can be incredibly dangerous; whether an officer tries to buy a large consignment of drugs or a small amount, there are always guns close by.

Enormous detail goes into a drug-buying operation. First and foremost, the officer must be a superb con man. He must totally unlearn all police mannerisms and assume, as skillfully as any actor, an entirely new role. If he makes even the smallest slip, he's likely to lose his life. He must be extremely quick-witted, with a glibness that allows him to adjust very quickly to changing situations. He must learn to act as if he were sampling a drug without actually doing so, which requires the sleight-of-hand of a magician.

All narcotics officers must also possess inhuman patience. They must be willing to work around the clock for weeks on end, lie out in a muddy field sometimes for hours, or sit in cramped, fetid quarters waiting for something to happen. Drug deals take an inordinate amount of time—time spent on surveillance, time spent on investigative background, time spent endlessly waiting.

Say an officer—we'll call him Mike—wants to buy fifty or one hundred kilos of cocaine. Mike starts checking around for someone who has that much to sell. He makes contact and the byplay begins. First, Mike must act suspicious of the drug dealer—like maybe the dealer is a cop. Then he must act suspicious about whether this person can actually supply what he says he can. So they engage in a bit of show and tell. Mike wants proof the guy has the drugs, and the dealer wants to see a little of Mike's money.

Which is where we ran into a big problem. At one time, you just had to show ten to twenty thousand dollars. Then it got to be a hundred thousand, five hundred thousand. And it had to be in cash. You can't go running to the bank at midnight. So we're thinking, *My God, what if we lose that money? What if half a million goes down the drain because we've lost control of the money?* Protecting the money and the undercover agent requires not only careful planning, but a healthy paranoia. We almost got to the point where we were as paranoid about losing the money as we were about losing the officer.

Naturally, we had a terrible time persuading the city to give us the money. Politicians don't like keeping half a million dollars in a safe where it isn't earning interest for them. I tried to get the Federal Reserve to turn over fifty million dollars to police departments all over the country, the used money that is taken out of circulation. It would serve as our "show money." But I couldn't get the feds to cooperate. So back to the city we went, begging for the money. The recent federal law on asset forfeitures, which allows law enforcement to keep a part of the money it seizes, finally served to rescue us.

When it's time for the deal to be done, the danger escalates. Since there is no honor among drug dealers, our man Mike has to be aware they may be setting him up to steal his money and then kill him.

We had one officer, Blackie Sawyer, who was supposed to meet a dealer in a hotel room. We had officers in the room next door. They thought they had him covered. But when the transaction went down, the guy with the narcotics pulled out a gun and shot Blackie point-blank before the other officers could get in there. He was the only undercover agent we ever lost that way—a pure "ripoff."

In time our tactics would change. We found it was more efficient to skip the long weeks of surveillance and setting up the deals by instead paying informants to lead us directly to the drug dealers. With money from drug seizures, we were able to afford this. Sometimes we had to pay as much as $50,000 for a big heist, putting us in league with some really terrible people. We kept an "unreliable informant" file, but even so, it always gets down to: How much can you trust an unsavory character?

We put them on a leash and we learned to check every piece of information they provided. Even if they came through for us once, we took the same precautions if we used them again.

For just when you think you can trust one of these guys, you'll get burned every time.

■

Once Scott was released from the L.A. County jail, he climbed right back onto his roller coaster. Over a period of six years he would be clean for a while; then he would start using. I continued my tough love stance, and became the villain to some in my family for it. They took pity on Scott, and Scott used that pity to con them all. When he was clean, his grateful sisters and friends bought him presents. Even though I warned and begged his concerned and loving grandparents not to give him money, they would end up feeling sorry for him and give their grandson another hundred dollars.

When I would find out, I'd almost go crazy.

■

Back on the streets our war against drugs escalated, as every clever tactic we devised was topped by one from the drug sellers. It became a war of technology. In the early eighties, when rock houses were just getting started, the front door would contain a slit. You pushed through your money; they pushed through the rock cocaine. Which foiled us completely. You can't arrest a hand. Unless there was something distinctive about the hand, we couldn't identify who it belonged to. So what we needed to do was to get inside quickly enough to seize evidence.

The doors got thicker. We would show up with a tow truck and a cable, lock onto the front door or a window, and storm in. The problem was, no matter how much skill and stealth the officers used, it took too long to get inside. By the time we did, the sellers would have taken the drugs into a bathroom—which would have a steel door—and flush them down the toilet. One household I saw had installed a commercial garbage disposal with a huge funnel top right in the middle of the dining room. It didn't matter that we had seen deals go down—or had earlier bought drugs ourselves. Without the drugs as evidence, we couldn't make an arrest that would result in a conviction.

Our next tactic was to use small explosives, called shape charges, to blow locks off doors. The cylinders, ten or twelve inches in diameter, would be hooked by wire to the lock, then detonated by remote control. But the ever-thicker steel front doors soon had locks in so many places that we had to put shape charges on the door itself and blow it off its hinges. There would be an explosion, off would come the door, and in would thunder the cops, scaring the hell out of the people inside. I used to go on these raids, and frankly, they worried me. The explosives seemed too dangerous, both to the officers and to the people inside the houses.

One raid I went on, the door was blown off and inside we found an absolute pigsty. It's hard to imagine the filth inside those rock houses; the litter of garbage, papers, and clothes on the floor, the stench wafting out of bathrooms so disgusting they made gas station restrooms look pristine. In the kitchen, where powdered cocaine would be heated with baking soda until fingernail-size "rocks" popped out of the broth, encrusted counters were piled high with refuse and ancient, half-eaten things. It reminded me of the day we took Nancy Reagan inside a crack house, and Nancy, raising her eyebrows skeptically, said, "Where's the furniture?"

There was none here, either. But right next door was one of the best-maintained homes I'd ever seen. It was owned by an elderly black couple who prided themselves on the care of that home. The man had done all the work by hand. Every pane in every window was set in very carefully, sanded just so, and painted beautifully. As careful as we were in placing the shape charges on the rock house, we managed to blow out this man's windows on the side of his house facing it.

I knocked on his door and apologized profusely. The man grinned. "Chief, I'm so happy that you came and did something about that house. If you'd blown up half my house I wouldn't have cared. Those people have destroyed my neighborhood."

We paid to fix his windows, but the incident once again warned me that we were engaged in something extremely dangerous. Many of the houses we blasted into were like heavily fortified, heavily armed bunkers. I decided we had to try something else.

SWAT had been requesting armored vehicles to use in situations like the Black Panther and SLA shootouts, but the city had refused to allow the police department to have military-type equipment. Shortly before the Olympics, SWAT discovered it could pick up two armored vehicles from the Department of Energy for a dollar each. The vehicles had been used for security at nuclear plants. And I thought, *Okay, what we need to do is to put this in the mode of being not an assault weapon but a vehicle of mercy. A vehicle that would* rescue *people.*

Without permission, we obtained the two vehicles and we painted them a nice blue to cover up their military look. And then we printed RESCUE VEHICLE on the side and slapped the city seal on the door. When we were finished, I told the Police Commission about our pretty new rescue vehicles. "For situations like the SLA shootout," I emphasized. And they said, "All right."

SWAT, which is clever about designing useful equipment, came to me and said, "What if we were able to devise a method of turning one of these vehicles into a battering ram?"

They had figured out a way to attach a battering ram to the front of the vehicle once they approached their target, so they wouldn't have to drive the surface streets looking like an invading army. They needed to practice, they said, but you can't just go up to somebody's house and try it out. So SWAT found some houses marked for demolition along the path of the new Century Freeway, and they got permission to use the ram on them. They learned how to approach a location, find and avoid the gas and electricity lines, then hit with precision the exact spot on the house they wanted to punch a hole through.

Again, I told no one what we were doing. But I went out and watched the practices. In my mind, the battering ram would be a far safer way to blast into a rock house than using explosives. And neither the city leaders nor the public had complained about those. The more I watched, the more I believed in SWAT's ability to use the battering ram expertly. Soon, they were able to ram a hole about three feet by four into the side of a house, move inside, and have everybody on the floor in eight seconds. It was an amazing piece of work.

In February 1985 we planned our maiden operation. The target was a rock house in Pacoima in the northwest Valley. Hours before, we went to an abandoned airfield for a final run-through. One more time, the SWAT team practiced getting the battering ram out and affixing it to the front of the rescue vehicle. We brought along two photographers—one print, one electronic—to record this great event and to serve as pool photographers for the rest of the media.

I had insisted on riding co-pilot, in part because if anything went wrong, I would be there to assume full responsibility. But also, there were times when I felt I had to show I was willing to crawl in the dirt with my officers. Somebody produced a bottle of Thunderbird and asked me to christen the rescue vehicle, imaginatively named *Thunderbird*. I did.

It was colder than the devil that night as we drove to our destination. All the surveillance work had been done earlier. An undercover agent had bought drugs from this pusher that afternoon. We had our search warrant. All we needed was the guy and his stash.

We stopped around the corner from the house and SWAT quickly attached the battering ram. As we approached the house we announced over a bullhorn our stated purpose and got no response. Then we pulled into the driveway, alongside a Cadillac convertible, and we blasted into the side of the house, right on target. The SWAT people were inside in seconds.

Meanwhile, the driver pulled back from the house and

out of the driveway, which was slippery. The vehicle swung sideways and hit the Cadillac, leaving a nice dent in its fender.

It was not our shining hour. The guy we had come to arrest had run out of rock cocaine and had gone out to resupply. No pusher, no drugs. Instead, what we had busted in on were two women and two little kids in the kitchen eating ice cream. One was the dealer's wife, along with his kid. The other kid belonged to a neighbor. I looked at them and said, "What kind of parents would allow little kids to be in a rock house?" Nobody answered me.

A moment later, the guy burst in. You might think he'd have run in and said, "Look at my house! Where are my kids? Is my wife okay?" But he didn't say that. Instead he started screaming, "You ruined my Cadillac!"

With no drugs in the house, no arrest, and one dented Cadillac, I thought, *Oh-oh, I'm going to have a lot of explaining to do.*

Plus, it was a nice house, with a fireplace in the living room and a den, in a nice neighborhood. I got on the phone fast. But none of the members of the Police Commission answered, nor did the mayor. Finally, I located somebody from the mayor's office.

Later, I did reach Commissioner Bert Boeckmann. "Um, you'd better watch the eleven o'clock news," I said.

Bolstered by photographs of the women and children eating ice cream, the *Times* and the *Herald* gave me hell. They emphasized the horror of the police busting in on this idyllic scene, never bothering to point out how horrible it was to have mothers and little kids in a rock house in the first place. Nor did they attempt to explain the elaborate steel fortification of a house in suburbia. They also disregarded the neighbors' expressed concerns about having a rock house on the street. Instead it was: "Here's Gates again—gone wild."

Typically, I became defiant. "I'm going to use this battering ram on every single fortified rock house in town," I proclaimed. And people said, "Sure, as long as it's in a black community." And I said, "Baloney. Show me a rock house in Bel-Air and I'll plow right through the front door. I don't care where the damn house is."

Despite the bad press, I garnered the support of some on the City Council. Dave Cunningham, who is black and who had castigated me over the chokehold remark, phoned and said, "Go right ahead, Chief. You do whatever you can to get rid of those rock houses. They're going to destroy the black community if you don't."

After we used the battering ram two or three more times—successfully—the ACLU dragged us into court. We argued that the court could not dictate our tactics. We explained we were trying to gather evidence, we had a court-authorized search warrant, and it was our decision how to proceed. The court came down with a half-assed ruling ordering us to come up with some guidelines and insisting that we obtain court approval for each mission when obtaining the search warrant. One thing they did not need to remind us of: We made certain through careful surveillance that no kids were in the house; if they were, we scrubbed the mission.

I continued to go on every raid. After one in south central L.A., I went into the crowd that had formed in the street to get a sense of what people in the neighborhood felt. For one hour and forty minutes, I stood on the sidewalk *signing autographs*. People were overjoyed that we were shutting down rock houses in their neighborhood. It was only the outsiders who made a fuss, people who never had to live in these areas.

Word about the battering ram spread through the streets like wildfire. Narcotics officers would knock on a door, yell, "Police officers, search warrant, let us in," and there would be no response. Then they would yell, "Get the battering ram!" and the door would fly open. It frightened even the hard-core pushers to imagine that at any moment a device was going to put a big hole in their place of business, and in would march SWAT, scattering flash-bangs and scaring the hell out of everyone.

In time, fortified rock houses began to disappear. Between 1987 and 1991, we closed 1,659 of them. They still exist—at any one time there might be 180 to 200 rock houses operating—but nobody's using steel doors anymore. LAPD still has the battering ram and they use it if they must.

Despite the criticisms hurled at us, we were able to

eliminate a terrible menace. No other city has yet accomplished what we have. Best of all, no one ever got hurt.

■

Scott's robbery of the Huntington Beach pharmacy resulted in a conviction on a lesser charge: grand theft property. He was sentenced to thirty-six months' probation and one year in jail. Once again he was put in isolation and was doted upon by all. While I was grateful in a way, I was also deeply concerned that he would not feel the full impact of jail life—and he didn't. Eight months later he was back on the streets.

My brother Steve, who had just been transferred from captain of Narcotics to captain of Southeast Area, felt confident he could help Scott. He had raised four terrific children, and Scott had always been fond of him. So Steve began working with Scott's probation officer, and Scott seemed to be responding. He agreed to enter Impact House in Pasadena, which operates one of the toughest and best rehab programs in the country. But again, it would become just another chapter of the same old story. Not long after leaving the program, Scott was back on his roller coaster.

Perhaps because of his inherent likability, Scott's ups and downs never seemed to affect his social life. He always had a girlfriend. Typically, these women saw in Scott a nice, handsome young man, a person with a problem that, with enough love from them, could surely be cured. They called me for advice.

I remember one in particular. I was, perhaps, a bit blunt. "You'd better hang on to your television set, hang on to everything you have," I warned, "because sooner or later he's going to steal from you. He will break your heart."

She became furious with me. Obviously, I was the reason Scott had these problems. At family gatherings she would excoriate me because of my cold attitude. But I knew the truth: how Scott, finding himself desperate, would do whatever he had to for a fix. She continued to call me, and I continued to warn her. "He will con you out of your socks, believe me. He will take anything he can get." And sure enough, she came home one day and he had stolen her TV and almost everything else. She never saw Scott again.

Hurt and disappointed, she phoned me. I should pay for her lost articles, she said. She was the third or fourth girlfriend whom he had stolen from, and all expected me to pay for their losses. Twice I did. But I had warned this woman and I had reached the point where I decided I had paid enough when he was a kid, every time he did something. Now he was a thirty-year-old adult-kid.

I wasn't going to rescue him anymore.

■

If we were making strides in cleaning up drugs in the bad parts of the city, we were getting nowhere in the high-rent districts. We were aware that many people in the film and music industries were using drugs, but we couldn't figure out how to infiltrate those circles. We had one undercover team—a man and a woman—and we dressed them up in flashy clothes and sent them out, to no avail. We quickly learned that the entertainment business was a small, closely knit community in which everyone knew everyone, and strangers couldn't just blithely waltz in.

The only believable approach would have been for us to get Guild or union cards—to actually put people in the business—but we didn't want to be accused of spying again. We did make one arrest: Dan Haggerty, the actor who played Grizzly Adams on TV, and it broke my heart. I liked that show. I felt like I was taking Yogi Bear into custody.

Those who lived in the fancier parts of town, who used drugs in the privacy of their homes, and who had the drugs delivered by messenger, were almost impossible to arrest. Sometimes we would get lucky. We would disrupt the sellers, mid-level dealers would go to jail, and that led us to bigger deals. But basically, we steered our efforts in a different direction. We targeted their products.

After all, Hollywood had so often targeted us. Starting with the Keystone Kops, the portrayal of the brutalizing cop, the bumbling cop, and the rogue cop had all been done in the movies. In 1949 a radio show called *Dragnet* became a summer replacement series. Jack Webb, the brains behind it and the voice of Sergeant Joe Friday, worked out an arrangement with then Police Chief Clemence "Jack" Horrall to do a true-to-life crime drama on a weekly basis. Chief

Worton cooperated too. Then Parker came along. Having had his fill of shows and movies in which the police were outwitted, or Machine Gun Kelly, Dillinger, and other gangsters were glorified, Parker wanted no part in the "Hollywoodizing" of a professional police department. But since agreements had already been reached with Webb's studio, Parker relented.

By the time *Dragnet* jumped to TV in 1951, LAPD was famous and, to Parker's amazement, remarkably accurately depicted. Webb not only used actual cases and situations as plot lines, but he built sets replicating rooms in the department right down to the exact placement of ashtrays. Webb's association with the department went further. He created the Police Academy Trust Fund and pledged 6 percent of the profits he made on the first showing of every new *Dragnet* and *Adam 12,* which he also produced.

Webb became a hero to more than just members of the real LAPD. I remember having lunch with him and *Los Angeles Times* sports columnist Jim Murray at Perino's restaurant one day. Jack had wanted to discuss an idea for a new show. Halfway through lunch, in walked Muhammad Ali. Totally ignoring Murray, who had probably written more columns about the champ than anyone, Ali blurted to Webb: "Would you say, 'This is the city . . . Los Angeles, California?' " Then, "Now say, 'My name's Friday. I carry a badge.' " After he requested a number of Webb's better-known lines, Ali, as excited as a kid, asked him to repeat them all again.

Over the years, Hollywood has returned again and again to the LAPD, either to depict it, to use our officers as "technical advisers," or as a place where actors can hang around to get the feel of what real police life is like. TV shows like *Police Story, Police Woman, Columbo,* and the short-lived *Cop Rock* reflected the LAPD. On shows such as *Rockford Files* and *Quincy,* "LAPD officers" played sidekicks. In the *Lethal Weapon* movies Mel Gibson and Danny Glover play LAPD officers. *Hunter* is an LAPD Metro sergeant. Twice I played myself on the show.

By the early eighties, Hollywood was increasingly portraying drug use in its films and TV shows as being part of ordinary American life. They were quite blasé about it.

Teenagers used drugs in movies, and so did their parents. *Saturday Night Live,* and most notably John Belushi, routinely got laughs when he joked about drugs. Until he died from them in March 1982.

I felt no sympathy for John Belushi at all. Although I enjoyed his (nondrug) humor, I could not forgive this public person's flagrant use of drugs. Overdosed, he died ugly, sprawled in a hotel room at the Chateau Marmont on Sunset, choking on his own vomit.

I set out to see if I could persuade the powers in Hollywood to act more responsibly.

In January 1983, I met with Lew Wasserman, the chairman of Universal, who probably wielded greater influence in Hollywood than anybody. Conjuring up the names of Belushi and every rock star I could think of who also had died from drugs, I asked that he urge his people to stop glorifying their use. Lew was most agreeable. "Hey, I'm all for it," he said. "I'll do everything in my power to turn this around."

I also met with Stephen Cannell, who has produced many TV shows, including *The A-Team, Wiseguy, The Rockford Files, Baretta,* and *Hunter*. He was very concerned. Richard Frank, the president of both Walt Disney Studios and the American Academy of Television Arts and Sciences couldn't have been more helpful. I talked to Hanna Barbera about the cartoon shows they were putting on the air for kids. All agreed they would help. Our intention, I said, was not to tell writers what to put in their scripts, or to censor them, but simply to ask them to consider the influence they had over the public.

Hollywood really came through. Suddenly, drug usage wasn't portrayed as cool, and it wasn't funny. Comedians changed their routines, making fun of drug users instead of getting laughs about drug use. Throwaway scenes in films, showing someone snorting cocaine, began to disappear altogether. The message was getting out at last.

At least it was on some homefronts.

■

In December 1986, my daughter Kathy phoned me from Hawaii, where she and her husband, Sam, were on vacation.

She said her alarm system had gone off, the police had been called, her house had been broken into, and a neighbor had spotted Scott in the area.

Hungry, dirty, tired, and broke, Scott had busted in. Kathy and Sam had always been good to him, slipping him money, feeding him, helping him out any way they could. A frequent visitor, Scott knew the alarm system, and once it sounded, he had been able to cut it off. He had forced his way in, taken a shower, dressed himself in my son-in-law's clothes, eaten some food, and departed—with jewelry and cashmere sweaters.

It was not the first time Scott had stolen from them. But the pain and the heartbreak never grow less. I told my daughter, "Prosecute him."

Furious this time, she called the Irvine police and filled out a crime report. She told the officers, "I know who it is. It's my brother."

But the Irvine police couldn't locate Scott. Disappointed and angry that his efforts had been for naught, my brother Steve went looking for Scott. He found him in a dilapidated, crummy hotel, wearing a pair of pants and no shoes. "I kicked in the door," Steve told me, "dragged him out to the patrol car, and handed him over to the Irvine police." He was whisked away to an Orange County jail and charged with one count of burglary in the first degree and one count of grand theft property.

Poor Kathy was a wreck.

"This is the best thing for him," I kept reassuring her. And she would break down and cry.

She was pregnant, which made it even more trying and more difficult for her, but she agreed to go through with the prosecution. My son-in-law didn't need to be coached; it cost thousands of dollars to fix his alarm system. "He didn't have to do this," Sam said. "We would have given him what he wanted."

But the longer Scott sat in jail, the more their anger wore off. "You have to go through with this," I urged. "He has to learn that he can't steal from anyone, and certainly not his family."

The Public Defender's office of Orange County assigned a case worker to Scott, and she took a strong liking to him.

She and the public defender hammered out a deal. He would plead guilty to second-degree burglary and would go to prison for a year in Arizona, where California has reciprocity.

That sounded fair. Steve and I, both seasoned police officers, knew there was absolutely no chance of a successful prosecution of first-degree burglary. His defense, we figured, would be: "Hey, I just wanted to get cleaned up, get something to eat. I didn't have a home and my sister always allowed me to come to hers. And yeah, once I was there, I saw the jewelry and I took it."

If this defense was convincing, Scott would get off on the burglary charge, which is a felony and a state prison offense, because it must be proven there was intent to steal *before* the intruder entered. Instead, Scott would likely be convicted of theft, which, considering the few items he took, would be a misdemeanor at best.

Personally, I thought it would help Scott to do real time in a state prison. But when the public defender offered the deal to the deputy district attorney, he flatly turned it down. "We're going to prosecute for first-degree burglary," he insisted.

The situation was ridiculous. Steve tried to intercede with the deputy D.A. We wanted the harsher route and the deputy district attorney, thinking we were trying to use influence, was insisting on prosecuting a case that wasn't going to go anywhere.

It was a bizarre form of reverse discrimination and it grew into a black comedy. In the first place, Orange County couldn't even find Scott. My brother did. My *daughter* was the one prosecuting him. *We* wanted him in jail, and the county was going to screw it up and get him off.

During a pretrial hearing, Kathy testified and broke down completely. She was seven months pregnant and I couldn't continue to put her through that. So I called the district attorney of Orange County, the first time I have ever called anyone for a favor.

"I'm not trying to ask for anything," I began, "except that you take a hard look at this case, because it's not going to go anywhere. Scott's defense will be theft, and the court will end up giving him time served. And here we have an opportunity for him to plead to second-degree burglary and go to Arizona for a year, which seems an appropriate sentence."

"Daryl," he said, "I'm concerned this will come back to haunt you. Somebody will believe you are trying to impose your influence on me or the system, so I'm not going to interfere. And I would advise you not to do anything either."

Afraid the media would indeed misconstrue my motives, I backed off. The trial took place. My daughter had to testify and almost made herself ill. My son-in-law had to get up on the stand too. It was just a horrible, wrenching ordeal for the entire family. In the end, the result was as we had predicted. The jury found him not guilty of burglary, guilty of theft, and the judge sentenced him to the four months he had already served. He walked out of court a free man.

For me, it was a sad lesson in how the judicial system breaks down. Even though I had spent forty years working in the criminal justice system, I suddenly experienced it from the public's point of view. Clearly, no one was considering what might be best for the individual.

■

It seemed to be a national disease. In the fall of 1990 the Senate Judiciary Committee was examining how federal funds could best be used in the fight against drugs. New York Police Commissioner Lee Brown and I testified together. Committee Chairman Joseph Biden noted that casual drug use was dropping and he believed that we needed to zero in on hard-core addicts. "Either they should go to prison," he observed, "or into rehabilitation."

I agreed. Then I added that I didn't understand the term *casual drug user*.

For years, drug researchers had been telling law enforcement that their market was 23 million mostly casual drug users. Whether those people used once a month or once a week mattered little to me. I considered them traitors to our whole effort to end drug use in this country, traitors in time of war. They, more than the estimated 6 million hard-core users, were keeping the drug sellers in business.

"The casual drug user ought to be taken out and shot,"

I told the Senate Judiciary Committee, "because he or she has no reason for using drugs."

I hadn't planned to say those words—like always, I just said them. I suppose I was borrowing a phrase my mother often used when somebody did something outrageous. She'd say, "Oh, they ought to take them out and shoot them."

When I made that statement, Lee Brown chuckled, Joe Biden didn't react, and I continued with my remarks.

Afterward, I spotted Ron Ostrow, the Washington correspondent for the *L.A. Times* and one of their very best reporters. He said, "Chief, you really didn't mean that we should take casual drug users out and shoot them, did you?"

I had just been interviewed by ABC and NBC, and not a word about my remark. But the *Times,* I thought—now here's an opportunity to get some attention for a very serious problem. So I said, "Yeah, Ron, I did. I understand the terrible burning compulsion an addict has for drugs. What I don't understand is an individual who is supposedly a 'casual drug user.' I'm not even sure there is such a thing. But if we have people who smoke a little pot or snort a little coke, who simply want to go out and party and use drugs, I think they ought to be taken out and shot, because if this is a war on drugs, they are giving aid and comfort to the enemy." It was obvious hyperbole, but I knew the *L.A. Times* would do its best to make something of it.

Predictably, most of what I'd said never appeared in Ron's article the next day. What did appear was the impression that the LAPD was going to round up all casual drug users, line them up against a wall, and shoot them. An officer sees a pot smoker—boom!—he blasts him on the spot.

The furor that erupted was extraordinary. Some liberals have such a cynical view of the police that they believe that because a chief makes a statement, all police officers are going to run around shooting up the city—totally ignoring the fact that police officers, more than anybody, know there is a death penalty for murder.

The usual detractors screamed into media microphones. Mayor Bradley declared, "I'm not going to dignify that statement by a response." Councilman Zev Yaroslavsky, never one to miss a photo opportunity, said of me, "He must have been smoking some pretty bad stuff. I think for a chief of police of any American city to make such a suggestion is outrageous and ridiculous." And I got letters from other Council members saying, "You draw evil attention to LAPD's aggressiveness on this narcotic issue with statements like that."

Using hyperbole to draw attention to a big problem, I had brought on a tidal wave instead. I remembered how Bill Parker—I suppose out of boredom—would stimulate controversy when things seemed too quiet. I always tried to calculate my situation: *Do I really want controversy?* And the answer would be: *Of course not.* Then another voice in me would say, *Hell, this is probably the most exciting time in your life,* and instinctively I would come alive every time a controversial issue popped up. But this "issue" was absurd.

Predictably, I was asked by reporters if I intended to take my own son out and have him shot.

"My son," I replied, "is not a casual drug user. He was led down a primrose path by casual users. Now he's an addict. I don't need to shoot him. He shot himself."

■

Scott's battle continued. In March of 1988 he was arrested for driving under the influence and was sentenced to three more years probation and ninety days in jail.

When he got out he went to live with my brother again. He began following a program and he looked terrific. He got involved in sports. An addict will always look for a substitute addiction, and Scott's became running and cycling. Soon he wanted to train for the triathlon and he needed a bike. Still the hopeful father, I went out and researched all the bikes. I finally settled on one that cost $1,300. I would buy it for him as a Christmas present.

I can always tell when Scott's using again. We will have developed a good rapport, talked often on the phone. When I am convinced he is sober, we open up our home to him. I assure him I am there for him, but only as long as he is clean and following the program.

As Christmas approached I noticed little things: The conversations changed; I began to hear the insincerities, the little lies your children will tell to make you think everything is okay. It was clear he was back on drugs. Scott knew he could not call me when he was on drugs. So the phone calls stopped. The visits abruptly ended.

I live day to day, wondering whether my son's going to make it. I will probably go to my grave believing there was something I could have done to prevent it—knowing, after all the analysis I've done, that there wasn't a thing I could have done.

Still, I can't help thinking that I failed too.

19

Guns and Gangs

Charlotte Austin stood in court Friday and looked right at the five gang members who fired 11 bullets into the body of her 13-year-old daughter.

"You took my child and shot her like she was an animal!" she shouted, her words carrying the strain of the past three angry, painful years. "Your souls are going to hell."

But as she spoke, two of the men laughed. Later, as convicted killer Deautri Denard stood to leave, he announced with a smirk, "Gangsterism continues," and flashed the sign of the Eight-Trey Gangster Crips.

So began a recent story in the *Los Angeles Times*. Although it was not an unusual one, it captured, more graphically than most, the vicious, near barbaric behavior of Los Angeles street gangs.

Charlotte Austin's ordeal had begun on May 9, 1988. A drug deal in south central L.A. had gone sour. Five members of the extremely violent Eight-Trey Gangster Crips set off to seek revenge by killing the drug dealer's sister. Armed with assault rifles and handguns, four men drove off in two cars, searching for the woman, who was driving a red car, they thought.

Soon they spotted a red Pontiac containing two girls who were on their way home from a hamburger stand. The Crips riddled the car with bullets, killing the eighteen-year-old driver and her thirteen-year-old passenger. Neither was the drug dealer's sister.

The five were convicted of first- and second-degree murder and of kidnapping another woman earlier for ransom. Four of the five were found guilty of raping the kidnapped woman. All were sentenced to two terms of life in prison without the possibility of parole. At the sentencing, Denard turned to Charlotte Austin and declared, "You don't deserve no respect. All you did was come in here and *instigate*."

Such episodes of senseless and depraved gang violence form the grim underbelly of the city of Los Angeles. In 1991 gang-related homicides comprised 29 percent of all homicides in the city; 77 percent of those murders were committed with guns. Thousands of rapes, robberies, burglaries, and cases of aggravated assault are also perpetrated by gang members, creating terror in black and Latino neighborhoods, occasionally slipping over into white suburbia, and driving the police to distraction. Most gang members are thugs of the lowest sort, empowered by automatic weapons and, often, the drugs they ingest. They act on twisted whims.

"Let's go shoot somebody."

"Who's got a car?"

"I got a car. You got a gun?"

Even some police officers have a hard time standing up to these criminals. Most officers entering the Academy today are college graduates from stable backgrounds although they come from all socio-economic levels. Many, unless they played football or boxed, don't even know what it's like to take a punch. We try to build training programs to prepare them. They run two miles, stop, fight with boxing gloves, run two more miles. The idea is to show them that they can be winded, punched, knocked down, and still get up, keep fighting and survive.

Nevertheless, some have trouble adjusting to the stressful, ever-changing demands put on them. Typically, we want them to be respectful, courteous, and friendly police officers. At the same time they must be ever wary, must understand what they have to deal with, and must be as hard and uncompromising as a gang member. When they are not, they often die. In seconds, they must be able to distinguish who is good and who is bad. Being human, they simply cannot process all the information flooding in and make the right decision every time.

Training decent human beings to think and act in such a way as to counteract the sociopathic personalities that make up the gangs is something we still haven't perfected. Being tough—no, being hard as granite—is as necessary to a street police officer today as is the need to be gentle to children and senior citizens and sensitive to the ethnic diversity within the community. It requires exceptional people.

■

" 'Course I got a gun. And some blow."

"Let's go blast someone. Get ourselves on the eleven o'clock news."

The history of gangs in Los Angeles is probably as old as the city itself. The earliest gangs were Hispanic. Romantics like to claim that gangs are part of the Mexican-American culture, formed to protect their turf. Most of their grievances were not with outsiders, but among Hispanics themselves. They fought wars over real or imagined slights: girlfriends, boyfriends, all kinds of things that rarely made sense to outsiders. When the police tried to intervene, they found they were not wanted. Hispanic society was a closed one.

Gang weapons, when I was growing up, consisted of chains, clubs, knives, and zip guns. The latter were crudely fashioned guns in which a rubber band acted as a spring on a piece of tubing. A nail served as the firing pin. When the person pulled back on the rubber band, creating tension, the nail would be pushed forward, striking a .22 caliber bullet and firing it. Inaccurate at best, the gun often didn't work at all.

I remember the time a kid from Highland Park unwittingly crossed into territory protected by a gang called the White Fence. Angered by this trespass, the gang swept into Highland Park, grabbed a kid from a malt shop, and beat the hell out of him with a tire iron. This infuriated my friends and we prepared to take this gang on. During the next few weeks on Friday nights, we'd go looking for White Fence members who dared to stray into Highland Park. Fear permeated the young people, generated by the weapons the Mexican gangs used.

Throughout my childhood and into my first years in the police department, this was the level of gang activity we saw. There were some black gangs, but they, too, were turf-oriented and reasonably quiet. It wasn't until the late sixties and early seventies that black gang members began to dress alike and adopted the vicious behavior we have come to know today.

The Crips was the first major new gang to burst onto the scene. In the late sixties and early seventies they began making a name for themselves in south central L.A. They were noted for walking around with canes. The Crips appeared to be a generic name for a group of gangs that clung to a particular territory. They didn't protect their turf as Hispanics had done; they just wanted a way to be identified with a particular neighborhood. Next came the Bloods, as a counter to the Crips.

Almost immediately, they presented problems we had not seen before. With Hispanic gangs, there would be a flurry of activity—a killing here, a killing there—after which nothing would happen for a long period of time.

But the Crips and the Bloods were mobile and extremely violent. Able to intimidate entire neighborhoods, they began attracting, or menacing, great numbers of young black kids. Kids who wanted nothing to do with gangs joined them purely out of fear.

LAPD responded immediately. By the mid-seventies we had put together our CRASH units. Actually, we tried calling it TRASH—Total Resources Against Street Hoodlums—as a way of demeaning gang activity. But some activists in the community objected. It was unseemly, they said, to call our units TRASH because we were dealing with human beings out there. Accordingly, we changed the name

to CRASH—*Community* Resources Against Street Hoodlums.

But going after gangs was not like going after the Mafia.
The Mafia is a well-regulated hierarchy and enforces rigid
discipline. Street gangs are a loose and shifting confedera-
tion of individuals with little or no organization. Their
identity is manifested mainly by what they wear, and this
seems to be the very reason for their existence.

The Mafia avoided the attention of law enforcement and
the general public. When it became necessary to murder
someone, "disappearances" were usually arranged without
visible traces of bloodshed. By contrast, the gangs specialize
in street shoot-outs with a total disregard for public safety.
That disregard intensified as drugs came increasingly into
play. With the invention of rock cocaine—known as
"crack" on the East Coast because when it is ignited in a
pipe, it crackles—the stakes grew larger. Rock cocaine
carries a bigger jolt for a much smaller price than powder
cocaine, and the streetwise criminals used gangs to set up a
lucrative narcotics distribution network. Gang members
were the visible part of that network; some sold the drugs;
others, with their guns, served as protective coating to scare
off anyone who tried to interfere. Although sworn enemies,
the Bloods and the Crips and other gangs would be found
working together in the name of making a dishonest buck.
Ordinary gang activities—the violent confrontations over
perceived slights, for instance—continued, but only to the
extent that these animosities did not interfere with drug
distribution.

As the face of L.A. changed, so did gang membership.
Since 1985 there has been a huge influx of Hispanics and
Asians. Hispanic gangs claim more than 18,000 followers,
and Hispanic gang activity now accounts for 50 percent of
the city's gang violence. The 37 Asian gangs have roughly
2,000 members; the various offshoots of the Bloods and the
Crips number about 15,000 members. Altogether, we have
identified 474 different gangs with a total membership of
35,000.

Fueled by drug activity, the growth of the gangs was
aided, too, by the enormous media coverage given them.
Hoodlums saw themselves on the evening news and came

away with a self-importance they had been searching for all their lives. If you're in a gang and you don't have a weekly killing, or a drive-by shooting, you're nothing. You don't get no news at eleven. You ain't gonna be a star.

Media coverage of gangs begat more acts of violence, increasing the tension in the community. That tension created a demand for the police to move in.

In the spring of 1988, I initiated Operation Hammer. This involved sending waves of as many as a thousand police officers into south central L.A. on an overtime basis for six months. We made hundreds of arrests. We drove drug traffickers underground. We restored safety to whole neighborhoods. We completely disrupted gang activity. And in 1988 we had one of the lowest homicide talleys in the last twenty years: 735, down from 812 the year before and down from 1,080 in 1980.

Pro-active as ever, we also stepped up our attack on drug activity. We used the "buy/bust" technique, where we'd buy the narcotics, then bust the seller. Or we'd take a buyer away from the scene, bust the buyer, then go back and get the seller. We used a slew of undercover techniques to get at the distribution networks and the wholesale markets, including the rock houses, and we made hundreds more arrests.

Other police departments were less than thrilled with our aggressiveness. Run out of L.A., the drug dealers began surfacing in other cities. When police chiefs in those cities complained, I told them with a straight face that it was part of our "cultural awareness" program for gangs. "We have a motto: 'Travel is broadening. Just get the hell out of Los Angeles,' " I would say.

Our hard-fought battles did gain us a bit of ground. Our buy/bust programs, our posing as sellers, our seizing drug buyers' cars for forfeiture, our disruption of the buyer-seller connection and flow-through, our operation to clean up the area and then maintain it with a uniform patrol, all have reduced the number of open markets for drug dealing from two hundred to less than half that.

Still, the enormous number of undocumented aliens who engage in drug-trafficking—many are El Salvadorian and Central American—continued to stump us. Our lack of control over these criminal immigrants became an almost insurmountable obstacle. Between 25 and 30 percent of all our arrests were undocumenteds, requiring 25 percent of the department's time. No sooner had we identified them than they would be out on the street, on bail, with a new name.

As the jail and the prison populations swelled, convicts were released early to make room for new arrivals. Once freed, they hit the streets and took up where they left off. Crime soared and detractors of Operation Hammer cried, "See! The tough approach doesn't do any good."

The city politicians, never quite wanting badly enough to support our efforts with adequate funding, kept reducing our overtime budget. Slowly we were forced to pull out our troops. But our intensive efforts produced at least one interesting result. Whereas burglary and robbery had always been considered preventable crimes, given enough police to stop them, conventional wisdom said homicide could not be stopped. Historically, most homicides were committed by family members or friends, either in a fit of rage or out of some personal motivation. Such crimes usually occurred indoors. But increasingly, people were being murdered senselessly, and many more were murdered out on the streets by unknown assailants. Now, for the first time, we showed we could curtail the number of murders, too, by heavy deployment on the streets where the murders were most likely to occur.

What was wrong with the crime-solving equation, we found, wasn't the police. It was the money to fund the police—and the laxity of the criminal justice system after the police had done their job. With jails and prisons over-crowded, there was not enough room to hold and control those who needed to be taken off the streets and kept for as long as possible.

■

It was also a matter of guns.

In today's Los Angeles, children wield fully automatic weapons designed for military use. Police officers carry one shotgun under the front seat of their patrol cars and another one in the trunk. Citizens are armed to the teeth with guns many don't know how to use. Two hundred years after its founding, America the great democracy has become one of the most oppressed societies in the world. Our national characteristic isn't freedom; it's fear.

What's changed is not only the proliferation of guns, but their sophistication. In the days of Machine Gun Kelly, John Dillinger, and the gangsters of Prohibition, the weapon of choice was the sawed-off shotgun. Because it was sawed off, the shotgun pellets would spread at very close range, acting almost like an assault weapon or an automatic gun. But outside the world of gangsters, such guns were rarely used.

Then came World War II, Korea, and particularly Vietnam—wars that produced deadlier weapons in great quantities. These semiautomatic guns expended bullets faster and required less skill to use. They were priced within reach of even low-level criminals; for $500 in a gun shop, or less on the black market, hoodlums or their girlfriends could buy a 9mm semiautomatic with a laser sight. Unlike revolvers, these are not fired by aiming through the sights; just train the laser beam on someone and the gun fires directly to that light. These types of weapons, which hold clips of fifteen rounds or more, were better than LAPD's and engendered a feeling of invincibility in their owners.

By the late 1970s the police were badly outgunned. Most LAPD officers still carried six-shot .38 caliber revolvers, updated but basically the same weapon that's been brandished by cowhands since the 1880s. Even in Ed Davis's time, officers were clamoring for more effective weapons. But some brass—including Ed Davis—and the Police Commission were reluctant. If we upped the ante on firepower, the thinking went, so would the criminal element, and the battle between cops and robbers would resemble a war between enemy nations.

Still, like the police in other cities, we were severely handicapped. Although most officers even now go through their entire careers without once firing their weapons, those who had to were able to squeeze off only a couple of shots to the ten or fifteen or more flying out of the semiautomatic or fully automatic in the hands of a criminal.

By 1986, I concluded that a gun was like anything else: a piece of equipment that could become obsolete. We began to study possible replacements and found that the 9mm

Beretta or Smith & Wesson automatics fit our needs best. I knew that getting permission from the Police Commission was not going to be easy. So I suggested a trial effort. We would allow a small number of officers to purchase the weapons and train with them, while we evaluated the results. At no cost to the city, how could anyone turn down a trial effort?

Once we tried them, we were convinced the 9mm automatics were more effective than our traditional service revolvers, and appropriate for use. The Police Commission agreed. The new automatics went through the department like wildfire. Officers didn't wait for us to purchase the new guns for them; they went out and bought their own. But by then, the arms race had escalated another notch. The criminals had discovered military-style assault weapons.

The UZI submachine gun, fully automatic and capable of firing thirty-two rounds per clip, turned up first. Soon, the less expensive but just as deadly AK-47 became the weapon of choice among the drug-dealing gang members in south central L.A. The AK-47 particularly affronted me. This is an assault rifle designed in the Soviet Union and built in Communist China. It was a weapon that had killed a lot of marines in the Korean War, and Americans—waving their flag of freedom—were clamoring to have this stupid gun. Seeing the number of AK-47's flooding into the country, seeing our officers picking them up off the street all the time, and burying two LAPD officers killed by assault-type weapons, I decided it was time to try to halt this nonsense.

Which is when I went on a personal crusade to ban them.

But trying to ban any kind of gun is an emotional issue. Hunters and members of the National Rifle Association felt strongly about their right to bear arms. There are also . . . well, I won't say "nuts," but a fringe element in this country that firmly believes that when the enemy forces come, they will be the ones to defend the United States. They, too, maintained it was their Constitutional right to own assault-type weapons.

Nobody was thinking clearly. Instead of trying to find a middle ground, the gun advocates and the gun-control advocates dug in at the furthest edges of the issue and went to war.

Both sides missed the point. In a complex urban society, there must be reasonable and responsible controls placed on the availability of armaments designed for use by the military. I could see no necessity in a free society for a lot of people running around with these things. While I have never been a gun-control advocate, nor believed gun control could be achieved by gun registration, I did hope we could bring *some* reasonable control to the situation. If we could raise the consciousness of the American public about the arms race that was occurring in our streets, maybe it could be brought to a halt. Liberty does not mean license.

I spoke; I wrote articles; I campaigned to ban assault weapons every chance I could. "Where are we going in this society of ours?" I railed. "Why do we keep arming ourselves? If we go to assault weapons, why not hand grenades, why not machine guns? I mean, where do we stop?"

Nobody expected this kind of talk from me—the hard-nosed, conservative chief of police in Los Angeles. Friends who belonged to the NRA were affronted that I would rebuke their perceived Second Amendment right to own any weapon they wanted to. Had I suddenly become a Communist?

One extremely conservative member of the NRA chided me: "You know, Chief, when you need help with the criminal element out there, you can call on us and we'll come to your aid. But after this legislation you want, you're going to have to go to the ACLU to get help, and you know what kind of help you're going to get from *them*."

"In my judgment," I quickly replied, "in a free society the police ought not to have to call upon armed citizens to help them. That's vigilantism at its worst. This isn't the wild wild West. If nothing else, I am hoping to bring some *civility* to the way we live our lives."

Liberals were stunned to find me in their midst, but I have always been a pragmatist above all else. So once again I went to Washington to speak my mind.

It was February 1989, and the nation had been shocked three weeks earlier by the random murders of five children in a Stockton, California, schoolyard and the wounding of twenty-nine others, plus a teacher, by Patrick Edward Purdy, a drifter with an AK-47. I appeared before a Senate

Judiciary subcommittee considering a ban on assault weapons.

"I am not a gun-control advocate," I reiterated. "But recent events have convinced me that we must stop thinking in terms of 'gun control' and start doing something about 'gun responsibility' and a *reasonable* right to bear arms.

"The Second Amendment to the Constitution reads: 'A well-regulated militia, being necessary to the security of a free State, the right of the people to keep and bear arms, shall not be infringed.' We should pay close attention to the words *well-regulated*. The Second Amendment gives no more of an absolute right to bear arms than the First Amendment gives anybody the right to yell 'Fire!' in a crowded theater or engage in child pornography."

I told the subcommittee that a coalition of criminal justice officials, including myself, had been working on legislation to prohibit assault weapons in California. I proposed similar legislation at the federal level: that the sale, manufacture, importation, and possession of assault-type weapons must be prohibited. So must the sale and manufacture of firearm magazines capable of holding twenty or more rounds of ammunition. "The NRA insists that guns don't kill people; people kill people," I said. "I agree. But assault-type weapons make it a whole lot easier for the cowards, misfits, and scumbags to do their killing."

That June, California banned the sale of a specific list of assault-type weapons. Those owned prior to June 1, 1989, could be kept if they were registered by December 31, 1990. Of the estimated 300,000 assault weapons in the state, fewer than 7,000 were ever registered. Federal law was never passed. George Bush, through presidential decree, did ban importation of AK-47's, UZIs, and other assault weapons.

In the end, it was too little too late.

■

In 1991, often with an assault-type weapon in their hands, gang members murdered more than seven hundred people in Los Angeles County. Never had the statistics been so grim. Never had so many children and innocent bystanders been the victims of gang-related shootings. If there was any common factor in these killings it was that the assailants, more often than not, directed their rage at those most like themselves. Blacks killed blacks. Hispanics killed Hispanics. They killed each other in their own neighborhoods—and those we arrested could never quite explain why.

20

To Protect and To Serve

Driving through Los Angeles with an aide at the wheel, I am often oblivious to the city as I try to get through the stack of material I must read daily. When I am not buried in papers but alert to my surroundings, I occasionally spot wrongdoing. Still a police officer at heart, my instinct is to take action.

"Pull over," I told Gene Arreola, my driver and security aide, late one afternoon as we sped along the freeway past a kid spray-painting graffiti on a wall. That really gets my blood boiling. "Wanna stop that guy."

"Okay," said Gene, not slowing down a bit.

"Pull over," I repeated.

"I'm trying to, boss—the traffic."

In a split second Gene, a fourteen-year veteran of the department, had envisioned the scene. We would pull up. I, in a suit and without a gun, would tell the kid to stop it. He would take off. I would pursue him. I'd catch him, he would take a swing at me, and I'd probably punch him. Or maybe the kid would pull out a knife or a gun. Gene would have his gun. Whatever ensued, it would produce a headline Gene figured we didn't need.

"Sorry, boss, I just couldn't find a way to pull over," Gene said eventually.

We had been through this kind of thing before. One night, returning home from a black-tie affair, I noticed a guy weaving dangerously along the freeway. "I think he's drunk," I said. "We'd better pull him over."

My security aide at that time, Thurston Bechtel, attached the red light to the roof of the Olds and off we went. After several miles the guy pulled onto the shoulder and stopped. I had taken my jacket off when I got into the car, so when I jumped out I was in a formal white shirt and black bow tie. Looking like a waiter, I approached the guy's car. He took one look at me and sped off.

We called for assistance, using my code name: "Staff One."

That produced results. Within minutes the poor guy was surrounded by five black-and-whites, one helicopter overhead, and two TV news crews who had heard the call from "Staff One" over their police band. To this day he's probably still wondering what caused the commotion.

Some things don't change, I often sheepishly remind myself. Then again, most things do. Like the city.

■

Driving to work in 1992, I pass through a Los Angeles that my parents would hardly recognize. The barren hills in Highland Park, down which Lowell and I once "sledded" on a flat waxed board, are crammed with nineteen separate condominium complexes, one of which I live in. The city ordinance that outlawed buildings taller than twelve stories was revoked in 1966, and now downtown and Century City, fifteen miles to the west, form two distinct towering skylines.

The faces in the windows have changed too.

The influx of Hispanics and Asians continues. Many of my condominium neighbors are Asian; other parts of Highland Park are predominately Hispanic. Throughout the city Caucasians are no longer a majority, but little more than a third of the total population. The black population has shrunk from 20 percent to 17 percent, causing the black leadership to worry that its political power will erode too. A full 40 percent of the population is now Hispanic; 7 percent, Asian. Hispanics and Asians have emigrated from dozens of countries, bringing with them a profusion of cultures and languages. In Rampart division, a crime-ridden twelve-square-mile area west of downtown, forty-one different languages are spoken.

Looking out the wall of windows in my sixth-floor office, I capture an odd tableau of old and new Los Angeles. Two new and as yet unoccupied federal government buildings rise up in the foreground. Between them, in the background, I can see a slice of Union Station, a reminder of the postwar bustle in a thriving downtown filled with department stores and ornate first-run movie theaters that long ago became decaying architectural artifacts. Beyond it, I have a view—smog permitting—of the San Gabriel mountains in the distance. It was Bill Parker's view too.

Parker's chair was planted in front of these windows, his desk facing into the room. Across the desk stood three chairs. Beyond them, along the opposite wall, were four more. That's where the deputy chiefs would be sitting when Parker would summon me from my desk in his outer office—"Gates!"—to make one of his salient points.

Tom Reddin got rid of that desk and had a new one built in, along the front wall of the office to the left of the doorway. When Reddin wanted to hold court, he invited his deputy chiefs or his visitors to join him at a round table at the far end of the office.

Two years later Ed Davis ripped out that desk and ordered a conference table. A disabled officer built it for him in the department shop, a twelve-foot oblong, walnut-stained table with the LAPD emblem emblazoned in the middle. Ed also installed a seven-foot-high glass showcase two feet in from the doorway. Visitors still have to dodge around it to get into my office.

Although I left the showcase, I didn't want a conference table; I wanted a regular old desk. The officer who built the table heard of this and was crushed. So I kept it. I sit at the far end, usually behind a pile of precariously stacked papers. Behind me is a console with my phone—and more stacks of reports, letters, and memos. Working there, seated at the head of this long table, surrounded by seven vacant black armchairs, I must look like a mad baron plotting to overthrow the throne.

Even before I get to my "desk" each morning, I have already scanned the overnight or weekend major-crimes report in the car.

To take a typical day, Monday, November 4, 1991, the following awaited me: shooting homicide of a forty-four-year-old Hispanic woman in Southwest division; shooting death of a black man in Wilshire division; stabbing death of a black man in Central division; shooting death of a black man in Southwest; stabbing death of a male Hispanic in Northeast division; shooting death of a black female in 77th division; a gang-related shooting death of a black male in Southwest; the vandalism of a car belonging to two Hispanics, with racial overtones (the word *Beaver* was spray-painted on one window) in West Valley division; and battery with hate or prejudicial overtones when an unknown suspect threw a large plastic bag filled with water at a crowd of homosexual demonstrators in west Los Angeles.

In addition, there were three officer-involved shooting incidents. One, in Rampart division, took place when an officer, while arresting a twenty-eight-year-old Hispanic male whom he had just witnessed in a drug transaction, noticed the suspect remove a handgun from his jacket pocket, pointing it at the officer. He shot him. The suspect's gun turned out to be a replica of a small hand gun. The suspect died.

In the second, two officers passed a car from which a passenger fired a shotgun at a house. The gunman then trained the shotgun on one of the officers. The officer shot his 9mm pistol at the suspect, missing. Two of three passengers in the car escaped. A seventeen-year-old Hispanic male was taken into custody.

Lastly, an off-duty officer, walking his dog, was stopped at gunpoint by two male Hispanics in the Valley. The officer drew his off-duty weapon and fired two rounds. He missed and the suspects fled.

The final weekend toll: seven homicides and one officer-involved shooting death.

Newspaper reporters, phoning our press relations people

for the same information, drum their pencils and say, "Just routine homicides, huh?"

There would be 1,025 of them in Los Angeles before 1991 was out.

■

Despite the gruesome numbers, Los Angeles, the second-largest city in the nation, ranks thirty-fifth in crime rate among major metropolitan areas—believe it or not. With the lowest number of police officers per population of any major city—two officers per thousand residents, compared to New York's and Chicago's four per thousand—and a geographical area second only to Houston's, LAPD has kept the number of crimes per population low because we have been both pro-active and creative in using our resources. For example, we have 14.9 officers per square mile; New York has 88.6. We average 3.1 violent crime arrests per officer; New York only 1.8. Yet the crime rate only keeps growing, with public apprehension growing even faster. In 1991, there were 24,020 people murdered in the United States. California led with 3,710. Los Angeles, with one eighth of the state's population, could boast one third of its murders.

Frightened citizens have responded in two ways. Some fortify their homes with expensive alarm systems, and their bedside tables with handguns. Seeing themselves as Dirty Harrys, they figure they'll take the law into their own hands because the police obviously can't be depended upon to do the job. Others simply cry, "More police!"

We have become an oppressed nation. We willingly trip off to war, depleting our material resources and sacrificing our young, to free other people who are living under oppression. Yet we continue to allow ourselves to be oppressed by the presence of a criminal army, which sucks up more and more of our freedom. Our answer: More police!

Which is idiotic. More money, more police, more courts, more jails—these are solutions that make no sense. Already the citizens of Los Angeles spend $1 billion a year on police protection; they are being soaked enough. This is not a police state; it's supposed to be a democracy. Do we want to go about our lives with still *more* cops looking over our shoulders? In America, the land of the free?

The present system of criminal justice is not working, and never really has. I've thought long, often, and hard about how the system can be improved. Here are some of my ideas:

1. *Identify the Enemy.* To fight a war on crime, shouldn't we at least know the size of the criminal army? When General Norman Schwarzkopf marched into Kuwait, he knew the exact dimensions of the enemy and the firepower it possessed. In America no attempt has ever been made to measure the number of burglars, robbers, murderers, or rapists. We diligently count crimes and arrests, but we pay scant attention to determining the number of criminals who perpetrate these crimes. Ask any police chief in the country to estimate the number of people he believes are committing burglaries, robberies, car thefts, and so on, in his community and he'll give you a wild guess. With a little study, and some help from all of our computerized systems, law enforcement has the ability to make some fairly accurate assessments.

Already we know that in the United States, 2.7 million adults were on formal probation and 531,000 were on parole in 1991. Add to these figures the number of adults in prison or in jail, and the total number of adults under correctional supervision was 3.7 million. On any given day then, 1 out of 49 adults was under some form of correctional supervision. That breaks down to 1 out of every 27 men, and 1 out of every 194 women. Throw in another million or more who have not been caught or who are awaiting trial.

Using this kind of data within each state and city, carefully organized by the types of crimes most likely to be committed, each police agency could begin to determine the dimensions of the criminal army it faces.

When I first came on the force in 1949 we arrested 110,000 drunks a year. It sounded like a huge number—my God, was everyone in Los Angeles tipsy? One day a sergeant said, "How come we have to fingerprint these drunks each time they're brought in? I mean, they bring old Joe in every other week."

It suddenly dawned on us that maybe we didn't have 110,000 drunks after all. Using old IBM punch cards, we were able to organize what we called our "drunk repeater file." When Joe would be brought in, we would look up his card and just add another thumbprint.

It turned out we had 22,000 or 23,000 people arrested on intoxication charges, not 110,000.

If you could extrapolate this system, using the sophisticated computer tracking equipment we have today, to the whole criminal army, you could determine its general and specific locations, the principle targets of its attacks, and greatly improve the chances of a counterattack. By organizing this information on a regional basis, I would have a way of forecasting, for instance, how many crimes would be committed in which parts of L.A.—and when.

Because we don't do that, the public now sees a seemingly endless stream of crime and believes the number of criminals behind those crimes is infinite. The number is not. Like a fountain in which the same water keeps coming over the top, criminals recirculate too.

With jails and prisons overflowing, those convicted rarely serve out their sentences. In California, state prisons release 20,000 of their inmates within three months; 40,000 are released after six months; and 60,000 in less than a year. Then they recirculate. In 1989, for instance, 11,040 parolees were returned to prison. The way the system is designed, the police, the courts, and the jails just keep coming in to perform the same job over and over. If you had a leaky pipe, you wouldn't keep calling a plumber to patch it up—you'd get a new pipe. It would be fixed, and the leak controlled.

We need to begin to control our criminal leaks, too, putting an end to the faulty patchwork.

■

2. *End Parole and Probation.* They're useless. Both ostensibly provide control over a convicted person while providing direction toward noncriminal behavior. It sounds good, but it doesn't work and never has. A recent study by the Rand Corporation determined that within two years' time, two thirds of those released on probation commit crimes that lead to their rearrest. Studies made in the 1950s produced similar results. Some progress.

Parole has the same failure. A bill signed into law by former Governor Jerry Brown limits parole in California to one year. Others convicted of crimes never serve any time and are sentenced to probation. Los Angeles County spends $300 million a year on probation and boasts some of the finest people in the field anywhere. But with an average caseload of four hundred offenders, how much control can one probation officer exert? It is impossible for one case-worker to keep tabs on the whereabouts, weekly, of four hundred probationers. Many disappear—until they are arrested again. Parole officers are saddled with the same unreasonable caseloads and aren't effective either.

Instead of these useless tactics, I have long advocated doing away with parole and probation altogether. Rather, depending upon the severity of the crime, how dangerous the person is, and his or her personal history, a judge would sentence the convicted person to "in-prison" or "out-prison" status.

This is a complex proposal, but in a nutshell this is how it would work: In-prisoners would go straight to prison to do their time, while those who would now be likely to be placed on probation would be given out-prison status. They would be sentenced to their homes and controlled by strict conditions of out-prison status.

At present, judges putting a convicted person on proba-tion make up their own conditions. They may suit an individ-ual probationer, but collectively they are haphazard and inconsistent, difficult for overloaded probation officers to monitor. Instead, out-prison conditions would be codified into the state penal code. They would have the force of law and provide for uniformity. In passing sentence a judge would select, from a menu, conditions in the penal code— A, B, D, F—that fit the particular out-prisoner. For exam-ple, this prisoner could only be out of his house between 6:00 A.M. and 6:00 P.M. to go to work; another prisoner could leave home between 7:00 A.M. and 4:00 P.M. to go to school.

Each convict's conditions of out-prisoner status would go into a central computer so that the information could be called up in every police station and every patrol unit. Out-prisoners would also carry an identity card listing the con-ditions of their status, which they would be required to show on demand to a police officer. By calling up the information on his mobile digital terminal, an officer could know instantly the exact conditions. A violation of any condition would result in a new status: "Go to jail."

Today, an officer questioning a suspicious-looking person—who is, in fact, on probation or parole—has no way to check that status except through the probation and parole departments, where such information may or may not be computerized. Often, the person is let go.

The out-prison system is not intended to be foolproof, but it would provide far tighter control on convicted persons and give police officers an extra bite on crime. In the beginning, it might add to prison and jail overcrowding, but in time it would do the opposite. Convicted persons would feel a control they do not experience now. It might just cause them to abide by the conditions of out-prisoner status, knowing the greater chances of their being found out and returned to jail.

In short, with every police officer acting as a prison guard, and homes serving as jails, the millions of dollars spent on parole and probation officers and on building prisons could be shifted to the front end of the system, where the flow of criminals might be stemmed right from the start.

■

3. *Crime Prevention Starts with Kids*. The front end of the system means the children. We are simply not doing enough to prevent so many of our young people from becoming criminals.

If all the talented parole and probation workers could be freed from their ineffectual supervision of criminals and reassigned to working with potentially endangered children, it would be like mining a bright, shiny vein of gold. Programs could be designed to work with children who come from unstable home environments or live in troubled neighborhoods. We could redirect vast resources from the tail end of the system to the front end. We could reach children before they became criminals, not afterwards. It would be a massive effort to stem the flow of new recruits into that criminal army.

LAPD has always run programs for kids. Our Explorer

Scouts attract young people under twenty, who work with the police in community-related activities. During a 10K race, for example, they will direct pedestrians along various routes. They help us search for guns—even bodies. They serve as the eyes and ears of the LAPD in nonthreatening jobs and get a taste of police life early to find out if they want to pursue it. In addition, every division has its own youth program, which might include soccer, boxing, and basketball.

Five years ago, LAPD started "Jeopardy," a program specifically aimed at kids leaning toward gang activity. Many kids reluctantly join gangs due to peer pressure, or because they are afraid not to, or because it's the fashionable thing to do. Officers will spot these "wannabes" hanging around gang members, pick them up, and talk to them about the downside of gang membership. They encourage the kids to think twice, offer them help and protection, and try to steer them toward LAPD's other youth activities. They also go to the parents and warn them that their child may be in jeopardy. "We think it's time for you to pay a little more attention to the situation," the officer will say, "and we'll help."

To provide that help, we tried holding community meetings. Sometimes we met with resistance, so we've had to develop new ways of encouraging parents to cooperate. We've held seminars for them and brought in experts who advise them on ways to turn their kids around. But there are some parents who are parents in the biological sense only, who know nothing of the true meaning of parenthood. Often they come from homes where that meaning didn't exist for *their* parents either. A lot of work needs to be done, but it can be, using the money and resources now wasted on probation and parole.

■

4. *Community-oriented Policing.* As law enforcement limps along, this is the hot idea of the moment sweeping police literature. Started in nineteenth-century London by Sir Robert Peel, community-oriented policing was nothing more than bobbies walking a beat. The concept is used effectively in Japan, where *Kobans,* or guard shacks, now

exist in every neighborhood. Inside sits the local police officer. People know they can go to that officer with a problem. Tokyo has thousands of *Kobans,* and the system has made the Japanese feel comfortable moving about their cities.

As this plan of forging an alliance between officers and the neighborhoods they serve spreads across America, the first problem is the need for more officers. Commissioner Lee Brown of the NYPD is a strong supporter of community-based policing. Already he has a department pushing 28,000 officers, in addition to the city's transit police, harbor police, housing authority police, and airport police. Now Lee is asking for 6,000 additional officers to put into neighborhoods. But again, how much more can taxpayers be asked to pay for?

Officers are only half of the partnership that needs to be formed. For this concept to work, the neighborhood must be actively involved, and many people don't want to bother. They want to come home at night, know they can rest safely, walk the streets after dark, and maybe say a friendly hello to the officer—but that's all the interaction with the police they want. Their attitude is: It's *their* job to stop crime—let *them* do it.

Los Angeles is a classic example. Ed Davis implemented community-based policing in the 1970s. Under his "Basic Car Plan" each division had a number of designated cars that patrolled the streets of its area. Nine officers, on rotating shifts, would man each car. Once a month the officers would sit down at a church or school in the community, have punch, cookies, and coffee, and talk about crime.

Only 150 to 200 people ever showed up. Mostly, it was the same 150—in a community of 30,000 that the basic car covered—which wasn't really cutting it. So we started holding smaller meetings in people's homes, where neighbors could gather with neighbors, with one officer attending. That was the start of the Neighborhood Watch Program, the first in the United States.

As an assistant chief, I implemented these programs for Ed. We dealt with the community on a broader basis than any police department at that time. We tried to learn what people wanted, what they thought the problems were, and then work out solutions together. But again, only a small number cared to get involved, and even those needed constant urging. Officers had to become extremely innovative to maintain "their" public's interest. Some people were annoyed.

One particularly vocal citizen marched into my office. "Will you please get your police officers to stop knocking on my door?" he said. "I have a nice house, a nice family. I have a *life*. I am an engineer, not a police officer. I pay taxes to have you people deal with crime."

Despite such resistance, activists continued to demand community-based policing. Because we were getting positive anecdotal feedback, we continued the program. We decentralized the department and empowered police officers to solve problems in their areas without a supervisor standing over them. Finally, we went into full team-policing. Individual teams of patrol officers, traffic officers, and detectives, headed by a lieutenant, were assigned to small areas and left to their own devices to solve problems within their communities and to keep the neighborhoods safe.

But before we could scientifically analyze the results, along came Proposition 13 in 1978. Due to tremendous cutbacks in personnel through attrition, we had to drastically pare down team policing. Refusing to abandon the concept completely, I have retained senior lead officers, the basic car, and the overall process. Communities that wanted to work with us could, and often crime was reduced in those neighborhoods, possibly as a result.

No police administrator would deny the benefits accrued through officers working in partnership with the community they serve. Often serious conflicts can be avoided. LAPD continues to explore better ways to gain the confidence of the public and to improve the process of working with them.

"Our senior lead officers who head each 'basic car' are the true chiefs of police," I would tell neighborhood meetings. "They can really make things happen. They know you, what you want, and how to get things accomplished. Not this old chief from downtown."

The problem is that too many people mistake community-oriented policing as a cure-all for crime. It is not. There is anecdotal evidence that it makes people feel better about the police, and the police, in turn, feel better about the people. It does bring the police and the community closer together—but that doesn't mean we're providing better service.

■

5. *Quality of Service*. A police department puts out a product, just as a company does. Our product is a service: to maintain peace and to reduce crime and violence so that people feel safe. Like that of any company in the private sector, our goal should be customer satisfaction. This is an area of law enforcement—indeed of government—that is routinely overlooked. Community-based policing is fine, but it doesn't go far enough toward satisfying our customers. Rarely do we even bother to find out what the customer wants. That's bad business.

The private sector is way out in front of government in this regard. Having obeyed my own preachings to "buy American" for years, I finally broke down and bought Japanese. Tired of the constant repairs my Oldsmobile needed, and the poor service it got, I succumbed and bought an Acura. Soon our mailbox was inundated with consumer-satisfaction surveys. Sam filled them out religiously. What did she like about the car? What didn't she? What improvements would she suggest on the next model? When we went to trade in the car for a new one recently, we were startled. The improvements had been made. It was as if they had tailored the car to our specifications. *My God*, I thought, *why isn't the LAPD being just as responsive to the public we serve?*

The public's perception of what needs to be done is often at odds with that of the police. People will complain about a panhandler begging in front of a store. They will raise Cain about drunks on a street corner where their kids must cross on the way to school, or about men who loiter outside a laundromat making jokes when women walk by. It is likely that none of these people actually present a threat, but the public feels intimidated nonetheless.

Graffiti on a subway car or bus makes passengers feel no one is in control. They may not be in any danger, but they feel as if they are. James Q. Wilson and George Kelling, in their paper "Broken Windows," speak eloquently to this phenomenon of public-disorder concerns. Perceptions of danger are often magnified by the media. In living color, a drive-by shooting in Los Angeles will come right into your living room; then there will be big headlines to suffer as you drink your morning coffee. The city can panic over too much, and too explicit, media coverage. Even though the chances of someone's dying in such a manner are remote, there comes the cry: "Where are the police? We need more police!"

Adjusting and melding the public's priorities with those of the police is a chief's job. I found, for instance, that pulling a drunk, who isn't going to hurt anybody, off a street corner does more for neighborhood psychology than putting away a burglar who, operating two blocks away, does real harm. Only the victims are aware of the burglar; *everyone* sees the drunk. Quality service requires that the police attend to both: Satisfy the concern over the drunk, but go after the burglar to assure safety to the community that is unaware of the danger. That is quality service.

The gang sweep in Los Angeles, Operation Hammer, was carried out as much to reduce apprehension by the public, to make people feel safer, and to show LAPD was not ignoring gangs, as it was to clear the gangs out. As one resident said, "The fear just tears at your heart and stays there." Though many we arrested were back on the streets the next day, I received hundreds of letters and handshakes from people saying, "Chief, thank God."

With the Japanese car survey still on my mind, I began to wonder why the police department couldn't survey its customers too? Cost is a barrier, but I believe it would be money well spent. The city has thus far refused to pick up the cost. I did survey the LAPD to gauge satisfaction within the department and to find out what else our employees might need to get the job done. Under the title "Focus on Service Excellence," we designed separate questionnaires for sworn officers and civilian workers. We asked questions about morale, ease of working with other divisions within the LAPD, job meaningfulness, and how did they feel about their ability to carry out specific functions?

Total quality management in pursuit of service excellence is a continual effort to improve and to provide better service to your customers—and to your employees, who, within the organization, are customers who must be satisfied too.

It was a start.

■

6. *Free the Chief*. It would be difficult for a CEO to run a company if he had to produce a quality product, yet had no control over the size of his budget or how it was allocated. Such is my plight, as well as that of most of the police chiefs in the nation.

Clearly, the amount of money allocated to policing is a policy decision that must be made by politicians. But the lack of control by the chief of police after that decision is made is appalling. I've often said to the political leadership: "Just tell me how much you are willing to spend on the police department and then give me some flexibility in how that money is spent." But that isn't the way it works.

First, an analyst from the City Administrative Officer's office studies the budget requests from all units within the department and recommends funding or not. Here is a guy—bright as he is but with no experience running an organization, let alone a police organization—saying no, the chief doesn't need more patrol cars; he needs flashlights. This person has no accountability for our success or failure, but has lots to say about what we can—and cannot—spend money on.

His recommendations, along with mine, are then presented to the mayor, who also substitutes his judgment for mine. "I don't think you need that, Chief," Tom Bradley will say. Again, here is a person short on experience in running a police department, but long on making critical assessments of it.

The budget now goes to a City Council finance committee. The members pore over every line item, as if they had any idea of what was good or bad for the department. Then on to the full Council for more debate. Once passed, the spending plan goes back to the mayor for approval—or veto—and then to the Council for final approval or, possibly, the overriding of some vetoed items.

Because this process takes forever, preparation for the annual budget begins one full year before it is enacted. Items that need no debate are debated. Take police cars. They are essential. They wear out. We know how long they'll last and when they'll have to be replaced. It really doesn't require a recommendation from LAPD or analysis from the City Administrative Officer, or examination by the mayor and the Council every single year. It shouldn't be difficult to forecast how many cars would have to be replaced annually, and put money for this purpose in the budget each year. This should be done automatically. Instead, we've created a whole bureaucracy to carry out these idiotic rituals of budgeting.

Even more senseless is the lack of flexibility that a chief has in spending the budget. Since 95 percent of the cost of running the LAPD goes for personnel, whose numbers are dictated by the mayor and Council, there is little room for input by me. I must submit an organizational chart that engraves every position in stone—a year in advance. Sometimes priorities change dramatically. But if I wish to redirect any amount over $25,000 within my budget, I must go through that long tortuous process again.

If I decide I need two more computer terminals and two people to run them in order to save time for ten police officers in the field, I have to go trotting across the street to harangue the City Council once more. Instead of my making that decision, some analyst in City Hall does. And if I fail to get a job done (because I am two computer operators short), then it's my fault, not the analyst's.

Similarly, if we have a series of disasters and use up all our flares, back I trek to the City Council. This process was so absurd that if the mayor authorized the hiring of more police officers, there was no accompanying financing for uniforms, guns, additional radio cars, or the expenses that go along with operating those cars. Finally, I got that changed. Now we get a complete budgetary package for each new officer. But to go over to the City Council every year and hear *them* quibble over how many cars or video display terminals we need is ridiculous. Actually, it is demoralizing. It has often reduced me to grumbling, to confrontations—to actually having to go over the heads of the mayor and the Council and plead my case to the public. Then I would be chided by the Police Commission for not supporting the mayor's proposed budget, and reminded that I was, after all, management.

Worse, if I couldn't get money for overtime or necessary equipment, I was a chief who had to lead a whole group of disgruntled employees.

It would seem far more logical to allow a police chief and other department managers to have some discretion on spending or allocating the money authorized them. Then, at the end of the fiscal year, the department head would be accountable for the management of his budget and the effectiveness of his department.

Lastly, chiefs could use a little independence from political control. They should be held accountable, of course, but the manipulation of chiefs and police departments by political leadership has become excessive and has long been the stuff that corruption is made of. One of the reasons the director of the FBI has been given a ten-year term is to avoid the attempts at political manipulation that occurred during Nixon's time. While I'm not advocating a total lack of political or civilian control of the police chief, I am simply speaking of that ounce of independence that will allow the chief to speak out on issues that might run counter to the positions of the politicians. The process of silencing chiefs in today's America is almost complete.

■

7. *The American Public Needs to Grow Up*. At some point, the public is going to have to adopt a more realistic view of the police. It needs to recognize what we are and what we aren't. The people pass laws to control traffic and pay the police to enforce those laws. Then, when we stop them for a violation, they get mad at *us*.

In Los Angeles we have strict laws regarding jaywalking. Fifty percent of all traffic fatalities involve pedestrians. Yet whenever a police officer writes a ticket for jaywalking, the person whines and carries on as if the officer had just stolen his kid. It always amazes me that grown-ups can't follow simple laws. We didn't enact them; we're just supposed to enforce them. Right, says the public, but enforce them against someone else.

The public also sadly lacks perspective. In the case of Rodney King, an ex-con who was driving while under the influence of alcohol—going way beyond the speed limit, being chased for several miles by police units with red lights flashing and sirens blaring—four officers were charged with improper use of force in subduing him. No one has tried to defend what those officers did. Yet the media's lopsided reporting (King was usually identified as "motorist Rodney King," evoking a picture of a guy just out for a spin) resulted in many people damning the *entire* LAPD.

We are the best police department in the world, but we are not perfect. We are men and women as imperfect as the society we are drawn from. Rodney King should never have been hit fifty-six times; yet many of the blows struck him were correctly placed so as not to cause serious injury, exactly as we teach at the Academy. Even in a situation where officers act entirely appropriately, as they did *not* in the King episode, when you are trying to subdue a moving, often violent suspect, one or two blows may miss their mark. This is the reality. It is the reality of police work in a world of guns and violence and sociopathic behavior that is almost beyond human understanding.

Some will say this is a chief who is minimizing police violence; I am not. I am just stating the facts. Judgments about the police come too quickly, too harshly, too often. The public is too quick to jump from the particular to the general, and there are always those in the media and in the political world willing to help the public make that jump.

In addition, the public must come to terms with what we do. Citizens ought to know they have a partnership with the police. When an officer stops a citizen, the citizen should not mistake demands for discourtesy. He should cooperate. At the same time, the officer absolutely must explain—with courtesy—why the person has been stopped.

People must also realize something else. Those who have disagreements with the government need to understand they're really suing the people. Juries are really fining themselves. When damage awards are excessive, which they are too often today, there are no winners except the lawyers.

The people lose in two ways. They will pay more taxes and get less service. When the police believe they've been maligned and unjustly accused, there is a human tendency to play it safe and to do less.

Over the years I have seen the best and the worst in police officers. But in comparison to others in government, you get more dedication, commitment, and overall ability to get a job done. In addition, the disciplinary system under which police officers operate has no peer in or out of government. We are tougher, as we should be, on police officers for their misconduct on and off the job. When a citizen is arrested for drunk driving, he pays his fine and does his time and that's it. When a police officer is arrested, he pays his fine, does his time, and then must face severe discipline by the department.

We don't flinch from the extra demands placed upon us, but we do believe the public should take that into consideration. We are not the enemy—we truly belong to you. We will do your bidding and try to do the best possible job. As Tom Reddin used to say, "To know us is to love us." Try it.

21

Outrage

Several feet along the back corridor from my office is a staircase known to only a few.

That's where I was headed at two o'clock on the afternoon of Tuesday, March 5, 1991, less than twenty-four hours after the Rodney King videotape had first aired. I had to be downstairs for the weekly meeting of the Police Commission. All exits from the sixth floor were barricaded by mobs of reporters and TV crews wanting to ask me about Rodney King. I needed to duck them.

With my two security officers, one in front of me, one behind, I hit the stairs on the fly. At sixty-four I was still able to outrun the media. I could hear their shrieks echoing down the stairwell from above as they realized their quarry had escaped. But when I reached the lobby, I saw that I had been outmaneuvered after all. Another crop of TV crews had sprouted outside the Commission's boardroom door.

As I approached it, and them, I knew I was in an awkward position. All morning long, a steady stream of assistant and deputy chiefs had flowed in and out of my office, responding to my orders to start gathering information and evidence about the King beating. Other aspects of our internal investigation into the incident were under way, but we were not nearly at a point where we could verify all that had taken place early Sunday morning. We were still checking to make sure the videotape was legitimate and had not, in fact, been tampered with.

For these reasons, I couldn't say much publicly. If any of the officers were to be punished within the department, as chief I would be their sole judge and jury. If we sent the case on to the district attorney for the filing of a complaint, I could taint the case by expressing an opinion prematurely. The last thing I wanted was to have a decision overturned because the chief had presumed right off that the officers were guilty of serious misconduct.

"Even if we determine that the officers were out of line," I told the mob pressing in on me, "it is an aberration."

Long ago, through bitter experience, we had learned how high-speed pursuits can heighten emotions and get the adrenaline flowing. Our department manual speaks to that: In the section "Post-Pursuit Discipline," it clearly states that a sergeant or a senior officer must be present to make sure no officer gets out of line. In this case, a sergeant had been there. Only, he had failed miserably to contain the situation, from what I'd seen on that video.

I should have said that. In retrospect, I should have been more candid about my feelings and less worried about the niceties of due process. The media and the public did not want reason; they wanted an emotion to match the pictures on the TV screen. Not speaking boldly of the horror I felt proved to be, in the final analysis, a significant error on my part—in dealing with a crisis that would only grow worse.

■

By Wednesday, March 6, matters were beginning to build to a crescendo.

King's lawyer and a neurologist who examined him were now reporting that King's injuries included eleven or twelve fractures in his head, including a fractured eye socket, several teeth knocked out, a broken ankle, and a fractured skull that might have caused air bubbles in the brain. Also, King might have suffered brain damage. "I don't think that

Mr. King will ever ever be a normal man, regardless of how long he's treated, by whom he's treated, or how successful the procedures,'' said Steven Lerman, his attorney.

The medical report issued by the L.A. County-USC Medical Center, where King was examined by Dr. David Giannetto, cited more moderate injuries: a fractured fibula in his lower right leg, a fractured right cheekbone, bruising and contusions on his back and on the right side of his chest. There were no missing teeth or any suggestion of brain damage. His blood alcohol six hours after his arrest was .094, which is over California's legal limit of .08.

Dr. Giannetto recited his findings to a grand jury, but although we made them available, I read nary a word in the newspapers. Again we were in an awkward position. While we were not trying to defend anything or justify the beating, we did want the public to have accurate information. They didn't get it.

Meanwhile, as CNN repeatedly broadcast the tape around the world, the word that formed on everyone's lips was "outrage." But we in the department were perhaps the most outraged of all. We felt betrayed, let down by our own. And as public indignation boiled over, a kind of gloom settled upon the entire Los Angeles police force.

That morning, I summoned the head of Internal Affairs, the commanding officer of Robbery Homicide division, the lieutenant in charge of our Major Crimes Unit, and two crack detectives to my office.

"I've decided to bifurcate the investigation," I said.

This was not normal procedure. Ordinarily, Internal Affairs investigates and if they find evidence of criminal activity, they submit their findings to the District Attorney. But a police officer being investigated administratively by the department does not have the same civil rights as a citizen being investigated. A police officer, if he is being investigated for a criminal offense, can refuse to talk to us, just as a citizen can. But he can't refuse to talk to us in an internal investigation if he wants to remain a police officer.

In the interests of speed, I wanted to run simultaneous investigations, with the criminal and the internal proceeding on parallel tracks. Having handled many crises before, I knew the best way to take control of a situation is to get facts out as quickly as possible and not to hide behind "an ongoing investigation."

"By tomorrow, or Friday morning at the latest, I want to present a criminal case to the district attorney," I said.

Lieutenant John Zorn, the officer in charge of Major Crimes, just rolled his eyes at me. "We can't do it. It's impossible. No way we can work that fast."

I said, "You will."

They all gulped.

"Sorry. This is what we're going to do and I don't want to hear *any* objections."

Addison Arce, a top-notch senior detective, sighed. "Okay, Chief, we'll do it. We will present that case by Friday."

I sensed Arce was just pacifying me. Given the hopeless timetable, I thought he was simply assuring me he would try his best to follow my instructions—to do the impossible.

■

Late the next morning, March 7, my detectives had truly done the impossible and *were* walking across the street to the D.A.'s office to present their case. Under the direction of Lieutenant Zorn, ten detectives had worked through the night interrogating the twenty-one LAPD officers at the scene, the two Highway Patrol officers, and two from the Unified School District. They talked to residents of the apartment complex who had witnessed the incident, and to George Holliday, the man who made the videotape. They had somehow located a bus filled with tourists from Tijuana which had stopped to watch the beating, and interviewed some of the passengers. They had gone into the lockers of the officers who had beaten King and had seized their uniforms and batons as evidence. They had collected medical reports from the doctors, and descriptions of King from the nurses who attended him. They had pulled recorded voice transmissions between the California Highway Patrol and the LAPD during the high-speed pursuit. And then they had typed up their report, according to the rigorous guidelines set by the D.A.'s office, to request the filing of criminal charges against the three officers who beat Rodney King—

Laurence Powell, Ted Briseno, and Timothy Wind. They were still investigating the sergeant, Stacey Koon.

What they got for their extraordinary effort was a cold reception, bordering on hostility. District Attorney Ira Reiner, vacationing abroad but apprised of the situation, summarily dismissed my detectives' case by long-distance telephone. Sounding as if he suspected a cover-up, Reiner refused to issue a complaint. "We are going to proceed ourselves," he announced.

Reiner's intentions were clear to me. District attorney since 1984, he's a political animal who always has one eye on the road ahead. Now, with the FBI coming in to investigate, civil rights groups up in arms, and every TV station and newspaper in the country glued to the story, he saw a golden klieg-lit opportunity.

"I intend to take this case to the grand jury," Ira Reiner said.

In fact, it was not a bad way to go. The grand jury could hear witnesses and issue an indictment within days. To go through a preliminary hearing, with all the attendant delays, could drag on for a year.

So I supported Reiner on that. What I did not appreciate was his office's unwillingness to work with my detectives. These are not police P.R. men, I reminded Acting D.A. Curt Livesay; they are dedicated, hard-nosed detectives who present cases to the district attorney all the time. But Reiner continued to act as if we were not going to provide adequate information for the filing of a complaint; that we were, somehow, going to thwart his office's efforts.

With morale in the department drooping and civil rights groups screaming for my resignation—the beating was not an "aberration"; it was department policy!—I taped a fifteen-minute video to be shown at police roll calls over the weekend. I said the Rodney King video "was two minutes that will go down in infamy in the history of this department. . . . The law says you will use only that force which is reasonable and necessary, so you *will* use only force that is reasonable and necessary. . . . People look to you for protection. They don't look to you for a beating. . . . And I am not going to resign. I will be here to make sure what I say is done and that the image of this department is restored and we can hold our heads high once again.''

I believed my words. Soon, I thought, the furor would die down. The appropriate officers would be dealt with and the city would see the incident for what it was: wrongdoing on the part of a few in a department that had a reputation as the world's best. Little did I suspect, even as the crisis continued to burn through the city like a raging brush fire, that I was playing out my hand with a stacked deck.

■

That same weekend, detectives worked around the clock sorting through the Mobile Digital Transmissions (MDTs) that were sent at the time of the King incident. Each patrol car is equipped with a computer terminal that officers can type on, to communicate with other cars or the dispatcher. Digital transmissions are faster than voice transmissions over the car radio, and they keep the airwaves from getting clogged. When we began using MDTs in 1983, we tried to monitor all messages, which are stored in our main computer in minute-by-minute chronology. But since one month's stack of printouts measures eleven feet high, and because we are perpetually understaffed, monitoring fell into disuse.

On Tuesday, March 12, a detective showed me a transmission from the car assigned to Laurence Powell and Timothy Wind shortly after the King beating. Officers tend to fall back on a kind of shorthand that renders most messages meaningless to anyone but them. I tried to make sense of this one.

1:12 A.M.

"Oops" was the initial message sent from their car to another.

"Oops what?" came the response.

"I haven't beaten anyone this bad in a long time."

"Oh, not again. Why for you do that?. . . I thought you agreed to chill out for a while. . . . What did he do . . .?''

"I think he was dusted, many broken bones later, after the pursuit.''

Dusted was police lingo for someone using the drug PCP,

which dulls the senses and at the same time gives the user the feeling that he has superhuman strength. When a suspect is on PCP, he often becomes extremely difficult to subdue.

My eye traveled up the roll of paper to another exchange made at 12:31, just before the Rodney King incident had begun.

". . . Sounds almost as exciting as our last call," read the Wind-Powell message. "It was right out of *Gorillas in the Mist*."

"What's that mean?" I asked, not having seen the movie.

One of my officers recalled a scene from the film in which African natives butcher an endangered silver-backed gorilla. Fearing that Powell or Wind might be referring to another violent episode, I had the detective check out the previous call the officers had answered. It turned out to have been a domestic dispute. The parties involved, who were black, said Powell and Wind had handled the problem with courtesy and professionalism. But the reference to *Gorillas* was clearly racist in nature, and while not said in connection with Rodney King, it suggested a possible bias on the part of the officer who had sent it.

I picked up the phone and told Mayor Tom Bradley in confidence what we had uncovered. Then I alerted the members of the Police Commission.

Shortly afterward, I was interviewed on the TV show *Prime Time*. During an off-camera discussion, I was asked whether any racial slurs had showed up on the audio tapes during the Rodney King pursuit. I said none had. A day or two later I was interviewed for the *MacNeil/Lehrer Newshour* on PBS and I was asked if it was true there were racial slurs on the audio tape.

Again, I replied, "No. Nothing on the audio tape."

Which was true. The audio tape had merely recorded officers' voices during the chase and contained no objectionable language. It was the *digital* tape from the computers that contained the reference to *Gorillas in the Mist*. Earlier in the day, two other reporters had innocently asked the same wrong question. Obviously the information had been leaked by somebody on the Police Commission or in the mayor's office. But whoever that was did not understand the difference between audio and digital tape. Not wanting to lead reporters astray, I went back to my office and called Ira Reiner. "I want to release those digital tapes," I said.

"I don't think it's proper, because they're under subpoena to the grand jury and I don't think you should release them," Reiner replied. "By law, evidence presented to the grand jury in a criminal matter is confidential until completion of their proceeding."

I debated releasing the tapes anyway. But then they'd say, "Gates released this stuff that is in the domain of the grand jury just to screw up the case."

I hung up the phone with a sigh. Maybe the pressure was getting to me.

■

Thursday, March 14. The grand jury indicted Sergeant Stacey Koon and Officers Wind, Powell, and Briseno on felony charges of assault with a deadly weapon and using excessive force under color of authority. Koon and Powell were further indicted for filing false reports of the incident.

"We will continue to investigate and present evidence to the grand jury regarding the other officers who were present at the scene of the crime," the district attorney announced.

Again, Reiner was grandstanding. A week earlier, I had pulled out my penal code and read it and asked some of my people if there was anything the seventeen LAPD bystanders could be charged with. There was not. I consulted Assistant D.A. Curt Livesay. Neither he nor his staff could come up with anything either. Nevertheless, Reiner vowed to press ahead with a criminal investigation of the bystanders, a move that every activist in town was clamoring for. In the end, the bystanders weren't charged. To which Reiner publicly editorialized: The officers' behavior was "irresponsible, offensive . . . disgraceful."

■

Just as the grand jury was preparing to announce the indictments that Thursday afternoon, the Police Commission was holding a special hearing, having issued an open invitation to anyone with an opinion on the King incident to stand up and express it. Four hundred angry people, predominantly black but with a few Hispanics and whites among them, squeezed into the Parker Center auditorium.

For three hours, as I sat pinned to my chair, the room attacked me. Reciting a litany of pejoratives—*bigot* and *racist* got a bit overworked, I thought—these people disregarded all decorum and civility, not to mention logic. What had happened to Rodney King, they asserted, was proof that I was running a police department whose mission was to beat up blacks. Melanie Lomax, the Commission vice-president, tried to manipulate the agenda so that only the most prominent activists would speak. But others didn't need a microphone to join in the verbal riot and, at a pitch usually reserved for football games, shouted their sentiments from their seats. The slightest word of LAPD support would bring hundreds to their feet, fists raised, yelling and screaming until the overwhelmed party simply sat down.

I was given no chance to respond. It was the citizens' turn to have their say, not mine. Even though I had sat through similar sessions, even though I recognized many in the audience as activists and agitators, even though I knew they did not represent most of the people in the black community, who had throughout the years supported the LAPD and voted overwhelmingly to pass our bond issues, the session left me drained.

As I walked out to the elevators to go back up to my office, I could see another gathering of protesters outside the heavy glass doors. They were chanting and yelling and waving hand-lettered signs.

One read: LAPD—HUMANS NEED NOT APPLY.

■

The next morning the *Los Angeles Times* published a story under the headline MAYOR'S OFFICE SEEN DIRECTING OUSTER EFFORT.

According to the article, "the behind-the-scenes campaign directed by Deputy Mayor Mark Fabiani is designed to exert so much political and public pressure on Gates that he eventually will give up his $168,000 a year post for the good of the police department and the community, said City Hall sources familiar with the effort. Within days, Bradley is expected to fill one of two vacancies on the Police Commission with an appointment intended to jolt the Parker Center Police headquarters.''

The story also said, ''The Mayor's current strategy of using Fabiani to bring pressure on Gates while he remains publicly silent on the Chief's status is a familiar one. The same approach was employed by Bradley recently in soliciting the resignations of three city department heads. . . .''

Bradley telephoned immediately. ''Chief, that is simply not true,'' he insisted. ''I don't know where they got that. I just don't know where that story came from.''

■

By now it was finally becoming clear to me that the King episode was having repercussions far beyond the unrestrained beating of a man.

The local director of the American Civil Liberties Union, Ramona Ripston, was blasting me every time she could find a TV microphone, for allowing—or ignoring—brutality in the department. Other civil rights activists lined up right behind her, and members of minority groups picketed daily outside Parker Center. Sadly, I watched years of hard work ripped apart at the seams.

In the aftermath of the Miami riots in 1989, I had organized the Black Forum and the Hispanic Forum to meet bimonthly. The Black Forum was made up of some of the most prominent leaders from the Urban League, the NAACP, and the Southern Christian Leadership Conference, as well as ministers, Muslims, business executives, Housing Authority representatives, and just plain folks. I, and members of the top brass, attended every meeting. My hope was that by opening channels of communication between the police and these community leaders, we could team up to prevent similar incidents from igniting here.

Indeed, the week before, aware that the Black Forum was scheduled to meet on Friday, March 15, I had sent a letter offering to discuss the King incident if they wished. In the past, we had provided police officers and police investigative files—whatever was asked for—in an attempt to address Forum members' concerns.

That Friday, the Black Forum met with me for an hour. But it didn't want to hear about Rodney King. Instead, it angrily castigated the department and demanded that I resign. Then it delivered the ultimate blow. I was no longer welcome to attend, it said—my Forum.

■

Discouraged and anxious to put the day behind me, I went home to try to unwind. For the first time in my career, I found I couldn't park my problems on the front doorstep. It wasn't the personal attacks that upset me; I have a thick hide. But I am thin-skinned when LAPD is attacked. My outrage followed me inside.

I am not much of a drinker. On Friday and Saturday nights I will have a glass of wine or a martini. Other nights, I run six miles to unwind, then I will usually cook dinner, because I like to and Sam doesn't mind. But since Rodney King, I had been coming home late, too tired to eat, too upset to watch TV, and just fallen into bed.

I slipped on a T-shirt and a pair of shorts. Ordinarily I run alone. But the rhetoric had turned so vitriolic that my security aide, Gene Arreola, a real runner, decided to go with me. It was dark and we ran along the sidewalk near my home. The roots of a large tree had pushed up the sidewalk and I, not watching my feet, tripped. I hit the cement sprawling, as if I'd been tackled by the Raiders' Ronnie Lott. I broke two ribs.

The next day I asked a doctor for a corset and hoped nobody would find out about my clumsy injury. "If anybody asks," I warned Gene, "I'm going to say that *you* tripped me."

■

Sunday was Saint Patrick's Day. I had been invited by a high-powered group of businessmen, doctors, lawyers, clergy, and politicians, called the Friendly Sons of Saint Patrick, to receive the Medallions of Merit Award, given annually to an outstanding leader. Since the invitation had been sent before the Rodney King episode, I asked Mary Miller to find out if they still wanted me. They said they did.

One thousand people were already seated in the ballroom at the Beverly Hilton as I nervously took my seat in the main row of a two-tiered dais and listened to the introductions. Because it was Saint Patrick's Day, everyone was laughing and drinking, not paying much attention, and there was only polite clapping as each honored guest rose.

Then it was my turn. I braced myself for the kind of onslaught I'd been getting all week. Instead, the ballroom exploded in thunderous applause. All the people jumped to their feet, chanting, "Four more years! Four more years!"

This did so much for me—for my self-esteem and my ego. It gladdened my heart no end.

The warm feeling lasted all of twelve hours.

■

First thing Monday morning, March 18, Phil Depoian, one of the mayor's staff people, phoned. "Just wanted to tell you, Chief, the mayor is writing a letter to the Police Commission ordering you to release those digital tapes."

"Has the mayor already written it?" I inquired.

"Uh, he's already sent it."

"You son of a bitch."

"We had a conversation with Ira Reiner," Depoian continued. "And he said he *never* told you that you couldn't release the tapes. So now the mayor's ordering you to."

"Screw you," I said. "And screw the mayor. I'm not waiting for some jury-rigged *order*."

My new press relations officer, Commander Robert Gil, called the media and handed out copies of the MDT messages. Meanwhile, Bradley's letter was circulating and so was his statement, saying the tapes showed a dangerous trend of racially motivated incidents running through the LAPD. The statement also said that my description of the King incident as an "aberration" was patently false.

The Police Commission complied with the mayor's request and officially ordered me to release the tapes, even though I had already done so. "This just proves Chief Gates was trying to withhold this damaging racial information," Commissioner Melanie Lomax declared. Melanie was one of the first I'd informed, and I became convinced she had been the leak to the media.

When asked, I told reporters that Ira Reiner had advised me to withhold the tapes.

When asked, Ira Reiner stated he had never been "opposed" to my making the information public. He was sorry, he said, if he had given me the wrong impression.

■

Tuesday, March 19. After another stormy and fruitless meeting with the Police Commission, I dragged home and was sorting through the mail when I came across an envelope addressed to me in handwriting and bearing a Marina del Rey postmark. I pulled out a sheet of paper and read the following typewritten message:

> If you don't resign by March 24 at 12 noon we will consider you a threat to society and we will then spend the next five years trying to assassinate you and your family.
>
> Checkmate

The envelope was not sealed. I glanced at my wife.

"I thought it was another letter of support," Sam said. "So I opened it."

"God, why didn't you call me?"

"I figured you had enough problems, I guess."

I felt a rush of anger. I had received many death threats before, twice from police officers I had disciplined, but never had these threats come directly to my home. And never had my family been singled out.

The next morning, I brought the note to work on the off-chance we could track the author down. But there were no fingerprints or other clues of origin. Concerned, my chief of staff ordered round-the-clock security for Sam and extra protection for me, which I hated. My security men, all from SWAT and doing what they are so well trained to do, stuck to me like leeches. Sam took her morning walk accompanied by one female officer from our crack Metro division, followed in a slow-moving car by another. She quickly found she enjoyed their company—and their protection.

I missed my privacy. After a month of this, I said to hell with it and sent all the security people away.

■

The tension continued to build. Not one civic leader stood up and took control of a situation that only grew more alarming. The whole fabric of the city seemed to be unraveling. Everybody was yelling at everybody else—provided a TV camera was present. Some who tried to register their support for the LAPD with the mayor's office complained they had phones slammed down on them. City Hall operators privately told us they were under orders to accept only anti-Gates or anti-LAPD calls. So the shunned phoned me. We had to hire extra people to handle the hundreds of calls that came pouring in. Thousands of letters arrived, too, from people all over the city declaring their support for me and the LAPD. But outside of Parker Center, nobody wanted to hear it.

Wednesday morning, trailed by twenty television news crews, I went before the City Council and tried to explain why it should support the LAPD too.

"This City Council, which is representative of all the people of Los Angeles, needs to stand up and do exactly that," I urged. "We are dealing with one incident, however horrible it may be. But let me point out that LAPD makes over three hundred thousand arrests a year, issues more than one million traffic citations. We stop thousands of people each year in a pro-active effort to deal with crime. In spite of the huge numbers of what could be negative contacts, only one arrest in a hundred results in *any* use of force, and only one in *eighteen hundred* results in a complaint of *unnecessary* use of force."

And, I added, "There isn't one of you who hasn't called to us for assistance and you know we've always been there for you. Now the officers need your support.

Up jumped Councilman Michael Woo, who represents Hollywood. "Are you threatening to withhold services to Council members who fail to support you?" he demanded.

Michael's father, Wilbur Woo, owns a bank in Chinatown and has been one of the stalwarts of the community for decades. I have always had a warm relationship with his parents, but Michael has his own political aspirations to consider: He wants to be mayor.

"That is the most insulting thing I've ever heard on this council floor," I said, showing my anger for the first time. "And I've been here a lot longer than you've been alive."

Michael sat down and shut up.

A dozen members of the public then took turns lambasting the department. One man accused us of trying to cover up the Rodney King incident. "Confidence in the chief is gone," he emphatically stated.

When the session ended, I left the marble-lined chambers of the City Council to a chorus of "Gates gotta go! Gates gotta go!" The strain, and the throbbing pain from my broken ribs, were wearing me down. I tried to move past the protesters and the phalanx of media lined up outside the Council chambers. But they pursued me along hallways, down stairwells, out of City Hall, and a full block to the front door of Parker Center.

I was prepared to talk reason with anyone, anytime. But no one seemed to be talking reasonably to me.

∎

That afternoon came the second half of the double bill: another public hearing before the Police Commission. Again the session was moved to the four hundred-seat auditorium and again the crowd overflowed into the hallways.

A dark-blue cloth had been draped over the table at which the Commissioners and I would sit. Moments before I entered the auditorium, Danny Bakewell, the head of the Brotherhood Crusade, marched in and cried, "Blue! No blue!" His beef was that police officers were wearing blue bow-shaped pins as a show of support for me and LAPD. Bakewell ripped the cloth off.

It was a replay of the hearing held Friday, only more rude and unruly, if possible. From where I was seated on the stage behind the table—hurriedly covered with brown paper—all I could see before me were hundreds of angry faces, screaming epithets, jeering, and yelling that I must resign.

No sooner had this "hearing" begun than the ACLU's Ramona Ripston dramatically carted in enormous boxes filled, she said, with 10,000 anti-Gates letters from people wanting me gone. She and her helpers plunked a dozen of these cartons in front of the table I was sitting behind.

Then a man elbowed through to the microphone. "As far as I'm concerned," he said, pointing a finger at me, "you're just white trash and you ought to be taken out with the other garbage."

Which more or less set the tone. Those who were allowed to speak were constantly interrupted by the chants: "Gates gotta go!" Even Melanie Lomax, who was presiding, could not finish a sentence. There was no decorum whatsoever. I mean, public officials were present and there is supposed to be some degree of dignity, or at least civility. There was none. One lady tried to speak *for* me and someone spat in her face.

I began to wonder if the group would erupt into physical violence. I could tell that the police officers present were becoming increasingly tense, registering the same concern. Only the barest thread of restraint seemed to contain the four hundred agitated people shrieking a few feet in front of me. I had been reading Tom Wolfe's *Bonfire of the Vanities* and I was suddenly reminded of the courtroom scene in which the mob, led by the Reverend Bacon, tries to take over the court and intimidate the judge. I told myself that most of these people had come at the behest of Bakewell and other rabble-rousers and represented no consensus other than their own.

This kangaroo court lasted for two hours.

I sat there in stony silence and waited for it to end.

■

As our Internal Affairs investigation into the King beating continued, I took steps to examine LAPD policies and training procedures, hoping to pinpoint what had gone wrong.

On Wednesday, March 27, I announced a ten-point plan. I ordered a study of our use-of-force policies. I asked Dr. Martin Reiser, the department's chief psychologist, to profile the officers involved in the incident, as well as other officers who had been accused in previous complaints of excessive force. I assigned a battery of sergeants to randomly monitor MDT transmissions for unprofessional or inappropriate messages. I instituted a twenty-four-hour hot line, to be staffed by Internal Affairs personnel, for use by the public to report complaints of excessive force. It could also be used by any citizen who wished a department representative to appear, to discuss or listen to community concerns. I assigned command officers to work night and morning shifts as my representatives to inspect, inspect, inspect the field, and to be there if officers needed them. There were other points as well, but most importantly, I asked retired California Supreme Court Justice John Arguelles to chair a five-member panel to study the LAPD's training and procedures as they related to use of force, and to determine if and how our training and control systems could be improved.

On April 1, Mayor Bradley announced his own panel. Instead of five members, his would have seven. It would be chaired by Warren Christopher, a former deputy Attorney General of the United States under Lyndon Johnson and a deputy Secretary of State in the Carter administration, and it would, Tom Bradley suggested, be far more objective and probing than mine.

Afterward, the mayor phoned and asked if I could meet with him at noon the next day. I said I had a luncheon—how about 11:15?

Although I had spoken to the mayor several times, I'd seen him only once in the month since Rodney King, and that was to discuss another matter. We were scarcely on speaking terms anyway. Over the years, our relationship had continued to deteriorate. Never once, in my opinion, had the man done anything remotely constructive toward the policing of this city during all my years as chief. In time, we learned to tolerate each other, barely—speaking only when we had to, mainly by phone.

I arrived for the meeting late as usual, not as a sign of disrespect but because I am forever running late. Accepting my apology and skipping formalities, the mayor got right to the point.

"As you know, Chief, I have not called for your resignation" was how he began. "I've been very careful in not doing that. But you are in the eye of the storm and because I don't think the healing process that needs to take place, can take place, I am today going to ask for your resignation."

In the first few days after the Rodney King incident

Bradley made several statements supportive of the department, which frankly surprised me, and for which I politely thanked him.

I should have known how long that support would last.

"In that case, Mr. Mayor, this meeting is over," I said. "I will tell you that my answer is, I will not, absolutely will not, resign. I won't retire."

Bradley said nothing.

At that moment I realized that Bradley had been insincere when he denied to me that he was working to get rid of me.

Many people have this picture of the mayor as a brilliant man, a great leader who loves the city, has the highest moral principles, and is totally committed to the underdog and the needy. This description may have fit him at one time, but not anymore. In recent years his probity has been questioned repeatedly.

In March 1989, the *Los Angeles Herald Examiner* disclosed that Bradley had served as an advisor to the Far East National Bank, for which he was paid $18,000. The *Herald* reported that Bradley called City Treasurer Leonard Rittenberg to inquire about the deposit of city funds at the bank. Although both men denied the phone call was an attempt to influence the treasurer, $2 million was almost immediately deposited in the city's account in the Far East National Bank. Bradley collected an additional $24,000 a year for sitting on the board of another bank that did business with the city. Bradley's ties to both banks—as well as other matters in which a conflict of interest had been alleged—were investigated by City Attorney James Hahn with the help of LAPD detectives.

When the investigation was completed six months later, Hahn did not file criminal charges based on Bradley's employment by the banks, but he noted, "The mayor clearly stepped into that gray area of law between factual innocence and a chargeable offense, but our system of justice rightfully gives him the benefit of the doubt." Hahn added that his report is "no vindication of the mayor's conduct."

Hahn did, however, file a six-count civil lawsuit against Bradley, alleging the mayor "intentionally or negligently" failed to report at least $222,000 in financial holdings as required by the state's Political Reform Act. Bradley agreed to pay a $20,000 fine for failure to fully disclose his investments. Wasting not a minute, Bradley jumped on TV to declare that the absence of any criminal charges meant he had been exonerated. A public opinion poll showed that 45 percent of the people surveyed disbelieved him, and many, many people came to me trying to elicit my support for his ouster. I stayed out of it.

Meanwhile, more allegations surfaced that some of Bradley's associates may have misused city resources and some of his supporters may have improperly raised campaign funds for him. Bradley agreed to return $55,000 in campaign contributions raised through a series of legally questionable fundraisers arranged by a Long Beach businessman who was trying to purchase city property. Again LAPD was called in to investigate. So was the L.A. County District Attorney. In addition, federal agencies were looking into the mayor's relationship with Drexel Burnham Lambert for possible insider trading violations in his stock dealings.

The Justice Department, in December 1991, terminated its insider trading probe without bringing any charges against the mayor. The D.A. is still investigating. So is the LAPD.

"You know," I said to Bradley, "last year when you were in deep, deep trouble, when you were being accused of dishonesty, lying, breaches of integrity, questions about some of your financial deals, a lot of people lost confidence in you. And *you* didn't resign. So why you think I should resign, I cannot understand. No one has directed anything personally toward me from the standpoint of integrity, but they did against you. And you just sat there and went through it."

Living up to his nickname, "Old Stoneface," Bradley didn't even blink.

No one," I emphasized, "is questioning *my* integrity. And I am going to stay because eighty-three hundred police officers want me to stay, plus a whole bunch of people out there who *you* aren't paying any attention to and never have in all your years as mayor.

"But most important," I went on, "are the police officers. They follow me, Mr. Mayor, and I guarantee they won't follow you. And they won't follow your Police Commission either. So you're going to have a leaderless group if I should leave. The best thing for the city is for me to stay, let the inquiries go forward, and then we'll see who's been derelict and who has not."

Bradley stared at me coldly. Frankly, I would have punched me for what I had just said, but the mayor remained silent.

I turned and walked out.

■

On April 4, Bradley attacked my other flank, using the Police Commission as his Trojan horse.

Over the years, I had dealt with twenty-two different commissioners. From time to time, the mayor has appointed to the Police Commission people I considered to be fine individuals who take great interest in the city and the LAPD. Whenever this has occurred, watch out. Somehow when they become too friendly with me or the Department it is not long before they become history. While I was chief, this happened several times.

In November 1990, it happened twice. Two members of the Police Commission—Steve Yslas and Robert Talcott, who had been thoughtful, concerned members—suddenly decided to leave the Police Commission. Talcott, in particular, had been a highly talented commissioner, bringing a well-balanced approach to the department and reining in the irascible chief. Unlike many commissioners, who know little about the workings of a police department—and never bother to find out—and, I suspect, have never even read the City Charter, Talcott and Yslas had done their homework. So much faith did I have in that Police Commission that I was giving serious thought to retiring in 1991, confident that it would select an able new chief.

All that changed. To fill their spots, Bradley appointed Dan Garcia, a longtime fund-raiser and political supporter of the mayor, and someone with whom I had crossed swords before and Melanie Lomax, a black activist lawyer who was like a ticking time bomb. Only months before, Bradley had appointed Lomax to the Airport Commission; during her confirmation hearings, a remark she had previously made was brought up: "I'm tired of goddam Jews telling people what to do." Lomax brushed aside the remark, insisting, "I have always fought for racial and religious equality," and everyone backed down.

In January, two more solid commissioners resigned. A new ethics law, passed, I believe, by the voters because of Bradley's questionable conduct, required full financial disclosure of city officials. One commissioner, Reva Tooley, felt to do so would unfairly expose the finances of her husband; similarly, the other, Bert Boeckmann thought his business partners' finances would be unfairly revealed. I am convinced that had Bert and Reva been able to remain on the Commission, most of the trouble to come would not have occurred. Bert, in particular, a very successful businessman from the San Fernando Valley, had the wisdom plus the political and financial clout to keep matters on an even keel.

After the Rodney King episode the balance tipped precariously. Bradley filled one of the vacancies with Stanley Sheinbaum, former chairman of the ACLU Foundation of Southern California, who had alienated the Jewish community by publicly hugging Yassir Arafat. Sheinbaum, who was apparently the appointee the *Times* suggested "would jolt Parker Center" made no secret of his desire to charge in and set the LAPD right, though his knowledge of police work was questionable. After several years of peaceful and reasoned dealings with the Police Commission, I sensed a renewed effort on Bradley's part to politicize it.

∎

That morning, April 4, I was summoned to a "special meeting" of the Commission.

Shortly after that phone call, I got one from John Ferraro, president of the City Council and acting mayor while Bradley was out of town.

"You're not going to believe this, Daryl, but the Commission is going to try to relieve you of duty," John said. "As acting mayor, I ordered Dan Garcia not to, but he ignored me."

"On what possible charge?"

"I don't think they have one."

I alerted my attorneys, Jay Grodin and Harry Melkonian, of the law firm White & Case, and at 11:00 A.M. the three of us walked into an office next door to the Police Commission board room.

In the office were three city attorneys who obviously had been summoned by the Commission. I told them that I foresaw a conflict of interest for them. If I had to go to court to fight the Police Commission's attempt to remove me, I said, they would be obliged to act as my attorneys as well as the Commission's.

Not true, they replied. In such a situation, they had to represent the higher authority, which in this case was the Police Commission.

"But clearly I have done nothing wrong," I argued. "What can they charge me with? Anything I have done is in the course and scope of my duty. And when it is in the course and scope of duty as chief of police, the city attorney has the responsibility to act as my attorney."

So the city attorneys went off to call their office. Then they came back. Right. It was a conflict of interest. If we went to court, the Police Commission would have to get private counsel, which the city would pay for. And I would have to get private counsel, which *I* could pay for. In the meantime, they would stay.

I raised a second conflict of interest. The LAPD, I told them, was currently conducting a criminal investigation of the Commission president, Dan Garcia. Based on reports carried in the *Los Angeles Times,* we had begun looking into allegations that Garcia, while a member of the City Planning Commission, had solicited questionable campaign contributions for Mayor Bradley. Some of those contributions may have come from builders who were bidding for city contracts, or seeking assistance in matters upon which the Planning Commission must act.

The attorneys ducked into the board room and spoke to Dan. He said he didn't believe he had a conflict of interest and he intended to stay put.

On that note, the proceedings began. Only three commissioners were seated at the conference table: Dan Garcia, Melanie Lomax, and Sam Williams, a one-time brilliant black lawyer who, due to a stroke, was not in good health.

Sheinbaum had gone off to Europe on a preplanned vacation. The fifth spot was, at the moment, unfilled.

Garcia got right to the point. "The purpose of this meeting is to inform you the Commission is considering placing you on a sixty-day administrative leave of absence, pending a review of certain aspects of the department and its management," he announced.

I stopped him right there. "Then I want all of the proceedings recorded."

A stenographer arrived and the meeting resumed.

My forced leave of absence, I was informed, was effective immediately. I would remain at my home during duty hours—on call, in case of an emergency of some sort, whatever that was supposed to mean. Otherwise, I was basically under house arrest.

House arrest? I was speechless. What they were invoking was a section from the LAPD personnel manual covering disciplinary cases, which allows me, as chief, to assign officers to their homes while serious allegations against them are investigated. By "serious," I mean things like narcotic use or some kind of criminal behavior.

"How can you do this?" I demanded.

"We're not trying to be punitive," they said.

"But you are. Historically, this section is used when there are major allegations against an officer. And there are none against me."

They ignored this.

"Then I want to retain my security," I told them, "and I want an answer now."

They said, well—what did that consist of, exactly?

"My security aide, who is with me when I am in public. And the car that we use." I told them about the death threat and how I wanted my family protected too. I didn't need security or a damn car. I was just being difficult.

They quibbled some more. Finally I got a grudging, "All right."

Next I asked if I could honor the commitments and appointments I had made for the next two months. I was heavily booked.

That started another debate.

In the end, I was told that each time I wished to keep an

appointment or attend a previously scheduled function, I would have to notify the acting chief in writing and *get permission,* which added to the humiliation.

After forty-two years in police service, including thirteen years as chief, it was all I could do to contain the anger I felt and the utter sense of betrayal. In each of those years, during my performance evaluation I had been given high marks by the Police Commission, *and* a pay raise approved by the mayor. Now, to be subjected to this: to have these complete neophytes, who had no experience with the Los Angeles Police Department, no knowledge of the LAPD, no understanding of what we were all about, making these kinds of pronouncements on me, the Chief of Police, with absolutely no supportive evidence whatsoever—practically charging me with malfeasance—was staggering to me.

"Now," said Garcia smoothly, "I will give you the order which we have signed."

I blinked. "May I ask when you signed this order?"

"Just when we got here."

"You signed it before you took the action?"

"No. We were sitting. We had taken a motion at our prior meeting, and we wanted to make sure—"

"You made it in a prior meeting?" Now my blood was really boiling. This whole meeting had been a charade. They had met in secret the day before, we were later able to show, in clear violation of the state's Brown Act, which prohibits secret meetings.

I'm thankful that my lawyers took over at that point, acting as my mouthpiece, for I'm not certain what I would have said. Harry Melkonian announced our intention of seeking redress in court the next day. Silently, I signed the order and left.

I was crushed. I felt stripped of my dignity and embarrassed beyond belief. You don't humiliate a person without just cause. You simply don't do that. I will never forget what they did, never.

I hope God forgives them, because I can't.

■

The next day it seemed as if all the lawyers in Los Angeles had been unloosed to untangle my situation. The

City Council met in executive session for four hours trying to figure out what to do. At one point Bradley came bouncing in. "Mayor, you've not been invited," John Ferraro said. "You'll have to leave."

Stunned, Bradley walked out.

Later, the Council summoned him back.

"Are you, Mr. Mayor, manipulating this?"

"Of course not," the mayor said.

Next they brought in Dan Garcia. Could he please explain why the Police Commission had acted as it had?

Garcia apparently gave an unsatisfactory answer.

Although the City Council had no authority to overturn the Police Commission's order, it did have the power to settle any lawsuits against the city. I prepared to file one. I would sue the city for violating my civil rights, my right to due process, and for causing embarrassment, humiliation, et cetera. I believe I could have won a great deal of money, but that is not what I wanted: What I wanted was my job back, and my dignity restored.

A deal was proposed and agreed to by the City Council. The Police Commission would withdraw its order against me if I would relinquish any claims against the city.

That was Friday, April 5.

By Monday, the Southern Christian Leadership Conference of Greater Los Angeles, Congresswoman Maxine Waters, other civil rights activists, the Board of Police Commissioners, and an attorney from the mayor's office had joined to file a taxpayer suit against the City Council. As a result, Superior Court Judge Ronald M. Sohigian found himself staring down at nine attorneys, all rattling separate sets of papers at him.

Unable to sort through them on the spot, he issued a temporary restraining order against the Police Commission's action. I could return to work while he spent the next three weeks shuffling through thousands of pages of legalese. A final decision on my status would have to wait.

I didn't. On Tuesday, I returned to Parker Center feeling like General MacArthur.

It took me forty-five minutes to get from the garage up to my office, as hundreds of officers and civilian employees cheered, waved signs, clasped my hand, hugged and kissed me, and shouted encouragement. As I edged through the crowd, Gene Arreola put it best: "Chief, we're on the damnedest roller coaster I have ever been on. One day we're way up on top—the next day we're down at the bottom."

On that day, April 9, I was jubilantly back on top.

22

The Long Goodbye

No sooner was I back at my desk than John Ferraro phoned to say he had arranged a meeting between Bradley and me. "I thought I could be a catalyst for bringing you two together," the City Council president said hopefully.

"I have no personal interest in talking with the mayor," I replied. "But I will be happy to sit down with him for the sake of harmony in this city, which has totally come unraveled."

At 4:00 P.M. I arrived at John's office in City Hall—neutral ground—and moments later in walked Bradley. We shook hands formally. John spoke of the need to get the city back together, to which we both agreed. "Okay," he said, "now what can we do?"

Before anyone else could speak, I did. I had a few things I wanted to say to the mayor, not to clear the air but to get them out of my system. I chided him for showing no leadership in the crisis we had brewing, or ever showing support for the police department in all the years I had been chief, or for as long as I could remember.

The mayor began to protest, but I cut him off. "Go out and ask any police officer what he or she thinks of you, and you'll find that they don't think much of you at all," I said.

Peacemaker John immediately spoke up. "Come on, let's talk about what to do."

Again I took the floor. I said we should cool the rhetoric on both sides, we should isolate the Rodney King incident, let the courts handle it, and we should let the two commissions—the mayor's and mine—do their work. At the same time, I said, we should let my ten-point plan go forward within the LAPD. And we should tell the public that we were going to cool the rhetoric while all these investigations and reviews of proper procedure went forward.

"Well, why can't we say all of that," Bradley broke in, "and then say that at the conclusion of this, once the chief has an opportunity to set things right, the chief will retire?"

For a moment I just stared at the mayor. Then I hit the ceiling.

"Who the hell do you think you are?" I demanded. "You want me to retire? Fine. Here's the deal. I'll retire right now, if *you* retire right now. Or, if you don't want to, then tell me you are *not* going to run for a sixth term."

Bradley said he would not do either one.

"The best thing you could do for the city is to resign right now," I persisted. "I'll leave the city at the same time. And have the Police Commission resign too. Then the police department could be restored and we could have a decent police department with you out of here."

At which point Ferraro interrupted. "Mr. Mayor, the chief wants to leave one of these days, but he's not going to signal his departure and I don't blame him."

"You know," I said, "if it wasn't for you being so absolutely stupid and your office so crass, you'd have known that this incident broke my heart. To see my officers out there flailing away on that guy, a total violation of everything I believed in and everything the department believes in—if you would have just supported the LAPD and let me put it back in order, I would have retired. I really would have. I have always put the department back in order. I've had murderers, I've had thieves, and I've put it back in order and you know that. But you had to put your grubby hands on the Los Angeles police department and just couldn't wait—''

"Look," Ferraro broke in. "If we're going to have any peace, we've got to stop this."

John was right. I was being a jerk, calling the mayor names, like a little kid.

"All right," I said, "let's get back to my suggestion that we simply say that we'll allow the various commissions and investigations to go forward and stop the rhetoric."

Bradley agreed and rose to leave. And still I had to have the last word.

"Tom, you know when you were a city councilman, we had a good relationship. When you first became mayor and I first became chief, we had a fairly decent relationship. But I'll tell you right now I resent you, and I'll never ever hold you in anything but contempt."

Even in spite of that, Tom Bradley extended his hand. But the gesture, like the words he spoke, meant nothing— nothing at all.

■

Our new mood of harmony was supposed to be consummated at a news conference. John wrote the press release and gave it to Bill Chandler, the mayor's press secretary. Bill added a line saying the Police Commission would continue its investigation of Chief Gates. When the release came back to me, I phoned Ferraro and said I would not attend the news conference if the sentence stayed in. The mayor refused to delete the line. John phoned him directly and said if he did not delete the sentence, neither he nor I would show up. The mayor backed down and changed the sentence to: "The Commission will continue its investigation"— which was okay with me.

I doubt that anyone who attended the news conference came away convinced that harmony had been restored. But I hoped our mere presence would set the stage for a return to some order in Los Angeles. When I spoke, I tried to point out that L.A. was a city of nearly 4 million people and very few, really, were involved in the antagonism that had resulted from Rodney King. Rather, the population of this city continued to depend upon 8,300 police officers to protect them—and those 8,300 officers badly wanted to do that job.

Any hope that the rhetoric would be toned down fizzled immediately. The Police Commission, as it waited for Judge Sohigian's ruling on my status, was in a shambles. On May 1 an attorney for the Southern Christian Leadership Conference, which had joined the taxpayers' suit, admitted in court that Commissioner Melanie Lomax had leaked to him copies of confidential memos concerning the case, written by the city attorney. That is, she had taken papers from a lawyer defending the city and given them to the SCLC, which was suing the city. A week earlier, when rumors of this leak first appeared, Lomax flatly denied culpability in a TV interview. But her lie was found out in court. "Based on what has happened," declared Commission President Dan Garcia, "I am very concerned about whether the credibility of the entire Commission has been damaged."

Six days later Garcia resigned. Publicly he blamed the City Council for interfering in Police Commission affairs, but privately he told me he couldn't abide Melanie Lomax. "She's out of control," Dan said. "I can't work in that environment, Chief. I did not want to put you on leave, believe me, but I was pressured by Melanie and Sam Williams." Others suggested he was more concerned about his law practice and keeping friendly ties with the City Council on behalf of his clients, who sometimes needed its favors.

Now the Police Commission consisted of Melanie Lomax, the ailing Sam Williams, and the newly arrived Stanley Sheinbaum.

City government continued to fall apart. The City Council, in a move unprecedented in recent times, rejected the mayor's new appointee to the Civil Service Commission. Bradley had removed one member, and the press was filled with speculation that he didn't trust her to vote a guilty verdict if I was ever brought up for a hearing on dereliction of duty. (The Civil Service Commission *could* fire me.) The mayor's proposed replacement would apparently do his dirty work for him. But the City Council, sounding tired of the mayor's shenanigans, resisted.

Then Bradley really screwed up. The City Council had been trying to place on the ballot a measure that would provide more authority for the Council to oversee the airport and harbor commissions and the department of water and power. This measure, which the Council had tried to get on the ballot before, was always vetoed by the mayor.

This time Bradley inadvertently signed it. When he realized his mistake, he called it a "clerical error" and asked the city clerk to revoke his signature. The city clerk would not. So the mayor went to court. The court ruled that Bradley was "negligent in the accidental approval of the measure." It further noted: "The mayor's signature is approximately five inches below the capitalized ballot title. One would have to not look at the document at all in order to have a misapprehension about what it was."

At long last, others were beginning to see what I had suspected all along: The mayor was clearly losing it. Here was a guy who, having come close to having criminal charges filed against him by the city attorney, was now making mistakes on a ballot issue. He had appointed a police commissioner who lies, and a Police Commission so biased that it was becoming hard to ignore. In short, in creating his own Tammany Hall, Bradley had brought to Los Angeles a rat's nest of impropriety not seen since the days of the Shaw regime of the 1930s.

■

In mid-May, Judge Sohigian ruled that I had reasonable grounds to demand reinstatement of my job, and valid claims against the city. The Police Commission had wrongfully put me on administrative leave, he ruled, since no specific charges were alleged.

The Police Commission appealed the decision—and lost that too.

■

Two months after the beating of Rodney King, it seemed everyone had had their say. I learned well the imperatives of the media, to seize an angle and hammer at it day after day—which they had been doing to LAPD with a jackhammer. Our side of the story, if it was reported at all, appeared in the final paragraphs of an article, jumped to an inside page.

But with my ten-point plan now in effect and the officers indicted, I honestly believed the tempest would blow away, the media would typically lose interest, the real facts would come out, and the LAPD's world-class reputation would be restored.

I couldn't have been more mistaken.

For the next two months, attacks on LAPD continued to appear almost daily in the *L.A. Times*. On June 18 a story raised the possibility that I had used my "secret files" to coerce City Council members into fighting the Police Commission over my forced leave of absence. Citing not a shred of evidence, the *Times* crafted a front-page story likening me to J. Edgar Hoover, and suggesting that I used secret files to control city government.

If that wasn't enough, the *Times* followed up the next day with an editorial: "Who Polices the Police?" Although the writer admitted there was no evidence to suggest I was using Hoover-like files, the piece concluded that it could happen because it had happened once already—in the 1930s! So help me. And the last paragraph read: "There is no evidence to support the allegation that there are files on local politicians, but the rumors aren't likely to die." Well, of course they weren't likely to die if the *Los Angeles Times* persisted in keeping the lie alive.

In the middle of all this, two LAPD helicopter pilots perished in a fiery crash. It was noontime when the engine failed, and they tried to land on auto-rotations. To their left was a school; to their right, parked cars. In an incredible act of bravery, to avoid the children in the schoolyard, Officers Gary Howe and Randy Champe veered right and rammed into a light pole. I went immediately to the scene and viewed the wreckage. They died on impact; never had I seen bodies so badly charred.

Two brave officers were killed in the line of duty, and although the *Times* reported the story on page one the next day, its follow-up story appeared in the second section of the paper, and its third-day coverage I finally located on page three of the second section—the sixth paragraph of a story about a group called Justice for Janitors suing the LAPD. While not averse to printing every innuendo, every rumor, every suspicion about the department, its blatant disregard for the value of these officers' lives galled me.

Their deaths sent me into a black mood I couldn't shake off. I snapped at everyone. It struck me then that if it weren't for the Rodney King controversy, the deaths of those two officers might have been the last straw. Having to search once again for something to say to their families—what?—and to present the flag to their wives at the funeral; it had become too much to bear. I didn't think I could make it through any more.

I badly wanted to quit. Okay, you bastards, here's my badge—shove it. But I knew I couldn't do that, not while LAPD was being destroyed piece by piece.

At the funeral, Randy Champe's wife, Sue, came up to me and said, "Randy thought you were the greatest chief LAPD has ever had. He had an I SUPPORT CHIEF GATES bumper sticker on his locker door. Please hang in there."

From the grave, Randy encouraged my heart. It was a wonderful thing.

Nobody, I vowed once again, was going to run me out of this office.

■

By mutual consent, the two commissions—mine and the mayor's—had been combined into one shortly after they were formed in April. Officially named the Independent Commission on the Los Angeles Police Department, it soon came to be known as the Christopher Commission, after the chairman, Warren Christopher. There would be ten members in all, seven from Bradley's commission, three from mine. Six were lawyers, two were professors, one was a college president, and one a corporation chairman. Although Christopher's credentials were above reproach, he had advised Bradley during his 1982 and 1986 gubernatorial campaigns and he continued to be a confidant of the mayor.

The duty of any commission is to investigate and ferret out problems and wrongdoing. For nearly two months the Christopher Commission—assisted by a staff of 103 lawyers and 10 accountants—took a superficial look into every nook and cranny of the LAPD. They held public sessions at different locations around the city. They interviewed community leaders, law-enforcement experts, and politicians. They visited some stations and locations within LAPD and talked to many inside the department. We had people working full-time churning out the information they requested as fast as we could. They reviewed literally millions of pieces of paper.

I understood that their findings would be critical of us; you don't spend two months investigating an organization and then award it a gold star. Although I had never met with Warren Christopher personally, he had said many times publicly that the chief of police would not be an issue in his hearings.

So, on June 14, I went before the commission, prepared to answer any questions they put to me. My first surprise was that all of the questions were asked by one person, John Spiegel, the chief counsel. We had already talked the day before. I had been expecting questions from commission members.

First he dwelled on MDTs, the mobile digital transmissions from one officer to another typed on their patrol-car computers. We had turned over 6 million transmissions to the commission and they had given us a list of 1,400 transmissions they found objectionable. I had glanced at them only cursorily and told the commission that some of them would undoubtedly shock outsiders. Most of the objectionable transmissions were just plain dumb locker-room humor spoken between two people, privately. To a police officer nothing is sacred, and unfortunately in these tapes there was a good deal of sexism, untoward jokes, and racial remarks. Actually, I can't say *racial*; *insensitive* would be better. I explained how we were going through the tapes and would discipline every officer who spoke out of line.

But I also tried to point out that if a doctor's office or a manufacturing plant were to be bugged, what might you hear then? The only bugged workplace I knew of had been in the White House, when Richard Nixon taped all of his conversations, and much of the same kind of "humor" and remarks were recorded.

"It's tragic. It's really dumb that police officers would talk like this, knowing we could call up that information," I said. "We haven't done the job that perhaps we should have."

As the interrogation continued, I realized there were

some questions for which I had no answers. The commission sounded as if it were looking for a perfect internal justice system, which simply doesn't exist. It wanted a system whereby, for instance, when a citizen complained about a police officer, we would be able to go out and learn exactly what the truth was, then punish the officer accordingly. "Why don't you do this?" Spiegel demanded. And I said, "Because it doesn't even exist in the criminal justice system."

I was stunned by that line of questioning. All we could do was carry out as thorough an investigation as we knew how. We had a long history of punishing officers when a preponderance of evidence proved the officer wrong. But the facts are often debatable; in those cases Spiegal seemed to expect us to go out and prove the officer wrong in every case in which a citizen complained. We have a tradition of seeking the truth—sometimes it is not to be found.

When he then raised the subject of community-oriented policing, I saw an opportunity to review the department's history with it. I explained how the mayor and the Police Commission had wanted to get rid of it when I became chief, believing, they said, it had been nothing more than a sly way for Ed Davis to build a political base in support of his planned run for governor. I also explained how Proposition 13 had drained the department of resources and reduced the number of officers to 6,500. And how, refusing to give up on community-based policing, I continued to use it in a viable and effective way.

After nearly two hours, Christopher smiled. "Chief, thank you very much. It's been a very important morning for us."

It would be an even more important afternoon.

■

Not realizing that his testimony would become public, Assistant Chief Dave Dotson, one of my closest confidants, went before the commission and really let me have it.

He prefaced his testimony with some polite disclaimers about the high personal esteem he held me in, how nice I'd been to him, how these were his personal opinions, the chance to influence the future of the department and the

city, blah, blah. He then made a whole variety of unsubstantiated comments about my lack of leadership. "I'm painting
with a very broad brush, but essentially in the last thirteen
years in the Los Angeles police department, with a couple
of very notable exceptions—we have not had, in my opinion,
at the top, very effective leadership." Outside of the Olympics and D.A.R.E., Dotson said, "We do not have clarity of
mission in our general operations. . . . We don't have a clear
understanding of where we're going and what our priorities
are, let alone how we ought to get there." He further
asserted that there was no accountability anywhere in the
department. "I told you Daryl Gates is a *very* nice man. I
love him! But he doesn't hold me accountable. I screw
things up and the worst he can do is to get a pained
expression on his face."

Five days later, Jesse Brewer, who had recently retired
as assistant chief, stepped up to the commission and had his
innings too. He amplified one of Dotson's complaints—that
my regularly scheduled meetings with the assistant chiefs
were often canceled or interrupted by my going off to take a
phone call or leaving for an appointment. This meant,
Brewer said, that the assistant chiefs had to make decisions
on their own.

Brewer was asked: "As a general rule, could the three
assistant chiefs work things out together?" Brewer said yes.

The next question was "And were your decisions communicated to the chief in some fashion?"

Brewer replied, "Usually in the form of an activity report
indicating what happened on a particular case."

"In effect he endorsed, he rubber-stamped . . . ?"

"Yeah," Brewer said. "We got feedback and usually it
was in the form of a note. If he disagreed, you knew about
it right away."

Brewer later said, "I would not give him a good grade in
his handling of discipline. I would probably give him a D."
Worse, he added, no one was accountable for the actions of
his subordinates.

Brewer continued to harp on my lack of leadership, even
when it came to matters under *his* control. After stating that
I had delegated complete authority to him to run his office,
Jesse turned around and criticized Assistant Chief Bob

Vernon for not properly preparing the field-training officers, which was Brewer's responsibility, not Vernon's. Never once had Jesse raised those issues with me. Rather, he had always assured me that we were doing a good job.

■

I was deeply disappointed by Dotson's and Brewer's testimony. They sounded like Frick and Frack and it was clear to me they had gotten together on their testimony. On a personal level, I felt betrayed. These were men I had been close to, whom I had believed in. I had trusted them implicitly, had encouraged them, promoted them, and above all else, I had been loyal to them. I was saddened by the way both Brewer and Dotson stepped back and disassociated themselves from the department in which they played such an integral role. I had delegated full authority to them to get things done within their scope of authority. If it was accountability they wished to apply, no one was stopping them. Dotson had charge of Internal Affairs. No one had more authority than he did to hold people accountable. In the end, both had absolved themselves of any responsibility. These men—perhaps through panic, fear for their future, or raw ambition—seemed willing to destroy LAPD, to harm its morale and to cast aspersions not just on me but on the entire organization. In my opinion Brewer and Dotson sold us out.

■

Looking back, I can discern an intricate web of opportunism, spun in City Hall and stretching across the street into Parker Center, woven in the aftermath of Rodney King.

The mayor wanted to get rid of me—fire me—and was unable to do so because he would have had to charge me with misfeasance or malfeasance, and there was neither. Long frustrated by his inability to control me, or to silence me, he and his advisers saw the King incident and the attendant uproar as their lever to pry me out.

Power, pure political power, motivated others. The driving ambition of some City Council members—Zev Yaroslavsky and Michael Woo in particular, and later the newly elected black councilman, Mark Ridley-Thomas—found a focus in the case, giving them a chance to make a name for themselves, whatever the cost to city harmony.

The black leadership in particular saw its chance. Locally, with rising Hispanic and Asian populations, blacks feared their hold on city politics was eroding. If Bradley did not seek an unprecedented sixth term in 1993, the black power structure would suffer tremendous losses. Lucrative contracts for black-owned businesses would fall away and so would many of the federal grants and funds that are directed toward blacks who have been empowered by a black mayor. Even though one officer who beat King is Hispanic, and the bystander police included Hispanics and a black, the incident catapulted into a racial issue. Those hungry for power fell on it as if it were a loose football.

The case also provided a golden opportunity for a new crop of activists and political wannabes to achieve recognition through the media: to get their names in the paper and their faces on TV. The prize for such exposure would be seats on the City Council, the County Board of Supervisors—perhaps even in Congress. The 1990 census showed a substantial population increase in the state and created several new seats in the House; both of California's U.S. Senate seats are up for election this fall. Even the Reverend Jesse Jackson couldn't resist the media spotlight created by the King case. Why else would he have made several trips to Los Angeles just to denounce me and the LAPD? It was power—raw power. It can seduce even the best.

Within LAPD, many saw the King incident as a way of achieving personal ambitions. I know Jesse Brewer had wanted to be chief. But realizing he had little chance to succeed me, he retired at the age of sixty-nine. Then, when I was about to be placed on leave, he was offered the job of acting chief. When the city attorney intervened, noting that people on pension could not be brought back to play a major role, the mayor's office instead offered Brewer one of the vacancies on the Police Commission. He accepted it on July 17.

In the weeks prior to Dotson's appearance before the Christopher Commission, Deputy Mayor Mark Fabiani telephoned Dave at home numerous times. The two men spoke again the night before Dave testified, according to Dotson's estranged wife, who told me this several months later. She overheard Fabiani and Dave going over what he would say, even to the point of indicating his affection for me. Dave made notes on index cards from this conversation, and Mrs. Dotson brought them in to us.

I believe both Brewer and Dotson struck a deal with City Hall in return for their testimony.

■

The 228-page Christopher Commission report, delivered to my office by a smiling Warren Christopher on July 9, would impress people with only a passing knowledge of police work. The gist of it was that the King beating raised fundamental questions about LAPD, among them grave problems of excessive use of force, issues of race and bias, and the difficulties the public encounters in attempting to make complaints against LAPD officers. Filled with facts and figures, the report was salted with dozens of noble-sounding recommendations.

I had expected there would be recommendations, and I was prepared to move forward in a positive manner. But reading the report quickly that morning with my attorney Jay Grodin and Deputy Chief Bill Booth, I was dismayed to see that the recommendations proposed many things we were doing already and had done for years. Furthermore, the commission often failed to indicate how it had reached its conclusions. Some of what I read was unsubstantiated, much of it misrepresentative. The commission had taken raw data, not bothered to analyze it or understand what it meant, then used it to damn the department. It was a travesty. It was exactly the kind of information that the lawyers on the commission would have rejected as unacceptable evidence, had they received it in their practice.

When we asked to see the backup for their report—what use they had made of LAPD data and their own research and interviews—they turned us down flat. To this day (except for the MDT messages) they have refused to provide us with the supporting data for their conclusions. It's a classic Catch-22. The commission told us to do what we believe we were already doing. But they wouldn't tell us

why they thought we weren't doing it or were doing it
wrong.

The one piece of backup we did see was illuminating.
The commission stated that having read through six months'
worth of MDT messages, or roughly 6 million transmissions,
the "vast majority" appeared to be routine police communications. But, it pointed out, there were a disturbing number in which officers "talked about beating suspects and
other members of the public."

I hadn't had time to delve into the messages before I
testified. Once we began to analyze the messages carefully,
we found an entirely different picture. For one thing, the
Christopher Commission had no knowledge of police lingo.
In one transmission, an officer typed, "We're going to kick
him, okay?"

"Yeah, kick him," was the reply.

Well, *kick* means to release a suspect. It does not mean
to strike the suspect with a foot. Other examples of our
"brutality" or insensitivity reflected nothing more than
sophomoric police humor. For instance, one officer was
cited for beating a woman. The officer had been delivering
food baskets on Christmas Eve. With one left, he spotted a
homeless woman. He got out of the car and offered it to her.
Then he typed on his terminal: "The last load went to a
family of illegals living in the brush alongside the pas fwy
[Pasadena Freeway]. . . . I thought the woman was going to
cry . . . so I hit her with my baton."

Of course he didn't hit her, as any officer would know.
It was just an example of how police officers talk among
themselves. Similarly, another exchange of messages between two cars went something like this:

"Where's the party?"

"We don't know."

"Could it be . . ." A certain place was named.

"We don't know."

"Typical Negroes—nobody knows nothing."

Well, how horrible, right? Only the parties involved
happened to be a husband and wife, driving in separate
patrol cars, and both were black. Sometimes people use that
kind of self-deprecating put-down humor. Shouldn't these
esteemed lawyers have checked?

In the end, after we went through all the messages ourselves, we came up with 277 that appeared to indicate misconduct. Of them, 44 were of a racial nature. But of the 44, 28 involved at least one officer of the concerned ethnic group. After checking those out, we found exactly 12 messages of a racial nature, where neither party was of the racial group referred to. *Twelve out of 6 million.* Could any other organization, if its employees' private lines were bugged, come out as well?

This same unanalytical approach was applied in the section concerning excessive use of force. Forty-four officers were cited. LAPD management, the report stated, had done nothing to deter these officers. But when we followed up with an exhaustive review of these officers we found adequate attention had been paid to them when appropriate. In many of the instances cited, the officers had been exonerated. The commission made it sound as if just having a complaint filed automatically indicated wrongdoing.

Sergeant Craig Lally wrote me a letter, upset that he had been identified by the commission as one of the top forty-four problem officers cited. Those in this group had six or more allegations of excessive force or improper tactics for the period 1986 to 1990. After listing the complaints and their dispositions—all "not sustained," "unfounded," or "exonerated," Lally wrote:

> The most upsetting portion of the commission report was that an example of my *brutality* is allegedly documented on page 43 of the report. I thoroughly read page 43 and none of the situations set forth on that page correlate to my complaint history. As a matter of fact, after reading the entire excessive force section numerous times, *none* of the examples given correlate to *my* complaint history. Either a "grossly negligent error" or a "blatant lie" was committed by the authors of this report.
>
> During most of the pertinent time period, I was assigned to Metro Division. We have the reputation of being an aggressive pro-active Division, carrying out our duties only in the most concentrated crime areas of the City. Additionally, the commission failed

to recognize that I have made in excess of 1,500 arrests in my LAPD career without a single sustained complaint.

I might also add this "problem child" has had 57 commendations in his personnel package. My reputation as a field sergeant has been severely damaged by the Independent Commission. There is no justification to put me on a "problem officer" list with the facts as stated.

Other statements critical of the department, many sweeping, were not substantiated at all. In a section critical of our Field Training Officers, this appeared:

"There are a number of highly committed, capable FTOs. However, our review of FTOs in these four divisions revealed disturbing evidence that many FTOs openly perpetuate the siege ('we/they') mentality that alienates patrol officers from the community. Flaws in the process by which FTOs are selected and trained allow too many FTOs to pass on to their trainees confrontational attitudes of hostility and disrespect for the public." The report did not present one single piece of evidence, or a single example, to back up these assertions.

Other statements reflected only one side of the story. Physical standards at the Police Academy had slipped, the report charged. A decade ago, only 60 percent of the cadets graduated; now the number was 90 to 95 percent. It said many of our recruits did not meet the high physical standards of past years. Yet I was stuck with lower physical standards as the result of a court-ordered consent decree mandating the hiring of more women and minorities. I had no choice in the matter. There was not one word of recognition that I, with these quotas imposed on me, had made the system work. Other police departments, handed similar quotas, simply designed less-rigorous training for less-physically skilled officers and suffered for it. We *added* programs to help them. That we have been meeting the quotas, and that we are continuing to turn out well-trained officers, was given no recognition at all. Instead, the report said we should *not* retain unqualified recruits for *any reason*. I agree. But the facts were that we kept only *qualified* recruits.

Nor was any credit given to us for following recommendations written in a report prepared by the Urban League and the National Conference of Christians and Jews ten years ago. We implemented every recommendation but one. No credit. In fact, positive statements made before the Christopher Commission rarely found their way into the report at all.

Perhaps the most damaging aspect of the report is that it was made without any opportunity for the department to respond to its conclusions. Even when an audit is done, the auditors give management an opportunity to review the auditors' findings and to comment on them before they are released. When I had asked the Christopher Commission for that opportunity, I was refused. Now the report will hang like an albatross around the neck of not just LAPD, but the city. Already it has become the source book for every attorney in town who has a client bent on suing the city. "Obviously the police department was derelict in not doing this—the Christopher Commission says so." Ultimately, city attorneys defending lawsuits brought against the city will have to confront that report in court. Perhaps the shallowness of the report's conclusions will be proved through discovery, depositions, and cross-examination. If the conclusions are not rebutted, they will become a plaintiff's guide to riches, coughed up by the taxpayer.

One other danger signal stood out. In its recommendations the Christopher Commission stated that the chief of police should be appointed by the mayor with the advice of the Police Commission and the consent of the City Council. The Police Commission would select three candidates in ranked order of preference and submit them to the mayor for a final choice. Moreover, a chief should be allowed to serve only one five-year term, renewable for another five years at the discretion of the Police Commission. The Police Commission could terminate the chief at any point, with the concurrence of the mayor. The termination decision would be reversible only by a two-thirds vote of the City Council.

If such a ballot measure passed, there would go an L.A. chief's small window of independence. The chief would be silenced by the politicians and subject to the mayor's every whim, just as they have been in Chicago, New York, Philadelphia, Detroit, and many other cities. LAPD would become politicized for the first time since the corrupt 1930s.

The Christopher Commission's recommendations are basically aimed at controlling the police. But it has no recommendations about controlling crime. It is dead-silent about how to deal with the crime and violence in Los Angeles today. LAPD is portrayed as being too hard-line, too aggressive, too pro-active, but the commission is curiously silent about a practical alternative.

I could have taken the Christopher Commission report apart page by page, but such was the mood of the city, I doubted anyone would listen. And so, because a distinguished lawyer lent his name to it, the report stands as a kind of modern-day bible on big-city policing. The commission tagged LAPD as a racist organization, composed of back-slapping cowboys out for a night of brutality on the town. Then they complimented us for our honesty and integrity.

■

The report hit the department like a Scud missile. Some officers, when they pulled over a motorist for a violation, were taunted unmercifully. ("Make my day, Officer. Beat me.") Others hesitated even to make an arrest. Many privately consulted their calendars and counted the time remaining until their twenty years were up. In a matter of weeks they had plummeted from being proud members of the esteemed LAPD right to the bottom. And unfortunately, there didn't seem to be a bottom. The media continued to berate us, continued to spotlight every blemish, every failure, every little chink in LAPD armor, anything that could take the shine off the department. The *Daily News* alone ran five hundred stories on the LAPD in 125 days, according to its city editor. What other organization, corporation or group of human beings could withstand that onslaught? The officers had been toppled into this bottomless pit. Their confusion and their anger were heartbreaking.

The flood of media attention given the report washed back on me. The entire LAPD had been convicted of racism, brutality, and gross mismanagement, and sentenced to a total face-lift—a new chief was needed immediately. The mayor, and others, yelled even louder for me to retire. On Wednesday, July 17, 1991, I phoned John Ferraro.

"The transition should begin," I told him. "But the recommendations they're suggesting on the tenure of the chief require Charter changes and therefore voter approval. The first step is up to the City Council. You have to decide if this is what you want on the ballot. I won't retire until you get that worked out. I won't have an interim chief."

"The next election is June second," John said.

"Okay. After that, I'll be out of here."

The next day John and Councilman Joel Wachs called me. Joel thought maybe they could hold a special election to decide the Charter issues.

"When?" I said.

"Right after the first of the year."

"You'd better find out how long personnel needs for the selection process to name a new chief," I suggested.

That night, I took the red-eye to North Carolina to attend a conference on D.A.R.E. Mary Miller phoned me the next morning.

"John Ferraro just announced that he and Joel Wachs are scheduling a press conference."

"On what?" I said.

"I think on you," Mary said.

I reached John at home. "I hope you're not going to announce my retirement," I told him.

"No, no. We're just going to talk about the transition process starting."

"Don't give a date," I cautioned.

"I won't."

Unable to resist, John and Joel said it looked as if I would be retiring after the first of the year. Which I had never said. When I got off the plane in Los Angeles Friday night I ignored the media, but on Saturday, I gave separate phone interviews to the *Daily News* and the *Los Angeles Times*. To both reporters I said that before Rodney King, I had intended to remain chief only until construction of a new Police Academy could begin. That would be in 1992 or, at the very latest, 1993. But now, I added, I would happily retire once the issue of a police chief's tenure was resolved. I didn't think it was fair to bring in a new chief who wouldn't know if the job was for five years or indefinitely, as it was now.

On Sunday the *Daily News* headline proclaimed: GATES PLANS TO STAY INTO '92. The *Times* headline said: GATES SAYS HE MIGHT NOT RETIRE UNTIL 1993. And a furor broke out again.

On Monday, July 22, I called my attorney Jay Grodin and told him I was drafting a letter designating a time for my retirement, to clear the air.

"You don't have to do this," Jay said.

By then, my disappointment brought on by the Christopher Commission report and by the betrayal of some of my top staff was so great that I no longer wanted to remain in office. It had taken the air right out of me.

"I'm ready, Jay. I've had it."

Late that morning I prepared to fax my letter to John Ferraro and the other members of the City Council. I said I would remain chief until sometime in April 1992, and that I would stay past April if the selection process for a new chief took longer than that. But before I sent it, I wanted to inform the police officers first. I went upstairs to the eighth floor of Parker Center and videotaped a reading of the letter to be shown at every roll call throughout the day.

Two thirds of the way into it, my voice broke. For a moment, I could not speak and I found that I was blinking back tears. Then I regained my composure and quickly finished reading the final two paragraphs.

■

Despite my disenchantment with the Christopher Commission report, I set about trying to implement as many of its recommendations as possible. The chief legislative analyst for the City Council identified 130 recommendations. But because some had subcategories, we at LAPD raised the number to 163.

The overriding message in the report was that LAPD was too pro-active and spent too much time arresting people and fighting crime. Armed with some vision borrowed from a professor at Harvard, and a few practitioners from elsewhere in the country, the commission declared that it had come up with *the* solution to policing the city of Los Angeles: community-based policing. That really gagged me. Did they honestly think that a bunch of cops grinning at people and patting kids on the head was going to prevent crime? We had been the leaders in community-based policing since the 1970s, and *we* knew the people of Los Angeles wanted more than that. They want their calls answered on time; they want something done about crime and violence. They want balanced policing, and that is what LAPD provided them.

Still, in flocked the academicians to tell us, its inventors, how to do community-based policing.

"Don't be tied to the 911—it simply doesn't work," they declared.

As if we didn't know that.

"Responding to people's calls really doesn't do that much good," they lectured. "You've got to convince the public that the police cannot be locked into responding to every call. You've got to stop the police department from handling barking-dog calls."

Well we hadn't handled barking-dog calls for the last forty years. We respond, on average, to 29 percent of the 911 calls we receive, the lowest rate of any major city in the United States. Chicago, for instance, tries to send a car out to every single one. We found this unproductive. Most calls can be handled by referring people to someone who can provide the real help they need. So we had greatly reduced our dispatching load, freeing officers to provide more valuable service. Like fighting crime.

Ignoring our expertise and my experience, the new Police Commission President Stanley Sheinbaum invited a professor to lecture the top brass on community-based policing. After an hour, I drifted out of the room.

I had better things to do.

Nevertheless, by December 31, 1991, I had taken action on most of the recommendations. Of the 163 we identified in the report, 105 had been fully implemented or were in progress. Another 43 were outside my authority; they included items to be negotiated with the union and changes in the selection process for chief, changes in the City Charter, or changes in the Police Commission. Five recommendations the department opposed, and some of the police commissioners opposed them as well. Ten were still under consideration.

By late January, I had announced the "beginning" of community-based policing in seven of the LAPD's eighteen divisions. Barely able to suppress their giggles, police officers said, "They think this is new?" It wasn't, if only the Christopher Commission had done its homework. The City Council reacted similarly. One by one, several Council members stood up and said, "I don't get it. Don't I have this in my area already?"

As any experienced chief executive would, I simply smiled and said, "Oh, but now we'll do it better!"

Although our "new" community-based policing will unquestionably lead to closer relations between the police and their neighborhoods, in the end I fear the people are being deceived. At some point, as crime continues to stalk this city, people are going to cry, "We don't want lollipops! We want arrests!"

Some cities have already revolted. In Houston, Elizabeth Watson, a fine chief of police and a proponent of community-oriented policing, was dumped because an audit of the Houston police department said not enough was being done about crime, and community-oriented policing was being overemphasized.

Nevertheless, eleven months after Rodney King, harmony in the city had finally been restored—at least for the moment.

■

By the beginning of 1992, I knew it was time to leave. I was bored. After fourteen years as chief, the challenges were gone; there wasn't anything I hadn't done. Given the resources I had to work with, I had kept the city reasonably safe. Always, I had emphasized crime-fighting, for I believed that's what people paid me for. I had made some inroads into curtailing gang activity. I had seen drug usage drop somewhat. I had paved the way for the birth of SWAT and D.A.R.E., both of which had been implemented around the world. The bright, happy days of the Olympics would forever form a chapter in the city's history. I had chaired the Major Cities Chiefs Association for four years. I had advised governors and Presidents. All along, I had tried my best to work with the community, implementing community-based policing where I could, and introducing programs such as Jeopardy, and many more.

I had my failures too. I was too combative. In retrospect, I should have been far more diplomatic, and I could have been with some of the police commissioners and the politicians. My problem was always a delicate one, for I was often speaking not just for myself but for my officers. We have a saying in the department: "You rolled over." It might have been better if occasionally I had—maybe not "rolled over," just compromised a bit more. But I could not let my officers down. In the back of my mind I dreaded the worst possible designation by police officers everywhere: the chief's a wimp.

Still, operating as I did, and despite the scattershot attacks on the department from the usual sources, I would leave knowing that I had been the chief of the best police department in the world, and I believe I helped to make it better.

There was nothing more to do. Voting on the ballot measure calling for changes in the selection of a chief would be held June 2, and I decided to leave by the end of the month.

I would miss the 3:00 A.M. phone calls, oddly enough, and the controversies. I would miss being a hostage for SWAT to practice on. I would miss acting like a police officer, responding to calls. But most of all, I would miss the men and women of LAPD—the support they always gave me, and their gratitude when I stood by them. They had been my strength, for they had encouraged my heart day in and day out, while God nourished my soul.

Everything else—forty-three years' worth of letters, scrapbooks, hundreds of photographs, dozens of plaques and mementos—I would pack in boxes as I gazed sentimentally out of the windows of my sixth-floor office.

Soon I would walk out of Parker Center as a sworn officer of the Los Angeles police department for the very last time.

I had stayed as long as I cared to. No one had run me out.

Afterword
August 1992

The peaceful scenario I had imagined for my departure didn't quite work out that way. Given my tumultuous career, I should have expected something, but this final episode was more than I needed; and tragically more than the city deserved.

Shortly after three P.M. on Wednesday April 29, I tuned the TV in my office to the courtroom in Simi Valley. The verdicts for the four LAPD officers accused in the Rodney King beating trial were about to be announced. The timing caught me by surprise.

Only three hours earlier I had met, as I often did, with Detective Addison Arce, who was assigned to the trial to assist the prosecution in any way he could. A highly experienced homicide investigator, Arce had put on hundreds of cases with the District Attorney. He was a master at reading juries and presenting a case. But he had received a cold reception from the District Attorney when he turned over our case to them. Throughout the trial, he told me, he was shut out of strategy sessions and treated like a messenger boy.

"Do you have any sense when the verdicts will come in?" I inquired.

"My feeling is two, three days," Arce said. "The jury has twenty-four exhibits to go through. Friday at the earliest." Now, suddenly, the end of the fourteen-month ordeal was at hand.

I had believed it unlikely that all four officers would be found guilty. In my opinion, the prosecution did a lousy job. Apparently worried that King carried too much "baggage" to be put on the stand, and that he would make a poor witness in any event, they had relied totally on the eighty-one-second videotape. What Deputy District Attorney Terry White should have done is flat out told the jury the truth: "Yes, I know Mr. King was previously convicted of armed robbery and was now on parole, that he had been speeding at over one hundred miles an hour on the Foothill Freeway, that he was very drunk, that he refused to pull over when chased by the highway patrol and LAPD units, that when he did, he resisted arrest, and that many of his statements after the event conflicted with the videotape. Nevertheless Rodney King should not have been beaten into compliance."

The second mistake White made was in not calling an LAPD use-of-force expert right away. When the defense called theirs first—Sergeant Charlie Duke—the prosecutors panicked. Arce phoned me from the courthouse. "Duke was brilliant on the stand," he reported. "Now the prosecution thinks *you* should hold a press conference denouncing what he said."

Well, of course I wasn't going to do any such thing, denounce a sergeant who had been subpoenaed to testify for the defense. Why should I offset the prosecution's mistakes? We had been trying for fourteen months to assist the District Attorney, and all they did was treat us like the enemy. Besides, for me to comment in the hope of influencing the jury would be highly improper, I thought.

I said to Arce, "Why don't they subpoena a department expert of their own? Tell them to get Assistant Chief Dave Dotson. He was in charge of personnel and training when some of these officers were taught use of force. Or Deputy Chief Bernard Parks, he teaches use of force." I was being facetious. Both Dotson and Parks were among the six canlidates to replace me as chief and neither would have wanted to be stuck on the hot seat.

Eventually, the prosecution lassoed Commander Mike Bostic, our resident use-of-force expert. What Mike tried to convey was: "This is what we teach our officers, and from an administrative standpoint we believe improper use of force was administered. We do not instruct officers to beat people into compliance." Mike explained that other tactics were available to the officers and he indicated several points in the videotape where, as resident expert, he believed the officers could have taken King into custody.

It was a bad situation all around. Because of a tactical error on the part of the D.A., Mike and the department were put in the awkward position of having to make up lost ground. It looked as if we had come to the courthouse to persecute the officers. We hadn't.

The jury was unmoved. It was clear that Charlie Duke had impressed them, and Mike's belated testimony, as good as it was, probably only irritated them.

Now, as the jurors filed into the courtroom, I predicted that Officer Laurence Powell, having struck the most baton blows, having typed the *Gorillas in the Mist* message on his mobile digital terminal half an hour earlier, and then, at the hospital, allegedly taunting Rodney King, would be found guilty of both assault with a deadly weapon and assault under color of authority. Sergeant Stacey Koon would be found guilty of filing a false report, although I didn't personally believe that he had. The other officers, Timothy Wind and Ted Briseno, would be acquitted.

Expecting demonstrations or outbursts of some sort, I felt certain that even one conviction would take the edge off the protestors' anger. But when the verdicts were read, I was stunned. Acquittals all around, save for the one count of excessive force under color of authority against Powell, on which the jury was hung.

Immediately after the verdict was announced, I put our emergency plans into play. I opened the Emergency Operations Center and reviewed deployment. The day watch of eight divisions was ordered held over; I checked on Metro Division, our free-ranging trouble-shooter division, and on SWAT. Two hours after the verdict, I went downstairs to the

Parker Center auditorium and told the media: "Whatever the emotions are, whether angry or happy, they ought to be channeled correctly in a positive way, not into a destructive or violent fashion."

Hours later, the city went up in flames.

■

We had been preparing for trouble even before the trial began. Although we could not know what the verdicts would be then, the emotions that had rent the city asunder for more than a year were smoldering still, ready to be ignited.

We prepared cautiously; the department continued to be beset by the unending attacks against it stemming from the King beating and the Christopher Commission report that followed. Sensitive to charges that we might be behaving provocatively, we called our planning sessions, Emergency Preparedness—Unusual Occurrence Contingency Plan, and made an effort to have the discussions cover contingencies such as earthquakes, floods, and antiabortion rallies as well as riots. The tactical manual for riot control I had written after Watts, which was still used nationally, was twenty-nine pages long. Every LAPD officer had been trained in the contents of that manual. Everyone was ordered to review it again. We held long discussions with the command staff to delineate step by step how to deal with a riot. At a dozen or more staff meetings of deputy chiefs and commanders, the last of which was held April 10, we went over elements of our standing plan. The plan is so basic, and so well known to the staff, I could see them getting impatient with me, as if I were a fretful father reminding the children to brush their teeth before going off to bed.

We did more than talk. Starting in September we had each division go through "tabletop" scenarios: this happens and this, what do you do? (Eerily, one of the scenarios practiced bore a striking resemblance to the televised incident at Florence and Normandie, where truck driver Reginald Denny was brutally beaten.) Officers were deployed on fake emergencies. Each of the four bureaus, which oversee the eighteen divisions, was required to review the plan. Rosters and officers' home phone numbers were updated for a callup if the department had to mobilize. Our Tactical

Planning section, responsible for all disaster-related planning, audited each division to determine its preparedness, and to look over our Mobile Command Post equipment. Checks were made to ensure that we had enough flares, film, ammunition, and yellow crime-scene tape. Almost always we came up short. For years we had lacked adequate equipment, particularly cars and communication equipment, but there was nothing we could do to solve that problem.

Finally, each area commander was given a list of gun stores and pawnshops in his jurisdiction that might become prime targets if looting broke out. Our mobile fleet, which is used for setting up command posts, was put into a state of readiness. I also established a liaison with the National Guard, alerting them they might be needed.

Against this backdrop I found myself once again doing battle with the Police Commission. Since the beginning of the year we'd had a number of retirements, and I felt increasingly uneasy about the serious holes left in our command structure, especially in the San Fernando Valley. Los Angeles sprawls across two basins divided by an east-west string of foothills; the Valley, with a population of more than one million, lies to the north of the foothills. There are five police divisions in the Valley and only two had a full complement of command-level officers.

The situation cried out for correction, and I set out to plug the holes. I moved three officers into high-level posts and two more to backfill those vacancies and was immediately accused of promoting people to hamper the new chief's ability to select his own staff. Which was nonsense. The City Council had imposed a hiring and promotion freeze throughout the city, so all I could really do was to move three men into higher positions without benefit of either a rank or pay upgrade. I left dozens of other positions for new Chief Willie Williams to fill, including those of all three assistant chiefs.

No matter. Stanley Sheinbaum, president of the Police Commission, sent me an order to undo what I did "and not make any new 'acting' appointments until further notice." This followed on the heels of a letter to the Police Commission from the mayor, using almost the exact same language.

"The mayor told you to do this, didn't he?" I said to

Sheinbaum. "Don't you realize that by giving in to him you are interfering with my duties as Chief?"

"Oh, the mayor doesn't tell *me* what to do," Sheinbaum said dismissively. "I haven't even talked to the mayor about this. But I have run this action by the city attorney and he has advised me that the Commission can lawfully order you to comply."

"I know the City Charter as well as the city attorney," I shot back. "And I'm telling you that you can't take this action as president of the Commission. It must come from a majority vote of the Commission in open session." I also warned him that he was interfering dangerously with my ability to properly administer the affairs of the LAPD. "In times of crisis, I need a properly functioning command staff," I said.

So Sheinbaum called a special session, during which they produced a boilerplate motion that ordered me to rescind my action and not make any more appointments without first consulting the Commission. I told them that while I understood the Commission had the power to order me to do this, I thought the city attorney ought to advise the Commission about the potential liability the city faced if the command structure was not adequate to meet a major disaster—and it would not be without those changes.

It was another tempest in a teapot, a meaningless controversy ignited by the mayor and allowed to reach the boiling point by his appointees to the Commission. When the media asked me if I was going to comply, I said they can "fire me, sue me, I don't care. I won't rescind those assignments. They are absolutely necessary to properly police the city during an emergency."

Later, when reporters confronted Sheinbaum with the suspiciously identical wording of his and the mayor's letters to me, Sheinbaum shrugged. "I just don't know how those words got into my head," he disingenuously said. And the media let this ACLU ideologue get away with it.

This kind of thing only saps your energy. And my battles weren't over yet. Several days later, when it became known that I had earmarked the last one million dollars in our overtime budget for use if a civil disturbance broke out, I was again criticized by public officials for fomenting trouble.

In addition, I made a five-minute video to be shown officers at roll call in which I said, "Each of us has a strong feeling about what [the trial] verdict ought to be, but whatever those feelings are they have to be kept inside, professionally and personally, while you're doing your job." I added that the reminder was necessary because "there are those in the community, some of them supposedly leaders, who have indicated that if the jury renders a verdict not satisfactory to them, some kind of uprising, some kind of violence, will erupt because of it. You must do your job calmly, professionally, maturely." The usual cast of activists and detractors—including City Councilman Mark Ridley-Thomas—attacked me for that, insisting I was only stirring up more trouble.

It was a sticky situation all around. We had to be prepared for a disturbance, but we couldn't give the impression that we were inciting one. To be truly prepared, we would have had to go into a full riot-control mode—putting all officers on twelve-hour shifts—at an additional cost of $1 million a day. From a practical standpoint, I couldn't do that. I didn't know when the case would go to the jury, when the verdicts would come in, or what they would be. Moreover, our limited budget prohibited this enormous expense, and if no riot had broken out, I would have been held accountable for having wasted the money. These were the very real considerations I had to take into account.

Even so, as word leaked out that we were making some preparations, reporters came to me, saying, "So-and-so says your actions are intended only to provoke." Every day it seemed as if I came to work only to face another controversy. It was exceedingly difficult to operate in this hostile environment. Each decision was looked upon as being somehow sinister.

■

As the trial wound down, intelligence reports warned us the real trouble would come from the gangs. Word was out on the street; "Crips and Bloods unite! Time to get the cops, kill the cops!" Graffiti all through South Central L.A. said "LAPD" with a line through it, or "Police 187," the number referring to the section in the penal code for murder. Other graffiti simply said "Kill Gates."

It was that kind of trouble that loomed in the back of my mind. We planned extensively for it. Fifty people were added to Metro, a pitifully small number in retrospect, but all our department could manage. Procedures for dealing with barricaded suspects and sniper- and crowd-control measures were reviewed and practiced daily by Metro. Ballistic helmets were brought in for SWAT. Within LAPD, we prepared for the worst.

What I did not expect was another Watts-type riot. Having suffered through August 1965, having witnessed the tragedy inflicted on so many people and knowing how that riot so impaired the community that it never fully recovered, I didn't believe in my wildest dreams that the people in South Central L.A. would ever allow it to happen again.

Yet I knew how deeply troubled the area was. The drugs and the violence and the total breakdown of family continued to grow alarmingly. We could see it as graphically as if the troubles were flashed in neon. In 1988, after then–Vice President George Bush visited my office, I sent him a letter suggesting ways to improve life in the inner cities. I wrote:

"I read with great interest your request for increased federal financing for minority-owned businesses to 'include those who have been excluded.' I applauded you. There are too many Americans who have been excluded and the next President must work hard to stop that continuing exclusion.

"Our past history in this regard can be likened to a rich father who does not really want to get close or involved with his children so he just throws money at them, trying to buy their affection. Instead of including them, he alienates them and they become even more distant. America must recognize that it has to get involved with its children before they become excluded, particularly its inner-city kids. Why we allow those beautiful little faces to turn into the faces of sociopathic monsters that we must arrest, prosecute and imprison is beyond understanding.

"We spend a great deal of money sending our Peace Corps volunteers to underdeveloped nations. Our hope is that we will improve the quality of the third-world people's lives. There exists the same need to improve the quality of life in our inner cities. Not by throwing money at them, but by throwing the weight of our social and technological expertise. Our past effort has done nothing but increase their exclusion from the American dream and to fuel an inner sense of alienation. We can send in a domestic version of our volunteer Peace Corps and pay them off in tuition to college or technical-vocational training—a kind of 'G.I. bill' for public service.

"This peace corps can begin to turn around the 40 percent to 50 percent dropout rate from our inner-city schools. They can teach and instill the necessary obligations that go with being parents and productive citizens. They can demonstrate how hard work and self-discipline will pay off in bright futures and good jobs. They can teach conflict resolution in an area where being the victim of a homocide is the leading cause of death for black males.

"Simply stated, we need to begin working on a front-end approach to good citizenship—not wait until we must defend ourselves by increasing the size of our police forces and building more prisons. It's a vision to be sure, but a vision whose time has come if we are to survive as a free society— free of crime, free of drugs, free of fear."

■

Still, even though we knew a time bomb was ticking, no one was prepared for such a massive breaking of laws—not only the laws of the state of California, but the very laws upon which civilized society is based.

■

The man I had counted on to plan for and take control if a riot occurred was Assistant Chief Bob Vernon. As head of Operations, he commanded eighty percent of all personnel. A talented and dedicated career officer, there was no one I trusted more to call the shots in times of trouble.

But by April 1992, huge cracks had begun to appear in the LAPD command structure. Top leadership had eroded substantially in the nearly fourteen months since the Rodney King incident. Two of my assistant chiefs, Jesse Brewer and David Dotson, not only maligned me during what they believed to be secret testimony given before the Christopher

Commission, they took some very cheap shots at their colleague Chief Vernon.

A Born-Again Christian, Bob was now being impugned for his religious beliefs. Brewer and Dotson maintained that Vernon's ideology influenced his operational decision-making and that he played favorites, looking more kindly on those who shared his beliefs. My own evaluation, and outside evaluations, found these charges to be absolute nonsense. Dissension among the top staff filtered down to the deputy chiefs too; two of Bob's deputy chiefs were almost openly defiant of him, others lukewarm. The situation worsened as internecine warfare broke out among assistant and deputy chiefs in their increasingly desperate attempts to win my job.

It was hurting how we operated. I raised the issue of top-level disaffection at almost every staff meeting. "If you don't believe in LAPD, its policies and practices, its values and principles, its personnel and their performances, then you don't believe in yourselves," I stated. "If you don't believe in yourselves, then none of you will become chief of police."

One deputy chief whined, "But we don't have a clearly defined mission."

"Of course we do," I said. "Every police officer fresh out of the Academy knows what our mission is. The mission of the LAPD is to achieve a safe environment free of crime and to promote the well-being of all people while demonstrating integrity, diligence, sensitivity, and compassion. Page twenty-two of our manual 'Human Relations in the Police Service.'"

Nevertheless, when a deputy chief is puzzled, you know you are in trouble. It was increasingly obvious that some in the top staff had lost their poise and their confidence. The crisis affected each in a different way, but it was clear that the strong, decisive, confident leadership that historically marked LAPD as exceptional did not exist as it had in the past.

Often I felt terribly alone. Even though some commanders, captains, and most lieutenants and those below were still functioning at top speed and in top form, they needed direction from above. But the would-be chiefs were too busy scrambling to get on the winning team. The problem they had was knowing who would emerge a winner.

The Police Commission's constant questioning of my authority and operation decisions, the carping by Bradley and some council members, and the constant barrage coming from the media made it less and less attractive for career-minded chief officers to line up behind me. They would not openly challenge me, for they knew the vast majority of department personnel were behind me. And though it was a day-to-day proposition, I could still usually garner a majority vote of the City Council when I needed to.

In retrospect, I should have been more aware of top brass falling apart under me. The first sign of trouble—the first time it became apparent that some of the top brass were catering to the more political leadership of the city—came during a series of gay rights demonstrations several months before. Governor Pete Wilson vetoed a gay rights bill and the activists took to the streets. These demonstrators were not peaceful. They broke the law and violated the rights of others. Yet LAPD response was tepid at best. Restraint became the operative word for officers in the field. Restraint is not a bad word. It means to act reasonably and with care; it does not mean to turn your back on obvious violations. And that's what they were doing.

I learned of this from complaints by citizens, and it was confirmed by field police officers who called me, knowing this was not my style. I immediately brought the top staff up short and demanded that they follow LAPD policy. Further demonstrations were handled correctly.

Nevertheless, the crack in LAPD's historically aggressive, pro-active enforcement policy had occurred and the signal was going out to those career-minded people within the department that "restraint" had a brand-new meaning.

That restraint would backfire in the opening hours of the upcoming riots.

■

On April 10 we held our last big riot-planning meeting. Bob Vernon said, "As soon as the verdicts come out, go full tac alert." A full tactical alert means no routine calls will be handled, freeing additional personnel to go into troubled areas.

Some at the meeting protested. "What if the verdicts are all guilty? Why waste the money?" Unhappily, Vernon relented. "Okay," he said, "as soon as we have a verdict, put your ear to the ground. I want you to be very sensitive to what is happening on the streets. If there are any problems, *any at all*, I want you to call a citywide tac alert." Later he phoned the District Attorney and the court, asking for advance warning of when the verdicts would come, if possible.

But on April 29 Bob was starting vacation pursuant to his retirement. With him gone, I chose Deputy Chief Ron Frankle to fill in. Right after the verdicts were read, I summoned Frankle to my office.

"You will be the department commander," I told him, in charge of the contingency plan for the entire emergency operation. He would be in charge of the four command posts set up throughout the city. He would be making balancing decisions in the use of personnel and equipment in order to meet the demands of the field commanders. He would operate out of the Emergency Operations Center in the fourth sub-basement of City Hall East.

"Keep in mind," I told him, "if we have an outbreak of *any kind* of violence, I want our people outfitted in riot gear and re-deployed in squads." A squad usually consists of ten officers. "We will have no one- or two-officer cars," I said, "I want four men to a car, two cars, with a sergeant and driver in a third car." Each squad would be deployed to a specific sector. "And keep them in their sectors," I emphasized. "Don't remove them for any reason." I also told him I wanted twenty-five to thirty motor officers put in buses or vans and deployed as Light Striking Forces to be called in to assist squads in troubled areas. We discussed our resource availability. He told me Metro was fully deployed in the South Central area.

This is the gist of any riot-control plan. Divide and constrict, hit them hard. It was, once again, kindergarten stuff, and he gave me one of those impatient "I *know*, Chief," looks that indicated to me he knew fully what to do.

■

An hour after the verdicts were read, isolated instances of rock- and bottle-throwing were reported, including the robbery of a liquor store at Florence and Normandie in South Central L.A., but no reports of widespread unrest filtered into my office. Minor incidents began flaring up sporadically across the city and they were being handled as routine calls. Already manpower had been increased. Day watches at three divisions in the South Central area—77th, Southeast, Southwest—plus Foothill Division in the Valley, site of the Rodney King incident, as well as four other divisions were held over.

In restrospect, I should have declared a citywide tactical alert right then, but you hate to take away police service from those who might need it, and we were still hoping to present a calm exterior, giving the impression of business as usual.

At 6:30 I left Parker Center to stop by a gathering for opponents of Proposition F—the charter amendment that would change the selection process and limit the tenure of the chief of police. A group of demonstrators had begun forming outside the building to protest the verdicts. I felt some apprehension as Gene Arreola pulled away, but from past experience with riotous behavior, I doubted anything substantial would happen until much later, or possibly the next day. Like the police, it takes rioters time to gear up too. Perhaps there would be demonstrations or picketing, maybe additional rock- and bottle-throwing, but I felt we were well equipped to handle that. Besides, I was not exactly out of touch. Armed with a police radio, a car phone, a portable phone, and a beeper, I was as accessible as I would have been behind a desk in my office.

I switched on KFWB, the all-news station. It was 6:45 and newscaster Pete Demetriou was just announcing that two or three blocks away from Florence and Normandie, big crowds were surging and throwing rocks. I reached for the phone and called my office. Commander Rick Dinse answered.

"It looks like some kind of major incident," he reported.

"Get Metro. Move 'em right now."

"Frankle's still here," Dinse said. "I'll go tell him."

Frankle indicated he knew about the problem and assured Dinse he would take care of it. He said Metro was going in now.

At this point we were on the San Diego Freeway heading north, not far, I thought, from our destination in Brentwood. Thinking I would stay for just a few minutes, I told Gene to keep going.

It was a big mistake.

Over the police radio, a tactical alert was being announced for Harbor Division, Newton, Southeast, Southwest, and 77th, plus South, Central, and West Traffic Divisions. It would be another twelve minutes before the tac alert went citywide.

I grew edgier and edgier. "Where is it?"

"We're almost there," Gene assured me.

In fact, the house was up Mandeville Canyon, a good deal farther than I realized.

■

In a riot situation, the first people in charge are the lieutenants, or watch commanders, known as the "first responders." Only if a problem grows bigger than the area are the command people brought in. The time line of events shows that the unrest built slowly but relentlessly, and for a while police units were able to handle the calls. At approximately 5:40, officers arrested three males for throwing rocks near Florence and Normandie. As they took them into custody, the crowd grew larger and uglier, the rocks and bottles beginning to fly.

The arresting officer called for assistance and about twenty officers responded. Most were not wearing riot control gear; already they were badly outnumbered. Some in the crowd were yelling, "It's Uzi time!"

Lieutenant Mike Moulin,* the watch commander at 77th Division, made a wise tactical decision. Surveying the growing chaos, he shouted, "I want everybody out of here, Florence and Normandie. Everybody get out!" A few minutes later, officers rescued a Latino family with head wounds, and escorted them to safety.

---

*Originally, I did not name the lieutenant. But since he has stepped forward and identified himself, I no longer feel the need to protect him.

Moulin immediately returned to the 77th Street Station to see his captain, Paul Jefferson. Moulin told Jefferson "we lost it out there." At that point Jefferson's and Moulin's accounts diverge. According to Moulin, Jefferson told him to go back out and make an assessment and then go to the command post. Jefferson would meet him there. According to Jefferson, Moulin said a tactical alert should be called. Jefferson says he told Moulin he was the field commander, and that if he needed to call a tactical alert, he should do so, telling him to go back out and handle the situation. Whatever the truth, a tactical alert was not called at that time.

What Moulin did was to order all units to the command post at 54th and Van Ness, a large Rapid Transit Authority depot several miles away. Two officers disregarded Moulin's orders and heroically went to the rescue of an Asian woman who was knocked unconscious in her car by a fusillade of rocks and bottles. One officer pulled the woman from her car while his partner held the crowd back with her gun drawn.

By now it was 6:16; forty-five minutes had elapsed since the first incident at Florence and Normandie. The problem was that once Moulin pulled his officers out, they were not redeployed.

Instead, as the officers pulled into the command post, sergeants formed them into squads and left them there. They sat, dumbfounded, as over the next half hour calls came in from other units reporting assaults around 71st and Normandie. Moulin reiterated his order that no units enter the area. Soon Captain Jefferson and Commander Ron Banks arrived. But rather than executing the standing plan—redeploy by squads into designated sectors—these command officers began ordering squads, one by one, to answer 911 calls, some of which were three hours old. This would go on for two hours, while increasingly frustrated officers and sergeants sat on the hoods of their cars—and just waited.

At 6:45, those glued to their TV sets were shocked by the sight of Reginald Denny being pulled out of his gravel truck and savagely beaten by at least three rioters at Florence and Normandie. In desperation, Denny reached out a hand for help, only to have one of the thugs bash him on the side of the head with a brick. As Denny lay motionless on the ground, another stole his wallet.

LAPD was nowhere in the vicinity—the officers who should have been there were still leaderless and stuck at the command post. Metro sent a small probe of ten SWAT officers to the intersection. Thirteen minutes after the Denny incident began, the officers pulled to within one block of the intersection. Only by then, both Denny and the truck were gone. Although those who viewed the beating on TV felt as if they had watched the horror go on forever, the actual time elapsed from the moment Danny was pulled from his truck until a few brave onlookers helped him back into it and drove off was six and a half minutes.

The drama of that piece of television will haunt us forever. Because all the TV helicopters had keyed on that one beating, viewers were left unaware that it was but one crisis point in the area, and they formed their opinion of LAPD's response to the entire riot by what they saw during that incident. But the area, which would become the epicenter of the massive riots that were now unfolding, actually covered thirty square miles. Outbreaks of violence were occurring all over the city. The demonstration outside Parker Center had turned riotous—windows were smashed and a guard's shack in the parking area set on fire. We had more than one hundred officers trying to control that situation, then part of the mob split off and moved down the street to City Hall while others began looting businesses up and down Broadway, the next street over. Incidents were also being reported twenty-five miles away in the San Fernando Valley. And the first of the 601 structural fires that would be set that night was already ablaze.

Still, I am convinced that if we had managed to have only one black-and-white charge into that intersection and rescue Reginald Denny, even if we had to use guns, which, given the hostile crowd, we probably would have, the public would not have castigated LAPD the way it did. The town would still have burned down, the looting would have gone on, but we wouldn't have had people saying that LAPD didn't respond. There would have been a different perception of the whole thing.

I had intended to stay at the Mandeville Canyon meeting only a few minutes and believed I had been there just five, but later discovered it was closer to twenty minutes. After touring some areas of the city that seemed to be peaceful, and looking in on the Parker Center demonstration, which was under control, I walked into the Emergency Operations Center at 8:15.

It was fully staffed with personnel: deployment specialists, operations and intelligence specialists. The EOC commander was on deck, and the various liaison people—someone from the Department of Water and Power, the California Highway Patrol, the Fire Department, and others—were in place. Deputy Chief Frankle was in the department commander's office adjacent to the EOC, but he could observe the continually changing status board through large glass windows.

I was immediately given a situation report on what was occurring in all parts of the city. I hadn't viewed what was on TV, hadn't seen Reginald Denny pulled out of his truck and beaten nearly to death. I was told that officers were being deployed. An order for full mobilization had gone out, meaning every officer was now on a twelve-hour shift. By 8:30, officers on the B shift, half of the department, were on their way to work. Some who had already worked twelve or fourteen hours were being sent home to rest up for the next day.

"We're trying to locate the mayor to call a state of emergency," Commander George Morrison told me. This is a piece of legal boilerplate that was long ago drawn up by a city attorney. Once the mayor signs it, the city may call upon any of its resources to deal with an emergency. It allows us to ban the sale of liquor, guns, and gasoline or to impose a curfew without having to pass a law. It also sets the stage for aid from the rest of the state, including a call for the National Guard. It takes a mayor's signature for that.

I called for a helicopter. I had learned from my experience during Watts, when Parker, ensconced in his office, kept barking out orders that did not fit the situation in the field. So as long as I had been chief, my command post was in my car or in a helicopter or on the street. It has always made more sense to me to be viewing firsthand what was going on than to wait for field reports. It allowed me to adjust and correct our field operations using on-site information. Now, as we flew over the city, I saw the situation report had not begun to convey the true dimensions of the riotous behavior. I could see dozens of fires raging and others being ignited. I was stunned. It was Kuwait all over again. That this kind of disorder could be full blown by nine o'clock was incredible.

"There's a fire over there," the pilot kept shouting. "Look, another over there. *Another* over there."

So much smoke was billowing up, it was causing thermals, adding to the difficulty of negotiating a sky clogged with a dozen news helicopters. I asked the pilot to go in low as I reached for a pair of high-powered binoculars. Crowds appeared sparse compared to what we had in Watts in 1965. I grew hopeful. "We can handle this," I thought. "We can deal with it."

I asked to be taken to the field command post at 54th and Van Ness. But when we were unable to get emergency clearance to land, I told the pilot to go back to the EOC.

By then Bradley was there and had signed the state of emergency order. Even though we had barely spoken in recent years, there was no animosity now. We had jobs to do and we have never let personal considerations get in the way. I told him: "I really get the sense we can deal with this, Mr. Mayor. There are a lot of fires, but not that many people on the street. If we can get adequate forces out there, we can bring it under control."

Bradley told me he had already phoned the governor to ask for National Guard troops, which was precisely the right thing to do. We made a conference call—the mayor, the governor, Sheriff Sherm Block, General Bob Thrasher of the National Guard, Dr. Andrews of the State Emergency Services, and me—and discussed plans to bring one thousand guardsmen into nearby armories right away. Once they were deployed, another thousand would be called in.

By now it was 10:15 and I decided to go back into the field. Accompanied by Gene and Commander Rick Dinse, we roamed the streets of South Los Angeles. As we drove, I had this terrible feeling. "Where the hell," I said, "are the police?" We couldn't find one officer anywhere. As I watched a man lob a Molotov cocktail through a store window, and noticed with relief that it didn't explode, I thought, "Maybe they're someplace dealing with *something*."

Arriving at the command post at 54th and Van Ness, I went to talk to Deputy Chief Matt Hunt. As the head of South Bureau, which encompassed Southwest, Southeast, 77th, and Harbor, this was his territory. Like me, he had been sidetracked earlier that evening. When the violence broke out, he was at the First African Methodist Episcopal Church in South Central L.A. with the mayor, other politicians, and community activists, where a peaceful rally was being staged in the wake of the officers' verdicts. Also present was City Councilman Mark Ridley-Thomas, who was videotaped, after word of the riots had reached the rally, saying, "Our instructions to the police were simply this: don't contribute to the crisis." He added, "An immediate display of force would precipitate rather than diffuse any situation."

In the meantime, with Hunt absent and officers from 77th and Metro pouring into the command post, utter stagnation had set in. Command officers were present and they should have taken charge. Some were trying to increase the flow into the field, but their efforts were insufficient. Finally, out of desperation, some Metro people decided to go out on their own, only to find their cars hemmed in. They tore down a fence and took off.

Earlier, when I'd met with Ron Frankle, we had discussed Metro's deployment. Metropolitan Division is our Crime Task Force. It moves anywhere in the city where we have a specific crime problem. These are highly trained and disciplined officers. They are LAPD's marines, split into three platoons, including "D" Platoon, which is SWAT. Frankle told me they would be heavily deployed in the South end. However, those who were responsible did not follow orders and deployed Metro all over the place. This is totally unlike Metro, which normally follows directions with precision. It was becoming a night when everything that could go wrong seemed to.

I walked over to the sector map. Oh, my God, I thought. "Where is everybody?"

"We've deployed them," said Hunt. "All of Metro is with the fire department." (Later I learned this was not accurate.)

"But where are *your* people?" I asked.

"Handling calls."

The way the riot-control plan works is that you deploy squads, sector by sector, until each is covered. Then, as more officers arrive, you send in additional squads, dividing the sectors in two, constricting the area. Once in place, the officers are not to leave for any reason. The next step is to start making arrests. More officers are sent in to take the arrestees to mass booking centers.

I stared at the map. The sectors had been drawn in, but not the squads. Thinking, "I know there's a scheme to this somewhere," I said, "No one's in any of these sectors."

"Well, they sent me fifty motor officers on a bus," replied Hunt. "I'm thinking of sending them out on the bus."

"No. Fill the sectors with squads."

"We don't have enough cars."

Which was absolutely the wrong thing to say. I blew up. "Two officers show up in one car," I said. "Then two more officers show up. You take the second two and put them in with the first two, Matt, and now you have an extra car."

I was so angry, I began yelling, which is not my style. You don't yell at a chief officer in front of his subordinates. But I couldn't help it. Matt had been trained up. He *knew* what to do. The plan is as basic as A-B-C. Everywhere else in the city the plan was being followed and unrest was being contained, but here, where most of the trouble was occurring, my talented deputy chief had suddenly turned hamhanded. Fortunately, at that moment my brother Steve walked in and, seeing how angry I was, he jumped in and started to work out the squads deployment. Literally shaking with anger, I stormed out.

For the rest of the night Gene, Rick, and I prowled the streets. Mainly I checked our deployment, which improved quickly after my outburst, but it became impossible not to get involved in some enforcement activity. As we drove along Exposition Boulevard, not far from the Coliseum, we noticed a liquor store that had been looted. We pulled up and out came some Koreans—it was their store. While we were commiserating with them, two guys with great big plastic bags came walking down the street. Rick, Gene, and I—still wearing suits—stopped them. Gene flashed his I.D.

"We're the police, and we'd like to talk to you. Put down your bags."

"That's no damn I.D.," one of them said.

Gene and Rick shook them down for weapons and checked the bags. One was filled with cartons of cigarettes. They became totally obnoxious.

"Leave your bags and go," Gene said.

"What right do you have to take our bags?" they shot back.

"Leave the bags or go to jail," I said. Angrily, they stalked off.

We continued our rounds of South Central. As the night wore on and more police finally arrived on the scene, arrests began to be made. But still we could not gain control. At one point I noticed a band of looters breaking into a market. I told Gene to stop and I jumped out. I know I am a target, I know my face is familiar to many, but I was so frustrated I didn't care. With Gene striding unhappily beside me, I walked toward the looters. Suddenly, one looked over and started to come my way. I felt Gene tense.

"Hey, Chief!"

Grinning broadly, the guy stuck his hand out to shake mine.

Then he turned on his heel and went right back into the market.

We called for assistance, but by the time it arrived, the man had gone.

■

At six A.M. I stopped by the EOC, was briefed thoroughly, and gave instructions for additional action to be taken to strengthen the South Bureau. Then we went home, showered, put on uniforms, and drove back to the EOC. I needed to get a sense of the rest of the city. I looked at our deployment and talked to deputy chiefs at their command posts. Unlike Watts, this riot was moving far afield from South Central L.A. Looters were moving north toward downtown Los Angeles and west to Wilshire Boulevard, West Los Angeles, Hollywood, and the San Fernando Valley. With the exception of South Central, the police seemed to have all other areas under control. Each chief voiced his concern about depleting his resources further by sending them to the South Bureau. As a result, I got back on the phone and said we needed the Guard deployed as soon as they were ready. Guardsmen had arrived in their armories but hadn't been deployed, and I didn't know why there was this delay. I called Bob Edmonds, Sheriff Sherm Block's number-two guy, and asked for additional assistance. He sent me one hundred deputies.

Later that morning I briefed the mayor in his office. The night before I had asked him for a sunset-to-dawn curfew to be imposed on South Central L.A. the next evening, Thursday. He agreed. But now I wanted it citywide. Bradley was reluctant. I declared that it was absolutely essential. At last he agreed, only to have second thoughts later on. Businesses were apparently complaining, citing losses of revenue. I said I understood but I sincerely believed it was necessary. I found myself almost begging him. Eventually, he said okay—for one night, then he'd probably lift it.

Meanwhile, I felt our deployment was still inadequate. I assigned three more commanders to South Bureau, directing each to take a major sector, to tighten security and speed up arrests.

The glitches of the night before continued to haunt me. The tac alert should have come much earlier, and there is no satisfactory explanation as to why it did not. And even though I was there for maybe twenty minutes, I shouldn't have spent twenty seconds at that political meeting.

Always in the first stages of a major disturbance there are glitches. Even in Operation Desert Storm—despite having prepared for months—they blew up people they shouldn't have. We had had our share of glitches. There could be no more.

■

I asked the California Highway Patrol to take over security of firefighters and paramedics. Originally, the CHP had been asked to cordon off the troubled area. But that was not

working; the rioters were springing up in other areas of the
city. The highway patrol proved to be outstanding, handling
any assignment quickly and efficiently.

At the same time, I learned the National Guard was now
held up waiting for, among other things, metal plates to
transform their automatic weapons into semiautomatic ones.
"Look," I said, "why don't you solve the problem by
putting only two bullets into a magazine at a time?" They
agreed; and that problem was solved.

After a series of meetings I went back into the field and
again stayed out until the wee hours of the morning. By
then, hundreds of guardsmen were on the streets. Their
presence, the curfew, and our rapidly increasing deployment
of officers was at last having an effect. Still, throughout
South Central, and now Hollywood, looters continued to
clean out stores and set them ablaze. Some 3,244 structural-
fire calls came in on the second day.

As we drove, we spotted looters cleaning out a furniture
store on Western Avenue. I told Gene to pull up and, really
incensed now, I jumped out of the car. Seeing a chair and a
coffee table sitting in the back of someone's van, I hauled
them out and brought them back into the store.

Later that night, cruising past a mini-mall on Figueroa,
we noticed two guys standing in front of a market. The
windows had already been smashed. As we pulled up, they
took off. I got out of the car. I could see them standing
across the street, glowering, waiting for us to leave. I started
toward them. I was ready. I'd had it. "Here it comes," I
thought darkly. "Rodney King number two. You're going to
jail, and it doesn't look like you want to go the easy way."
But just before I got to them, they jumped in their car and
sped off.

Finally, after thirty-six hours without sleep, I went home
and allowed myself two. Then I showered and went back to
work.

■

By Friday, the National Guard was pouring in, more than
one thousand patrolled the city. The night before I had
requested four thousand guardsmen and Sheriff Sherm
Block, two thousand. Despite this, I was being accused in

the media of resisting National Guard troops. Blind quotes attributed to "people close to the mayor" were making these statements. At my Friday-morning briefing with Bradley, I said, "This is not the time for confrontation between you and me. Tell your people to back off."

He said he couldn't imagine who had said such things, but he agreed this was hardly the time to be sniping at each other. Immediately, the "people close to the mayor" shut up.

Unbeknownst to Sherm and me, Bradley and Governor Pete Wilson were cutting a deal with the White House to bring in Regular Army and Marine personnel, to federalize the National Guard, and to dispatch one thousand federal officers. We said, "Why?" We were a little put out, since we had the responsibility for stopping the riot. We now had the situation under control from an enforcement standpoint, and the National Guard was deployed to watch areas that had not been hit. Besides, I recoil at the idea of federally controlled Regular Army and Marine personnel, trained to fight a foreign enemy, being deployed on Los Angeles streets. Theirs was a political gesture that had no other effect, and I resented it.

The federal officers became a problem. DEA agents, immigration people, and others showed up wearing funny uniforms, or no uniforms, and because they are not trained in riot control, it was hard to know how to deploy them. I said to my commanders, "You will greet them and you will use them. They have been uprooted and sent here to do a job. I am appreciative. However, I'll do my best to get rid of them." Far more helpful were the police officers sent in from small cities as far north as Fresno and as far south as Orange and San Diego counties. By Friday night we had seven thousand people on the streets. The mayor agreed to extend the all-city curfew one more night. The city started to calm down.

■

After another night on the streets, and two more hours of sleep, I was in the shower around seven o'clock Saturday morning, when the phone rang. I turned off the water and grabbed it. It was my ex-wife, Wanda.

"Scott's in the hospital," she said. "He's critical. His pulse rate is down to twenty and they're not certain he'll make it. I'll call back when I find out more."

She didn't say drugs—but I knew.

Slowly, I replaced the receiver. I hadn't seen my son in a while, or talked to him, but I had heard that he seemed to be doing quite well on methadone. Now my heart was, once again, breaking. The old feeling of helplessness overwhelmed me. Dressing blindly, I left a note for Sam, who was still asleep, telling her what had happened. Then, needing to be at EOC for an eight o'clock briefing, I walked heavily out the door.

The day became a blur. I told Mary Miller to check with the hospital and keep me informed. The only other person I confided in was Tom Bradley. "If I have to disappear for an hour," I said, "I want you to know why." He was very sympathetic. And the next day when I spoke to him, the first thing he did was to ask about Scott.

For a while on Saturday I couldn't actually locate Scott. The hospital Wanda had mentioned insisted he wasn't there. Wanda never called back. While Mary was phoning all the hospitals in the area, I was in my car, checking the streets, checking our deployment, with Leslie Stahl of *60 Minutes* camped in the backseat. I know she must have thought I was stupid at times, because my mind wandered and I couldn't concentrate on her questions. Mary phoned periodically, trying to relay information in a way that I could respond to without letting on that anything was wrong. Scott, it turned out, was in the hospital Wanda had mentioned, after all. Because he was unconscious, he couldn't tell the medical staff what drugs he had ingested. All they could do was keep pumping his stomach—and keep their fingers crossed.

My worry clashed with my anger. Of all the times he's used drugs, of all the times for him to wind up on his deathbed, he had to pick now, I thought, while I'm trying to keep the city together. I was angry with him, with myself, with what was happening to my city.

For two days Scott languished. Then, being Scott, he pulled right out of it. With Sam and his sisters and Wanda at his bedside, he wrote little notes. "I love you." And, "Does

Dad know?'' The next day he was released, worrying only—typical Scott—about how he looked.

■

In the end, it took about thirty-six to forty-eight hours to put down the riots, less than half the time it took us to quell Watts. But in those hellish days, at least forty-five lives were lost, hundreds of millions of dollars of damage done, and untold lives and psyches hopelessly wrenched and thrown into despair.

Predictably, the media and others have focused their attention on what the LAPD did wrong—why the slow response, why no plan, why did the chief attend the political get-together? As I rerun the events in my mind, here is the analysis I am able to draw.

We did have a plan. Decades old, it is detailed and the strategies it entails are appropriate. In most areas of the city, the plan was executed properly and civil unrest was contained. What went wrong involved the initial execution of that plan in the South Central portion of L.A., where the rioting began. And here a number of factors need to be examined.

The anti-LAPD mood of the city, which had engulfed the department since the Rodney King incident, served as a backdrop against which we had to operate. For fourteen months officers were under attack from citizens and political leaders alike. They felt as if they were working under a microscope, every move subject to review. And that scrutiny showed up in our statistics.

Although largely ignored by the Christopher Commission, the data for 1988, 1989, and 1990 showed the number of use-of-force incidents as reported by LAPD officers had dropped fifty percent. For example, the average use-of-force per officer in 1988 in Rampart Division, our highest crime area, was 1.8. Use of force can mean anything from a baton blow to a wrist lock. The next year it dropped to 1.3. In 1990 it dipped to less than one. This was something to be proud of, because arrests and numbers of contacts between police and citizens stayed the same. But after Rodney King use-of-force incidents dropped sixty percent more—in Rampart to .3 or .4 per officer—and arrests plummeted too

Clearly, officers had decided that if force became necessary, they wouldn't use it except in extreme situations. How much this lack of overall aggressiveness has impacted the safety of the city is impossible to ascertain. But I suspect the public is paying a price.

Privately, many officers told me they decided using force wasn't worth it. They no longer believed their superiors would back them even when they were within their right to use force. Although I saw no evidence that this climate affected officers and sergeants once they hit the streets during the riots, it's possible it affected the department command structure. People dislike making career-impacting decisions.

Indeed, the day before the riots, Deputy Chiefs Matt Hunt and Bernard Parks had been cautioned by some black leaders. "What we stressed was not to have an over-response to whatever happens," Mark Ridley-Thomas was quoted as telling them. "We do not want a repeat of the mistakes of the past." Did some of my command staff lean over too far?

To an extent, the tugging and the pulling of the community did affect me. I was being attacked on all sides, from the media, the Christopher Commission, and the Westside liberals, to the people in South Central who claimed police brutality. I had been trying to rebuild the department to make everyone happy, and I was trying to be measured in what I did. We all were. As a result, we may have been overly cautious. I was under siege from a citywide budget deficit and from the constant berating of the department on the whole use-of-force issue. In the months before the verdicts, everything I did drew an accusation that I was precipitating trouble. On the very day the riots broke out, the *Daily News* ran a story headlined "Activists Ask LAPD to be Calm: Post-Verdict Reaction Toward Public Feared," while the *Los Angeles Times* headed its story "Black Leaders Accuse Gates of Inflaming Racial Tensions."

How these factors affected the scheme of things remains unclear. More clear is that what went wrong in the early stages of the riots involved a chain of command. And even here, there are questions that may never be answered.

One. When I was in my car and heard that crowds were

collecting near Florence and Normandie, I ordered Ron
Frankle to deploy Metro immediately—and was assured
they would be. Why were they never deployed? Assistant
Chief Vernon told me later: "In my opinion, they were
afraid to deploy Metro." Bob is too nice to say it, but what
he meant was they were afraid because they knew Metro
would kick ass. "It's the old Hiroshima-Nagasaki argu-
ment," Bob theorized. "You drop the bomb and you kill
hundreds of thousands of people and today the United States
is still criticized for that. But if we hadn't, if we had invaded
Japan instead, at least a million lives would have been lost.
If Metro had gone in and used deadly force, maybe killed
ten people to disperse the rioters at Florence and Normandie, what would the public have said to that?"

Two. Lieutenant Mike Moulin has told us why he initially
pulled his men out and I can support his decision to do so.
But it's still not clear why his men were not formed into
squads and redeployed right away, or why a tactical alert
was not called at least an hour earlier.

Three. I am still perplexed as to why Captain Paul
Jefferson and Commander Ron Banks did not correct the
situation. Both are experienced people. Some within the
department have privately wondered if both men, who are
black, may have been influenced by some of our black
leaders who pleaded caution. While my heart tells me no,
my head asks me "How come?"

Four. The next up the chain of command was Deputy
Chief Matt Hunt, who is in charge of South Bureau. In
January, trying to satisfy the Christopher Commission's
recommendations, I selected six of our eighteen divisions to
switch over to full community-based policing. In order to
make those divisions more accountable to the people they
served, I put the captains in charge and told them to report
directly to me, cutting out the deputy chiefs as middlemen.
Matt was unhappy to lose two of his four divisions, Harbor
and Southeast. Then Councilman Mark Ridley-Thomas
complained that 77th Division was not included and should
be. I had wanted to wait for some results before I included
77th, but he went to the Police Commission. It begged me
to include 77th in the program. I gave in. Now Matt's
command load was reduced to only Southwest, South Traf-

fic, and South Bureau Homicide, and he was visibly un-happy. "Matt," I said, "for once I have had to make a political decision. Don't take it personally."

But at our April 10 strategy session, Matt kept saying, "If trouble erupts, who'll be in charge?" I said, "Matt, the captains will be in charge. If we need to consolidate, we have commanders available. And probably you will wind up in charge if things get really bad."

Indeed, one of the first things I did after hearing the verdict was to put Matt in charge of his old territories. Yet, when the riots broke out, Matt, too, held back. "He was at the church when the riots started," Vernon reminded me. "Frankly, I think he was intimidated by Mark Ridley-Thomas and others who were there. I think Matt was liter-ally paralyzed and didn't know what to do."

Five. Many have pointed a finger at me, actually accusing me of purposely holding back as some kind of screwy power-play in which I figuratively gave a finger to the city. This is such an evil thought, I can't even deal with it. If nothing else, I am a thorough professional. I have always moved in as hard as possible, that's my nature. And when have I ever put my department's reputation—or my own—on the line to score a political point?

Six. We have been criticized because some of our cap-tains were at a seminar in Ventura and others in the com-mand staff were off duty or on vacation. But that wasn't a problem. You want only half your command staff on duty during a twelve-hour shift, with the other half ready to take over. All were in place when we needed them.

Seven. Should we have been even better prepared? In retrospect, of course we should have been. But no one, not me, not the mayor, not even the community's activists, foresaw the explosion of the rioting. A citywide tactical alert, put into effect as the verdicts were read, could have speeded our response somewhat. I might have speeded it even more had I not spent those twenty minutes at that meeting, or been able to land at the command post at 54th and Van Ness. Still, it must be said that none of us could or would have been in front of a TV watching Reginald Denny get beat up. If any of my officers in 77th had seen the Denny beating on TV, they would have used deadly force to enter the area and rescue him. Had we responded to that six-and-a-half-minute episode, I doubt that the torrent of criticism would have been heaped on us.

■

We are, historically, a little bitty police force spread out over 467 square miles. At the time of the riots, we were down to 7,900 officers. Geographically, the city of Chicago cannot fill the San Fernando Valley which is only a portion of Los Angeles, yet Chicago has twelve thousand officers. New York has eighty officers per square mile, Philadelphia fifty and Los Angeles fourteen. When the riots broke out, even after holding over a number of day watches, we still had only one thousand officers on the streets. At full strength during any twelve-hour shift—with half the department off and many assigned to other necessary policing duties—we still could field only twenty-five hundred officers. Given the spontaneous combustion across Los Angeles, the hundreds of fires being set, the lack of police officers to accompany the firefighters, the numerous incidents of rock- and bottle-throwing by hostile crowds, followed by the wholesale looting—we simply did not have enough fingers to stick into the bursting dike. In the end, it required thirteen thousand law enforcement and military people to put the riots down.

By comparison, in September of 1992, when a New York County grand jury voted not to indict a police officer in the killing of a Dominican drug dealer two months earlier in Washington Heights, NYPD was able to send two thousand uniformed officers into the tiny area to maintain peace, while three thousand more waited in a parking lot nearby.

■

At midnight on June 27 I officially retired as chief of police. But already a thorough internal investigation of our response to the riots was under way, ordered by me in their aftermath. Dozens of staff and command officers were interviewed, as well as supervisors and a cross-section of rank and file employees; MDT messages were scoured, plans and procedures reviewed, a log of events scrutinized. The report was presented to Chief Willie Williams on July 8, and most of it confirmed my own findings. This is some of what it said.

"The vast majority of line officers interviewed perceived a lack of support by City Government leadership and by some Department management following the release of the Christopher Commission Report . . . This, coupled with the constant barrage of negative information by the media about the Police Department, caused many police officers to question their authority to use any force and to do their job to the best of their ability."

The report confirmed instances of political and special-interest criticism of the department for planning for civil unrest. It found instances of political leadership strongly advising police management to maintain a low-key role following the King verdict.

It said: "The Department's policy of arresting all violators was not reemphasized at this time. It was the perception of a large number of supervisors and officers that the Department had taken on a low-key approach of restraint . . . These factors not only did not assist the Department in planning and preparing, but very probably developed a mindset of restraint to the point of inaction at some leadership levels."

The report criticized Lieutenant Moulin for not initially following the "basic fundamental LAPD plans for a response to a civil disturbance. He failed to exercise his authority and take appropriate action," it said. Of the unrest at Florence and Normandie, while noting that Moulin had no knowledge of the Reginald Denny beating, the report found that Moulin "did have sufficient forces at his disposal to respond quickly . . . and at least stop the life-threatening criminal activity, and he certainly had the authority and responsibility to request additional personnel immediately in order to respond appropriately. It was further determined that the failure to request a tactical alert, or to request additional personnel immediately, critically impeded the Department's ability to respond quickly."

In conclusion the report found: [In the first six hours] "the fast-moving and widespread unrest impeded the Department's ability to focus on any significant overall response. However, there was an opportunity to respond to extremely violent acts at the initial stages of unrest using existing Department strategies and plans. Unfortunately, for a variety of reasons, mainly human failure and possibly the political climate, this opportunity was lost. Planning was made an issue by some Department personnel; however, sufficient plans were in place to deal with the initial outbreak, but the appropriate execution of that plan never occurred. The lack of mental preparedness might have had a role in the lack of execution but planning most certainly did not.''

∎

I still maintain that when you subject human beings to harsh, unending, and relentless criticism, as LAPD has been, you demoralize them. A demoralized police force is not the strongest bulwark against the kind of civil disorder we had on April 29. The main reason I stayed on as chief, despite calls for my resignation, was to try to protect the LAPD and rebuild it, address its deficiencies, and put the heart back into it.

In the end, we must remember that the police did not cause the riots. Our society must face the harsh realities that confront it, and root out the anger, hate, prejudice, and desire for vengeance that did cause them. We must also abandon the misconception that everyone rioted; hundreds of thousands of people live in the area of the riots, and most of them did *not* attack or loot or burn.

We must also throw out the notion that a police department can have great impact in the early stages of a full-scale uprising. It is going to take at least a few hours to get the operation rolling. Unless a department is fully mobilized, the sad truth is there is going to be a lot of property damage and injuries and some loss of life. Given the conditions, given the circumstances, I believe LAPD will come out looking fine. There was preparation. There was a plan. Many executed it beautifully.

Yet, as always, there are so many things I wish we had done.

Acknowledgments

These are only a very few of the incredible people that made LAPD great. I acknowledge them, but in doing so, I have neglected literally hundreds of others who have touched my professional life and made LAPD what it is today.

I would like to thank my personal secretary, Mary Miller. Twenty-two years of putting up with me is above and beyond the call of duty. I ask all the time where or what would I be without her. My thanks also to Deputy Chief Bill Booth, who served thirteen tumultuous years as my press relations officer and confidant and without whose encouragement this book would not have been written.

Mary's assistants, Rosa Torres and Chieko Shimokaji, have been marvelous. My security aides and partners, through the good times and bad times for the past fourteen years, have been Gene Arreola, Bruce Vermaat, Gerry Sola, Thurston Bechtel, Mike Moran, Pete Weireter, Bob Guzman, Steve Madden, Frank Virgallito, Ken Lockwood, John Vach, Gene Fretheim, Pat Connelly, and Rod Bernsen.

My adjutants and executive officers, who have done my work and always made me look good, are Lieutenant Betty Kelepecz, Lieutenant Kathleen Murcott, Captain Gary Brennan, Captain Russ Leach, Lieutenant Gary Williams, Captain Rick Wahler, Lieutenant Ken Colby, Lieutenant Don Farrell, Commander Robert Gil, Lieutenant Greg Vasquez, Captain Terry Dyment, Commander Rick Dinse, Commander Maurice Moore, and Lieutenant Jack Mahon.

I express my deep admiration for the present and past members of the Family Support Group and their loved ones. They will always have a special place in my heart.

And of course, there were the great chiefs, Bill Parker, Tom Reddin, Ed Davis; Thad Brown, chief of detectives and interim chief; Deputy Chief Lynn White; "Old Venerable" Roger Murdock, deputy chief and interim chief; Bob Rock, assistant chief and interim chief; Assistant Chief Jack Collins, "Mr. Integrity," and his wife, Sergeant Margie Collins; Assistant Chief Robert Houghton, head of the Special Unit Senator Task Force; Assistant Chief Robert Vernon, a much maligned guy, who stayed loyal throughout the darkest days; Captain Jack Donohoe; Inspector John Powers, an unsung hero; Inspector Ken McCauley, a hard-nosed guy whom everyone loved; Deputy Chief John McAllister, a great friend, and father of Colonel Branford McAllister, U.S. Air Force, and Detective Julie McAllister, a Los Angeles police officer; Assistant Chief George Beck and his daughter Megan McElroy, an LAPD officer, and his son, LAPD Sergeant Charlie Beck; Assistant Chief Dale Speck and his wife, Connie Speck, the first female captain on the LAPD; Captain Carl Calkins, former chief of police of Long Beach; Deputy Chief Jim Fisk; Officers Chuck Foote and Larry Moore, LAPD's athletic coordinators; Commander Pete Hagan; Lieutenant John Kauzor and Lieutenant Pete Bagoye; Commander Paul Gillen; Lieutenant Chuck Higbie; Captain Roger Moulton, now chief of police of Redondo Beach; Commander Jim Chambers; Captain Pierce Brooks; Lieutenant Bill Hall, investigator of hundreds of officer-involved shootings; Lieutenant John Borunda; Detective Ed Lindsey and his sons, Brian and Eddie, Jr.; Captain Tom Hays;

Officer Tom Hazelton and the "Centurions"; Commander Jim Munger; Deputy Chief Jim Hardin; Officer Shilah Johnson; Captain Jim Glavas, later chief of police of Newport Beach and Santa Barbara; Captain Merrill Duncan, later Chief of Police of Orange; Assistant Chief Barry Wade and his sons, LAPD Officers David, Gordon, and Douglas Wade; Commander Walt Mitchell and his wife, Cindy; Captain Don Vincent; Commander Sid Mills, and his son, Captain Sid Mills, Jr.; Deputy Chief Charlie Reese; Commander George Morrison; Sergeant Fanchon Blake; Officer Audrey Fletcher; Joe Wambaugh, a former police officer who is a brilliant writer and a hell of a nice guy; Gene Roddenberry, creator of *Star Trek*; Deputy Chief Steve Downing, now a successful executive producer, and his son, Lieutenant Michael Downing; Commander Joe Gunn, a successful writer and producer; Deputy Chief Richard Simon, a man I loved dearly; Deputy Chiefs Harold Sullivan and Benny Caldwell, both traffic experts for the police department, who went on to head up the California Highway Patrol as commissioners; Commander Ray Ruddell, a classmate of mine; Commander Larry Binkley, later Long Beach chief of police; Deputy Chief Bill Rathburn, now chief of police of Dallas; Commander Thom Windham, now chief of police of Fort Worth; Inspector Nate Iannone, author and lecturer; Assistant Chief Marvin Iannone, now chief of police of Beverly Hills; Inspector James Lawrence; Inspector Ed Walker, original press relations officer for LAPD, and an incredibly wonderful man; Captain Lou Ritchey, one of my field commanders during the Watts riots; Captain Charles Crumly; Captain Earl Sansing, who was, in my opinion, probably the greatest captain of all time in the Los Angeles Police Department; the Howe brothers, Captain Charlie Howe and Deputy Chief Mert Howe; Assistant Chief Wes Harvey, one of the best assistant chiefs I ever had.

Outstanding police commissioners have been Dr. Reynaldo Carreon; Dr. Francisco Bravo; Michael Kohn; Emmett McGaughey; Frank Hathaway; Al Hudson; Marguerite Justice; Sal Montenegro; Max Greenberg; Steve Gavin; Bert Boeckmann and his lovely wife, Jane; Reva Tooley; Robert Talcott, president and a very positive force for the Commission; Steve Yslas.

Others who should be thanked include Johnny Grant and Bill Welsh, both great and constant supporters of LAPD; Fred Dryer, who made the *Hunter* series reflect a professional LAPD; John McMahon, creator of the Johnny Carson *Tonight* show but, more importantly, the Los Angeles Police Memorial Foundation; Bob Hope, who has been a rock in supporting me and the LAPD and has always been there when we needed him; and finally, Jack Webb, who made this department famous and gave it the professional image in both the *Dragnet* and *Adam 12* series. Jack never turned his back on us; he was a positive contributor in every way. He did an incredible job of producing an image for the Los Angeles Police Department and putting us in the homes of people across the nation. I will be forever grateful to Jack for all he did for this department.

A special tribute to Steve Delsohn, a fine writer, who created the theme for this book.

And, a special thanks to Peggy Rowe Estrada and all the members and supporters in "CISCOP" (Citizens in Support of the Chief of Police).

Lastly, I must acknowledge the incredible help of the staff of Bantam Books: Lauren Field drove us crazy, as most lawyers do, in requiring us to justify every word—but she drove us crazy in such a *nice* way; Betsy Cenedella, whose careful scrutiny as a copyeditor eliminated all the errors of style; Linda Grey—without her faith in the project it would never have happened; Stuart Applebaum, whose enthusiasm for the book helped us carry on; Genevieve Young, our tough-minded, no-nonsense, slave-driving editor—dear Gene—who added just the right touch and direction at just the right sentence and paragraph. If the book becomes a success, Gene must share in it.

Index

ABOUT THE CO-AUTHOR

DIANE K. SHAH is a contributing editor at *Esquire*. Her articles have appeared in *GQ* and *The New York Times Magazine;* for six years she was a sports columnist for the *Los Angeles Herald Examiner*. Ms. Shah is the author of the Paris Chandler mystery series, which began with *As Crime Goes By* and continues with the recently published *Dying Cheek to Cheek*.